Grandpa & Grandma & Di
Merry Christmas '94
Best Wishes to y'all in ...
Love Always
Mike

FRIDAY NIGHT
FARMERS

THE HISTORY OF THE LEWISVILLE FIGHTING FARMERS

BY GARY D. KERBOW

FARM PRESS
LEWISVILLE, TEXAS

Printed by
Taylor Publishing Company, Dallas, Texas

Jay Love, Publishing Consultant

Anita Stumbo, Design and Typography

Photo credits

Front Cover: *Lewisville Daily Leader–Lee Baker, Lewisville ISD Public Information Office Lewisville Fighting Farmer Football Booster Club, Lewisville Band Booster Club, Dave Lane.*

Back Cover: *Lewisville High School, Russell Kerbow.*

Photos by and courtesy of: *Lewisville High School, James Polser Collection, Squire Haskins Photography, LISD Public Information Office, Peggy Cook, Henry Vance, Johnnie and Helen Tucker, Max Goldsmith, Judy Sparks Goodman, Everett and Kathy Denison, Lewisville Fighting Farmer Football Booster Club, Walt Garrison, Ron and Kathy Aljoe, Bob and Judy Camp, Gary D. Kerbow, Lewisville Band Booster Club–Dave Lane, LISD Athletic Department, Lewisville Daily Leader–Lee Baker*

─────────────── ❖ ───────────────

FARM PRESS
P.O. Box 962
Lewisville, Texas 75067
817 · 424 · 3533

© 1994 Gary D. Kerbow

All rights reserved. No part of this book may be reproduced in any form without written permission from the publisher.

ISBN 0-9644462-0-0

To the honor and memory of all the young men whose dream began under the heat of the August sun and continued through those cold December nights. Those who endured bus rides to places like Sherman and Wichita Falls, Waxahachie and Bryson. From those who did battle on the unrefined surface of the Degan lot, to those who defended the honor of the Farmer at Goldsmith Stadium under the bright lights . . . the pages following are for you.

The "Farmer" is symbolic of the spirit of L.H.S., a spirit that creates in each of us an unwavering determination to succeed.

— Foreword from the 1947–48 LHS Yearbook

"We took it in the ear from every direction. Lewisville High School, from a town north of Dallas, went to the state finals and claimed it actually was America's team."

—Roger Staubach
Time Enough To Win

CONTENTS

Foreword by Bill Shipman 9
Preface by Randy Galloway 11
Introduction 13

I	Where It All Began	17
II	A Farming Community	27
III	Down Through the Years	34
IV	Founding Farmers — Famous Farmers	57
	The Coaches · The Players · Famous Farmers · The All-Americans	
V	A Bank Robbery	93
VI	Some Lean Years	101
VII	The Band That Marches With Pride	105
VIII	1972 — A Season to Remember	123
IX	Growing Up — Moving Up to 4A	171
X	The Wilson Years	178
XI	Big Plays	199
XII	A Dream Realized	209

Appendix 293
    Year At a Glance 294
    Farmer Mascots 295
    Schedules and Results 296
    Coaches Career Records 311
    Band — Year At a Glance 312
    Nicknames of Farmers Opponents 313
    Top Ten Wins in Farmer History 315
    All-Time Roster 316
    Post-Season Honors 329

FOREWORD

When Gary Kerbow asked me to write the foreword for this book, I immediately agreed to do so. Almost three decades ago I was fortunate enough to become a small part of the ongoing tradition of the Fighting Farmers. To this day, I get chill bumps when I hear the strains of "Big John" or am lucky enough to catch the Fighting Farmers on TV, or—once in a great while—in live action. To me, and to many others, the Farmers will always be special.

Why? Why are the Fighting Farmers special to so many—even to some who have never seen them in action? I think one reason is that they are for real. The history of Lewisville is basically the history of real farmers; honorable, hard-working, conscientious, conservative farm families who worked hard, played hard, and stayed together—whether it was getting the crops in, playing a Sunday baseball game in a pasture, or—eventually—competing with great success in organized school sports.

To me, it is only natural that "Big John"—the peaceful, powerful, and mystical Farmer—has become the symbol for the many teams that now represent Lewisville High School in competitive endeavors.

I could write at length about Big John and Farmer success, but numbering and extolling Farmer victories is not my task. Gary has done that very well in the pages ahead. You will find many interesting facts, fancies, and wonderments in those pages. There are details about the great Farmer team of 1972 which was led by the unbelievable Paul Rice—the greatest runner I have ever seen, at any level. You will learn about Coach Raymond Mattingly's fine teams of an earlier time, and of many other fine teams, players, and coaches. There are stories of Lewisville's own Walt Garrison, the Oklahoma State University All-American and—in my mind—the greatest Cowboy of them all. You will become better acquainted with Max Goldsmith, the football and track legend that Lewisville is lucky enough to still have in its midst. You will learn about the great teams of the Neal Wilson era. And finally, you will read about Coach Ronnie Gage and the fantastic Texas State Champions of 1993—probably the best Farmer football team ever.

But—again—the pages ahead are Gary's, and he has done a wonderful job of researching and writing. Gary—himself an ex-student and player—is a good example of the men—young and old—who have done so much to initiate, build, and further Farmer football tradition. I congratulate him for his completion of the difficult task of researching and writing this book. I commend it to all who are true believers in the Maroon and White: Go, Fighting Farmers!

—BILL SHIPMAN

Preface

They come, they go. They talk the talk for awhile. They boldly put in a claim about being "the best." Eventually, however, truth and common sense prevail. Realizing they can't walk that talk, they wisely shut up.

There is now silence in Pennsylvania. Ditto for California. Give it awhile and the same will apply in Florida.

Over the last several decades, those states have all bragged about replacing "us" as America's mecca of high school football.

Impossible, of course. Forget it, you people. It hasn't happened. It won't happen.

We invented high school football in Texas . . . well, probably we did. And even if not, we perfected it to such a level that no Pennsylvania, California or Florida can ever duplicate it, much less surpass it.

OK, so I'm prejudice on the subject. But that doesn't mean I'm not right. Growing up in Texas in the late '50s and early '60s, the high school game became part of my blood and my heritage. The same applies for every Texan.

And over the course of 30 years at the *Dallas Morning News*, I've also had the opportunity to talk to major college football coaches from coast to coast.

Just ask—they'll tell you. Texas high school football is the best.

Stop by a city like Lewisville on a Friday night in the fall and you can see for yourself. Friday night with the Fighting Farmers is what this book is all about. About being a part of the very best.

—Randy Galloway
Dallas Morning News, 1994

INTRODUCTION

Once in a while extraordinary events occur, inspiring those of us fortunate to witness them, and motivates us to record the happenings for safe keeping. Such is the case with me in reference to the 5A Division II State Championship captured by the Lewisville Fighting Farmers from the Aldine MacArthur Generals at the Astrodome on December 18, 1993. Not only was I able to witness this game, but I was also present for the 1972 near miss at a state title against Uvalde in Austin. The agonizing memory of that contest is what made the eventual 1993 championship that much sweeter, as those who were there 21 years earlier will confirm. It was my observation, however, that the majority of those who witnessed the state championship, certainly those who played, were not around in 1972 and do not know just how great that team was, nor where the winning tradition we currently enjoy at Lewisville began, which is what prompted this book.

First let me tell you what this book is not. It is not an attempt to compare the three most successful teams since 1970, those being the 1972, 1979 and 1993 Fighting Farmer football teams. The truth is it's difficult to compare any two teams from separate times in history, simply because there are too many variables involved that make it unfair to declare one team superior to another. About the only way to determine which team is better, apart from public debate, is to line 'em up and let 'em play. If there was a Jurassic Park type experiment that could be performed to resurrect the best teams throughout Lewisville

Farmer history and pit them against one another, maybe it could be determined which team was the best. No, this book is not about declaring an all-time best team, for there are arguments both for and against each candidate.

Also, I do not profess this book to be a complete work, although that was the intent initially. Some of the information I sought was unavailable to me due to loose reporting requirements to the University Interscholastic League office in the early days, or priorities other than sports reporting in the early editions of the Lewisville Enterprise. There was a war going on during some of those early years that required more attention than the outcome of the Farmer football games on Friday nights, consequently some information on the Farmer games went unrecorded. This work, though exhaustive, is, at best, incomplete. More accurately, it is mostly in tact with a few holes here and there, prohibiting this from being a complete work.

What I've tried to do with this book is preserve as much of the history of Lewisville Fighting Farmer football as possible, both as a tribute to the 1993 State Champions, as well as all those young men who have had the good fortune to call themselves "Farmers," once upon a time. In an attempt to link the present with the past, as many rosters as possible, beginning with the early 1920s to present, have been included in the appendix, along with season records, dates, opponents, locations, scores and coaches. The standings in district each year are included when available. I have also included all-district selections by year according to the coaches' picks. I apologize for any omissions or inaccuracies in advance as I am certain somewhere, in the long line of maroon and white faithful, a few pieces of information have evaded me.

But mostly, this book is about Farmer football history from its origin to the present. You will read about people named Hoss Williams, B.F. Tunnell, Niles Ladehoff, Chad Nelson and Paul Rice. You will read about more famous players, such as Walt Garrison, Jesse and Teddy Garcia, and Mike Aljoe. You will read about exciting games in 1968 against McKinney, 1969 against Plano and 1970 against Gainseville, the exciting comeback in 1972 against McKinney, the season saving catch in 1979 by Eugene Corbin against Abilene Cooper, and a game-saving interception against Sherman by Jason Cotten. And, since no work about Fighting Farmer football would be complete without it, there's even a chapter about the "Band That Marches With Pride," the award winning Fighting Farmer marching band. If you're not a Farmer fan before you read this book, hopefully you will be one when you put it down.

Finally, I am much in debt to some fine folks who enthusiastically share my passion for the remembrance of Farmer football, and have freely offered information from days gone by, entrusting me with valuable photographs and artifacts to include in this publication. Thanks to Mr. J.K. Delay for the countless interviews and recollections; also to James Polser for his expertise on the historical perspective of Lewisville. My undying gratitude goes out to Henry Vance and Hoss Williams for their muses from the early 1930s, and to Max Goldsmith for a lifelong perspective on Farmer football from his days as

Introduction

a player in 1938–39, and as a coach and athletic director from 1967 to 1983. To Neal Wilson for his support and contributions, and to Ronnie Gage for the many hours spent in capturing the 1993 season in print, I extend my deepest appreciation. And to the countless others who have contributed to this work with either information, confirmation of content, photographs or encouragement, I deeply thank you. Finally, to my wife, who allowed me the freedom to go gallivanting about the state to undertake this project, I especially thank. It could not have been possible without her.

But mostly what I want to accomplish with this book is to bring back memories to those of us in the past who were blessed to have worn the maroon and white under the Friday night lights, and to give to others a glimpse of what it means to be a Farmer. I hope you enjoy it.

. . .

CHAPTER

WHERE IT ALL BEGAN

As A FRIEND AND I pulled into the parking lot of Houston's Astrodome on December 18, 1993, one of the parking lot attendants, a young fellow in his early twenties, approached me and asked where we were from, since there were no external markings on my Mazda indicating my allegiance, unlike the multitude of motorized shrines of metal and shoe polish inscribed, with phrases like: "We're No. 1" and "State Bound," which could easily be altered to read "State Champs" with the wipe of a wet rag and the scribble of some close-at-hand shoe polish. In fact, many of the estimated 15,000 fans from both teams on hand that day were armed with glass cleaner and shoe polish in hopes the particular message on their vehicle could be changed to the enviable one that read "State Champs '93," signaling to all on the trip home that in their community abode the newly crowned Division II 5A State Champions.

FRIDAY NIGHT FARMERS

Actually, his question was, "Are ya'll from Lewisville?" of which I proudly responded in the affirmative. He then went on to inquire as to how Lewisville came to be known as the "Farmers." I quickly answered by leading him on with the tail that, years ago, Lewisville's football team was scheduled to play a neighboring team, but were short of players due to the cotton harvest that had to be reaped so, on the way out of town to the game, the bus stopped by a cotton field and picked up enough farmers to complete the team. When they got off the bus, most of the players were still dressed in overalls and straw hats, since they came right from the fields, and the other team taunted them saying, "We're gonna play a bunch of farmers!" Well, Lewisville went on to win the game in spite of their lack of preparation time and unorthodox uniforms. The attendant said, "Really? That's wild." I hated to bust his bubble, but I had to come clean and admit my misinformation. I then gave him the explanation that was given to me years ago.

I told him that somewhere in the history of Lewisville there was a close association with Texas A&M, since Lewisville was a farming community, and it was not uncommon to name the school mascot after something identifiable to the community from which it came. I gave him the example of the University of Miami and its close association with hurricanes, thus being nicknamed the Hurricanes. The same with Arkansas and the well-known razorback pig indigenous to that state, and so on. Therefore, Lewisville was called the farmers from that day forward. I added that since A&M was maroon and white, the same colors were adopted as well. I was satisfied with my explanation and the parking lot attendant seemed to accept it, so I went in the stadium to select a seat for that afternoon's contest. After the game was over and all the excitement dwindled, I began to wonder if that story I had detailed was actually true, or a fabrication of the truth. That's when I began to investigate for myself the origin of this unique mascot.

According to life long Lewisville resident and historian James Polser Lewisville, being primarily a farming community, derived its school's mascot name from just that. The settlement of Lewisville was a day's ride on horseback from Ft. Richardson in Greenville to the east, and Jasckboro to the west. Both were dispatch sites for Confederate soldiers, consequently, Lewisville was a good place to rest your horse and stay the night. With the combination of that and the variety of sand and black dirt conducive for various types of farming, Lewisville emerged as a prolific farm community. Seven gins were located in Lewisville after its settlement in 1845 and all the cotton crops in Denton, Collin and Fannin Counties were ginned there, as well as much of Tarrant County's crops. Naturally, those who lived in Lewisville and attended Lewisville High School were, indeed, farmers, so the name naturally evolved.

Former Superintendent John Keith Delay concurs with this account of the origin of the naming of the Farmers. Delay was the Superintendent of LISD from 1942 until 1966, and was himself the head coach, and only coach, from 1942–47. According to him organized football in Lewisville began in either

Where It All Began

1923 or 1924, and then Superintendent B.F. Tunnell was influential in naming the Farmers. School personnel were scarce in those early days and wore many hats to fulfill the requirements of the state in providing a well rounded education, and Tunnell was no exception. He was the vocational agriculture instructor as well as Superintendent. According to Delay, "Tunnell was an A&M man. When it came time to pick a name for the team he influenced the decision in favor of the Farmers since Lewisville was a farming community and all the kids came off of farms." The late Sam Salmon, who played on the football team from 1921–25, told a reporter in 1973, "the football players got together one day and voted on a mascot and colors for the team," no doubt influenced by Mr. Tunnell.

So both of the stories I told the parking lot attendant were essentially true, the latter being more accurate, but the former more fun to tell. As for the colors of maroon and white, there is really no clear cut answer. Polser could not recall any significance to selecting maroon and white, but did recall in the 1910s and 1920s class colors for Lewisville High School being green and white, "but the school colors have always been maroon and white." Mr. Delay did not recall any symbolism or special reason for our current colors, as well. Regardless of the reason for maroon and white, Lewisville is not alone with this color combination. One hundred twenty-seven other high schools in Texas have maroon and white as their school colors, several of which have competed against the Farmers, creating a bit of confusion to the less familiar fan. The most notable maroon and white opponent of the Farmers has been Plano. Often when these two teams meet, there appears to be one big wave of maroon and white, including the bands, drill teams, and cheerleaders.

So we really do not know what reason, if any, is behind the selection of the colors that have flown over the city of Lewisville for seventy-plus years. Perhaps it can be speculated that Mr. Tunnell equally influenced the color selection to match that of his alma mater, Texas A&M. This seems likely, but will probably remain unknown as fact, unless further research reveals the answer.

Although the Farmers have an unusual name, it is not entirely unique. In fact, only two teams in Texas own the name Farmers, the only other being Farmersville, for obvious reasons, although the Robstown Cotton Pickers and Roscoe Plowboys are distant cousins. Farmersville is located in Collin County 30 miles east-northeast of Lewisville, midway between McKinney and Greenville. Other nearby neighbors to Farmersville are Plano and Allen. McKinney, Plano, Greenville and Allen have been or are regulars on the Farmers schedule, however, only one time in history have both Lewisville and Farmersville engaged in battle, that being in 1950 for the Regional Championship. The Farmers won 17–9 to claim title to the championship of Region 5 of class B, which is as far as class B teams played in those days. By the way, it was the Lewisville Farmers who won that title, capping a perfect 11–0 season.

Along with the name Farmer came a mascot donning overalls and a straw hat, although in the early days of Farmer football a young citizen of Lewisville, often a younger brother of one of the players, coaches or faculty members usually filled this role. Only recently did the Farmer mascot, currently known as "Big John," occupy a space on the sidelines alongside the Farmer cheerleaders. This tradition began in the fall of 1970 with Scott Jackson serving as the mascot in both the 1970 and 1971 football seasons. Jackson dressed in overalls, a straw hat and an old game jersey, and Big John has essentially not varied much from his debut 23 years ago, although in the fall of 1983 he took on a different image with the addition of the current mascot's costume.

Although Jackson was the first Farmer mascot to accompany the cheerleaders in pep rallies and on the sidelines during games, the tag of Big John did not arrive until the fall of 1972, the following fall after Jackson graduated. Head coach Bill Shipman, in an attempt to build up spirit in a program that finished 2–7–1 the previous year, invented a character of legendary proportion, and told of heroic feats accomplished by the extraordinary being. This character he named Big John influenced by the former Jimmy Dean hit song of the same title. Naturally, the song fit right in with the spirit Shipman was trying to create and, thus, became the Farmer's theme, which is still heard on the sidelines and in pep rallies to this date.

The image of the Farmer was emblazoned on the water tower located in the northeast quadrant of the intersection of Interstate Highway 35 East and Main Street, behind the old Piggly Wiggly store, bearing the image of the profile of a Farmer wearing a straw hat with a piece of wheat or cotton protruding from his mouth. That Farmer symbol has evolved over the years, taking on various shapes and forms, but maintaining the spirit that has surrounded LHS since the crude beginnings of its football program in 1914.

The first symbol of the Farmer arrived on the scene in 1923, just a year or so after Lewisville adopted its nickname of Farmer. Edwin Neely and Jack Bonds, both students at LHS in the early 1920s and members of the football team, were in study hall class on the third story of the building which housed the entire student population of LISD, a site where present day College Street Elementary resides. Neely was an artist and thought it necessary that LHS have a symbol to represent the newly named Farmers. It was during that study hall period that he and Bonds joined forces to draw the first Farmer mascot, a profile of a country farmer from the chest up, outfitted in a flannel shirt, vest and straw hat, complete with a five o'clock shadow and the familiar straw between his teeth.

Since the first yearbook did not get published until the spring of 1942, the image drawn by Neely and Bonds remained the official logo of LHS until the 1942 annual was produced. The symbol adopted at that time borrowed the same components of the original Farmer, however it was reduced to just the profile of the Farmer's head, with the hat, straw and unshaven face in tact.

This Farmer was more animated than Neely's, and struck various poses

Where It All Began

The first Big John, Billy Merritt, in 1972, along with cheerleader Carrie Bailey.

T.J. Koehler as the Farmer mascot in 1974.

The first Farmer as drawn by Edwin Neely and Jack Bonds in 1923.

The Farmer symbol as it appeared in the 1942 yearbook.

The many poses of the 1942 Farmer.

From the cover and inside the 1944 yearbook.

throughout the 1942 yearbook to introduce the different sections of the first annual, but the expression remained the same.

This Farmer lasted through the mid-'60s, but other depictions of the LHS mascot were introduced periodically, with several overlapping as complementing symbols of Lewisville's Farmers. Altogether, 18 different symbols have been identified in the history of Farmer football as representatives of the Lewisville Maroon and White, the latter one coming on the scene in 1983. Although the current Farmer is a far cry from Neely's Farmer composed in 1923, the spirit is the same.

In 1943 two other depictions of the Farmer mascot were constructed, capturing the image of a younger, healthier Farmer. Both appeared in the 1943–44 yearbook, one on the cover, and one inside the front cover. The Farmer on the cover showed a full front view of a young Farmer, obviously after a hard day's work, leaning on the plow he had no doubt just used to plow a good bit of acreage earlier that day.

The other was the traditional view from the shoulders up with a strong countenance, high cheek bones, a wide brim hat, but no five o'clock shadow. This Farmer captured the trend in community growth and reflected the strength of the up and coming town which lay north of the Dallas-Ft. Worth Metroplex.

In 1947 the Farmer was drawn plowing a field, instead of leaning on that plow. This image, or some variation of it, was around as late as 1964, and was obviously one of the favorite symbols of the Fighting Farmer spirit.

Although other symbols emerged, the Farmer plowing the field was retained as the primary logo. For example, in 1947 two identical versions of another Farmer appeared, both featuring the head of a weathered, but friendly face of a Farmer with a hat more like a cowboy hat than the familiar straw hat. The only difference between the two versions was that one had a cotton boll in his mouth, while the other did not, linking the new image with that of Neely's original Farmer. These two portrayals were visible off and on until 1958, and faded away as other symbols became more popular.

In 1949 and 1950, two additional logos were added to the expanding Farmer gallery, again, both being just the head, and retaining many of the features of their predecessors. The '49 model was an imitation of the 1941 Farmer, but not as refined.

The 1950 depiction was somewhat similar to the one introduced in 1948, but had a straw hat instead of the cowboy hat. Both of these images served as transition symbols of the Farmer mascot as they gave way to other, more popular ones, disappearing after their respective years, never to reemerge in later years.

One of the most popular and lasting versions of the farmer was introduced in 1955. This Farmer took on a totally different appearance than those of the past in that he was a harmless looking fellow, with a broad smile, Ben Franklin glasses, and a sparse goatee beard on a head that was too big for his body, on

Where It All Began

One of the favorite symbols — the Farmer steering a plow — displaying silent strength and determination.

Two versions of the 1947 Farmer.

The 1949 Farmer (left) and 1950 Farmer were only used once.

Beginning with the 1955 season, this depiction remained as one of the most popular in the history of the Lewisville Farmers.

The Farmer's Harvest banner as it first appeared (left) and in later years.

A new look for the Farmers in the 1960s.

The Farmer logo adopted in the 1987–88 school year.

Friday Night Farmers

Big John interacting with some players on the sideline and up close and personal.

purpose. He also bore a pitchfork in his right hand, as well as the familiar straw hat and stalk of wheat emerging out from between his teeth behind the friendly grin.

He appeared more like Fred Ziffel from television's Green Acres than any Farmer in the past. This version of the Farmer was depicted on a banner area merchants and townspeople would hang in their windows that read, "Home Game Tonight—Support The Farmers." In fact, one of these banners still hangs in James Polser's office at the Lewisville Feed Mill in Old Town, Lewisville.

The next lasting depiction of the Farmer appeared in 1960 as a part of the banner of the weekly school newspaper, the Farmer's Harvest.

This symbol was enhanced in future years, but remained basically the same with the comical smile, straw hat and wheat stalk, with a pencil resting above his ear, reflecting the merge of journalist and school mascot. This symbol was retired as part of the banner in the mid '80s as the school paper was revamped to accommodate the trend toward modernization in journalism.

In 1966 the Farmer emblem took on an image unlike any before or since. He traded in his overalls and plow for a football uniform and pitchfork, complete with brogans and a helmet. This Farmer was so popular it replaced the one on the water tower in 1966. In 1968 Hollis Henry, of Henry's Signs in Lewisville, painted the image on the newly constructed locker room.

Henry's stepson, Mike Riley, was an all-district member of the 1970 and 1971 Farmers, and Henry was a booster club member. He volunteered his time and materials to give birth to the new Farmer image on the field house. This image remained until 1983 when the Farmer got a face lift and took on a mean, more determined demeanor.

Where It All Began

Although not officially adopted until the 1987-88 school year as the school mascot, the image of Big John was changed in 1983. Some old time Farmer fans resisted the change, and still do today, but, as LHS teacher and Bell Crew sponsor David Wright explained, the change was to broaden the mascot to fit all school sports and activities, not just football. The new Farmer mascot lost the football uniform and regained his overalls and jersey for a new look which appealed to a younger, growing Lewisville.

The current school song has been so since 1950. Prior to that another song, "The Ole Maroon and White," served as the school song. Its origin is uncertain, but it lasted from about 1920 until the fall of 1950. Lewisville was growing and the Lewisville I.S.D. was expanding to accommodate it. The student population had outgrown the three story building at College Street, and the school board and town voted to build a new high school. The new high school was constructed on Purnell Street, which is now Delay Middle School, to house the 200 or so high school students, and it seemed fitting that along with a new school should come a new song. The school song from Cornell University was adopted as the new LHS school song, and Dorothy Taylor composed the familiar words to the current song:

Far down in a town so noble,
Challening the eye,
Stands a school above all others,
Stands our Lewisville High.

Lewisville High to thee we shall be
Ever loyal and true.
Fighting always to do service,
For Maroon and White.

There aren't many who recall the words to the original song, however, they were discovered in the 1942 Farmer yearbook:

We're loyal to you, Lewisville High,
We're Maroon and White, Lewisville High,
We'll back you to stand, against the best in the land,
For we know you will stand, Lewisville High, Rah! Rah!

So step out that ball, Lewisville High,
We're backing you all, Lewisville High,
Our team is a fame, protect your home, boys,
For we expect a victory from you, Lewisville High.

Life-long Lewisville resident, and 1935 graduate of LHS, Gertrude Sigler, recalled the original words to the school song as being slightly different:

We're loyal to you, Lewisville High,
We're Maroon and White, Lewisville High,
We'll back you to stand, against the best in the land,
For we know you have sand (grit), Lewisville High.

Friday Night Farmers

So snap out that ball, Lewisville High,
We're backing you all, Lewisville High,
Our team is the fame protector, oh boys,
For we expect a victory from you, Lewisville High.

Some variation of this version functioned as the school song from 1920 to 1950. There was no band in Lewisville until 1958, so the pep squad was the primary performer of the song.

The current fight song has been the Farmer fight song since as far back as anyone can remember. The tune's official name is "Washington and Lee Swing." No one knows where the words originated, but the familiar hymn is popular with fans old and young:

Oh, when that L-H-S team falls in line,
We're gonna win, boys, win another time,
And for that football team we love so well,
And for that football team we'll yell and yell and yell.

We're gonna fight, fight, fight for every yard,
We'll circle in and hit that line so hard,
We're gonna put those (next opponent) in the sod, on the side,
Farmers fight!

So the question of the origin of the name and colors of the Lewisville Fighting Farmers is somewhat satisfied. Although the answer is not inscribed in some historical book for reference by armchair historians as myself, the consensus is that our common link with Texas A&M, then called Farmers, is what most likely influenced the naming of the mascot of Lewisville High School. Regardless of why or how Lewisville High School selected its name, one thing is certain; a rich tradition of spirit has remained from the early 1920s until today, captured by the spirit of the farmer.

. . .

CHAPTER II

A Farming Community

LEWISVILLE WAS ORIGINALLY SETTLED as part of the W.S. Peters Colony of north Texas in 1844. In order to attract settlers in the somewhat newly formed Republic of Texas, formed in 1836, large parcels of land were offered as inducements to groups of men, called impresarios. The function of these impresarios was to assemble willing settlers, either immigrants or citizens from other states in the country who had not had luck in establishing themselves in land ownership. The purpose in granting the land to the newcomers was for them to settle and become tax paying citizens in the young Texas Republic. A bill passed in the Congress of Texas in 1841 provided for the granting of these large tracts of land, usually 640 acres, to be settled for farming or some kind of mercantilism, attracting both rich and poor alike to settle in Texas.

The first of these impresarios was headed by William Smalling Peters, and his three sons: W.C., Henry J. and John. Peters, along with 20 other investors, formed the Texas Agricultural, Commercial and Manufacturing Company with the intent of uprooting from their native Louisville, Kentucky, home and relocating to Texas to take advantage of the generous offer of land. Peters was awarded a contract on August 31, 1841, six months after the bill passed. The contract gave the Peters Colony Settlement "wild land in North Texas," covering all or part of 26 counties that exist today.

Denton County was one of those counties. In exchange for the land, Peters was required to survey and parcel the land into tracts, and petition the Republic of Texas for land titles. In turn, the individual settlers were to dwell on the land no less than three years, requiring a minimum of fifteen acres per tract to be farmed. The allocation per family was 640 acres, with half that for single men age 17 or older. After the three year requirement was satisfied the land could be sold or traded. To give an idea of the value of a parcel of land in today's prices, at $2.00 a square foot a single acre would bring $87,120.00, and each family had 640 of them. So in exchange for transplanting their families and, in essence, their lives to Texas, the early settlers were given an opportunity at land ownership and the chance to carve out an honest living. The opportunity was not without hardship. There were Indians, pestilence, the acquisition of goods and supplies and medical needs, not to mention the sheer work necessary to turn wild, uncultivated land into a livable, producing homestead.

The land office operated by W.S. Peters was located in what is now the southeastern corner of Denton County. The land there was attractive, with varied soil types, and the Elm Fork of the Trinity River divided it, making a natural choice for Peters and company to set up shop in the newly acquired territory. To the west of the office, approximately one mile, lay the budding town of Lewisville in its embryonic stage.

The earliest settlement in Peters Colony was by John W. King and his son, Augustus G. Their settlement was the heart of the current day Lewisville, covering the area currently known as Old Town. In the fall of 1844 settlers from Platte, Missouri, John and James H. Hallford, settled the area west of King's settlement, which soon became known as Hallford's Prairie. Much of the territory that is now the town of Flower Mound is located in the Hallford's Prairie territory. An error in the writings of an early Denton County historian, Edward Bates, has the spelling of Hallford as Holford, but the original spelling is Hallford. Consequently, the errant spelling was retained throughout the historical accounts and the territory became known as Holford's Prairie. That explains the street named Holford's Prairie, after the early settlement, east of Lewisville across from the Lewisville Fish Hatchery on state Highway 121.

The next settlers to stake claim in Lewisville were the Fox, Rawlins and Craft families in 1845. It seems these families brought with them 50 or 60 slaves, making the area of Lewisville one of the largest slave selections in the country. Local citizens referred to the area as the non-politically correct "Niggerville," due to the large slave population. The area was also called Hallford's Prairie as well, after the settlement. In 1855 a wealthy surveyor,

A Farming Community

Basdeal W. Lewis, came to Hallford's Prairie, bought huge amounts of land, divided it into town lots, and named it Lewisville, although it took a while for the name to stick. Mr. Lewis remained only two or three years, then left a much wealthier man. The name remained, however, and that's where the town of Lewisville was born.

After news spread of the fruitful land and opportunity available in Lewisville, other settlers began to migrate to the developing area. Most of the town's activity built up around the area in north Lewisville on the site of Old Hall Cemetery. In 1862 a two story log cabin was erected, through a community effort, to serve as a general meeting hall. All church denominations met there, along with a school, on the bottom floor. The Free Masons occupied the second floor. The structure was officially named Hallford Prairie Hall, but was shortened to Old Hall, along with the adjacent cemetary, which still bears the same name today. The cemetary is located on McGee Lane's east side, midway between Valley Ridge and F.M. 407 in north Lewisville.

The town's activity began to move southeast in 1881 with the Missouri, Kansas and Texas Railroad's construction through the eastern edge of Lewisville. The Dallas and Wichita Railroad was authorized by the Republic of Texas to construct a railroad from Dallas to Wichita Falls in May 1873. The contract required 20 miles to be completed by July 1, 1875, or else the company would have to forfeit its charter. It barely retained its charter by completing the 20-mile section at midnight of June 30, 1875. The point of completion fell approximately one mile south of Lewisville. The project seemed to have stalled at that point, however, T.M. Smith apparently sold some land to the railroad to continue construction, provided the track be built within one-half mile of Lewisville. Later, the Dallas and Wichita Railroad—now changed to Missouri, Kansas and Texas Railroad, or MKT Railroad—began construction again in 1881, eventually reaching Denton in 1882. The railroad, still existent in the eastern part of Lewisville, approximately one-quarter mile from Main and Mill streets, enticed the migration to that area of the newly settled town, and businesses began to crop up along Main Street. Dry goods stores, gins, saloons and grist mills dotted both sides of Main Street, and merchants began carving out decent livings by serving and supplying the droves of people seeking land and opportunity in the fast growing town 21 miles north of Dallas.

The main function of the merchants of the town of Lewisville was twofold: (1) to sell supplies to the settlers, and (2) to provide entertainment. General stores carried a variety of essentials, such as seed, fabric, furniture and other supplies necessary for setting up and maintaining homesteads. Saloons provided relief from a hard day's work for the tired farmers. They could take a belt off a bottle of whiskey or corn liquor and get to know other farmers, sharing experiences and getting advice on what to grow and how to grow it.

The main industry in Lewisville was farming, as one might guess. Fertile lands and favorable climates were well suited for the growth of corn, cotton, wheat, grain and peanuts, and harvests were plentiful in the newly settled

Main Street in Lewisville on July 4, 1911. Many of the buildings pictured above still exist.

land. Naturally, gins and mills were opened and operated to process the crops from the farms of Lewisville, allowing them to maximize their earnings by not having to pay a middle man to transport their harvests to a gin in some neighboring county or halfway across the state. The gins were so successful they began ginning for other counties, and soon were ginning all crops from Denton, Fannin and Collin counties, and most of Tarrant County. This provided much needed revenue to support this emerging community.

The presence of waterways on three sides of Lewisville, the Trinity River and Denton Creek to the north, and Timber Creek to the south ensured a sufficient water supply, not only for raising crops, but for use in households as well.

Although several wooden framed buildings were constructed into what is now the downtown area, the first brick building was built in 1875 by W.D. Milliken Sr. It was located on the north side of Main Street, midway between Mill Street and North Poydras Street, in the space now occupied at the approximate location of Michael's Music Shop.

In 1877 funds were allocated for the first public school in Lewisville, although teachers taught privately in their homes for a small fee prior to this time. Each community eventually had a community school, such as Double Oak, and Donald, to the west, Round Grove and Bethel to the south, and

A Farming Community

The heart of Lewisville as shown in 1957. Old Town was still the hub of activity as businesses were lined along Main Street.

Causey, McCurly, Midway, Lake and Hebron to the east. Soon after, other buildings of brick began to emerge on Main Street, showing signs of stability in the young town of Lewisville.

Besides being a choice area for farming, Lewisville was a hub of receiving and transporting goods to those who lived in Hallford's Prairie, now Flower Mound, and other areas to the north and west. By 1883 Lewisville's population had grown to 300, but the commercial, or down town area reflected more than that due to the influx of travelers passing through. By this time Lewisville had two hardware stores, two hotels, two doctors, four grocery stores, three dry goods stores, a wagon maker, a general store, two drug stores and a grist mill. A lot of commerce for so little population. However, Lewisville was on the road, almost midpoint between Ft. Richardson in Greenville to the east, and Jacksboro to the west, a dispatch for civil war soldiers, and was heavily traveled. The smooth, gently rolling terrain, laced with plenty of water, made it an attractive path through the north section of the state, so Lewisville was frequented by hundreds of travelers, all needing supplies and a place to stay.

The little town of Lewisville was a welcome site to the tired, thirsty vaga-

The budding town of Lewisville in 1962, before the population began to increase in the early '70s. Construction west of IH-35 was in its infancy.

bond with his pockets full of money, and the merchants were more than eager to receive him—and his money.

The majority of supplies were to assist the farmer, the main source of revenue, so Lewisville became famous for its farming community. The population was distributed primarily between the area of what is now Mill Street and Charles Street, east and west, and Purnell Road to the south, and Justin Road, or F.M. 407, to the north, although the area of Lewisville stretched from the line which is now Kirkpatrick Lane, north of F.M. 1171, and Garden Ridge, south of F.M. 1171, to the city limits of The Colony to the east, leaving plenty of room for high spirited farmers to cultivate land for growth. Roads conducive for travel were constructed throughout the city, and later named after some of the early settlers, providing access to and from the downtown area, now secured in the heart of Lewisville.

The spirit of the farmer is what made Lewisville a success, beginning in 1844. The population continued to grow after 1883 by huge margins. From 1883 to 1930 the population grew to 853, an increase of 553 citizens, 90 percent of which lived and worked on farms. Each decade thereafter indicated steady growth as depicted in Table 1.

A Farming Community

Table 1: Population of Lewisville by decade

Year	Population	% Increase	Year	Population	% Increase
1930	853		1970	9,264	134.2%
1940	873	2.3%	1980	22,000	137.5%
1950	1,516	73.7%	1990	46,000	109.1%
1960	3,956	160.9%	1994	51,450	12.0%

Source: Lewisville Chamber of Commerce

Although not incorporated until 1925, Lewisville was well established by this time. As the population increased, Lewisville expanded its city limits west of Interstate Highway 35E in 1960 and began growing westward, away from the Old Town area to accommodate the influx of citizens.

The construction of the Dallas/Fort Worth International Airport, located six miles southwest of Lewisville, continued to attract urban dwellers as major businesses began to relocate in the north Texas area, and the Dallas/Fort Worth Metroplex in particular. Yet with the growth, Lewisville has not lost the spirit of its roots; the spirit of the farmer. Rather than being pushed aside with the arrival of new faces, the reverse seems to be true. It is not long after a resident moves to Lewisville that the spirit of the farmer moves to adopt the new citizen, making him or her a child of its own heritage. So it is no surprise when it came time to choose a mascot for its high school football team that "Farmer" was the natural choice. After all, that's the spirit that founded this thriving area, and the same spirit that sustains it.

. . .

CHAPTER

III

DOWN THROUGH THE YEARS

A look at Farmer Football before 1972

THE LEWISVILLE FARMER football program has enjoyed enviable success in recent years, capped off by its first state championship in the fall of 1993. The 1972 season serves as a milestone for the Farmers as the football program made a major turn upward, narrowly missing their first state title against the Uvalde Coyotes, losing 33–28. From that season until 1993 the Farmers have owned a remarkable winning record of 170 wins, 71 losses, and only nine ties. This calculates to a winning percentage of .690 during the 21 year span from 1972 to 1993, rivaling the winning traditions of Plano, Brownwood and Odessa Permian in Texas high school football. During this time period the Farmers captured eight district championships, and made 11 playoff appearances, with only four losing records. In fact, the last time the Farmers had a losing season was in 1980, 13 years prior to their state championship season, with a 4–5–1 record. Ironically, the Farmers were picked number one in many preseason polls based on the 1979 semifinal playoff appearance.

Down Through The Years

Not much is remembered, or at least not talked about prior to 1972, however winning in Lewisville did not begin then. Perusing through the trophy case at Lewisville High School, much evidence can be found to show that the winning tradition began many years earlier. The first district championship for the Farmers, on record, was 1932, and from 1932 to 1957 Lewisville won 12 district titles, five bi-district championships and two regional trophies. They would have won another title in 1941, however, the Farmers were forced to forfeit all but one game due to the use of an ineligible player, spoiling what would have been a 9–1 record and a 13th district crown.

Texas high school football began in 1894 with the first game between Galveston Ball High School and Texas A&M College. This may seem to have been a mismatch, however A&M only won by a 14–6 margin. The eligibility rules for players were extremely lose in those early years, and the roster for Galveston Ball included a few high school students, some teachers and students from the nearby Galveston Medical College, so the contest was more evenly matched than it initially appeared. It wasn't long after that Lewisville began its football program. According to the Lewisville Enterprise, the male students at Lewisville High School formed an Athletic Association in September 1914, and began playing competitive football, although no records or rosters are available. The University Interscholastic League was not formed until 1920, so no official records across the state were kept before this year, and even after then many records are incomplete. Therefore, information on the Lewisville Farmers from 1914–1935 are sketchy, at best. Information from 1936–93 is complete and in tact, and paints a total picture of Farmer football from the post-depression era to present.

The earliest data available regarding the outcome of a Lewisville Fighting Farmer game comes from 1920, with Lewisville losing to Grapevine 40–6. Many teams in the 1920s played limited schedules, due to the shortage of teams available nearby to compete against. The athletic departments, which usually consisted of only a single coach who, more often than not, was also the high school principal and sometimes even the superintendent, were not as sophisticated and had different problems that are nonexistent on the same scale today. Along with budgets and eligibility requirements, early coaches had to deal with scheduling and transportation problems, not only of vehicles but also an inferior infrastructure; not just finding a team to play, but a road that led to it. Perhaps the 1920 Farmers could only find one opponent to play that season, although other teams during this era played complete schedules. It is more likely that not all results were reported to the UIL, and no records were retained in the athletic office or at the high school. Since no yearbooks were published at Lewisville High School before the 1941–42 school year, and due to the unavailability of newspapers prior to 1946, many of the results are simply nonexistent, unless by chance one happened to be fortunate to, by chance, discover a score or two while researching other items, or obtain some information in conversation with a relative of a former player.

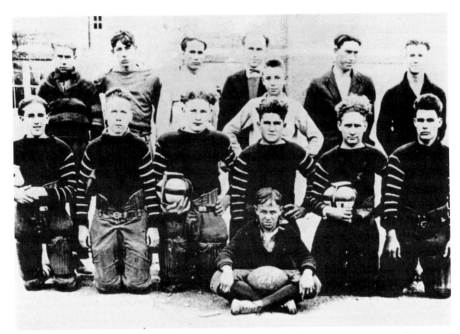

The 1921 Lewisville High School football team. *Top row:* John Henry Hoskins, Sultan Boyd, Charlie Whitlock, Coach Lee Preston, Otho Silk, Sam Salmon. *Standing* in front of Preston: Raymond Emery, manager. *Kneeling:* Edwin Neely, Jack Bonds, Howard Cobb, Garland Orr, J.T. Watson, Otis Shaw. *Front:* Carl Ratliff.

So from 1914 to 1935 only a handful of results are available. For instance, from 1920–1924 only five scores are available, including the 40–6 loss to Grapevine in '20. The only score available in 1922 was a 66–7 loss to Plano. This was the most points given up by a Lewisville Farmer team on record. The Farmers dropped a 34–0 contest to Highland Park in 1923. From research of memorabilia it was discovered that the Farmers were 5–3 in 1924, but only two of those scores are available. Lewisville lost to Gainesville, 64–0, with the second highest points surrendered by a Farmer team, for one of the three losses on the year. Lewisville defeated Sanger 20–13 for one of the five Farmer victories. There does seem to be a conflict, as a trophy at LHS indicates the Farmers defeated Sanger 20–19 for the county championship in '24. It is not certain if this was a separate contest for the county championship, or if by virtue of the regularly scheduled game victory the championship was awarded to Lewisville. If the latter is true, there is a conflict in the scores, one being 20–13 and the other being 20–19. In either case, the Farmers finished 5–3 and won the Denton County championship over Sanger, the first championship of any kind credited to a Farmer team.

In 1925 the Farmers finished 1–3–1 under head coach Ed Lowe, who had become the coach in 1924. In Lewisville's five games in '25, they defeated

Down Through The Years

The Lewisville Fighting Farmers of 1924

only Sanger, 6–0. With losses to the Masonic Lodge Orphans Home of Ft. Worth, 21–0, and a 25–0 revenge victory by Sanger, the Farmers tied Grapevine 0–0, before losing to them in a re-match, 48–0, to close the season. No results are available for the 1926 season.

In 1927 the Farmers boasted a 7–2 record, good enough for a second place district finish to Grapevine. One of the losses Lewisville suffered was to the North Texas State Teachers College (now University of North Texas) freshman team, 12–7. The best finish for the Farmers from 1914 to 1935 came in 1932 where Lewisville defeated Whitesboro 14–0 for the bi-district championship. The team, coached by R.O. Davis, went 8–0–1 on the season, setting up the bi-district face off. The only blemish on the record was a 0-0 tie against Sanger.

Sanger was a rival of Lewisville's since 1923, and proved to be an obstacle to the Farmers that day. Lewisville, who relied primarily on a somewhat unorthodox passing game, was plagued by an unusually high wind that day. Henry Vance, who played left end for the Farmers from 1931–33, recalled the extreme gusty conditions as being detrimental. "Sanger had a pretty good team in 1931 and 1932 and was one of the oldest rivals of Lewisville," according to Vance, "and the wind made Sanger extra tough that day in 1932." It was all the Farmers could do to hold them off and prevent them from spoiling LHS' unbeaten season. Although the Farmers did not score themselves, they were able to keep Sanger off the scoreboard, playing to a 0–0 tie. This was as close as the Farmers came to a loss that year as they posted the 9–0–1 record, and both district and bi-district championships.

The 1932 Bi-District Champions

The Champions in formation. *L–R Back Row:* Dick Hayes, Woodrow Sigler, Hoss Williams and Bud Waldrip. *Front:* Pal Boyd, Doyle French, Cornelius Sonntag, Woodrow Bays, Lee Bond, Robert Jasper and Henry Vance.

Down Through The Years

The 1932 Farmers outscored their collective opponents, 190–6 on the season, the only touchdown allowed in the third week of the season against the Justin Texans. Unfortunately for Lewisville, Class B teams played only to the bi-district level. There are some that think this team could have won a state championship, or gone deep into the playoffs if a playoff format had included a state championship as its ultimate prize.

The next season, 1933, the Farmers finished 3–6–1 under a new coach, Roger Elms. Elms' predecessor, R.O. Davis, coached from 1931–32, notching the bi-district championship in 1932. Elms came in and coached for the 1933 season alone after Davis left to take a coaching job at Highland Park Junior High. Although the Farmers finished with just three wins, the season was highlighted by a 72–12 victory over the Celina Bearcats in the next to last game of the season. This is the third highest offensive output in Farmer history, coming in a less than spectacular 3–6–1 season. Had the Farmers redistributed their points among the losses from the 72-point season high scoring game, they may have secured yet another district title, as Lewisville outscored their opponents 131–122 in 1933.

Taft Dunsworth became the Farmers' coach in 1934 and continued through the 1935 season. Not much is available in the way of scores, schedules and standing in district for these two seasons. In fact, the only results available are in 1934, with a 19–0 loss to Grand Prairie, and in 1935 with two losses by the Farmers, 12–0 and 25–0, both to the Grapevine Mustangs.

R.E. Mattingly became principal at LHS in 1936 and took over duties as coach as well. Mattingly was one of the most successful coaches in Farmer history as he amassed a 49–5–3 record during his tenure from 1936–1941 for an overall winning percentage of .907. Mattingly's Farmers captured three district championships, one district co-championship, and two bi-district championships. The only two seasons in which the Farmers did not win the district title under Mattingly were 1936 and 1941. In 1936 the Farmers were 7–2, and in 1941 they finished 9–1. Their 9–1 record was sufficient for another district title, however the eligibility of one of the players came in question, and after further investigation, the player was deemed ineligible, forcing Lewisville to forfeit all but one of their games, leaving them with an official 1–9 record.

Many positive things developed from the Mattingly era, including the emergence of an All-District quarterback of 1939 by the name of Max Goldsmith. After playing quarterback for the Farmers in 1938 and '39, Goldsmith went to North Texas State Teachers College on a track scholarship. After a three year stint in the United States Navy, Goldsmith went to Andrews, Texas, coaching track and football. He returned to Lewisville in 1967 to coach the offensive line under Head Coach Bill Shipman, who he had coached with in Andrews, and later became Athletic Director in 1970. He served in this capacity until his retirement in 1983.

The Farmers had a limited schedule in 1942 brought about by several factors. Mattingly and Superintendent H.G. Vick both resigned shortly before the

Mattingly's Teams

The 1936 Fighting Farmers — R.E. Mattingly, standing to the left of Reveau Stewart (19) and his first District Champions at Lewisville. They finished the season 7–2.

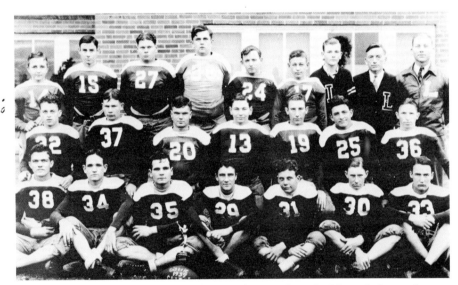

District Champions 1937 — The winning continued with an 8–1 record.

Down Through The Years

District Co-Champions 1938, a title they shared with the Grapevine Mustangs, featured players like Max Goldsmith (44) and Mutt Garrison (31).

The first of two Bi-District Championships under Mattingly.
The 1939 Farmers defeated the Howe Bulldogs 32–6 for the crown.

The 1940 Farmers — Mattingly's second Bi-District Champions defeated Howe again for the title; this time 46–6 at Denton.

beginning of the 1942–43 school year. With World War II gaining momentum, most available coaches were serving their country in some military capacity, leaving the Lewisville School Board hard pressed to find a replacement on such short notice. After coming up empty on filling the coaching vacancy, the board decided it best to cancel the football schedule and suspend all athletics until after the war was over, at which point the program would be reinstated.

On October 1, 1942, the school board solved its vacancy dilemma for superintendent by hiring John Keith Delay to fill that position. Delay reported for duties on that October 1 morning, and was working away in his new office at becoming oriented with the job that would be his until 1966. No sooner had he begun organizing his desk and files than a knock came at the door. When Delay answered the knock, there stood three young men with determined looks on each of their faces. They weren't interested in getting to know their new superintendent or changing their English class. They wanted to play football and insisted that Delay coach, find opponents to fill their vacant schedule and convince the school board to reinstate the athletic program, or at least the football portion of it. After a bit of resistance, Delay finally agreed to the demands of the young men, more to cease their persistence than his desire to coach, and he was able to get approval from the board to compete. The Farmers could only manage to get three opponents scheduled for the '42 season, with the first game scheduled for October 30. Remarkably, uniforms and equipment were issued on Monday, October 26, practice began the next day and continued the remainder of the week, and the Farmers took on Frisco's

Down Through The Years

The 1938 team in formation. Goldsmith (back-right) led the way from his quarterback position.

Coons on Friday night of that first week of football. Lewisville defeated Frisco 14–7, but lost their two remaining games to go 1–2 on the season. In spite of their losing record, the 1942 Farmer season was a success as they were able to salvage their football program after the adversity of losing their successful coach.

So the 1942 school board filled two positions in hiring Delay as superintendent. He continued coaching until 1947, exactly six years longer than he had planned. The next three seasons, 1943–45, the Farmers went 9–8–3 under Delay, with their best finish coming in 1943 with a 5–1–1 record and the district championship. Due to the war, schedules were shortened, and the Farmers averaged playing six or seven games each season instead of the normal ten games.

Full schedules resumed in 1946 and the Farmers finished with a near perfect regular season record of 10–2. Two of the Farmer victories were forfeits by Sanger and Boyd, both due to flu epidemics. These two forfeits, preceded by an open date, gave Delay's Farmers of 1946 a month long break between games, resulting in two consecutive losses to wind up the season. The final one came against Pilot Point, 21–0, for the bi-district championship. Lewisville did win the district title that season, however, the second of three Delay would lead the Farmers in obtaining.

In 1947 the Farmers picked up right where they left off the previous season as they finished 13–0 with the second of four unbeaten records in their history. Along with the 13 victories came the second District 13-B title for Delay, along with the bi-district and regional championships. Again, Class B teams played to the regional level only under the playoff format prior to 1980, consequently the regional title was equivalent to a state title for the 1947 Farmers, in essence, although not in reality. In winning the 13 games the Farmers outscored their opponents 445–27, with 12 of those points surrendered against the Richardson Eagles in the regional championship game won by Lewisville,

1943 District 9-B Champions

13–12. Ironically, after his resignation from LISD in 1966, Delay took a position with the Richardson I.S.D. until his retirement. Delay maintained his residence in Lewisville while employed at Richardson.

A.J. Hudson coached the Farmers in 1948 for only one season. Under Hudson the Farmers finished 6-3-1 and third place in District 13-B. Losses to Bridgeport and Boyd, along with a tie against Saint Jo, cost Lewisville their third consecutive district title.

The following three seasons, 1949–51, brought the Farmers a new coach and a new found success. J.H. Bronaugh lead Lewisville to a 27–3–1 three-year record, but only managed to squeeze out one district title in 1950. In 1949 the Farmers fell behind 13–0 in the first half of their first contest of the season against Valley View High School of Iowa Park. The Farmers came back to shut them out in the second half, but could only score 12 points themselves, losing the game 13–12. Lewisville never trailed the remainder of the season and finished 9–1 on the year, but with their victory over the Farmers, Valley View finished 10–0 and won the championship. Regardless of the disappointing second place finish, the Farmers put up some impressive numbers as they scored 233 points and allowed only 25, 13 of which were given up in the initial contest.

The Farmers bounced back the next season, completely dominating their opponents and capturing not only the district championship, but continuing on to win the Regional 4-B championship. That championship game featured both Farmers vying for the title, that being the Lewisville Farmers and Farmersville Farmers. That contest marked the only time in Texas high school

Down Through The Years

The 1946 Farmers fell to Pilot Point in the Bi-District game, but won the District Championship with a 10–1 regular season record.

football history where the only two teams nicknamed "Farmers" played each other, with Lewisville winning, 19–7.

The 1951 season for the Farmers was decided in their final game against Grapevine. Lewisville's first loss of the season came in week four against the Lake Worth Bullfrogs. The 12–6 loss ended a string of Farmer victories at 24, with the last loss coming two seasons earlier in the first game of 1949. Lewisville went on to tie Sanger two weeks later, 12–12, setting up a do-or-die situation in their final game against the Mustangs. Although it was close, the Farmers lost 7–6, and with the loss missed the district championship by the narrowest of margins.

The following season ushered in a new coach, who would lead the Farmers from 1952–1954. When A.L. Kay left the Farmers after the 1954 season, he had compiled a 22–8 overall record, but managed no better than three second place finishes. The 1952 Farmers finished 6–4 and tied for second place under the new head coach. District losses to Grapevine and Lake Worth matched the only two district losses Lewisville experienced the previous year, giving them their second place finish behind Grapevine, tying them with Lake Worth. In 1953 the Farmers finished a respectable 7–3, but again could not manage the Grapevine Mustangs, losing the game 7–6, and the district title along with it. This was the third consecutive loss to the Mustangs with Grapevine capturing the title each of these three seasons.

A new district champion was crowned in 1954 in District 10-A, but is was neither the Farmers or the Mustangs. Lewisville got off to a roaring start with convincing victories over Frisco, Sanger, Northwest, Plano, Mesquite and

Delay's 1947 Farmers defeated Richardson 13–12 for the Region 5 Championship, capping a 13–0 season record.

Carrollton by a combined score of 166–26, with the closest of these victories coming against Plano 14–2. The Farmers defeated Azle in game seven by a mere score of 7–0, but took their only loss of the season against Pilot Point, 21–20. The Farmers won their final two games against Bridgeport and Grapevine, hoping for some help from the rest of the district against the Bearcats. That help did not come, however, and the Farmers' 9–1 finish, although impressive, netted only a second place finish to Pilot Point's perfect 10–0 record.

Aside from the game against Pilot Point's Bearcats, the Farmers completely dominated district 10-A in 1954, outscoring their opponents 232–53. Minus the 21 points allowed against Pilot Point, the most points given up in a single game was the seven against Bridgeport in week nine of the season. In four contests Lewisville surrendered just six points, and logged three shutouts as well. They would have had another, but a safety allowed to Plano for their only points cost the Farmers a fourth shutout. Offensively, Lewisville averaged 23.2 points per game and surrendered a measly 5.3 points per contest, proving the Farmers were prolific equally well on both sides of the ball, with 10 Farmers being placed on the All-District team.

Lewis McReynolds joined the Farmer coaching staff in 1952 as an assistant under Kay. He remained the assistant coach until Kay's resignation created a vacancy, and was named the head coach for the 1955 season. With three seasons as an assistant, the stage was set for McReynolds to experience one of the greatest era's in the Farmers' history. Many of the starters from the explosive 1954 team returned for the 1955 season, including the Farmers' first All-American, Gordon Salsman. Other standouts like R.L. Crawford Jr., Mike

Down Through The Years

Denison, Walter and Richard Morris, Clarence Myers, Pete Underwood, Don Smith, Scotty Stubblefield, Terry Don Parks, and Dan Talley returned after getting a taste of winning big, but coming up short the previous year. Their combined efforts provided one of the most spectacular seasons in Lewisville Fighting Farmer history.

The Farmers cruised through the five non-district games, defeating the likes of Frisco, Grapevine, Plano, Mesquite and Carrollton. The narrowest margin of victory in these five games was 20 points, that coming against Carrollton with a 41–21 win. Altogether the Farmers scored 188 points and defeated their first five opponents 188-46 in just the first half of the season. The 1954 powerful offense scored 232 points for the entire season, only 44 points more than the '55 team had amassed in only the first half.

The Farmer offense continued to explode as the district portion of the schedule approached and showed little mercy on their hapless opponents. Lead in the backfield by Salsman, the Farmers averaged just over 65 points per game for the remainder of the regular season, including a 93–6 punishing of Justin Northwest. This stands as the highest scoring offensive output by the Farmers in history. In fact, three of the top ten scoring games in Lewisville's history occurred during this five game span, the others being a 65–0 defeat of Azle and a 60–0 spanking of Springtown. Perhaps even more impressive than this volatile offensive five-game display was the mere 12 points allowed defensively.

Needless to say, the Farmers ended the regular season with a perfect 10–0 record, ready for their first playoff appearance in five years. Their opponent would be the Chilicothe Eagles, with the game slated to be played in Wichita Falls at Coyote Field, the day after Thanksgiving.

Heavily favored, the Farmers expected to demolish the Eagles with their powerful offense, anchored by Salsman's All-American effort. In fact, many thought this game was but one rung on the ladder toward the first ever state championship for Lewisville, and the Farmers' hopes were high. Those hopes were dashed early in the contest, however, as on the game's eighth play Salsman's leg was broken, and with it most of the Farmer offensive scheme. This unfortunate mishap knocked Lewisville off-balance and they simply were not able to recover. For all practical purposes, the Farmers' season ended with Salsman's fracture, and they lost 20–7 to a team that hardly anyone from Lewisville believed had a right to be on the same field with the 10-A representative.

Aside from the premature exit from the playoff picture, the Farmers reached several milestones in the area of Texas High School football, as well as in the Lewisville high school record books. With their seven points against Chilicothe, the Farmers were the state's highest scoring team in 1955, outscoring their opponents 522–78 in only 11 games. This offensive point total stood as a Farmer record until the 1993 state champions amassed 555 total points on the season, allowing 208. What highlights the 1955 effort is that it was accomplished in just 11 games, where the 1993 point total stretched over 16 games, including

FRIDAY NIGHT FARMERS

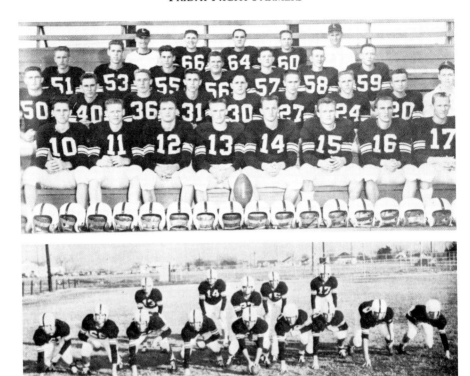

The 1955 Lewisville Fighting Farmers — the state's highest scoring team with 522 points.

the six playoff games. Also, the 1955 Farmers only allowed 78 points on defense, 41 of those coming in two games. The 1993 Farmers allowed 208, 347 less than they scored, indicating the ability to outscore their opponents rather than rely on a strong defensive battle.

Also in 1955, the Farmers had their first players named to an All-State team; Billy Sisk and Gordon Salsman. Sisk was an offensive lineman while Salsman played fullback from 1953–55. Salsman was also named to the 1955 All-American team as a result of his outstanding season. In this record-breaking season, Salsman scored 203 points to lead the Farmers' offensive effort. Only Paul Rice's 218 points exceeds Salsman's total as a Farmer record, this with his 36 touchdown season in 1972.

The 1955 district championship would be the first of three consecutive titles Coach McReynolds would win at Lewisville. En route to the 1956 district title, the Farmers again finished 10–0 in regular season play while competing in their first year of 2A competition, and displayed offensive power akin to that of the previous season by scoring 315 points. The Farmers had to travel to Wichita Falls again for bi-district, this time to battle the Burkburnett Bulldogs.

Down Through The Years

Like the 1955 Farmers, the 1956 team dominated their regular season foes. The closest game for Lewisville was against Grapevine, winning 18–6. As far as scoring, the Farmers scored over 50 points twice, between 30 and 50 twice, and no less than 18 points in each of the other six games. So there was no doubt Burkburnett would be their toughest foe of the year. This proved to be true as the Farmers dropped the bi-district game 28–19 to finish 10–1 on the year. The Farmers also landed 10 players to the All-District team, including one first team All-Stater, Joe Anderson, and two All-State honorable mention candidates, Dan Smith and Scotty Stubblefield.

Things appeared a bit dismal for Lewis McReynolds' Farmers to open the 1957 season, as they lost the opening two contests to Bowie and Richardson, 12–6 and 12–7 respectively. Lewisville finally got on track in week three, trouncing Alvord 46–0. Originally, the Farmers were scheduled to battle Plano in their third game of the season, but a flu epidemic throughout Plano High School forced the Wildcats to cancel the game, leaving the Farmers with a potential second open date of the young season. McReynolds was able to schedule Alvord to substitute for the ailing Plano team, giving the Farmers their first victory of the season. The Farmers would go on to win the next seven games also, going 8–2 on the season and finishing with a perfect 6–0 district record. With his third district title in hand, McReynolds headed into his third bi-district contest, again to lose out, this time to the Electra Tigers, 32–7. This would be the final opportunity McReynolds would have to capture anything more than a district title with the Farmers, as he would leave after the following season to become the head coach at Sweeney High School, located south of Houston near the Gulf Coast of Texas.

The UIL shuffled the district alignment for the 1958 season, and the Farmers wound up in district 12-2A, where they would remain for four seasons. With the new district assignment came new district opponents, such as Whitesboro, Bonham, Commerce, Richardson and Plano. Lewisville and Plano had not been in the same district since 1946, but had been regulars on each others pre-district schedules during the previous 12 years. They would be a thorn in the Farmers' side in 12 of the next 14 years, managing only a 3–9 record against the Wildcats from 1958–71.

The Farmers did defeat Plano in '58, 23–6, along with three other district foes, losing only to the Bonham Purple Warriors 28–7. Unfortunately, Bonham beat everyone else to snag the first district crown in the newly aligned District 12-2A.

More than Plano, Bonham would prove to be the Farmers' toughest opponent since 1958 when their series began. Each year they played, beginning with the '58 season, the Farmers lost, and it was not until 1972 that the Farmers actually won, 26–0, although there were several close games during this series; 2–0 in 1962, 13–12 in 1961 and 6–0 in 1967. There have also been some blowouts dealt to Lewisville by the Purple Warriors; 32–0 in 1963, 41–0 in 1969 and 35–6 in 1971. Bonham last appeared on the Farmer schedule in 1973, and the two teams have not met since in either regular season or the playoffs. Altogether the Farmers are 3–13 against Bonham, so shaking them after the 1973 season was a fortunate move for Lewisville by the UIL, as the Farmers were moved up to 4A competition, leaving the Purple Warriors behind.

With the loss to Bonham in 1958 the Farmers were 4–1 in district, finishing second place behind the Purple Warriors. This was also the final stanza for Lewis McReynolds as head coach with a four season record of 34–9, and a winning percentage of .791, making him the second "most-wins" coach in Farmer history behind Mattingly (1936–41).

Things were a bit bumpy for the Farmers over the next 13 seasons, going 51–78–1 under four different coaches. Ben Harmon was at the helm from 1959-63 finishing no better than 5–5, which he did back to back in 1961 and '62. In 1959 the Farmers finished 4–6 in Harmon's first season, and 3–7 in 1960. In his final season, 1963, the Farmers went 4–6, giving Harmon an overall record of 21–29 from 1959–63. Although the Farmers were not as successful as in years past, a bright spot did emerge during this period that would not be evident until several years later.

In 1959 a sophomore suited up as a Farmer for the first time, as his father had done in 1936–38, and his brother would do later from 1968–70. As a running back and linebacker he saw limited action his first year but emerged as a prominent member of the Farmer offense his final two seasons. Although the Farmers had limited success during his tenure at Lewisville, this player managed to be named to the All-District honorable mention team in 1960 and 1961 due to his efforts, at a time when Farmer dominance was wavering.

Upon his graduation this bullish football player received a scholarship to Oklahoma State University in Stillwater, Oklahoma, where he eventually earned All-American honors. Upon graduation from OSU, this running back was selected in the draft by the Dallas Cowboys, then under the direction of Tom Landry. Initially he backed up Carl Perkins at the fullback position, but became the starter after Perkins' resignation. It was during this time that one of the favorite Cowboys of all times, Walt Garrison, would be an instrumental part of a Dallas Cowboy team that dominated the National Football League in much of the 1970s. Garrison would play nine seasons with Dallas, playing in two Super Bowls, after getting his start as a Lewisville Farmer in the early '60s.

Harmon became principal of LHS in the Fall of 1963, leaving a vacancy at head coach of the Farmers which was filled by Sherrill Bottoms. Bottoms originally joined the Farmer staff as an assistant under Harmon in 1963, coaching with him for two years prior to his head coaching assignment. Under Bottoms the Farmers immediately improved over their 4–6 finish the previous season with a 6–4 record. During the '64 season the Farmers earned their first victory over a 3A team on October 2, defeating Azle 16–8. Azle and Lewisville had been regular foes off and on since 1946. Azle was promoted to 3A for the 1964 season, however, and the Farmers were familiar with their style of play. In fact, since 1946 when the teams first met, the Farmers have had great success against the Hornets, defeating them 12 consecutive times, with only one loss, which occurred in 1963. The Farmers would lose to Azle only one more time in the following season, and the teams would never meet again after 1965.

The Farmers lost district games to Rockwall, 21–13, and Plano, 49–20, and non-district losses to Dallas' Bishop Dunne, 7–0, and Bonham, 20–6, for a respectable 6–4 record in the 1964 season, finishing in the middle of the district standings. The 1964 season marked a milestone for the Farmer football program, which had nothing to do with rushing records or season totals. It had to do with racial equality. Prior to the 1964 season Lewisville schools were segregated, as were many of the other public schools across the south. In Lewisville there was one black school and three white schools for elementary levels, but black junior high and high school students were bused to Denton. Fred Moore High School was an all black high school which Lewisville's and other black students in the county attended, until the Civil Rights Bill of 1964, which forced schools to end segregation. Black Lewisville students wishing to play football played for Fred Moore High School until 1964. Players like Earl and Bill Chew, and Edgar and Willie Redmon are some of the black Lewisville students who played at Fred Moore High.

That changed in 1964, however, and Edgar Redmon and Bill Chew were the first two black athletes to play football for the Lewisville Fighting Farmers. These two notable black athletes paved the way for other blacks to participate in the Lewisville Fighting Farmer football program; names like Manuel Champion, Ronnie Cummings, Mike Nichols, Mathis Dunn, Curtis and Joe Bishop, Floyd and Sammie Voss, Zachary Turner, Alvin Turner, Milton Burel, Paul Rice, and countless other black athletes that have made a considerable impact on the success of the Farmer football program through the years.

The following season was a rough one for Bottoms and the Farmers as they finished with a 2–8 record, managing victories only against Northwest and Wilmer-Hutchins. The Farmer roster fell from 37 players in 1964 to only 21 players in 1965, contributing to the dismal performance for the '65 stanza.

The growth in the Lewisville student population paralleled the community growth, and with that, the Farmers were placed into 3A competition for the 1966 season. This would be a season of many changes for Lewisville football. Along with a new district came a new head coach, Bill Shipman, who would bring a new approach to coaching. Shipman retained Jerry Cantrell and Ronnie Davis as coaches from the 1965 staff, and added six others to specialize on specified areas of the team instead of general offense and defensive formations. Shipman's staff would dissect the defense into secondary, linebackers and defensive line, and the offense into quarterbacks and receivers, offensive line, and running backs. This approach would allow coaches and players to concentrate on individual position play, then bringing all units together to work on team offense and defense play.

This new approach did not pay dividends immediately, however, as

Shipman and the Farmers floundered for the next two seasons, finishing 2–8 and 1–9, respectively. 3A competition did not treat the Farmers kindly during these two seasons as Lewisville defeated only Grapevine and Mt. Pleasant in 1966, and Mt. Pleasant again in 1967 for their three victories in Shipman's first two seasons.

The two consecutive victories over Mt. Pleasant were somewhat prophetic to the Farmers, in general, and Shipman specifically. After the 1967 season, Lewisville and Mt. Pleasant went their separate ways, each remaining in 3A but realigned in different districts. The next time the Farmers and Tigers would meet would have to be in a playoff situation, due to the shuffling of district assignments. However, with both programs rapidly sinking to the basement, it was unlikely they would meet anytime soon.

It took five years for both programs to succeed and reach the playoffs, but they finally did meet in the state playoffs in 1972 at Forrestor Field in Mesquite. Both teams were bigger, faster and stronger, setting the stage for a fierce quarter final showdown. So on November 30, 1972 the Farmers and Tigers met for the third and last time, with the Farmers emerging victorious, 20–14, in one of the season's better playoff contests, giving both Lewisville and Shipman a 3–0 record against Mt. Pleasant.

The 1967 season represents the bottom, as far as the Farmer football program goes. The 1–9 record was the worst finish for Lewisville in the team's history, forcing the Farmers to make changes in its program in order to be more competitive. The Farmers remained in district 6-3A for the next six years, beginning in 1968, with Plano, McKinney and Gainesville alternating as the dominant teams. Lewisville finished a surprising 6–4 in '68, highlighted by a 17–14 upset of the McKinney Lions, costing the Lions the district title. This would be the last victory Lewisville would deal to McKinney for several years as the Lions completely dominated the Farmers from 1969–71, outscoring them 91–15 during that three year span. In fact, it would be the first of only two victories the Farmers would enjoy over the Lions in the eight game series from 1966–73.

1968 was an important year for the Farmers for another reason as well. The Lewisville I.S.D. constructed a new high school to house the continually growing student body, and it opened in the fall of '68. The old high school, which is currently Delay Middle School, was constructed in 1950, and sufficed for 18 years before westward expansion forced the school board's hand into building the new facility. Along with it came a brand new stadium, then called Farmer Field. According to Max Goldsmith, Lewisville Athletic Director from 1969–83, one of the most exciting plays at the new stadium in 1968 came in the first home game against the Waxahachie Indians. Waxahachie apparently had won the coin toss on that September 20 evening, and received the opening kickoff. Lewisville held on the first series to open the game, forcing the Indians to punt from inside their own end of the field. Fred Sullivan and John Allen joined efforts to block the punt, giving the Farmers the ball at

Down Through The Years

the Waxahachie 35-yard line. On the first play of the drive — the first play for Lewisville in their brand new stadium — quarterback John Garrison, Walt's younger brother, dropped back and fired a pass to split end Lawrence Johnson which covered 35 yards and the first touchdown scored in the newly erected Farmer Field. The Farmers went on to lose 21–7 in that contest, but gave the history books something to record that evening.

Farmer Field, now Goldsmith Stadium, has been good to the Farmers since 1968. One hundred forty games have been played there by Lewisville with the Farmers winning 99 games, losing only 34, while tying seven from 1968–1993. This is an astounding .707 winning percentage, making the turf at Goldsmith Stadium a den of defeat for those who dare to enter the feared arena.

Shipman left coaching after the 1968 season, but remained with LISD. He was assigned the position of principal of Lakeland Elementary, where he remained for two years. Don Poe, an assistant under Shipman, took over duties as head coach for the 1969–70 seasons where he lead the Farmers to a 11–9 two year record. What intensified the naming of Poe as head coach, within the confines of District 6-3A, was that his twin brother, Ron, was the head coach of McKinney, setting up a twofold rivalry between the two schools during the two seasons Poe coached the Farmers. The Lewisville Poe was on the losing end of both contests against his brother, losing a close one in 1969, 10–9, then being routed the following year, 49–0.

The Farmers finished 6–4 in 1969, and 3–3 in district, finishing somewhere in the middle of the District 6-3A race. The Farmers defeated North Dallas High School, 34–16, that year, the first 4A team Lewisville played since entering 3A competition. The most memorable game of the '69 season, however, came against the Plano Wildcats.

The Farmers and Wildcats rivalry dates back to 1922 when Plano soundly defeated Lewisville, 66–7. The Wildcats have dominated the Farmers in the 19 games played between the two from 1922–1969, leading the series 11–7–1. The Farmers lost 31–0 against Plano in 1968, so the game in 1969 was especially important to Lewisville, for pride as well as district standings.

Lewisville was 1–2 in district play going into the '69 game against the Wildcats, having lost to McKinney and Bonham, and was virtually out of the district races. The Farmers were fresh from a homecoming victory over the Grapevine Mustangs entering the Plano game, which was scheduled for Farmer Field. With revenge in their minds and determination in their hearts, the pesky Farmers lined up in a defensive struggle against Plano, with Lewisville edging the Wildcats in a 7–6 victory. This win, along with a final game victory over Gainesville, 27–14, served as bright spots to an otherwise lackluster season.

In 1970 Lewisville went 3–4 in district play, with a 5–5 record overall. Again, the Farmers finished in the middle of the road in the newly remodeled District 6-3A. District 6-3A remained virtually the same since 1966 when Lewisville joined it. Bonham, McKinney, Gainesville and Lewisville were the core of this district, along with Mt. Pleasant, Lake Highlands, Sulphur Springs and Greenville. Plano and J.J. Pearce of Richardson were added to the district in 1968, along with Grapevine, while Sulphur Springs, Lake Highlands, Mt. Pleasant and Greenville were shuffled off to other districts. In 1970 the South Grand Prairie Warriors were added in place of J.J. Pearce, along with Richardson Berkner, to complete one of the toughest districts in the state.

Although the Farmers were not in contention for the district title in 1970, they were a factor in determining who would capture the crown. Going into the second-to-last game against Gainesville, the Farmers had won two of the last three games and were improving each week. Traveling to Gainesville, the Farmers and Leopards engaged in a muddy, defensive battle. The afternoon and evening rains interfered with the usual offensive attack, making it a sloppy defensive struggle. Turnovers cost the Leopards severely as they fumbled six times, losing two costly ones to the Farmers, while Lewisville managed to lose only one. The game was a defensive seesaw battle through three quarters in a ho-hum contest that appeared to produce no winner, as both teams were more concerned with holding on to the ball instead of trying to score with it. The entire game, as it stands, was played in that fourth quarter as both teams sensed that the one fortunate enough to score in any fashion might just snatch a victory.

Gainesville finally broke the ice on the initial play of that final period on a 4-yard run. With the field unfit for place-kicking, the Leopards felt their chances were no worse in attempting a two-point conversion. Gainesville succeeded and went ahead 8–0 with the conversion. That score stood until just under five minutes left in the game when the Leopards committed a costly turnover, fumbling to Lewisville on their own 6-yard line. The enthused Farmers ultimately scored and added a two-point conversion themselves, with both scores supplied by senior, and four year starter, Ronnie Cummmings. With the game knotted 8–8 and less than a minute remaining, the Leopards, in their own end of the field, were content to run out the clock and accept the tie to remain undefeated in district play, given the unfavorable field conditions. Instead, however, the Farmers' Mark Reynolds forced the final Leopard fumble from his linebacker position, allowing nose guard Dennis Vorin to recover on Gainesville's 28-yard line.

Earlier in the slippery contest the Farmers had attempted a field goal, but due to faulty footing the attempt went awry. Now Lewisville had the ball with five seconds to go and 28 yards from paydirt, forcing the Farmers into another field goal attempt. The results were different this time, though, as John Garrison's kick traveled through the uprights for a three point Farmer victory, spoiling the Leopards' undefeated season and any chance at the district trophy.

Ronnie Cummings had been a starter for the Farmers since he was a freshman in 1967. He had been a standout throughout his high school career, as both a wide receiver and a defensive back, in a day where most players played offense and defense. He also made an impact on special teams as a kickoff and punt returner due to his incredible speed. Once, while only a freshman, Cummings was clocked in the 100-yard dash with the nation's fastest time, thus he had a bright career ahead of him. Going into the final game against South Grand Prairie in 1970, Cummings was ready to wind down his brilliant high school career, having been named to the All-District teams in 1968, '69 and '70.

In the midst of the game Cummings was either returning a kickoff or a punt, when one of South Grand Prairie's Warriors, in an attempt to catch the swift Cummings, did so, but not in the conventional way. While being blocked, the tackler reached from the side and caught Cummings at full speed by the facemask, giving it a hearty yank. The effort brought Cummings to the turf, along with a 15-yard penalty. Cummings, however, lay motionless on the sod, unable to move. No one was sure of the extent of his injury and eventually he was carried off the field on a stretcher.

The kickoff return would be the final athletic feat of his career as Cummings suffered a twisted spinal column. Although able to walk normally, Ronnie Cummings would never be able to run again, ruining not only a potentially stellar collegiate career, but also extinguishing any hopes of competing as an Olympian in track and field. Many had thought him an Olympic hopeful for the Summer Games in Munich, West Germany in 1972, but those hopes were dashed on that fateful November 20, 1970. The tackle of Cummmings set off several following conflicts throughout the remainder of the game, including a bench clearing brawl, as the face mask incident appeared to be intentional. The Farmers eventually lost, 24–14, giving them their fifth loss on the year and leaving a bad taste in their mouths to end the season.

Poe accepted the head coaching position at Sulphur Springs the following year, leaving a vacancy in a program that was in desperate need of revival. Bill Shipman was renamed head coach of the Farmers for the 1971 season, bringing with him an entirely new coaching staff, including David Visentine, Tommy Shields and Don Harvey. This new staff did not experience instant success, however, as the Farmers finished 2–7–1 on the season, only one game ahead of the Raiders of North Garland High School, who had replaced Grapevine in district 6-3A beginning in 1971.

The 39–7 victory over was the only district win for Lewisville that year. It was the Farmers' biggest offensive output of the year allowing them to escape the 6-3A cellar, thanks to the Raiders' dismal performance in their new district. Although the Farmers lost a total of seven games in 1971, it was not as bad as it might seem. Of the seven losses, five of those were lost by a total of 17 points, including the opening season loss to Saginaw Boswell, 16–13, a 19–14 loss to Gainesville, and a 13–12 loss to South Grand Prairie to end the season. Combining these close losses with the third week tie against Wilmer-Hutchins and the Farmers could have easily gone 6–4 instead of 2–7–1, had they been able to find another 10 points somewhere.

But things were not different for the Farmers, and the 2–7–1 record stood in the minds of the coaches and players throughout the off-season. With a relatively young team in 1971 that featured two sophomore offensive weapons, Randy Cade at quarterback and Mike Nichols at tailback, the Farmers were determined to use the losing record the previous fall to motivate them to improve their play for the 1972 season. In fact, 17 players were to return the following year, including 11 starters. With Plano moving to the 4A division, McKinney and Gainesville were the odds on favorites to capture the district title. No one paid much attention to what the Farmers were building in 1971, or what impact it would have on the district race in 1972.

Although a drought in winning district titles occurred from 1957 to 1971, history indicates that the Farmers and winning were not strangers. From 1920 to 1971 they captured 12 district titles and five bi-district championships, with an overall record of 245–143–14. Although the latter stages of this era ended on a downward trend, overall the period of Farmer football from its inception in 1914 through 1971 reflect a rich heritage of spirit and unity, and a foundation for success.

. . .

CHAPTER

FOUNDING FARMERS— FAMOUS FARMERS

HIGH SCHOOL PROGRAMS throughout the state of Texas have rich heritages with roots stretching back into the early 1900s, and are products of the vision of those who preceded them. The Fighting Farmer program is no exception. The successes enjoyed in recent years are a tribute to the likes of those whose names are unfamiliar, but whose spirit is the same. Many players, coaches and administrators have laid a foundation for the current Lewisville Farmer program, and others after have built upon it. Together, all have contributed to the tradition of Fighting Farmer football.

FOUNDING FARMERS: The Coaches

B.F. Tunnell
The first Farmer forefather was neither a player or a coach. B.F. Tunnell was Superintendent of Lewisville schools in the early '20s, among other things, and was a huge supporter of the football team at LHS. Although unnamed, football was important to the tiny farm community, and when it came time to select a name for its team, Tunnell, no doubt, exercised his influence.

Mr. Tunnell was a graduate of Texas A&M in the late 1910s and was still an A&M man at heart. His connection with the farm community of Lewisville was a natural one, being the vocational agriculture teacher as well, in whose class 90 percent of the male students were enrolled. When the thoughts turned to selecting a name for the team, Tunnell suggested the name "Farmers," as it both characterized the community in which they lived and the school near and dear to his heart. Prior to being nicknamed the "Aggies," A&M boasted the tag of "Farmers," a spin-off of the educational pursuit for which it was founded. The colors of maroon and white were a natural choice in following with the A&M example, thus the spirit of the Fighting Farmers was born, with much thanks to Mr. B.F. Tunnell.

Lee Preston
The earliest coach on record of a Farmer football team is Lee Preston. Preston coached from 1920 to 1923, and although his overall record is unknown, his early Farmer teams took some real beatings from neighboring Grapevine, Plano and Highland Park. Under Preston the Farmers experienced the worst loss recorded, with a 66–7 defeat by Plano in 1922. The lack of success was not due to Preston's inability to coach as it was from the complications characteristic of a new program.

Ed Lowe
The first winning season for the Farmers came in 1924 under first-year coach Ed Lowe. Lowe's 1924 team finished 5–3 and defeated Sanger, 20–19, for the Denton County championship of Class C teams, recording Lewisville's earliest title of any kind. The following season Lewisville finished a disappointing 1–3–1 in Lowe's second, and final, season as Farmer coach.

Darrell Jones
In 1926–27 the Farmers were coached by Darrell Jones, who had great success as the Farmer mentor. No results are known as to how the 1926 team finished, but the '27 team boasted a 7–2 record, recording losses only to the North Texas State Teachers College (now the University of North Texas), 12–7, and Grapevine, 14–0. Lewisville avenged the loss to the Mustangs two weeks later, 14–6, to give the Farmers their first real taste of success in football.

R.O. Davis
Lewisville won its first district championship in 1932, finishing 8–0–1, and continuing on under Coach R.O. Davis to win the bi-district title. Davis came from Itasca, Texas, to coach at Lewisville and did so from 1931–32. Davis' district championship would be the first of many the Farmers would win throughout their history.

**Coach Davis
1931–32**

Founding Farmers — Famous Farmers

R.E. Mattingly
Certainly one of the most successful coaches in Farmer history was Raymond Mattingly. Mattingly, who was also the principal of LHS, coached at Lewisville from 1936–41, posting a 49–5–3 overall record. The Farmers were district champions under Mattingly from 1937–1940, while winning bi-district titles in 1939 and '40. They would have won the title in '41, but the use of an ineligible player caused the Lewisville to forfeit all but one of its games, giving the Farmers an official 1–9 record for the season. The four district championships under Mattingly ties the most won by any Farmer coach in history through the 1993 season.

J.K. Delay
John Keith Delay came to Lewisville as Superintendent to replace H.G. Vick, who had resigned the first day of school in 1942. Also vacant was the coaching job resulting from Mattingly's acceptance of a coaching position in Bowie, Texas. Faced with no coach, and no men available to coach due to World War II, the school board voted to suspend all athletics until after the conclusion of the war so that a suitable replacement could be hired. That was the situation Delay found the Farmer football program in when he arrived as Superintendent and had no notions of changing it. Or so he thought. Several boys from the 1941 team visited him on the first day he reported to work and asked him of his intentions for the football team. When he told them he did not have any, they insisted that he coach, schedule some teams and get the school board's approval to reopen the athletic program. After much persistence, Delay agreed, more for peace of mind than anything else, and the 1942 Farmer football program was salvaged. He was able to schedule three games that season as several teams were forced to cancel their programs because of the war effort, creating vacancies the Farmers could fill. Lewisville managed to beat Frisco, 14–7, in Delay's first game as coach, but lost the other two in the first year of what would be a memorable coaching career in Farmer history.

Coach Delay
1942–47

Under Delay the Farmers won three district championships, the first in 1943, and the other two in back-to-back seasons of '46 and '47. Lewisville lost their bi-district bid against Pilot Point in 1946 but followed it with a perfect 13–0 record and the first regional championship for the Farmers. The win came against the Richardson Eagles in a dramatic 13–12 victory and would be the final game in the successful coaches career, as the superintendent replaced Delay as head coach for the '48 season. It seems that Delay's 23–2 record from '46 to '47 displeased the superintendent so much that he replaced him the following year. But remember—Delay himself was the superintendent.

Delay explained that he never really expected to coach past the 1942 season, much less the five years after that. "We were trying to build a building to keep up with our growth, and I didn't have time to coach," explained Delay as his reason to quit coaching. For someone that never really wanted to coach the Farmers, his 33–12–2 overall record continued a winning tradition that had begun first under Davis, and later under Mattingly. Delay remained as the superintendent until 1966, when he resigned to accept a position with the Richardson I.S.D., but retained his home in Lewisville where he still resides.

Lewis McReynolds
Lewis McReynolds first came to Lewisville as an assistant under A.L. Kay in 1952 and took over as head coach in 1955. McReynolds' first season was one of the most memorable ones in the Farmer chronicles as Lewisville was the state's highest scoring team that year, outscoring their opponents 522–78. The legendary Farmer running back Gordon Salsman was a senior on that team and led the Farmers to a 10–0 regular season record, setting up a showdown with the Chilicothe Eagles for the bi-district crown. It's likely they would have won had Salsman not gotten his leg broken on the game's eighth play.

McReynolds led the Farmers to district championships in the following two seasons but never advanced past the bi-district level, each time losing to a West Texas team. His final season as head coach of the Farmers was in 1958 when they finished a respectable 6–4, to give McReynolds an overall record of 34–9–0. McReynolds retired from the Sweeny I.S.D. where he completed his coaching career after leaving Lewisville.

Bill Shipman
Bill Shipman spent two stints as Farmer head coach, the first from 1966–68, and the second from 1971–73. Shipman first came to Lewisville from Andrews, Texas in 1966, after spending five seasons as an assistant for the Mustangs. Prior to that he spent time at Bowlegs High School in Oklahoma, then at Irving and Denton. Shipman did not experience success as the Farmer head coach until the 1968 season, when his team finished 6–4, and 3–3 in district— twice as many victories as in the two seasons before. In

Coach Shipman 1972

'66 Lewisville finished 2–8, winning only a single district game. Shipman's team finished a dismal 1–9 in '67 before turning things around in the '68 season. After a three year record of 9–21, Shipman took leave from coaching and became Principal of Lakeland Elementary School in the Lewisville I.S.D. for two years.

Coach Shipman reentered the coaching ranks for the 1971 season, but had little success. Lewisville finished with a 2–7–1 record, and the Farmer football program appeared to be spiraling downward. Before it went into a tailspin, the talent level increased tremendously for the 1972 season, and Shipman

Founding Farmers — Famous Farmers

led the Farmers to a 12–2 record and their first state final appearance ever. Shipman was able to blend the talents of players like Paul Rice, Joe Martin, Mark Angeli, Allen Fox, James "Red" Bishop, Eddie Mullins, Steve Coker and a host of others, using a two-platoon system, to reach the championship game. Under Shipman's leadership the Farmer football program took an upward turn in preparation for the promotion to 4A competition, which was to follow after the '73 season. Lewisville, after losing to Uvalde in the '72 finals, was upset by McKinney in the final game, snatching the district crown from Lewisville in 1973 in a game marred by questionable officiating. In his first four seasons as the Farmer head coach Lewisville finished 11–28–1 under Shipman; in his final two they were 21–3, bringing his career total at Lewisville to 32–31–1.

After the '73–74 school year Shipman resigned and accepted the head coaching job at Abilene High School. He spent two seasons there before heading to Denton as head coach of the Broncos, also for two seasons. Shipman completed his high school coaching back at Andrews from 1978–83, after which he retired from coaching. He entered a brief second career as manager of the Andrews Chamber of Commerce until 1987. After four years in that capacity he retired for good.

Shipman did not remain idle, however. He spent several seasons as a volunteer high school coach in Vail, Colorado, but the highlight of his post-career coaching was in coaching American football in Germany. Shipman spent the spring and summer of 1992 and '93 coaching the Hamburg Silver Eagles, compiling a two season record of 18–8. American football is not a school sponsored sport in Germany, but rather is compiled of players in their 20s. The sport was introduced in 1982 and continues to increase in popularity.

Of the coaches in Farmer history, clearly Bill Shipman was one of the most charismatic and popular. He, too, is fond of the city of Lewisville. "I've always thoroughly enjoyed coaching and enjoyed the Lewisville kids as much as you can," remembers Shipman. He attended a reunion of the 1972 Fighting Farmer football team in 1985 and still keeps in contact with some of the players and coaches from that season.

Neal Wilson
From 1978 until 1985 the Farmers were directed by Neal Wilson. During that span the Farmers compiled a 67–19–5 record, winning four district championships while making five playoff appearances. Wilson's best finish as Farmer head coach came in 1979 with Lewisville reaching the semifinal round, losing to the eventual state champions, the Temple Wildcats, 3–0. The 12–2 finish matched the record of the 1972 Farmer team that reached the state finals as a 3A team.

Wilson's home town is Era, a small community in the southern portion of Cooke County in North Texas. His parents, Irving and Dixie, were both in education when Wilson was growing up. His mother was a teacher and his father was Superintendent at Era, and Wilson always knew that coaching was his calling. "I always knew it; that I would be a coach, and worked toward that. I never considered anything else." While at Era, Wilson started at quarterback for the Hornets all four seasons, earning All-District and All-Area honors in three out of the four years. After graduation from high school he attended North Texas State University and also played quarterback, lettering his senior year. Upon graduation in '65 Wilson began his career in coaching.

Neal Wilson began his coaching career at the same place he ended it—at Lewisville. Wilson came to Lewisville in 1965 as the eighth grade football and basketball coach at Lewisville Junior High School. He finished 5–1–1, beating Plano 7–0 for the district championship and setting the stage for a successful career in the ranks of high school coaching. His first stay at Lewisville was brief, as he left Farmer territory after the school year ended in '66 for an assistant coaching spot at Decatur. After two seasons as an assistant, Wilson became Decatur's head coach, a position he held from 1968–70. Altogether Neal Wilson spent five seasons as an Eagle coach, and four out of five of those seasons resulted in district championships. Decatur reached the regional round in 1966 and '67 and lost bi-district games in '68 and '70. The only season the Eagles did not make the playoffs under Wilson was 1969.

While at Decatur, Wilson coached a young man in 1969 and '70 named Ronnie Gage. Gage would later join Wilson on the Lewisville coaching staff in 1978 as a coach of the sophomore team, joining the varsity staff in 1980. Gage eventually was named head coach of the Farmers for the 1991 season, following in Wilson's shoes.

After the 1970 season Wilson was named head coach at Eagle Mt.-Saginaw's Boswell High School, where he fielded competitive teams from 1974–77. During his early years at Boswell, Wilson's team fell victim to the explosive Farmer teams of 1972 and '73, losing three times to them in two seasons. Lewisville defeated the Pioneers in the first game of 1972, 14–7, for Boswell's only loss of the season. They continued on to win the District 5-3A championship and met the Farmers again in the bi-district round of the playoffs. This time Lewisville crushed the Pioneers, 35–0, on their march to the state finals. The two teams lined up again to begin the '73 campaign, and again Wilson's Pioneers fell to Lewisville, being shutout, 34–0. As the Boswell head coach, Wilson was 2–2 against his future team, and experienced considerable success in his seven seasons prior to coming to Lewisville. The Pioneers were district champions or co-champions in each of his seasons there. Wilson was one game shy of a state final appearance in 1977, losing to the Brownwood Lions and the legendary Gordon Wood.

Highlights of the coaching career of Wilson at Lewisville include winning the district championship in 1978, his first season as Farmer chief. Beating the number one ranked Abilene Cooper Cougars in 1979 stands out as the most exciting game he coached, but victories over Odessa Permian in 1981 and Plano in 1982 helped the eight-year head coach post an overall career record of

153–39–6, an outstanding winning percentage of .797. Aside from the 4–5–1 1980 finish, Wilson never had a losing season at Lewisville. He and his wife, Donna, have three sons, two of which Wilson had the chance to coach. Darrell and Lance, his two older sons, each played under their father. Darrell played defensive end in 1983 and '84, while Lance alternated at quarterback with Randy Peters in 1985. Wilson's older son, Colby, played in 1989–90 under Chuck Mills, but he was able to watch his youngest son closely. In 1983 L.I.S.D. Athletic Director Max Goldsmith retired, and Wilson was named as his successor. He did double duty as Farmer head coach and athletic director from 1983–85 but gave up his coaching responsibilities after the '85 season.

Wilson's philosophy of coaching is simple, but breeds success. "It is essential to construct and maintain a successful program, but being competitive is the biggest thing. As long as you're competitive you have a chance to win," related the 21-year coach. One of the accomplishments as athletic director achieved by the successful football mind was in overseeing the construction of the million dollar athletic complex at LHS named after the previous athletic director, Max Goldsmith.

Wilson's accomplishments as a coach did not go unnoticed. He was the district's Coach of the Year in 1978, '79, '81 and '85, and the Metro Coach of the Year in both 1977, as head coach of Boswell High School, and in 1979 with the Farmers. His most cherished honor, however, occurred with his induction into the Texas High School Coaches Association Hall of Honor on July 27, 1994, including him as one of the legends in Texas high school football.

Ronnie Gage
Ronnie Gage was hired to replace Chuck Mills as head coach of the Farmers in 1991, and the Fighting Farmer football program has continued to progress. In just his third season as the Lewisville head coach, Gage led the Farmers to the Class 5A Division II 1993 State Championship, the first state title in the history of the Farmers. Over three seasons as the Farmer mentor Gage has compiled a 32–7–2 record, including a Lewisville High School record 15 wins in 1993.

Gage was raised in Decatur, Texas, graduating in 1971. He was a two-year member of the Decatur Eagles varsity squad as a two-way starter. Gage played center on offense and defensive back on defense, earning All District Honorable Mention honors his senior year. Gage played for Neal Wilson in Wilson's final two seasons at Decatur and began a relationship that would extend for more than two decades. He attended Texas Tech University and Weatherford Junior College before completing his college education at North Texas State University in 1976. After spending two seasons as a junior high coach with the Keller I.S.D., Gage rejoined Wilson as a member of the Farmer coaching staff in 1978, where he coached the freshman football team, along with Vance Perkins and Gary Walton. In 1979–80 Gage coached the sophomore team before joining the varsity staff in 1981.

Gage spent six seasons as an assistant on the Farmer staff before feeling the urge to seek a head coaching position for himself. After putting out applications in several places, Gage accepted an offer at Northwest High School in Justin, Texas. This would prove to be a challenge, as the Texans had not won a single game in over two years prior to his arrival.

Nor did they in Gage's first season. The Texans finished 0–9–1 in the new coach's inaugural season, including a 55–0 loss, which Gage recalled was the worst feeling he experienced in all of his 19 years of coaching through 1993. Northwest had just moved up to the 4A classification and had only 47 players report for two-a-days for both varsity and junior varsity. Twenty-three of those kids suited up for the varsity (the Texans finished the season with just 20), which contributed to Gage's winless start. As a Farmer assistant Gage experienced winning by contributing to two district titles and a third playoff appearance; losing as he did in '87 was something he wasn't accustomed to. After the season Gage questioned both his decision to move to Northwest and desire to continue coaching. His wife, Stephanie, was a source of encouragement during those dark days and snapped him out of his post-season depression. The following season Gage led the Texans to a 4–3–3 finish, the first winning season in a long time, and the town responded to the new-found success. The three losses were by a combined total of 17 points, indicating the competitiveness of the program that had, only a season earlier, been the doormat of the 4A division.

The Texans turned the corner the next season as they finished 8–2–1 and runner-up to Wichita Falls Hirschi, making the playoffs for the first time in 27 years. With each week's success, the citizens of Justin turned out in increasing numbers, filling the stands that were empty only two seasons earlier. Although they lost to Ft. Worth Brewer, 42–0, in the bi-district round, Gage was encouraged with his future at Justin, but there remained limited resources with which to work. With only two students above the 720 enrollment required for 4A competition, the player pool was limited to 30 players on varsity, making it difficult to remain competitive at that level. In 1990, Gage's final season at Northwest, the Texans were upset by Azle, 7–6, costing them a spot in the playoffs. They had beaten The Colony, then a 4A school, and the always tough Gainesville Leopards, but losses to Azle and Wichita Falls Hirschi spoiled their hopes of reaching the playoffs for the second consecutive season.

The loss to Azle affected Gage in a negative way. He personally took responsibility for the loss and felt as if he let the program at Northwest down after so much progress had been made. He again questioned both his ability and desire to coach. Shortly thereafter, the head coaching job at Lewisville opened up, and Gage pursued it in hopes of fulfilling a goal he had set early in his coaching career. Gage had set his sights on being a 5A head coach someday, secretly hoping for the chance to head the Fighting Farmer program.

A multitude of quality applicants indicated an interest in the Lewisville

Founding Farmers — Famous Farmers

A head coach experiences many moments throughout a season, as did Ronnie Gage during the championship drive of 1993. *Center:* The Farmer head coach awaits the departure for Houston. *Clockwise, from top right:* Gage sends Farmer quarterback Chad Nelson in with a play at Texas Stadium; meeting the public after the championship parade; a dejected Gage looks for answers at halftime; an enthusiastic post-game speech; visiting with the media after defeating Temple in the Semi-Finals; Ronnie Gage displays a proclamation received from Lewisville Mayor Bobbie Mitchell at a ceremony honoring the 1993 Division II State Champions.

vacancy, compiling a sort of Who's Who list of high school coaches. Athletic Director Neal Wilson narrowed the field to three choices: Robert Woods from Wilmer-Hutchins, Eddie Brister, a former coach at LHS and head coach at Willow Ridge High School, and Ronnie Gage. Each candidate endured a final interview before the selection was finalized. Once the decision was made,

Wilson picked up the phone and called Gage. "Gage, it's yours if you want it," was how the Lewisville Athletic Director offered the position to his prodigy, and Gage immediately accepted. He had made up his mind to accept the head coaching job at Lewisville during the final phase of the interview process, if it was offered to him. With Gage set to take over the reins beginning in 1991, a new chapter in Farmer history had opened.

FOUNDING FARMERS: The Players

Lewisville has been blessed to have had many players rich in talent and full of dedication and pride to establish and sustain the football program since its inception in 1914. Though all have played an important role in the development of what is now known as "Farmer Pride," a handful stand out as players who's efforts paved the way for writing an important chapter both in the history of Lewisville and Texas high school football.

E.A. Sigler
One of the first to wear a Lewisville football uniform in the early years was Emery Sigler. He, along with Lloyd Carlisle and Ray Lester, were among a group of Lewisville High School boys that created an athletic association for the sole purpose of competing in athletics, particularly football and basketball. Sigler, along with the other two, were the first to play on a football team compiled of Lewisville High School students, beginning in 1914, giving birth to a program that has been in existence for eight decades. It is likely the boys coached themselves, or perhaps a faculty member lent his assistance, but Emery Sigler was among the first gridsters at LHS. Although not called the Farmers until 1923, no doubt the same school spirit and pride was around in those early years.

After graduating from LHS, Sigler completed college and entered the coaching field. He eventually went to Plano as a coach and eventually Superintendent, where he remained for 40 years before retiring from the field of education. With Plano as a rival of Lewisville through most of his tenure as their chief administrator, Sigler was torn when the two teams met on the field, especially when his nephews were members of the Farmer football squad. Billy (1941), Larry (1956–58), Sammy (1958–61) and Dale Sigler (1961) were all nephews that Emery Sigler watched throughout his 40 years with Plano before winding down his career.

Emery was the first of several Siglers to play football for Lewisville in the early years. His younger brother, Fred, came along a few years later, and Woodrow, the next sibling, was the first Sigler as a member of a Fighting Farmer team from 1931–32. He was a member of the first district championship team at Lewisville High School. Foster, the last of the early Siglers, played running back in 1934 under Taft Dunsworth before attending North Texas State Teachers College, where he played for one year. The Sigler family tree grew under the union of Foster and Gertrude Sigler, and three of their sons became Fighting Farmers in the later '50s and early '60s. Larry Sigler played from 1956–58 as a running back for the Farmers. Sammy Sigler was a four-year member of the Farmers from 1958–61, while Jimmy wore number three for Lewisville in 1968 and '69.

Emery Sigler was one of the founding Farmers as a member of the first Lewisville football team, paving the way for other players to share in the Farmer dream.

Hoss Williams

From 1930 to 1933 Fred "Hoss" Williams was a four-year mainstay in the Farmer backfield, where he started at quarterback the last three seasons, including the 1932 bi-district championship. Williams was small and fast and led the Farmer offensive attack under Coach R.O. Davis, playing in the same backfield with Dick Hayes, Woodrow Sigler and Bud Waldrip. The Farmers ran a wing-T offense out of the shotgun formation, with Hoss responsible for calling all the plays. Since there were only 11 starters, each playing offense and defense, there were no substitutes to shuttle plays, consequently Williams was relied upon to direct the offense from the field.

Things were different in other ways as well. They did not huddle between plays, so Williams called all the plays from the line of scrimmage. Coach Davis designed a simple system for Williams to communicate with the players, making it less complex than imaginable to run the offense without a huddle.

Basically, the Farmers ran every play from the same formation, so it became a simple matter of communicating the play and snap count to the offense without letting the defense know what play was going to be run. And it was very simple, according to Williams. He explained that each play in the Farmer game plan had a number assigned to it, and the first two numbers he called out at the line of scrimmage added up to the number of the play he wanted to run. For example, a sweep to the right might be play number 60 in the Farmer repertoire, so Hoss would call out "58-2," and so on, with the first two numbers adding up to 60. "I tried to keep it simple so the rest of the guys could add it up real easy," confided Williams. "After all, we were there to play football, not do math." Determining which play to run was only half the job; setting the snap count was the other half, which was easy enough. After calling the two numbers which added up to the desired play, Williams would ramble off a series of meaningless numbers designed to do nothing more than confuse the defense, but when he called out the actual number of the play, that was when the ball was to be snapped. So a sequence of events would go like this, if play number 60 was to be run. Williams would call out, "58-2-23-96-14-58-9-60," and the ball would be snapped, beginning the play. If, by chance, the defense broke the Farmers' code, it could be altered slightly to get the desired effect.

Altogether the Farmers had 25 or 30 plays in their arsenal, each designed to utilize the speed and quickness of the Williams-led offense. Williams scored many times himself during his four seasons as a Farmer, leading the way in the 1932 bi-district championship season, the first one for the Farmers. Lewisville outscored their opponents 190–6 that year, including a scoreless tie against Sanger in week eight. That was the closest the Farmers came to losing that season.

Besides being a quarterback, Williams also had the chore of kicking off, and he played linebacker or cornerback on defense in a day where the players had little protection. Williams recalled that they did not play with helmets until his junior season, and even then, some players opted not to wear them, citing their discomfort as the main factor. "It's a wonder we hadn't gotten killed out there without the pads like they have today," chuckled Williams. "I guess all that whole milk I drank kept me from getting my bones broken." The shoulder pads utilized in Williams' heyday barely covered the shoulders, and the knee and thigh pads were, "felt, sewn right into the pants," according to the swift signal-caller from the 1930s. "It wasn't much, but we didn't know any different. All we wanted to do was play football."

One might think the nickname of "Hoss" would be attributed to the size of a man, as visions of Hoss Cartwright of television's "Bonanza" come to mind, portrayed by the bulky Dan Blocker. Instead, Williams got his nickname from one of his grandfathers when he was but a toddler. "I stayed with one of my granddaddy's one day when he was outside shucking corn. He wasn't paying much attention to me and I would wander off. He came and got me several times, but I'd just keep getting away. Finally he tied me up to a tree to keep me from running off, and gave me an ear of corn to keep me busy. It wasn't anything cruel or anything. In fact, they (my parents) thought it was kind of funny. My granddaddy said, 'yeah, there's my little hoss,' and the name stuck."

In addition to playing football, the fleet footed Williams was a track star, capturing the second fastest time in the 100-yard dash in Denton County one year. After a brief stint in the Army, Williams was medically discharged, and he returned to Lewisville, assisting Coach Taft Dunsworth in coaching the Farmers on his own time.

Williams was the biggest Farmer fan after his graduation from LHS. He lined and chalked the field at the Degan Gin lot, where the team played its home games, and supported the Farmers in many ways. Max Goldsmith, a member of the Farmers in 1938–39, recalled that, "Hoss was always around the team helping out the coach and tending to equipment. He used to paint the helmets maroon and painted the white stripes on them for us. He chalked the field, too. We appreciated his efforts in supporting us."

Williams indisputably owns the record for consecutive attendance of Farmer football games. Beginning with the 1935 season, Williams attended every Farmer game, home and away, until 1990, when his health did not allow him to continue his streak. But he still listens to them on the radio, and caught them on television for the state championship game in 1993. The spirit, pride and enthusiasm displayed by Williams during his playing days, as well as his days as a fan, is unparalleled, symbolic of the pride and tradition which characterizes what the Farmer football program strives to achieve.

Max Goldsmith

One of the players who made a big impact on Farmer football was Max Goldsmith. As a player from 1938–39, he led the Farmers to two consecutive district championships as quarterback. In 1939 the Farmers also won the bi-district title with a 32–6 victory over the Howe Bulldogs. The bi-district crown was the second such title for the Lewisville Farmers in their young history, completing a 9–1–1 season under the legendary Farmer coach, R.E. Mattingly. Goldsmith directed the Farmers to a two-season record of 17–1–2, with their only loss coming against the Frisco Coons in 1939, 7–0. The loss to Frisco forced a tie for the championship, as the Coons had lost to the Era Hornets earlier that season. "Instead of a coin flip to determine who advanced," Goldsmith recalled, "we played an extra game against Frisco at Carrollton. We won that game, 19–13, and won the district championship with it."

Goldsmith was also a member of the only Farmer team to play on a Monday night. To close the season the Farmers traditionally played Grapevine, however, the December 1 contest in '39 scheduled for that Friday evening had to be postponed due to extreme muddy conditions caused by heavy flooding earlier in the week. Rather than cancel the non-district game, the two coaches agreed to play the contest on the following Monday. The two teams struggled to a 0–0 tie, the second tie between the Farmers and Mustangs in as many seasons. Four days later the Farmers beat the Bulldogs for the bi-district championship. Goldsmith earned an All-District first team selection for his play in 1939.

Goldsmith recalled the game of football being much different when he played as compared to today. "When we played, the game lasted 60 minutes instead of 48, like it is now. If you left the game for any reason, for an injury or just to get a breather, you couldn't go back in until that quarter was over." With the depth of players minimal, Goldsmith and the others made certain that their need for substitution was absolutely necessary before leaving the field.

There was no field clock either. The referee kept the time on the field, unlike the sophisticated scoreboards of today. In fact, not much was sophisticated about the early days of Farmer football when Goldsmith played, including the playing field. Lewisville played all their home games at the Degan lot (or gin lot, as it was often referred), a piece of land adjacent to a gin owned and operated by the Degan family, one of the oldest families in Lewisville. Goldsmith remembers the rough terrain of the playing surface peppered with "goad heads," a grass burr of sorts, but much larger and harder. It was no fun to get tackled and land on a patch of these. It was difficult enough battling the opposition, much less having to combat the hazardous vegetation, so Goldsmith and the other players would rid the field of the prickly substance as best they could. "We took tow sacks and filled them with hay to where they were full. Then we would roll them all over the field and the goad heads would get caught in the sacks. We got as many off as we could, but we couldn't get all of them. We had to wait until November before they all died before we got any relief."

As for the rest of the playing field, Goldsmith remembers, "there wasn't any grass on it except by accident." Nor were there lights until 1938 when Charlie Whitlock, a local electrician, donated his services and materials to provide lighting at the Degan field. That's when the first night game was played at Lewisville. Goldsmith recalled that instead of the traditional brown football, they used a white football because it was easier to see under the dim lighting. By comparison, Degan field, where Goldsmith spent his playing days, was a far cry from the current Farmer stadium that bears his name today.

Goldsmith graduated from Lewisville in the spring of 1940 and attended North Texas State Teachers College in Denton, Texas, on a track scholarship. In 1943 he joined the U.S. Navy and returned to NTSTC in February 1946 after his discharge, where he ran track once again, winning the Lone Star Conference as a sprinter. After graduating from NTSTC he landed his first coaching job at Andrews High School, coaching football and track through the 1966 season. In his final two seasons Goldsmith was head football and track coach, coaching track teams that set several Texas records for the 440 and mile relay.

Goldsmith and Bill Shipman first connected at Andrews, as Shipman was an assistant on the coaching staff along with him. Goldsmith joined the Farmer staff one season after Shipman was named head coach in 1966, and he remained as an assistant through the 1969 season, after which he took over duties as Athletic Director. He remained in that position through 1983 and retired after 36 years in the coaching field.

Besides hiring coaches and drawing up schedules for LISD athletic teams, Goldsmith took personal responsibility for the care and upkeep of the football field. He did everything from planting seed and fertilizing, to watering and mowing, ensuring a quality playing surface for the Lewisville Farmers at Farmer Field, a task he continued until the field was resurfaced with artificial turf in 1989. It was no surprise that when it came time to rename the stadium to accommodate both the Farmers and the Marcus Marauders, the board of trustees approved the name of Max Goldsmith Stadium, as a tribute to the man who had given so much of himself to the athletic program of Lewisville.

Goldsmith has seen some memorable moments while at Lewisville regarding the Fighting Farmers, including the first play of the 1968 season at Farmer Field. It was their first home game that year, and it was also their first season in the newly constructed stadium. After blocking a punt, the Farmers took over at their opponent's, the Waxahachie Indians, 35-yard line and scored on their first play from scrimmage in the new stadium. The play, a 35-yard pass from quarterback John Garrison to flanker Lawrence Johnson, is one of the moments that sticks out in Goldsmith's mind. John Garrison's last-second field goal to defeat the McKinney Lions in 1968 also brings a smile to Goldsmith when reliving it. "It was McKinney's first district loss in 10 years," recalled Goldsmith, who witnessed the game as a member of the coaching staff.

Of course, the most vivid recollection of a Farmer game was the dramatic 1972 come-from-behind victory against McKinney for the district title. It had been the first district championship since 1957 and was the most remarkable win he had ever been a part of in his 36 years in athletics. Getting to see running backs like Walt Garrison, Paul Rice and Freddie Wells marks individual efforts that, Goldsmith claims, have helped Lewisville grow, "from a doormat program in the '60s to a perineal contender."

His contribution in helping to accomplish that is what Goldsmith is most proud of. He named Paul Rice among the best backs in Texas high school football history from his near half-century of observing the sport. Among his other contributions to the Lewisville Farmer program was the hiring of Neal Wilson to take over as head coach of the ailing program in 1978.

For his achievements not only as a coach and athletic director, but also as an athlete, Max Goldsmith was inducted into the Texas High School Coaches Hall of Honor, an award richly deserved.

Marshall Durham
Marshall Durham played for the Farmers from 1947–50 and was a standout as a member of the offensive line, which yielded a 39–4–1 record during his four seasons. Included in this time span were two district championships, along with two regional championships. Unbeaten records in 1947 and 1950 earned the Farmers the regional crowns, and Durham was an integral part of that team. He earned All-District honors in 1949 and 1950.

Durham graduated from LHS in 1951 and attended North Texas State College, where he received a bachelor's degree in education. After spending several years in the military, Durham returned to Lewisville where he assisted Lewis McReynolds on the Farmer staff for two seasons from 1957–58. He later moved into the administrative level, serving as a principal at both the elementary and junior high school level before being named Assistant Superintendent of Operations.

Durham passed on his athletic abilities to two of his sons, as both became members of the Fighting Farmer offensive line in the 1970s. Rudy Durham played offensive guard in 1972–73 and was a member of the state finalist team in 1972. Rory Durham played center for the Farmers in 1978–79, reaching the semifinal contest in 1979. The Durham's third son, Rody, became Assistant Athletic Director for the Lewisville Independent School District in the spring of 1984. Rudy and Rory join their father as two-time All-District recipients in each of their respective seasons as members of the Fighting Farmers, with Rory earning first team All-State honors in 1979.

Don and Dan Smith
From 1949 through 1956 the Farmer backfield featured a pair of brothers that were instrumental in leading Lewisville to three district titles and no worse than a tie for second place in the other five seasons. Don and Dan Smith both were running backs, each one a four-year starter in the backfield, but never at the same time. Don played from 1949–52 then graduated in the spring of 1953. Brother Dan stepped in the following year, 1953, and continued through the '56 season, and both were standouts on the Farmer offense.

Don earned first team All-District honors in each of his final three seasons as a Farmer, as he led the way to a four-season record of 33 wins, 7 seven losses and one tie, including the 1950 regional championship. That came in his sophomore season, and would be the only Lewisville district championship team he would be a part of. The worst record Don endured as a Farmer was a 6-4 finish in '52, his senior year, and good enough for a second place tie in District 10-1A. In fact, the Farmers finished second in Don's freshman and junior seasons as well.

Dan Smith followed in his elder sibling's footsteps in the Farmer backfield from 1953–56. During his four seasons as a Farmer, Lewisville finished 36–6–0 and captured two district titles. Dan earned All-District honors in 1954–56 as a compliment to the legendary Gordon Salsman in the Farmer backfield, including the record setting team in 1955.

Besides being a football star Dan excelled in track and field as well, earning a trip to the state meet in 1957, competing in the shot put event. A throw of 46-feet-6-inches garnered him the opportunity to compete at the state level, along with teammate R.L. Crawford Jr. Dan went on to continue his football career, joining his brother, Don, at NTSC, as a product of a football factory at Lewisville that continually supplied quality athletes to the Denton college during the mid '50s. He joined a local fraternity at NTSC called "Geezles," along with other former Farmers who had chosen to obtain their post-high school education while playing football for the Mean Green. Others, like Terry Don Parks, R.L. Crawford Jr., Gordon Salsman and Pete Underwood, were members of this distinguished group of Farmer alumni that regularly met to continue the relationships they had begun in high school, as well as become acquainted with other athletes from surrounding areas.

Dan Smith

Pete Underwood, a Farmer from 1954–57, recalled one of Dan's more outstanding performances coming against the Grapevine Mustangs in 1956. The Mustangs offensive attack featured All-State quarterback Jerry Pair, and had hopes of dethroning the Farmers from atop the district throne. Instead, Smith

Founding Farmers — Famous Farmers

and company capitalized on several Grapevine mistakes, spoiling their homecoming, 18–6. Although he did not score a touchdown, Smith led the way on both sides of the ball from his fullback and linebacker positions. His punishing style of running gave the Mustangs all they could handle as he led the way to the Farmers' first district title at the 2A level that season.

Sleepy Reynolds

Everett "Sleepy" Reynolds made the varsity as a freshman in 1951, as did many freshmen in the early '50s, and started at quarterback beginning in 1952, continuing through his senior year in 1954. He wore number 10 as he led the Farmers to a three-year record of 22–8 but never captured a district title. As a sophomore in '52, Sleepy directed the Farmers to a second place tie for the District 10-1A title, finishing with a 6–4 record and a 4–2 district mark. Losses to the Lake Worth Bullfrogs and Grapevine

Sleepy Reynolds
1953

Mustangs threw the Farmers into a tie with the Bullfrogs for second place, while Grapevine captured the crown. In '53 Reynolds again led Lewisville to a second place finish behind the Mustangs, turning in a 7–3 season record. The '54 Farmers finished 9–1, their best finish under Reynolds, and had hopes of knocking Grapevine off the top of the District 10-1A heap, but neither the Farmers or the Mustangs won the title. Lewisville's high powered offense outscored their opponents 240–54, but a 21–20 loss to Pilot Point in week eight of the season spoiled their run at a perfect record. The Farmers had a 20–0 halftime lead but allowed the Bearcats to score 21 unanswered points in the second half, costing them both the game and the eventual district championship.

Reynolds earned All-District Honorable Mention in '53 and was selected first team All-District in '54, despite not leading the Farmers to the district crown. After graduating from LHS in 1955, Sleepy Reynolds attended Northeast Louisiana University, where he played for the Indians for four seasons. Six games into his freshman year Reynolds got the starting nod at quarterback, and he remained at that spot throughout the rest of his collegiate career. Reynolds was named to the All-Conference first team his senior year to climax an outstanding eight year football career as a player, but his interest in athletics did not end with his final snap at NE Louisiana.

Upon graduation from college, Reynolds entered the coaching ranks at Pine Tree High School in Longview, Texas, where he remained for 12 years. He resigned from Pine Tree to accept the head coaching position at Carthage High School, and continues his career there, beginning his twenty-second season in the fall of 1994. Through the 1993 season Reynolds compiled a career 156–78–9 record for a winning percentage of .670. In the fall of 1993 he was inducted into the Northeast Louisiana University Hall of Fame to highlight a brilliant career.

R.L. Crawford Jr.

Another member of the powerful Lewisville Farmer football machine in the mid-'50s was R.L. Crawford Jr., who played both receiver and running back from 1954–57. Crawford's speed made him a valuable weapon in the Farmer offensive attack, complementing the powerful running combination of Salsman, Don and Dan Smith, Walter Morris and Larry Sigler, during his years as a Farmer. Besides receiving, Crawford handled all the kicking duties his senior year in 1957.

R.L. Crawford Jr.

As a sophomore Crawford played left halfback on both offense and defense, allowing him the opportunity to gain experience during the 1955 record-setting scoring season. In fact, Crawford contributed to three district championships in 1955, '56 and '57 with swift running and reliable hands, earning himself All-District honors in 1956 and '57 and being named to the first team his senior year, his best as a Farmer. Crawford scored eight touchdowns in 1957, six of them on pass receptions and the remaining two on the ground. Remarkably, Crawford caught only 13 passes all season, with just under half of them resulting in scores. His 291 yards in receiving led the team, and his 181 rushing yards netted a 5.8 average, revealing just how much of a dual threat he really was.

The Presbyterian Backfield
R.L. Crawford Jr. (11), WalterMorriss (12) and Pete Underwood (36).

Crawford, along with quarterback Pete Underwood and right halfback Walter Morriss, compiled what the Lewisville Enterprise dubbed the "Presbyterian backfield," as all three were members of the First Presbyterian Church of Lewisville. The trio served as captains of the 1957 team as well—a tribute to their leadership on and off the field. Besides football, Crawford lettered three years in both basketball and track, proving to be a versatile athlete year around. He earned a trip to the state meet in the 880-yard run his senior year after winning the regional meet, posting a 2:07.4 time in that event. A severe bout with the flu spoiled his hopes at placing at the state level, ending his high school athletic career on a disappointing note.

Crawford's high school activity was not spent entirely on athletic endeavors, however, as he was president of his senior class and was voted "best all-around" the same year. He even was a member of a singing group, along with other athletes, to display another of his many talents. The group, known as "The Rockets," included Crawford, Bobby Kimmel, Don Kennedy, Terry

Founding Farmers — Famous Farmers

Parks, Dan Smith and Billy Parker, with LeNore Aly as the only female member. The group was so popular that they appeared at several functions and dances, including a television appearance on Jerry Hayne's Juke Box on the WFAA station. They even had a five-year recording contract with two Dallas producers, proving they were capable artists.

Crawford attended North Texas State College on an athletic scholarship. After graduating, he entered the business world in the insurance industry, establishing his own agency in Lewisville.

FAMOUS FARMERS

Hundreds of thousands of athletes play high school football each year across the nation, many of which continue playing in college. Many collegiate athletes aspire to enter the professional ranks, but with only 28 teams in the National Football League and about 1,400 jobs available, not all who hope to land a spot in the pros do. Many high school football programs feel fortunate to produce players that are able to play at the college level; few are able to realize the dream of carving out a living at the sport they love so much.

The Lewisville Farmer football program has been fortunate to have had many former players represent it at the collegiate level, with three continuing at the professional level. Others have achieved feats that make them more than just a legend in the Farmer history books; they've become national figures.

Walt Garrison

Without a doubt the most famous Farmer is Walt Garrison, recognized more for his nine seasons as a Dallas Cowboy than his three as a Fighting Farmer. Garrison played for the Farmers from 1959–61 during a time when Farmer football was less-than spectacular. In the years that Garrison played the Farmers finished a combined 12–18 with their only real threat for a district title coming in 1961. The Farmers finished 5–5 that year, and 3–2 in district. A final game loss to arch-rival Plano is the only thing that prevented them from capturing the district championship that season.

Walt Garrison
Fighting Farmer

As a Farmer, Garrison started out playing tackle but was later moved to tight end to utilize his quickness and blocking ability. Ultimately he was shifted to linebacker, where he finally earned a starting roll as a senior. Walt was a captain of that Farmer team in '61 as well. Although he garnered All-District Honorable Mention recognition in both his junior and senior years, Garrison's career as a football player at Lewisville was, at best, average. He is the first to admit there was nothing special about him as a player at Lewisville. "Making second team honorable mention is like being on the fourth team somewhere. It's nothing to brag about," recalled the former NFL great.

Garrison did earn a football scholarship to Oklahoma State University in Stillwater, Oklahoma, although not primarily for his accomplishments on the playing field. While in high school Garrison worked at the American Nut Company where he spent summer days and evenings loading and unloading 130-pound bags of peanuts, which helped him keep in shape. His boss, Zan Burroughs, thought a lot of the young Garrison and saw to it that the youngster at least got a chance at a college education. Burroughs knew that Garrison's family could not afford to send him to school, nor could he earn enough money at the nut factory to pay his way through school. Neither could Burroughs, for that matter, but he did the next best thing. His brother was governor of New Mexico, so he made a phone call to him and secured an athletic scholarship for Garrison to New Mexico State University. Burroughs assured his brother that Walt was a hard worker and would more than earn his scholarship as an Aggie. With everything set, Garrison prepared to head west to Las Cruces, New Mexico for his freshman year in college.

Between the time the former Farmer received his scholarship and the day he was scheduled to report for the first day of practice, the National Collegiate Athletic Association (NCAA) placed New Mexico on probation and removed all scholarships, including Garrison's. The governor, feeling somewhat obligated to the youngster, called another friend of his, who happened to be the governor of Oklahoma. Between the two they worked it out where Garrison would, instead, receive a full scholarship for athletics to Oklahoma State University, so he enrolled as a freshman and reported for two-a-day workouts in the fall of '61.

Originally Garrison was slated to play linebacker, the position he excelled at while at Lewisville. His forte' was defense and he saw only marginal time at fullback while a Farmer. As a hay hauler and bull rider, Garrison had a toughness about him that lended itself to being a prolific defensive player. In short, he liked to hit people, a desirable quality in a linebacker.

Unlike college football of today, players in the early '60s still played both offense and defense, and Garrison's offensive position was fullback, largely due to his quickness and stocky build. "Everybody had a position on offense and defense, and linebackers on defense were usually fullbacks or centers on offense," recalled Garrison, which turned out to be a blessing in disguise. Garrison's first love was defense, but his services were needed on offense. In his sophomore year Head Coach Phil Cutching engineered Garrison's move to fullback, although he still played linebacker in goal line situations. He backed up George Thomas on offense his sophomore year but started at fullback his junior year. Although the team was unsuccessful, posting only a few wins, Garrison led the Big 8 Conference in rushing, which began to catch the eye of writers and coaches around the nation. "I have no clue as to how many yards I gained that year. It didn't really seem to matter because we didn't win

Founding Farmers — Famous Farmers

Left: As an Oklahoma State Cowboy, Walt Garrison gains good yardage against Oklahoma in 1965. The Cowboys beat the Sooners, 17–16, for their first win over OU in 20 years. *Right:* Garrison breaks a tackle against the Cardinals' Roger Worely (22) as a Dallas Cowboy.

much. Hell, if we won the coin flip we had a celebration," Garrison said, recalling his unpleasant memories of the 1964 season.

Oklahoma State lost heavily to the University of Oklahoma that season, as they had done the previous 20 times they met. The Cowboys' losing streak to the Sooners dated back to 1945, and it became a goal for OSU to beat them in '65, if they beat no one else that season. They managed to do just that, with Garrison leading the way. The burly senior paced the Cowboys to a slim, but certain, 17–16 victory over their intrastate rivals and mustered enough momentum to nearly defeat the eventual Big 8 champ, the Nebraska Cornhuskers. Garrison logged his second successful season on the ground as well, finishing second in the conference in rushing as an integral part of the rebirth of the OSU football program to a level of prominence it had not seen since Harry Truman was President.

Besides making an impression on opposing defensive backs, Garrison made an impression on NFL scouts, too, with the 1966 draft around the corner. One such scout was Gil Brandt of the Dallas Cowboys, recommending that they make Garrison their fifth round selection. "The Cowboys needed someone to back up Don Perkins at fullback, so they picked me in the fifth round," explained the Lewisville native. He was also picked by the Kansas City Chiefs in either the 14th or 15th round in the draft of the now defunct American Football League. Being both a Texas native and Lewisville boy, he opted to sign with the Cowboys to remain in Texas and play for the legendary coach, Tom Landry.

Garrison spent three seasons backing up Perkins before moving into the starting lineup after Perkins' retirement. He played in the backfield with other distinguished Cowboy running backs like Perkins, Calvin Hill, Dan Reeves and Robert Newhouse, as well as the controversial Duane Thomas. He lined up behind lengendary Cowboy quarterbacks Roger Staubach, Craig Morton and the colorful "Dandy" Don Meredith, who was also a Texas product. Meredith once spoke of Garrison's reliability as a ball carrier. "If you needed four yards, you could give the ball to Walt and he'd get four yards. If you needed 20 yards, you could give the ball to Walt and he'd get you four yards," the comical Meredith said of Garrison on Monday Night Football, where he was a color commentator for many years.

Garrison played with the Cowboys from 1966–74, making the playoffs in eight of those nine seasons. 1974, Garrison's final season with Dallas, was the only year they did not make it to post season play while he wore the familiar number 32. Garrison completed his professional career with 3,886 yards rushing on 899 carries for a 4.3 yard average per carry. He scored 30 touchdowns rushing and another nine receiving, as an instrumental part of the birth of the Cowboy dynasty that reached into the late 1970s.

As of the completion of the 1993 season, Garrison is sixth on the all-time Cowboys rushing list, behind Don Perkins, Calvin Hill, Robert Newhouse, Tony Dorsett and Emmit Smith. His most prolific day as a Cowboy came against the much hated Washington Redskins on December 9, 1972. Dallas beat the Redskins, 34–24, in an offensive showdown, and Garrison gained 121 yards on just 10 carries to provide a big piece of the offense that day.

WALT GARRISON'S CAREER TOTALS AS A DALLAS COWBOY (1966–1974)					
RUSHING:	Attempts	Yardage	Average	Longest	TDs
	899	3,886	4.3	41	30
RECEIVING:	Number	Yardage	Average	Longest	TDs
	182	1,794	9.9	53	9
KICKOFF RETURNS:	Number	Yardage	Average	Longest	TDs
	41	813	19.8	36	0

Founding Farmers — Famous Farmers

The true cowboy — Garrison wrestles a steer in rodeo competition, one of his lifetime hobbies.

In his nine seasons with the Cowboys, Garrison played in two Super Bowls. Dallas lost the first one to the Baltimore Colts in 1971, 16–13, on a last-second Jim O'Brien field goal. They came back the following season to finish with a 14–3 record and captured the franchise's first Super Bowl, securing the championship ring for Garrison before he retired three seasons later.

After retiring from professional football, Garrison did not become idle. He began his second career in 1972, three years before retiring, as the vice president of Southwest Promotions for Skoal-Copenhagen, traveling throughout the Southwest Region as the spokesman for the smokeless tobacco product. In conjunction with his duties the popular Cowboy was featured in national television commercials touting the product he had used while participating in his hobby of bull riding and calf roping. It was his authenticity as a real cowboy that attracted the people at Skoal-Copenhagen to use him as their spokesman; the fact that he actually used their product made it a natural connection.

Garrison now offices on Main Street in downtown Lewisville, in the building once occupied by the Liberty Picture Show, a place he frequented as a Lewisville youth. "This place once was the Liberty Picture Show and, much later, a Karate studio. After that it was condemned, then we bought it and remodeled it into what it is now," explains Garrison.

As a teen Garrison and some friends worked for his Uncle Leroy at the Diamond R Ranch, breaking horses, riding bulls and hauling hay. The experience toughened Garrison and made him a better football player. It also laid the ground work for his current occupation, as well as other pursuits. Besides representing Skoal-Copenhagen, Garrison owns and operates an indoor arena in Benbrook, Texas, south of Fort Worth, which features rodeo activities and bicycle motorcross six days a week.

Walt attributes much of his success to his roots, being raised in a small Texas town. "Growing up in a small town and working at the nut mill, hauling hay and breaking horses and anything using my muscles—it all helped me stay in shape. We also played everything; football, baseball and basketball. There weren't enough of us to go around so everybody played everything. It definitely helped me," recalled the former Dallas Cowboy.

Upon reflection, Garrison was uncertain of his football future after he graduated from LHS and enrolled at Oklahoma State. "I didn't think I could play in college. When I got there, I realized I was in a room full of all-staters," tells Garrison. But things turned out just fine for the Lewisville native who was first a Fighting Farmer, then an OSU Cowboy, next a Dallas Cowboy... but always a true cowboy.

Jesse and Teddy Garcia
The Farmers were strengthened by the kicking talents of brothers Jesse and Teddy Garcia from 1977–1982, with both demonstrating consistency that allowed them to reach the professional football level.

Jesse kicked for Lewisville from 1977–78 and was a part of Neal Wilson's first district championship in '78. While a junior in 1977, Jesse nailed a 57-yard field goal, by far a Lewisville Farmer record and the fifth longest in the state, a record he shares with four other Texas high school placekickers.

Jesse made first team All-District in '77 and '78 as a soccer-style kicker—the first in Lewisville history. The elder Garcia brother gained his kicking skills as a soccer player for the Lewisville High School soccer team. Those skills translated into football skills when the Farmers, suffering from an inept kicking game, went on a search for someone to handle the placekicking chores. Jesse Garcia was that person and became one of the few bright spots for the Farmers in '77, the final season under David Visentine as head coach.

Jesse spent the first half of his college career in Lubbock, Texas, playing for the Texas Tech Red Raiders under Coach Steve Sloan and joining Farmer teammate Dale Brown. Two seasons later other Farmers would be added to the Red Raider roster, but Garcia would not be there. Eddie Tillman joined Garcia and Brown at Tech in 1979, and Freddie Wells in 1980, to become the first of a steady flow of players the Farmers would supply the Southwest Conference university in future years.

But Jesse transferred to NE Louisiana his junior year, following former Lewisville greats such as Gordon Salsman and Sleepy Reynolds, and played his final two seasons for the Indians. It was Jesse's switch to NE Louisiana that would attract his younger brother there three years later.

Founding Farmers — Famous Farmers

Jesse pursued a professional career after graduating from the Southland Conference school and headed to Thousand Oaks, California for a shot at the kicking job with the Dallas Cowboys. Garcia had hopes of beating out Rafael Septien for the position and gave him a good fight. Jesse made it to the final cut before being let go, narrowly missing out on a chance to play for the NFL's dean of coaches, Tom Landry. Content with his effort, Garcia did not pursue a chance with another professional team, and his football career ended with the Cowboy tryout.

Teddy Garcia earned a spot on the varsity from 1980–82, battling for the kicking duties with Steve Bernhard in '80 before winning the job. Teddy experienced a dismal season in 1980, as the Farmers finished 4–5–1, but contributed to two district championships in 1981 and '82. Like Jesse, Teddy made the transition from the soccer field to the football field to bring a consistency to the kicking game, an aspect of the Farmer attack that was lacking the year before. The inability to connect on three makeable field goal attempts in the 1979 semi-final game cost the Farmers the game and, many think, a state championship had they won. In 1982 Teddy made the All-Metro team but was overlooked when the All-District honors were made during all three of his seasons with the Farmers.

The younger Garcia graduated in 1983 and attended Northeat Louisiana University in Monroe, Louisiana, competing in the Southland Conference. Garcia's decision to go to NE Louisiana was due to Jesse's influence. It was a move that paid off for Teddy, who played for the Indians for four seasons.

With Teddy Garcia as their place-kicker, the Indians won the 1987 Division II National Championship against Marshall College of Idaho. Garcia provided the winning margin with a last-second field goal allowing the Indians to claim the national title. Garcia carried All-Conference honors in his last two seasons before being drafted by the New England Patriots in the fourth round. He was cut by the Patriots the following season and tried to capture a spot on the roster of the Minnesota Vikings, but Rich Karlis beat him out for the job.

Garcia then went to Houston and beat out Tony Zendejas to become the Oilers' place-kicker. He played for Houston for a single season before losing out to Al Del Greco, then he played in Spain for the Barcelona Dragons of the short-lived World Football League. No longer in football, Garcia returned to Monroe, Louisiana to make his home.

Mike Aljoe

As a sophomore Mike Aljoe was a key player in the Farmers' bid for a state championship, which was spoiled by the 3–0 semi-final loss to Temple. Aljoe played two more seasons on the offensive line for the Farmers, earning first team All-District honors in his senior year. He earned an Honorable Mention to the All-District list in '79 as a sophomore, but what has been forgotten about him was his second team All-State selection to wrap up his senior year.

Perhaps his All-State selection got lost in the mix and went unnoticed by the local press. After all, he was one of 10 Farmers selected to the first team All-District team, and one of 28 Lewisville players receiving post-season accolades. He apparently impressed others throughout the state, as he was named to the North All-Star team and played in the annual battle in the Astrodome which climaxed the Texas High School Coaches Association convention.

Aljoe played on the offensive line for Greg Sherwood's North squad, as a 208-pound guard who was asked to go up against 260-pound defensive linemen. But Aljoe didn't mind. He considers it an honor to have been asked to play. Sherwood confided to Aljoe, after the conclusion of the 7–3 North victory, that, "you're the best pulling guard I've seen." Sherwood, then head coach of the Plainview Bulldogs, had seen plenty of them.

As a somewhat silent, but effective member of the Farmer offensive line, Aljoe was one of the top 15 blue-chip linemen in the state his senior year and was destined for a collegiate career in the sport. He was heavily recruited throughout the southern region but accepted Barry Switzer's offer from the University of Oklahoma to play for the Sooners. "I wanted to travel and see more of the country than the Southwest Conference had to offer," explained the former Lewisville standout. "At the time Oklahoma was one of the top 15 football programs in the country, unlike many other schools where I could have gone," realized Aljoe.

That decision turned out to be a beneficial one for both him and Barry Switzer. Aljoe played on some of Switzer's best teams at Oklahoma from 1982 to 1987, including three Big 8 conference championships, three Orange Bowl appearances and a national championship. Aljoe received a scholarship as a student athlete in the fall of '82 but was red-shirted that season. The Sooners fell to Arizona State in the Fiesta Bowl that year but came back two seasons later to make the first of three consecutive Orange Bowl appearances, all of which Aljoe was a part of.

After losing to Washington in the '84 Orange Bowl the Sooners and Aljoe defeated Penn State in '85, 25–10, to win the national championship. Mike had completed his academic requirements for graduating in the fall of '86, playing his final season for Barry Switzer and the Oklahoma Sooners. They defeated Arkansas 42–7 in one of the most lopsided games in Orange Bowl history, as Aljoe completed a collegiate career as a part of one of the most successful Oklahoma Sooner teams in the university's history.

Aljoe did not pursue a professional career, although he felt it would have been possible, had it been what he wanted. "I could have probably given a valiant effort to be a free agent, but I would not have been drafted by any team. I did not get the visibility necessary at OU to have much of a chance at a pro career," explained Aljoe. The political climate at OU did not give him the national exposure he needed to become a draft prospect. "I played behind some pretty good athletes at Oklahoma and was swallowed up by all their publicity. I got injured in '83 in a system where four people played two

Founding Farmers — Famous Farmers

Mike Aljoe as a member of the Fighting Farmers (left) and Oklahoma Sooners. Aljoe played for the University of Oklahoma from 1982–86, including three Orange Bowl wins and a National Championship.

Mike Aljoe competes in a qualifying run on the United States 4-man bobsled team in 1987. Aljoe (rear) and Brent Rushlaw (inset) prepare to make a run in the '88 Olympics in Calgary.

positions," related Aljoe. The platooning, while good for the Sooners, was not necessarily good for Aljoe's national exposure, and he was overlooked.

But Aljoe's athletic career did not end with the Orange Bowl appearance on January 1, 1987. Five days later he was in Lake Placid, New York, trying to earn a spot on the United States Bobsled team that would compete in the 1988 Olympics in Calgary, a task that was to be a challenge. Aljoe was not the traditional U.S. bobsledder, at 6-foot-2-inches and 230 pounds.

Historically, the U.S. Bobsled Committee elected to utilize small, quick athletes to push the sled, theorizing that larger ones could not be coordinated to fit into the tight confines of a sled with another human being. But Aljoe set a new trend in American bobsledding in '87 with his combination of size and speed that would earn him a place on the U.S. team. Aljoe was quick, as characterized by his 4.62 speed in the 40-yard dash, and that quickness allowed him to push-start the sled at a world-class pace. Once in the sled, his 230 pounds worked in his favor, allowing it to travel faster due to the combined forces of gravity and friction. At year's end, Aljoe was ranked as the number one brakeman and pusher in the United States, only a year after he had removed his Oklahoma Sooner jersey for the last time.

During the qualifying year of 1987 Aljoe traveled the world as a member of the World Cup team, competing in places like Cortina, Italy, Winterbery and Karl Marx Stadt in East Germany, Innsbruck, Austria and Switzerland. In October he secured his spot on the team and would be joined with veteran driver Brent Rushlaw.

Aljoe had broken into the sport with Randy Will as his driver, but Will had been beaten out by Rushlaw, and so the two were paired. Rushlaw had engineered sleds in the 1976, '80 and '84 Olympics and was entrenched in the "old school" of U.S. bobsled competition. Instead of emphasizing fitness and athleticism, Rushlaw tended to put more emphasis on the machine, depending on a sound design rather than a sound body. Aljoe was just the opposite, as he felt the necessity to train physically was at least as important as maintaining the equipment. "Brent's idea of training was to stop drinking and smoking," according to Aljoe, which made it curious as to how he had been so successful in the sport thus far. "He really wasn't considered a world class athlete but was a fantastic driver. What he lacked as an athlete he more than made up for as a driver," explained the former Farmer-turned-Sooner-turned-Olympian.

So Aljoe and Rushlaw comprised the team that would occupy the USA One two-man bobsled that would compete in Calgary in the '88 Winter Olympics, but not without a controversy. Willie Gault, the all-pro receiver who was then with the Chicago Bears, had taken an interest in the sport like Aljoe, and decided he would put his name in the hat as well. Although his motive for competing was uncertain, it was clear that his presence was a disruptive force in the qualifying process. "Willie would fly in one day, then fly out, and fly in a week later, expecting to be given a place on the team. He was a nice guy, but him coming and going led to disharmony in the bobsled community and created loopholes in the selection process. It was like having a player on a football team showing up for the games but not at practice," recalled Aljoe.

Aljoe resented Gault's cavalier approach to the sport, but it did not disuade him from achieving his goal in making the team. He and Rushlaw competed in the two-man event, but had to withdraw after the third heat because of an injury to the driver. Rushlaw and Aljoe were in 23rd place after the second heat but had climbed to 16th with their third run. Rushlaw suffered a pulled hip flexor muscle during, what would be their final run, and did not finish the competition.

Regardless of the disappointing finish, Aljoe had impacted the sport of bobsledding with his size and quickness. Future teams would begin to search for the larger, quick man to anchor the U.S. bobsled teams instead of the traditionally smaller types. Aljoe was a prototype of things to come in the sport of United States bobsledding.

And it all began at Lewisville. "I remember moving to Lewisville when I was in the fifth grade. We drove by a sign that read, 'Welcome to Lewisville—Home of the Fighting Farmers.' I turned to my Dad and said, 'What have I gotten myself into?'" reflected the fiery competitor who was voted Lewisville's Male Athlete of the '80s. "Paul Rice was my inspiration to play football at Lewisville. After going to see the Farmers play and seeing Rice run, I knew I wanted to be a Farmer." And what a Farmer he was.

THE ALL-AMERICANS

Gordon Salsman

In 1955, the season in which Lewisville was the state's highest scoring team, a Farmer running back ended his high school career in an unfortunate way, but not before he wrote himself into the Lewisville High School record books as its first All-American. On the eighth play of the 1955 bi-district contest against the Chilicothe Eagles, Gordon Salsman got his ankle broken, ending his high school career, and with it, the Farmers' bid for at least a bi-district championship.

**Gordon Salsman
Defense 1953**

Salsman was a four-year letterman in football from 1952–55, earning All-District honors in three of the four seasons. In 1953 he earned second team honors but achieved a first team selection in '54 and '55. Also in 1955 Salsman was named to the All-State first team, along with teammate Billy Sisk. They were the first two Farmers to be recognized among the state's best.

Salman's efforts as a fullback is what led the Farmers to a 32–9 record during his four seasons on the Lewisville roster, including the record-setting season of '55. Salsman's straight-ahead power running paced a 522 point

Salsman on the move in 1955.

The All-American

production that season, 203 of which Salsman contributed. Besides his fullback duties he also handled all kicking chores, allowing him several ways to increase his overall point total. One of the most memorable contests Salsman recalled was a 93–6 shellacking of the Northwest Texans.

Playing at home, the Farmers had secured the victory over the Texans by the end of the first period, and Coach Lewis McReynolds began to call off the dogs. Unable to prevent frequent scores, the Farmers began punting on first down in the second half, ensuring they would not add to their big lead. The coaches had already agreed to cut the time of the quarters from 12 to eight minutes in hopes of ending the massacre. Salsman scored five or six touchdowns himself, but said it would have been much worse. "Our quarterback, Terry Don Parks, had six or seven touchdowns called back or it would have been a lot bigger score," recalled the former fullback. In fact, 327 of the total 522 points on the season came in the five district contests. Overshadowed by the offensive output was the tremendous defensive effort turned in by Lewisville. During the same district stretch the Farmers allowed only 12 points, and 78 all season. Salsman played defense as well, contributing to the team's success on both sides of the ball.

After graduating in 1956 Salsman attended North Texas State College, starting and lettering for two seasons as an Eagle. Following the '57 season Salsman transferred to Northeast Louisiana, rejoining former teammate Everett "Sleepy" Reynolds in the Indians' backfield. He lettered for Northeast Louisiana, earning All-Conference honors both seasons.

Founding Farmers — Famous Farmers

Salsman had an opportunity to play professional football, being heavily wooed by the Dallas Texans. Hank Stram, then head coach of the Texans, and Abner Haynes came to visit him to try to seduce him into continuing his football career. Haynes shared the same backfield with Salsman while at NTSC and convinced Stram that Salsman was a professional caliber player, pursuading him to make the "sales call" to Lewisville. Stram and Haynes were not able to convince Salsman to join the Texans. Salsman, being somewhat skeptical of the newly formed American Football League, passed up their offer. Haynes went on to star with the Texans, and later with the Kansas City Chiefs, as owner Lamar Hunt moved his team from Dallas to Kansas City in 1963. Salsman has no regrets for not accepting the chance to play professionally, as he chose to enter into the business world after leaving Northeast Louisiana.

Paul Rice
The Farmers have been blessed to have featured some of the state's top running backs in their offensive schemes over the years, but when the subject arises, the name of Paul Rice quickly emerges to the top of the list. Rice played at Lewisville from 1972–74, leading the way in rebuilding a program that had been in a shambles for 15 years. Rice rushed for 2,359 in 1972 as a sophomore and scored 36 touchdowns to lead the Farmers into the state title game; their first chance ever. Behind fullback Mike Nichols' blocking, Rice's achievements were impressive enough to earn him a first team spot on both the All-District and All-State rosters. To culminate the success he experienced that season, he was named to the All-American team, being recognized as one of the nation's top backs.

Rice duplicated his achievements in his remaining two seasons as a Farmer, becoming the first, and only, three-time All-American to be produced from the Lewisville High School football program. He is one of the state's best backs and among the leaders in several categories in Texas high school football history. His career season-high 2,359 rushing yards in 1972 was a 3A record that stood for 13 years before Tomball's Bubba Greely broke it in 15 games in 1985. Rice's season high is currently fifth on the all-time rushing list at the 4A level, after the records were adjusted to accomodate the division realignment in 1980. His 218 point-total that year is the third highest individual total in the state's history.

In 1973 Rice added to his career rushing total, setting a pace to exceed what he achieved in 1972 in 14 games. His numbers were cut short, however, as the Farmers' bid for a second consecutive district title came to a screeching halt against McKinney. The Farmers lost to the Lions in McKinney, 28–21, a game in which Rice rushed for 229 yards and scored one touchdown. Several questionable calls by the officials nullified another estimated 150 yards for Rice, costing him a shot at another record, but more importantly, the district title and a chance at a state championship.

Rice secures the ball against Richardson Berkner in '72.

The Lewisville All-American charges into the line against McKinney in 1973.

Rice eludes an Irving Tiger in 1974, his final season at LHS.

Behind Mike Nichols (35), Joe Martin (8), and Terry Wilcox, Rice gets outside against North Garland in 1973.

1,000-yard rusher: Paul Rice gained 5,270 yards rushing in his three seasons as a Lewisville Farmer, leading them to a state final appearance in 1972.

Against Boswell in the playoffs, Rice speeds through an open lane.

Rice rushes for good yardage at Farmer Field.

Founding Farmers — Famous Farmers

The 1974 season was the final one for Rice, and a difficult one for both him and the Farmers, as they moved up to 4A competition. Rice, who had attracted a lot of attention nationally, became the target of the new district's defenses, as he was the only true weapon the Farmers returned from their 1972–73 arsenal. His numbers went down considerably, but he managed to reach the 1,000-yard plateau, gaining 1,069 on 244 carries. He scored 12 touchdowns, one-third the number he scored his sophomore season, to bring his high school career total to 69—by far an LHS record.

Rice achieved the "triple-crown" of post season honors for the third consecutive year, earning a first team selection on the All-District and All-State teams, and being named to the All-American team. He was highly recruited nationwide, with offers from everywhere, including the University of Southern California, Notre Dame, the University of Oklahoma, the University of Texas, Southern Methodist University and Texas A&M University, to name a few. At first, the attention Rice received was flattering to him but soon became a nuisance, as hoards of phone calls, letters and personal visits disrupted his daily routine. The recruiters popped up everywhere, hounding Rice all hours of the day at his home and on campus. He finally signed a letter of intent with SMU, more to stave off the intruders than fulfill a desire to play for the Mustangs. A week later he signed a national letter of intent with USC, hoping to bring to a halt the parade of headhunters once and for all.

Rice graduated from LHS at mid-term of the 1974–75 school year and ventured out west to the Southern California school to get a jump on the competition for the starting tailback position. He was forced to play behind eventual Heisman Trophy winner Ricky Bell and saw little playing time that initial season, a position Rice had not been used to. The prospects were not good for Rice either, as Bell was only in his junior season, and a hot prospect was due to arrive on the scene to intensify the competition at the coveted tailback spot. Charles White came in as a freshman behind Rice and eventually took over after Bell's final season. In the meantime Rice, impatient to wait another season for the position to open, transferred to a junior college to log some playing time, hoping to return to the Trojan roster for his junior year of eligibilty.

He never got the chance to return to USC, however, and bounced around to several other Division I schools before ending his collegiate career. After leaving California he attended Ranger Junior College, but remained there less than a semester. He had an altercation involving a weapon with one of the other players and was dismissed from the team. He returned to the metroplex and visited with new SMU Head Coach Ron Meier. He and Meier reached an agreement, and Rice shared the backfield with Arthur Wittington that season. Rice, the larger of the two, was inserted at fullback and used primarily for blocking, a skill he excelled at but a roll he did not bargain with Meier for. He wanted to run with the ball, utilizing his natural speed, power and quickness. He was displeased with the number of times he carried the ball and left the team after the sixth game of the season. He concluded his collegiate career at

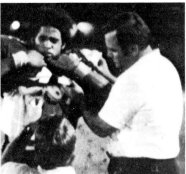

Paul Rice in 4A competition against Irving (top left), getting medical attention from Vic Rucker (top right) and breaking out of the pack against Trinity (bottom).

East Texas State University in Commerce, Texas, a far cry from the glamour of USC.

Rice's 5,270 career rushing yards at LHS from 1972–74 was a 5A record that stood until Converse Judson's Jerod Douglas broke it in the 1993 season. Douglas rushed for 6,189 yards from 1991–93 and led his team to consecutive state championships in '92 and '93, and a semi-final appearance in 1991. Douglas bested Rice's 21-year old record in 44 games — 10 games more than Rice played to achieve his rushing title. Had he been able to play another 10 contests like Douglas, it is unknown how many yards he would have gained. Another factor to consider was Rice's partner in the backfield in his first two seasons. Mike Nichols gained 2,580 as he shared the running chores with Rice in 1972 and '73, easing the youngster's load a bit.

Together the two gained 6,850 yards rushing in two seasons, indicating that Rice was not the only one capable of carrying the ball for the Farmers. Nichols' presence in the backfield aided Rice tremendously, as the Farmer

Founding Farmers — Famous Farmers

offense featured a more balanced attack than the lone running back teams like those Douglas played on at Converse Judson.

The Farmers have had their share of outstanding running backs in their history; runners like Woodrow Sigler and Hoss Williams from the early '30s, to more recent stars as Gordon Salsman, Dan and Don Smith, Joe Bishop, Dale Brown, Freddie Wells, Terrance Miller, Eddie Tillman, Bert Jones, Andre Brown, Metrick McHenry and Dwayne Brazzell. But none were more explosive or exciting than Paul Rice, who dazzled and impressed high school football fans from 1972–74.

Brian Camp

Lewisville's third All-American came, not from the running back position, but from the offensive line, as Brian Camp earned the honors in 1980. Camp was a 6-foot-5-inch, 250-pound starter for three seasons on the Farmer offensive line, contributing to two district titles. The massive offensive tackle was a part of the 1979 team that knocked off the highly acclaimed Abiline Cooper Cougars and reached the semi-finals. He was a big part of the offense that sprung running back Freddie Wells for more than 1,000 yards that season before narrowly losing to the Temple Wildcats, 3–0, to end the season. He earned a selection to the first team All-District team in each of his final two seasons as a Farmer.

Brian Camp wore No. 76 as a Farmer from 1978–80

Besides his obvious athletic talents, Camp finished 21st in his class of 519, with an average of 94 percent, ensuring he could attend any college or university of his choice. And he had plenty to choose from. Coaches from all across the country would love to have had his combined size, strenth and savvy anchoring their offensive line. He received letters from practically every known football program, including personal visits from well known figures like Barry Switzer of OU, Lou Holtz from Notre Dame and Grant Teaff at Baylor. Due to his deep religious conviction and lifelong affiliation with the Southern Baptist denomination, Camp had predetermined he would attend Baylor University in Waco, Texas, although he admits it was enjoyable to receive the various offers. Several years later his younger brother, Gary, was similarly recruited, and the two compared the letters each had received. "One day we got our letters out and weighed them to see who had more. We each had about 60 pounds apiece," joked the elder Camp.

Brian lettered four seasons at Baylor, starting his final two, including an appearance in the Bluebonnet Bowl in 1983. The Bears played Oklahoma State University, coached by Jimmy Johnson. Baylor lost, but it was a memorable experience for Camp, receiving a traditional bowl ring as a souvenir.

Although Camp never made All-Conference athletically while at Baylor, he did earn All-Conference honors academically, carrying a 3.9 grade point average. He graduated magna cum laude in 1985 from the distinguished Southwest Conference university, gaining skills that would serve him equally well in the business world.

Camp recalled facing some prominent athletes while playing tackle for Baylor. He remembers playing against the notorious Brian Bosworth when Baylor played Oklahoma, but his best recollection was of his effort against Texas A&M and his battle with defensive tackle Ray Childress. The 6-foot-6-inch, 272-pound Childress is now an All-Pro with the Houston Oilers, but "I got the best of him when we met while I was at Baylor," remembers Camp.

Brian Camp is the last on a short list of All-Americans to play for the Lewisville Fighting Farmers, completing his high school career in 1980 on a team that finished a disappointing 4–5–1. Inspite of the dismal finish, Camp was a bright spot in the Farmer line-up, earning the All-American honor. He first learned of his selection after reading it in the newspaper, but was eventually notified by the various sponsors of the prestigious choice, receiving plaques from Sports Illustrated, the Carnation Company and Scholastics Magazine, the tri-sponsors of the award. By making the All-Conference academic list Camp defied the stereotypical image of football players, earning a bachelor's degree in economics upon his graduation from Baylor in 1985.

. . .

CHAPTER

A BANK ROBBERY

The Day the Farmers Foiled a Bank Robbery Attempt

ANYONE WHO HAS BEEN a resident of Lewisville for any length of time and has followed the Farmers, no doubt has heard about the 1946 Farmer football team — not for their football ability on the field, but rather for an incident that occurred one Monday afternoon on the last day of September. The story has been recounted numerous times, but no history of the Farmers would be complete without its reconstruction included. On the day when the verdict of the famous Nurenberg trials was handed down, where 12 Nazi war leaders were convicted and sentenced to death by an international tribunal for inhumane war crimes, the citizens of Lewisville were concerned with a more immediate crime.

The story, as it goes, begins on Monday, September 30, 1946, at around 4:00 p.m. The Farmers, fresh from a 6–0 victory over the Alvord Bulldogs the

Then and now — The Lewisville State Bank (above) shortly after its construction in 1910. (Right) That same building in 1993.

previous Friday, were about one-third the way through the afternoon's workout when Coach J.K. Delay joined them. Delay, who also happened to be the superintendent, joined the team each day after school let out, once his official duties as superintendent were completed for the day. After about 30 minutes the town's fire alarm rang, signaling that there was a fire, or some community emergency, in the small, agricultural town of Lewisville. Coach Delay and the team disregarded it. After all, they were in preparation for the coming Friday's game against the Frisco Coons, so they left the worry of fighting fires to the local volunteer fire department and continued with practice.

As it was, about 4:45 p.m. a young man from Sherman had slipped, unnoticed, through a side door of the Lewisville State Bank that opened out to Mill Street (Highway 77), making a withdrawal of $1,046.00. The problem was this young man did not have an account at the bank, and the only withdrawal slip he had was a .22 caliber revolver. Consequently, he directed bank President G.C. Hedrick, along with Cashier Arthur Hayes, Assistant Cashier Ben Savage and Junior Bookkeeper B.L. Dungan, into the bank vault. After forcing the quartet into the vault, he asked Hayes how to lock the door, and where the money was kept. Hayes locked the door himself, surrendered his key to the robber and pointed to a cash drawer, still filled with the currency from the day's activities. A fool proof plan, or so the robber thought.

While the felon turned to help himself to the cash, Hayes rejoined the others in the vault, fortified with 20-inch thick cement walls, slamming the door behind him to ensure their safety. It seems Hayes, or whoever oversaw the construction of the bank, had foreseen an incident like the one taking place, and had a phone installed inside the vault, which he promptly used to call the town's lone operator, Miss Willie Sparks. Hayes instructed her to sound the fire alarm and contact the sheriff regarding the robbery attempt. She also called city hall and, apparently, her mother, Mrs. Sam Sparks.

In 1946 the city of Lewisville stretched from where Main Street and Highway 121 now intersect, on the east side, to Main Street and Interstate 35E to the west, Purnell Road to the south, and 407, or Justin Road, to the north. The

A Bank Robbery

The downtown area of Lewisville, much like it was in 1946.

population of Lewisville was approximately 1,150 then, many of whose families had money on deposit at Lewisville State Bank. At that time the bank was located on the southwest corner of Main and Mill Streets, in the building now occupied by the Victorian Rose Antiques shop and the Bridal Balcony. The football field lay where the parking lot of Lewisville Center is currently located, which was in close proximity to the bank. It ran north to south, bounded by Elm Street to the north, and adjacent to the western most row of buildings in Lewisville's oldest shopping center. Parallel to Main Street one block south, Elm Street ran west from Mill Street, behind the row of buildings on the south side of Main. It also bordered the north side of the football field.

Apparently the alarm frightened the robber's accomplice waiting outside in the getaway car, and she drove away, leaving the young man afoot. And run he did, out the east door of the bank, turning west behind the bank down a back alley in between Main and Elm Streets, then south on Charles Street, where he continued running toward where Delay Middle School is now located. His path lead him on the west side of the football field while practice was in still in session. That's where the Lewisville Farmers entered the scene.

Mrs. Sam Sparks, the operator's mother, lived above Whatley's Store on the south side of main Street, diagonally across from the phone company where her daughter worked. After learning of the hold up, she ran out to her balcony where she saw Coach Delay and the Farmers in the midst of heavy toil. When she got there she noticed a figure running westward between where she stood on her second story balcony and the north end of the football field. She yelled down to Coach Delay, informed him of the plight and sought his assistance.

Several of the team members appraised the situation, calculating out loud to their coach of both their ability and willingness to pursue the thief and recover what loot, if any, he had taken from the citizens of their hard-working community. Coach Delay expressed his objection to the thought of allowing his squad of twenty teenagers to give chase, given the possibility of some sort of weapon involved. Instead, he suggested they go atop the bleachers on the west side of the field to keep the robber in sight. The team complied and Coach Delay lead his squad to the bleachers to keep an eye on the villain until the sheriff arrived. The team had a different idea, however, and continued past the stands in pursuit of the robber, leaving a bewildered Coach Delay behind.

At this point in the story things usually vary, depending on who tells it and how it is remembered. Like the fish that gets bigger and bigger with each repetition, some would have us believe that Lewisville's Farmers filed through a corner phone booth along the way, donned white suits with a maroon cape and an "L" on their collective chests and gang tackled the robber, torturing him until he cried, "uncle," or "Farmer," or whatever word or phrase defined surrender. The fact is, there was no physical contact made with the robber by any member of the team; the closest they came to him was about 50 yards.

The robber, identified as 22-year-old S.A. Brueggemeyer, had entered the bank that afternoon with a grin on his face, looking harmless. Hayes, Hedrick and the others had not noticed him until he entered the cashier's cage, flashed the .22 pistol he had purchased for $18.00 earlier that morning from a Dallas pawn shop and stated, rather boldly, "I mean business. This is a holdup. Get busy." That's when the activity began. He quickly gathered the cash in a paper sack he had procured at a nearby store, and fled.

By the time the Farmers got involved, Brueggemeyer had a decent head start in his getaway attempt. After passing the south end of the football field he went to a gin, located approximately where the old post office on Charles Street is located, and attempted to force two of the workers, W.W. Sherrill, a co-owner of the gin, and G.E. McCombs, to drive him out of town to, no doubt, squander some of his recent booty. Sherrill and McCombs had emerged from the gin to see what the emergency was after they heard the alarm.

The robber first encountered McCombs, pointed the gun at him and ordered McCombs to drive him to the highway in a nearby pickup truck. McCombs declined, stating the pickup was not his and that he didn't have the key. Brueggemeyer then turned to Sherrill and repeated his demand. Sherrill moved toward the truck and started to get in, but turned to the robber in defiance, saying, "You can't bluff me. I'm not going with you." The response apparently surprised Brueggemeyer and he, weighing his options, elected to continue on foot, which he did, through a cornfield south of the

A Bank Robbery

The robber's path

gin, and headed back east toward the highway to find some other means of escape. That is where he encountered the football team again, still in pursuit.

From there the chase lasted only about one-half mile. As the Farmers closed the gap other citizens joined the chase, and Lewisville began to resemble a scene from the Keystone Cops. Members of the football team yelled to Roy Rogan and Heath O'Briant, two mechanics busy working under an automobile at nearby Thomas and Sons service station on Highway 77. After sorting out what the players were saying, they immediately jumped in a vehicle and drove toward the fleeing robber.

Meanwhile, Bob Hilliard, who had been relaxing on that early fall afternoon in front of Whatley's Store, from where Mrs. Sparks notified the team, borrowed a double-barrel shotgun and hitched a ride toward the highway, attempting to head off Brueggemeyer. He was the first to intercept the robber.

Hilliard bolted from the car in front of the robber, still running from the fleet-footed Farmers, led by Eugene Matthews and Jimmy Carpenter. Hilliard dropped to the ground and aimed the borrowed shotgun at a point that would soon be occupied by the robber. As Brueggemeyer came into sight he collapsed, partly out of fear and partly out of exhaustion. He then gave up. "When he saw me hit the ground with that gun he started begging for himself," Hilliard told a Dallas Morning News reporter during the aftermath. "He said he didn't want to hurt anybody."

Rogan and O'Briant, along with Dick Hayes, a former Farmer star in the early '30s, carefully confronted the felon, under the protection of Hilliard's well-aimed weapon, and apprehended him, as the rest of the team caught up with the commotion. It seems as if the robber's naval training had failed him as he gave into his exhaustion with no struggle at all. Rogan said, "He was pretty well worn out and didn't put up any fight. We had a shotgun in the car, but it wasn't loaded and we didn't take it out." Denton County Marshal Arthur Cozby and Coach Delay arrived shortly after the chase ended. Delay had gone north to Main Street when the team went south, and flagged down Cozby, who had just happened to be on patrol in the area. The two then drove to where the squad, along with Rogan, O'Briant, Hayes, Hilliard and the robber, were milling around. With the suspect in custody, this crime would be solved in a matter of minutes.

As Brueggemeyer was searched, however, it was discovered the money and the gun were missing, two key elements to make a case. That's where another citizen, J.W. Wolters, figured in the case. Wolters, a carpenter, had been in the bank earlier and left only a few minutes before the crime. He had noticed a young man, along with a female, parked in a black sedan outside that side door, just before he entered the bank. They were still there when he came out. He thought nothing of the couple, unaware of what they were plotting. Apparently they were waiting for Wolters to leave before perpetrating the crime.

After the alarm sounded, Wolters learned that the bank in which he had

A Bank Robbery

recently transacted business had been robbed. He, too, hitchhiked, post haste, to where the felon was nabbed, and when he arrived he learned that the bandit did not have a gun or the money. Wolters retraced the robber's trail through the cornfield, but several of the football players had already found both the gun and the money in the sack, ditched in haste at the bottom of a utility pole. Matthews, Wallace (Trap) Travelstead and Jackie Reynolds discovered the money, along with the gun used in the robbery, and returned them, solving this crime in only a matter of minutes.

Matthews recalled the encounter 48 years later, especially the chase. "We chased him from the football field to where they caught him. At first we didn't know why we were chasing him. We knew he had run by the field, but we didn't think anything about it. When the lady (Mrs. Sparks) screamed, we figured out something was wrong and took out after him," recalled the former split end. Matthews remembered the pursuit being somewhat peculiar. "He went into the gin to try to get some men to help him get away and had already come out when we started after him. He acted kind of strange. He would run about 50 yards or so then stop . . . and then we'd stop. Then he would start running, and we'd start running again. This happened several times. We knew he had a gun and thought maybe he was trying to get it out of his pocket to use it. We stopped because we didn't want to get too close," detailed Matthews.

It was later discovered that Brueggemeyer had worn gloves while committing the crime and was stopping to remove them while being chased. Reynolds recalled the event in different detail. "He (the robber) kept putting his glove in his pocket, but we thought he was getting his gun. As we got closer he'd taken his gloves off and put them in the bag with the gun and the money. He must have thrown it down by the telephone pole when he passed by it. That's where we found it," explained Reynolds. When asked if he was scared, Reynolds replied, "we weren't really scared of him so much. But what we were afraid of the most was that others who had come to catch him from the other way would shoot us in the crossfire."

The sack used by Brueggemeyer was the most damning of evidence collected as it contained a note in the robber's handwriting that read:

> *I want the biggest bills you have put in this sack.*
> *I mean business. I will shoot to kill.*

This, along with the gun, prompted a confession out of the robber. Brueggemeyer, whose father was a police sergeant in Sherman, had been medically discharged from the Navy in 1943. The money, he said, was to pay off some rather sizeable debts to banks and finance companies in Dallas and Gainesville. Copies of notes in his wallet substantiated this claim. Brueggemeyer was taken into custody and transported to the Denton jail, where a charge of robbery with firearms was filed the next day by Denton County District Attorney W.K. Baldridge.

Friday Night Farmers

The holdup had been the third in Lewisville history, but the first thwarted by the Lewisville Fighting Farmers. The last robbery attempt came 11 years earlier in 1935 when Raymond Hamilton attempted to rob the Lewisville National Bank. In all three robbery attempts the would-be villain was caught and all monies recovered within 24 hours.

Eventually the team returned to the field, but was too excited to concentrate on practice. Coach Delay, out of frustration, announced, "Okay! We've had a little excitement, now let's get back to work! If I hear another word about it, you'll have to run 20 laps." That declaration held the players' attention and practice continued, but the threat lasted only 20 minutes or so, and the excitement of the day's event dominated the rest of the players' thoughts. Finally, a frustrated Coach Delay called off practice and dismissed the team amidst the buzzing recount of the afternoon's adventure.

This story was picked up by Dallas, Ft. Worth and Denton papers, and eventually spread across the country, via the wire service, from Portland, Oregon to Boston, Massachusetts, about how a 20-man high school football team called "Farmers" in a sleepy little Texas town called "Lewisville" ignored certain danger and spoiled an ill-planned bank robbery. In fact, this story turned out to be one of the Top Ten stories of the year in 1946 by the *Dallas Morning News*.

Incidentally, the Farmers went on to defeat Frisco that Friday, 7–0, and continued on to win the district championship.

. . .

CHAPTER

VI

SOME LEAN YEARS

FROM 1932, WHEN LEWISVILLE WON its first district title, to 1957, the Farmers wrapped up 12 district championships, a handful of bi-district district titles and two regional crowns, with an overall record of 177–46–10 through the 26-year span. Folks in Lewisville had become accustomed to winning, and winning big. The Farmers started out in the Class C division of the Texas high school football classification and had climbed to class 2A by the time Lewis McReynolds won his last district title at the reins of the Farmers in 1957. It would be 15 years before the thriving community of Lewisville would experience the thrill of capturing another district crown.

The 15-year drought, beginning in 1958, was the widest margin between district titles for the Lewisville Fighting Farmer football program. Even during the first few years at the 4A level when Farmer football was struggling, only six years passed between the final district championship in 3A, in 1972, and the first district crown at the 4A level in 1978. The 15-year valley represents the all time low in Farmer history, as the harvest was lean for Lewisville in the area of winning during this time span. Oh sure, there were victories, 57 of them to be exact, along with 82 losses and one tie covering 14 seasons, but the gap between them resembled the teeth of a carved halloween pumpkin—too few and far between. While the Farmers enjoyed a remarkable record from 1932 to 1957 with only four losing seasons, conversely, from 1958 to 1971 Lewisville posted only four winning records, along with two 5–5 finishes.

There is really no accounting for the downward trend beginning with the '58 season. Although the Farmers won the district title in their first year in district 10-2A, they would win no more at this level. Of course, the competition increased at the 2A level, but the enrollment at LHS was increasing in population, theoretically providing a player pool which would keep pace with the competition. Where once they were atop the ladder in 1A competition and dominated their foes, the Farmers experienced what it was like to be on the other end of the spectrum.

Following the 1958 season, in which the Farmers finished 6-4, they would post losing seasons in three of the next five years. The only bright spot, if it could be considered so, came in 1961 as Lewisville managed a 5–5 finish, good enough for a second place district finish. What a difference a year makes. The following season, 1962, the Farmers also finished 5–5, but only managed a fourth place finish in the district standings.

In 1963 Lewisville compiled a 4–6 record, including their third consecutive loss to the Plano Wildcats. This would be the third of six consecutive losses to Plano, and eight of nine defeats from 1958 to 1971 during the Farmers' wilderness experience.

Things got a little better in 1964 as Lewisville finished 6–4, with three of the six wins by a combined margin of four points. Lewisville defeated Grapevine and Seagoville in two low-scoring games, 7–6, and, 8–6, respectively, and Wilmer-Hutchins in a 41–40 slugfest. With the 6–4 record in 1964 the Farmers won more games that year than they would win during the next three seasons.

From 1965 to 1967 the Farmers won just five games, losing 25, with three of those victories coming in district competition, one in each season. In 1965 and '66 Lewisville had identical records of two wins and eight losses, bottoming out in 1967 with a 1–9 record. This marks the all-time worst record in Farmer history for a 10 game season. This three season stretch marks the poorest three season record in the history of Fighting Farmer football.

With the plummeting performances of the Farmers during the mid to late '60s, the attendance was adversley affected. Prior to the 1958 season, one could hardly find a ticket to a Farmer game; during the drought it was beginning to look like it would be some time before the bleachers would be filled again. Aside from the throngs who attended to see the award winning Farmer band, Lewisville fans were beginning to find other things to do on Friday nights.

Some Lean Years

The Farmers appeared to pull out of their nine-year slump in 1968, finishing 6–4 both in 1968 and '69 and matching their highest season totals in the lean 15-year duration. The 17–14 upset of Mckinney in '68 highlighted the 6–4 season as the Farmers struggled to adjust to 3A competition, where they had been promoted two seasons earlier. In '69 Lewisville nipped Plano, 7–6, for their only victory over the Wildcats from 1958–71, thwarting Plano's chances at a district title and allowing the McKinney Lions to capture the crown.

Lewisville slipped the following season with an even 5–5 season record and a 3–4 district finish. Again, the Farmers were the spoilers in the district 3A title race with an 11–8 last second victory over Gainesville, preventing the Leopards from advancing to the playoffs. This victory overshadowed back-to-back losses to Plano and McKinney, 48–0, and, 49–0, to open up district play for the Farmers with an 0–2 mark.

A primary reason the Farmers fared poorly from 1958 to 1971 was that six of those seasons were spent in district 6-3A, where Lewisville was sentenced to serve from 1966 to 1973 before graduating to 4A competition. District 6-3A historically has been viewed as one of the toughest in the state. From 1966, when Lewisville joined, until 1974, one year after the Farmers escaped from it, four teams from district 6-3A made it to the state championship game. In 1966 McKinney, representing district 6-3A, was defeated 30–6 by Bridge City for the 3A state title.

Four years later in 1971, the Plano Wildcats defeated Gregory-Portland for the state 3A crown in a close contest, 21–20. This would be Plano's final season in 3A competition, giving both the Farmers and district 6-3A some relief. It took the Wildcats only six seasons in 4A competition to capture a state championship at that level, defeating Port Neches-Groves, 13–10, in 1977. In 1974 Gainesville's Leopards lost to Cuero's Gobblers, 19–7, in their attempt at capturing the state title. Cuero's victory was their second consecutive state crown, defeating Mt. Pleasant the previous season, 21–7, for the 3A title. The Gobblers were not satisfied with back-to-back championships as they, again, made it to the title game in 1975, narrowly missing their third straight state crown by losing to Ennis, 13–10.

The fourth team from district 6-3A to make it to the state title game from 1966 to 1974 was the Lewisville Fighting Farmers, when they came from nowhere in 1972 to battle a tough Uvalde Coyote team to the final gun, losing 33–28, in Austin. So competing in District 6-3A strengthened teams, especially from 1966 to 1974, preparing the victor for the playoffs.

At its peak of strength district 6-3A was in tact, beginning in 1967, one year after the Farmers joined it. With the addition of the Plano Wildcats that year, 6-3A became one of the state's fiercest groupings, similar to the American League East baseball division, or the National Football Conference Eastern Division, both with reputations of producing champions in their respective sports. The AL East has produced consecutive World Series Champions, the Toronto Blue Jays, winning the Series in both 1992 and '93. Likewise, the Dallas

Cowboys' back-to-back Super Bowl wins also in 1992 and 1993 indicate the strength of the NFC East.

So with the Wildcats firmly in place, district 6-3A would produce several state contenders from 1966–74. The core district members were McKinney, Bonham, Plano, Gainesville and Lewisville. Greenville, Richardson J.J. Pearce, Richardson Berkner and North Garland all either came or went during this time, but were no real factors in contention for the district crown during the 14-year span. Bonham, Gainesville and McKinney had already been dominant forces at the 3A level, while Lewisville and Plano had much success at the 1A and 2A levels, adding strength to this already powerful district when they were aligned in 6-3A. Three years prior to joining 6-3A, Plano won its first state championship in 1965 against Edna, 20–17, and in 1967 won its second state title against San Antonio Randolph, 27–8, before being moved into its new 3A home the next year. It was no surprise to see teams from district 6-3A do well in the playoffs from 1966–74, with a rich heritage of successful programs representing it.

The Farmers finished 2-7-1 in 1971, with only one district victory against North Garland. The only consolation for Lewisville was that the victory over North Garland kept the Farmers out of the cellar as the Raiders were winless in '71. Other than that, things were dark for the Farmer football program from 1958–71, with little evidence of improvement.

. . .

CHAPTER

THE BAND THAT MARCHES WITH PRIDE

FROM 1958 UNTIL 1971 there was little for the Farmer contingent to cheer about; their combined 57–82–1 record evidence of that. Sure, there were bright spots during the dry spell to keep the hopes of the Farmer faithful alive, but not enough to produce a winner that Lewisville fans had been accustomed to. Upset Farmer victories in 1968, '69 and '70 over McKinney, Plano and Gainesville were satisfying, but those were the exceptions, not the rule. And yet, Farmer fans still turned out on Friday nights, a tribute to their faithfulness to the football program and the spirit it had generated.

Perhaps there was one other factor that contributed to the throng of fans present on Friday nights. As the football team's success began to dwindle, the LHS marching band began to succeed and grow into one of the top rated bands in the state, which produced a huge following of its own. Coincidentally, it was not until 1958 that the first marching band was formed at Lewisville High School, the year the Farmers began their 14-year slide.

Friday Night Farmers

Gordon Collins

Gordon Collins was the first director of the Farmer band. It was a first for many things associated with the infant band program that year, including the first marching contest appearance. There was no music program to draw on, so Collins' task of establishing a band program in junior high and high school involved the dual task of teaching music theory and marching. A solid program at the junior high level would give the Farmer band experienced musicians in later years as the band membership increased.

Vivian Claytor was the first drum major selected to lead the Farmer band in 1958. Claytor repeated as drum major the following year as well. She was the first of only eight drum majors to serve for two years through 1993. No one has served more than two years in the history of the band.

With the inception of the band program in 1958, there would follow the entry into both events which compiled the Sweepstakes award; marching competition, and concert and sight-reading competition. These two events were established by the University Interscholastic League as a device to measure both the quality of musical ability of a band, as well as the marching style and uniformity. The competition served as a goal for the newly formed band to shoot for and gave Collins a gauge with which to measure the progress of the Farmer band.

In the first two years of marching contest it is unknown how the Farmer band fared. No information was available as to if they competed, or how they did. In 1960 the band received a first division in marching contest, the highest rating a band can achieve, and the first of many it would receive. Linda Banks had the privilege of being drum major for the Farmer band's first "one" rating in their young history.

The first Farmer band in formation with Vivian Clayton as drum major.

The Band That Marches With Pride

The band on the field during halftime of the 1963 game against Northwest (above) and Kathy Rankin, drum major 1962–63 (right).

In 1961 and '62 the band received a second division rating in marching competition each of these years under two different drum majors. Carolyn Stewart led the Farmer band on the field in 1961, followed by Kathy Rankin in 1962. Although not a first division, a rating of two was respectable given the five year history of the Lewisville High School band.

Rankin was drum major again in 1963, but the Farmer band had a new director. Vernon Denman replaced Gordon Collins as band director for the 1963–64 school year, and the band received the first of 25 consecutive first division ratings in marching competition, a string that would stretch over three decades. Although they received a one rating in marching competition, the Farmer band was not able to garner a "one" in concert and sight-reading, the second element of competition, and did not earned a Sweepstakes award in its short history. That would be the next milestone the Farmer band would need to accomplish in order to progress as a band.

Denman only remained one year as director, however, as William Brady was named chief of the Farmer band in 1964. Brady brought with him a military style of marching, combined with a bit of pagentry, to elevate the Farmer band to new heights. The band continued the string of first divisions in marching contest begun by Denman the previous year and were able to earn the elusive first division in concert and sight-reading competition along with it to receive the coveted Sweepstakes award for the first time. Jill Morris served as drum major during this memorable year.

William Brady

Brady remained at LHS for seven years, from 1964 until 1970, each year guiding the Farmer band to, not only a one rating in marching competition, but a Sweepstakes trophy as well. Altogether, the Farmer band won seven Sweepstakes awards under Brady. Doug Coyle became the first male drum major for the Farmer band in 1965, followed by Mary Stewart in 1966 and '67.

FRIDAY NIGHT FARMERS

Mary was the second of three Stewarts who would lead the Farmer band as drum major. Carolyn, the first Stewart, led in 1961 under Gordon Collins, and Debbie would earn the spot as a co-drum major for the 1972–73 school year.

Carolyn, Mary and Debbie are the children of Reveau and Jane Stewart. Reveau himself was a star of the Fighting Farmers from 1935–37, so they had been raised with Farmer spirit. It was no surprise that they would excel to leadership positions as members of the Farmer band. In fact, the Stewart's other four children would follow the same path of leadership as well. Eileen, the second child, was named Homecoming Queen in 1964. Kathy, the youngest daughter, was a varsity cheerleader in 1972 and '73. The two youngest children were boys and followed in their father's footsteps. Bo was a back-up quarterback for the Farmers in 1973, and started at that position in 1974 and '75. Hal, the youngest Stewart, blended the two activities of band and athletics together. As one of the starting quarterbacks for the Fighting Farmers in 1978 and '79, he was an accomplished musician with the trumpet as well. At the Homecoming game of '79, Stewart, after the first half had ended, emerged from the locker room at halftime, still clad in his football uniform with the number 9 on it, grabbed his horn in time to step on the 50-yard line and blasted a solo to a standing ovation. This performance defied the myth that athletics and band could not co-exist. Conversely, many members of the football team were accomplished musicians, the most notable one being Mike Nichols.

Nichols was a stand out running back throughout his football career at LHS. As a sophomore, Nichols was a star at tailback. The following season he was overshadowed by the speedy All-American Paul Rice's 2,359 total yards rushing. Nichols had 1,400 rushing yards of his own at fullback, a new position for him. He made second team All-District in each of his last two seasons, as well as All-State band, truly an accomplishment, and a testimony of the mutual respect the football and band programs had for one another.

In 1968 Sandi Smith was drum major for the Farmer band, and led them to their sixth straight marching contest trophy. With their success, interest grew in the band program, with the band growing in members each year. Although the football team's success was dwindling, the band's entertainment was enough to keep fans coming out of Friday nights.

With the size increasing, Brady named two drum majors to lead the Farmer band in 1969. Rodney Barton and Glenda Bassinger became the first co-drum major team to lead the Farmer band. With the increased number of marchers and the formations spreading farther apart, it was necessary to add a second drum major so that the entire band could see a director on the field. The combination proved successful as the Farmer band won yet another marching title, and continued on to win the Sweepstakes award.

Rodney Barton and Glenda Bassinger

The format for trying out for drum major involved two phases: the preparation, or training phase, and the tryout phase. Individuals who aspired the office of drum major would undergo a four-week period of training on Tuesday and Thursday afternoons. The training involved learning drum major responsibilities, commands and field directions. After the four weeks of instructions, the tryouts would begin. The tryouts consisted of three parts.

First, a candidate would undergo a marching test to reveal whether or not he or she possessed suitable skills in basic marching ability. It would be difficult to lead on the field without having mastered those skills. The second part was in issuing commands. This test was designed to evaluate a candidate's ability to bark or whistle the commands necessary for a drum major to successfully communicate to the 80–100 or so bodies spread across the football field, covering 40 yards of the playing surface. The final portion of the selection process consisted of an interview by a panel of past drum majors, band officers and the band director. This involved putting the candidate in various hypothetical situations to evaluate how he or she would respond.

It was required that a drum major serve one year as an assistant before taking full responsibilities the following year. Consequently, the tryouts were limited to only freshmen and sophomores in order to satisfy the one year apprenticeship requirement. Indeed, it was rare for someone to be selected as drum major during their freshman year.

In 1970 Ronny Haygood and Cindy Mikel served as co-drum majors, and again the band won a Sweepstakes trophy. This year would end on a rather sad note, however, as Brady announced his resignation as director of the band that had come so far in so little time. Altogether, Brady directed the Farmer band seven years, leading them to seven consecutive Sweepstakes awards. More importantly, he instilled a standard of excellence and tradition which has been preserved through the years.

Rex White was selected as band director to replace Brady in the fall of 1971. He had been an assistant under Brady in 1969–70 after coming to Lewisville in 1966. White began his career at Lewisville as the Jr. High director from 1966–69 after graduating from North Texas State University in Denton, Texas. White built upon the foundation of the military style of marching established by Brady, continuing the standard of excellence. White's tenure at LHS lasted from the fall of 1971 to the spring of 1978. During this time frame the band earned a first division in marching competition each year to sustain the streak begun under Brady's leadership.

Rex White

White saw the band grow in several ways under his direction. As the population of the city increased, the number of students interested in the band programs increased as well. When White joined the LISD faculty in 1966, the band marched only 66 students. In 1977, his final year, the number of marchers nearly tripled to 180. White even remembers marching as may as 186, presenting quite a challenge to chart a halftime show to encompass the huge number of musicians. Also, the string of first divisions in marching contest continued, standing at 15 at the time of White's departure. Unfortunately, the Sweepstakes string was broken at 10, coming to an end in 1974. The Farmer band was unable to earn a first division in the concert and sight-reading segment of the contest, narrowly missing the Sweepstakes honors by earning a second division mark.

Cindy Mikel and Kathy Cochran

The first female duo of drum majors led the band in White's first season as director. Cindy Mikel, in her second year as drum major, was joined by Kathy Cochran to lead the band in 1971. The following year featured a new duo of drum majors. Debbie Stewart, the last of the Stewart family to serve as drum major, was named co-drum major, along with her counterpart, Mike Kerbow. Aside from the thrill of continuing both the marching contest streaks and Sweepstakes awards, they had the thrill of leading the Farmer band during the 1972 "Cinderella" season in which the Fighting Farmers competed for the state championship at Austin's Memorial Stadium, losing a heartbreaker to the Uvalde Coyotes, 33–28. Kerbow and Stewart felt the band was the number one organization to supply spirit for the football team. With the band positioned centrally in the student body section, Kerbow saw it as their responsibility to initiate cheers in between songs. To further demonstrate their spirit during the '72 stanza, White included a special segment in the halftime show of the thrilling McKinney game that brought the house down. Each member of the marching band purchased a shirt enscribed with "Beat McKinney!" and wore it under their regular band uniform.

As the band formed the traditional LHS salute to the student body at Lewisville High, they laid their instruments down, unbuttoned their jackets, displaying the "Beat McKinney!" message in unison, and drawing a rousing applause from the Lewisville crowd.

The traditional LHS salute in 1974...

The Band That Marches With Pride

The interlocking LHS, which traditionally ends each halftime show, began under Brady in the late sixties. It was somewhat of a challenge to supply enough band members to form all three letters in a fashion where they could be identified, but with the assistance of the drill team they were able to stretch out far enough to compose the salute that continues today. With over 160 marchers in 1993, the Fighting Farmer Marching Band was amply able to form the LHS calling card all throughout the state, from as far north as Sherman to as far south as Houston, with many points in between.

It is quite impressive to witness the Farmer band as they make their way into the LHS, adorned on one side by the drill team and by the flag corp on the other. Once in the formation, the band strikes up a chorus of the Farmer fight song, continuing to play it as they march off toward the sidelines. No true Fighting Farmer fan can resist jumping to his or her feet and clapping in rhythm, while singing the familiar anthem that unifies Farmer fans young and old.

In 1973 Cindy Houston and Russell Kerbow served as drum majors, the final year Lewisville High School was to be classified as a 3A school; the following season would be the school's first year at the 4A level. Russell Kerbow was the younger brother of Mike Kerbow, and the two served as drum majors in consecutive years, the first, and only siblings to do so. In fact, only three families have supplied more than one drum major of the Farmer band. The Stewarts supplied three, with Carolyn, Mary and Debbie, and Mike and Russell Kerbow served in the consecutive years of 1972–73 and 1973–74. Terri and Kristi Keith were the other family members to serve as drum majors. Terri led the band in 1979, while Kristi served in 1984, five years later. No other family has produced more than one drum major, although marching and leading in the band has been a family affair. Kathy Rankin, drum major in 1962 and '63, had a younger sister, Mary, who was a majorette in the late '60s. Linda Harmon was also a majorette at about the same time as Cochran. Her sister, Mary Harmon, was drum major during the 1977–78 school year.

. . . and the salute at Texas Stadium in 1993.

Friday Night Farmers

L–R: Suzy Schlegel, Dale Benson and Shirley David

These are just a few examples of younger brothers or sisters who marched in their elder sibling's footsteps.

The Farmer marching band received a new look the following year along with the school's move into 4A. Besides the two drum majors, White added a third position of leadership for the band. Dale Benson was named mace carrier to compliment the drum majors. A mace is a baton longer than the standard drum major's baton, and Benson's height made him a logical choice for the new position. The band featured mace carriers from 1974–76, skipped a year, and resumed for the 1978 season.

The decision to include a mace carrier had to do with the qualifications of those trying out for drum major. In 1974 it was difficult to decide between two of the three leading choices, those being Benson, Shirley Davis and Suzy Schlegel. Rather than make the choice, White decided to name all three as leaders of the Farmer marching band. The trend continued in 1975 with Jeff Herro carrying the mace alongside drum majors Shirley Davis and Mike DeSimone. Mark Bogle was mace carrier in 1976, flanked by Sharna Milheder and Elma Rios as drum majors. The inclusion of the mace carrier had no adverse effect on the quality of marching by the Farmer band as they continued the streak of first division ratings.

The 1977–78 school year was White's final year as director of the Fighting Farmer Marching Band. The mace carrier was absent from the leadership of the band, with Mary Harmon and Terry Whitmer serving as drum majors during White's closing year. Throughout his tenure the Farmer band changed in several ways. The year after the mace carrier was added White also added a flag corp to maximize the involvement of the growing band. Since the band's beginning in 1958, the Farmer band featured a majorette line that led each rank. Primarily a leadership capacity, the majorettes twirled as well in a few shows, but not each week. In the mid-'70s the majorettes discontinued their twirling, but were retained as a marching line. In lieu of the majorettes twirling, Lewisville had its first featured twirler in 1977. Kim Peck first twirled that season and continued to do so until her graduation. After graduating, Peck attended Notre Dame University and was a featured twirler with the Fighting Irish Band.

Ann Anderson (front) was a member of the first flag corp.

Carol Allen was named band director to replace White for the 1978–79 school year. She had been an assistant in the Lewisville I.S.D. for several years

The Band That Marches With Pride

The band marches at halftime. Majorette Cheryl Inmon leads a file.

before taking over the helm. Mark Lee and Mark Sessumes served as drum majors in Allen's only season as director, and John Nyquist was the mace carrier as Allen again utilized three leaders of the marching band.

Although Allen only served as director for one year, White credits her with valuable contributions that helped maintain the standard of excellence established by Brady and sustained under White. It was Allen's suggestion to institute a band camp, which began in August 1973. The camp was designed to grant the band a concentrated period of time devoted to learning how to march and working on the fundamentals of marching, with limited distractions. To get the most out of band camp, freshmen and newcomers were required to assemble at the school each morning the week before camp to learn the basics of marching. Once camp began, the band would concentrate on learning the halftime show for the opening game, as well as the contest show. Initially, the band traveled to Ruston, Louisiana, where camp was held at Louisiana Tech University. Besides being a capable musical director, Allen was a staunch disciplinarian, which, no doubt, was a contributing factor in another first division marching award.

Allen resigned after the 1978-79 school year for a career in the insurance business, but kept her hand in music as the Director of the Grand Prairie Community Band. Several LHS graduates joined her as members of the band, including one of the 1973 drum majors, Cindy Houston.

Bill McMath became the next director of the Fighting Farmer Marching Band and held that position through the 1982-83 school year. During McMath's stay the Farmer football team began improving, giving the Farmer band a much larger audience than they were accustomed to, highlighted by the semifinal appearance in 1979. It was not his first look at a Farmer playoff team, however. He and his wife, Dixie, LHS health teacher and cheerleader sponsor, came to Lewisville in the fall of 1973. Prior to that they both taught in the Eagle Mt.-Saginaw School District and saw the district's Boswell High School Pioneers lose twice to the Farmers en route to their state-final appearance. There they also first met head coach Neal Wilson and were reunited when Wilson was named head coach of the Farmers in 1978. When McMath first came to Lewisville he was the head band director at Hedrick Middle School

CONTEST DAY: The Fighting Farmer Band competes at Birdville Stadium — then the waiting begins. The wait is ended with the judges' decision announced as Lewisville earned another first division.

The Band That Marches With Pride

The band assembles before entering the field for a halftime show.

through the 1977–78 school year. After that he assisted Carol Allen in 1978–79 before being named the director the following season.

During McMath's tenure the marching contest first division ratings continued to pour in, extending the streak to 20 in his final year. Under McMath, Terri Keith, Bobby McKenzie and Elizabeth Rau served as drum majors in 1979, with Rau repeating in 1980. She was joined by Jackie Walker. Walker served a second year in 1981 along with Darla Mosely and John Moates. Kristen Strobel and Alyson Wood led as drum majors in McMath's final year as director of the Farmer band. Under McMath, the band grew to a point which featured 250 marchers, a considerable increase from the 66 under Brady two decades earlier.

In 1983 there was a concert and reunion commemorating the 25th anniversary of the Farmer band, which featured band members and directors covering the entire 25-year span. McMath was primarily responsible for organizing the function, giving the opportunity for a quarter of a century of Farmer band members to assemble to reminisce and get acquainted.

Bob Brashears took over for McMath in 1983 and continued through the following season. Brashears assisted McMath, and White before him, taking over the jazz band and turning it into an award-winning ensemble. As the head director, Brashears continued the level of excellence that became commonplace for the band boosters and admirers in Lewisville, and the band received two more first division marching contest awards. George Howard and Tim Germann led as drum majors in Brashears' first year, followed by Kristi Keith and Tom Krauss in 1984–85.

The 1985–86 school year ushered in a new director and a new era in the Lewisville High School Fighting Farmer Marching Band, which would last eight years. Bill Morocco was hired as director of the LHS band and remained through the 1992–93 school year, the longest tenure of any Farmer band director. Under Morocco's leadership the string of consecutive first division rat-

The Farmer band marches in the Homecoming Parade in 1992.

ings was extended through his first three years. DeAnne LaGrone and Craig Partin were the drum majors in Morocco's first season, leading the Farmer band to a 23rd first division in marching contest. Becky Jameson and Tanya Richardson duplicated the 1985 efforts, effectively commanding the Farmer band the following year. In 1987, Sharon Alderman and Michelle Roberts were drum majors in Morocco's third year, bringing home yet another first division marching trophy, and the string of first division marching awards stood at 25.

In l988, Morocco's fourth year in command of the Farmer band, things began to fall off a bit, negatively affecting the band's "on the field" product. Rachel Elizabeth Dye and Mary Lou Moreno Larios were drum majors that season, hoping to capture a 26th marching contest trophy. As the streak began in 1964 and continued into the '70s, it was apparent that Collins, Brady, White and the founders of the band program had built something special. Once the streak reached 10 the level of expectation perpetuated throughout the band program at LHS and dipped into the junior high ranks as well. The musicians had always taken pride in developing their halftime show through discipline and many hours of preparation. Their efforts, while always outstanding, began to attain equal status with that of the football team.

In fact, it was the band that experienced the most success in the '60s and most of the '70s, save the 1972, '73, '78 and '79 seasons. Along with the success came the pressure of sustaining the level of excellence established by the Lewisville High School band program. Each year became a challenge in itself, not so much in achieving a higher quality of performance, but in not breaking the streak. No band wanted to be the one remembered as the one that couldn't cut the mustard, and certainly no drum major team wanted to leave that as their legacy. Consequently, although contest was exciting and eagerly anticipated, the pressure was compounded each year, especially for the director and drum majors.

The Band That Marches With Pride

Filing into Max Goldsmith Stadium at Lewisville to the tune of the Fight Song.

Unfortunately for Morocco and his band, that remarkable streak came to an end in October of 1988, as they received a second division rating in marching contest, their first since 1962. The student population at LHS was depleating since 1982, with the opening of the Edward S. Marcus High School as well as The Colony High School, and along with it the band program became somewhat of a challenge for Morocco to maintain. In l985 the number of marchers dropped below 100, a dramatic decrease from McMath's peak of 250 in 1982 just three seasons earlier. By 1988 the numbers increased to around 120 marchers, but the loss of students no doubt hurt the band program. In fact, it had an adverse effect on the Farmers, as well, as they tied Marcus, 20–20, in the third Battle for the Ax, but lost the game on the basis of first downs. Both teams had three penetrations each, but the Marauders held the edge in first downs, 17–15, to win the ax and begin a three year winning streak over Lewisville.

Morocco turned things around the following year as the Farmer band received a first division in 1989 to begin a new streak. Nikki Razey and Heather Sutton helped turn things around as drum majors that season. Razey returned as drum major in 1990, along with Brandi Davidson and Neil Grant, to lead the Farmer band to another first division, making it two in a row, and 27 in 28 years. But the streak would end there as the band fell on hard times the following two years.

In both seasons the band achieved only a second division rating, reaching an all-time low in the school's history. In fact, the band narrowly escaped an unheard of third division in 1992. Marching contests are judged by a panel of three judges. In order to achieve a first division rating at least two of the three judges must award that score for a band to receive it. In 1992 two judges awarded the Farmer band a two, while the third judge awarded them a three.

The band performs at haltime against L.D. Bell in 1991 during the playoffs then forms the traditional LHS.

Earning a second division rating was less than acceptable; a third division rating would have been a disaster.

The 1992–93 school year spelled the final year for Marocco at Lewisville High School, leaving the band program in disarray. To have a marginal football season was somewhat forgiving; after all, a team cannot be expected to win it all every year. But to have a marginal band program was unheard of, especially at Lewisville High School. It was a source of pride. When thinking of Odessa Permian, Southlake Carroll or Plano, state championships and winning football immediately come to mind. When talking about outstanding marching bands, thoughts turn to the rich heritage at Lewisville High School and its "Band That Marches With Pride." The citizens of Lewisville would not be content very long with a mediocre marching band.

The Band That Marches With Pride

Following Morocco and beginning his first season as head band director, Brad Kent was hired to rebuild the interest in the band program. Brandon Harvey and Josh Schnitzius served as drum majors in Kent's first year, proving to be a successful combination as the band returned to its roots, earning a first division in marching competition after a two year drop-off. That gave the Farmer band 28 first divisions in the band's 35-year history.

Since the band's existence, beginning in 1958, several traditions have become a part of the rich heritage which reveal the pride and discipline involved in being a member of the Farmer band. One of the earliest traditions was initiated by the band officers, with Cindy Mikel primarily responsible for its beginning. Each year the band would meet several weeks before school started and begin working on marching fundamentals and the beginnings of the first halftime show. At the end of the summer rehearsal, on the final evening, the band would conclude practice by marching, single-file, from the practice field to the band hall where the officers awaited them clad in full uniform. Once all had arrived the officers commenced with a program simply called, "The Ceremony."

White described it as an initiation, and it was conducted by candlelight to increase the dramatic setting. McMath viewed it as a rite of passage from the upperclassmen to the freshmen to communicate to them what it meant to be a member of the Farmer marching band. Each officer played a part in the ceremony, reading or reciting a part that spelled out different privileges and responsibilities of each band member. If it was not understood how serious it was to be in the band during rehearsals, it was extremely clear after The Ceremony.

In 1971, due to the growth of the band, marching assistants were named with the important task of instructing newcomers how to march. Normally the assistants were unsuccessful drum major candidates, but who were quite capable marchers and adequate at teaching others how to march. Utilizing marching assistants spread the responsibility for instruction and expanded the leadership. These officers were jokingly called, "band aids," and were the forerunners to the section leaders in today's band. Initially there were four marching assistants, but that number increased in proportion to the size of the band.

Other traditions which endured revolved around contest day itself, more for luck than anything else. It is customary for band members to place a penny in their left shoe before contest for good luck. The reason it is placed in the left shoe is because the first step is always taken with the left foot when marching. Also for luck, band members take a right hand glove, turn it inside out and wear it on their left hand throughout the day.

Perhaps the longest running tradition, at least the most memorable one, occurs on each out of town game. On the bus ride to the games, once the bus reached the city limits of the opposing team, band officers on the bus would lead the band members in singing the Lord's Prayer, followed by the school

The Farmer band performs at contest at UTA's Maverick Stadium in 1992.

song. After completing the school song silence was observed until arriving at the stadium. According to McMath, "The silence allowed for each band member to concentrate on their assignment for the show." McMath described the silence as "eerie" for those not participating in the show. The school song was sung again on the return trip, once the buses reached Main Street, as a tribute to Lewisville High School. This tradition still exists today.

The band program at Lewisville is special, to say the least. Spawning successful programs at Marcus High School and The Colony High School due to the expansion of the Lewisville Independent School District, the Fighting Farmer band has produced outstanding musicians who have gone on to excel in the field of music. Mary Stewart was the first All-State musician at LHS. Stewart, now Mary Skipworth, chose a career in music education, and is band director at Winnesboro High School. And there have been many others; musicians such as Mike Hall, Steve Nehle, Ronald Rutherford, John Schlegel, Cindy Mikel, Mary McKinney and Mike Kerbow to name a few. Cindy Mikel, drum major in 1970 and '71, went on to direct bands at Copperas Cove and A&M Consolidated. Cindy Houston, 1974 graduate, now directs band in the Arlington I.S.D. Harden Robertson, who played in the Brady era, went to teach band in Arkansas.

The LHS band program has also produced several professional musicians as well. David Bush, graduate of LHS in 1970, went on to a career as a professional pianist, as well as a piano teacher at Southwest Texas State University in San Marcos, Texas. Mike DeSimone, although an outstanding baritone player in the Farmer band, is now a studio guitar player, having also played the guitar in the LHS Jazz Band. Mike Harcow entered the United States Air Force and played in the legendary Air Force band. Upon discharge he became a professional french horn player. John Holt, a 1977 graduate, attended the University of Miami, Florida, and later became a symphony player, traveling throughout Europe. Mike Bogle, now an assistant in the Jazz depart-

The Band That Marches With Pride

The Farmers' biggest fans — the band plays at Texas Stadium during a playoff game, then cheers after an exciting play.

ment at the University of North Texas, had a jazz arrangement nominated for a Grammy Award in 1993.

And there are many more outstanding musicians that have been produced by the LHS band program. "But," according to White, "what made the band so successful was not good players so much as it was so many good kids contributing to the success and traditions of the band. It's good to see the tradition and quality turn around to the way it was for so long."

The relationship between the band and football team at Lewisville High School has been one of mutual respect and support, unlike it is in many other high schools in which the relationship is adverse. Athletics and band do not mix in many school districts, and it's even discouraged in some, viewed as conflicting interests. However, many students have been both Fighting Farmers and members of the Band That Marches With Pride, with the support of both the head coach and the band director. Mike Nichols, an All-District and All-State player on the football team was also an All-State saxaphone player in the same year. He was a member of the state semi-final team in 1972.

Hal Stewart, Rory Durham, Eugene Corbin and Eric Ferris were all key members of the 1979 semi-final team, and were also outstanding members of the band. These four even attended band camp, although they were not required to since they would be unable to march. They even attended marching practice on Tuesday and Thursday afternoons after football workout, showing their support for their fellow band members. As a tactic to instill quality and friendly competition, each squad was required to create and perform a show of their own. This group of athletes, not to be left out, created a program that resembled a half time show, and performed it to the delight of all.

In 1972, when the Farmers were driving for the opportunity for a state championship, Mr. White was asked by Coach Bill Shipman to give a pep talk to the team before one of the playoff games. Earlier in the year, when the band was set to enter marching contest that fall, Shipman gave a motivational speech to the band to let them know how much the football team appreciated them and that they were proud of them. In fact, Shipman jokingly referred to the football game on Friday nights as, "the activity that took place before and after the half-time show," which captures the sentiment that LHS, and the community, has for its band.

. . .

CHAPTER

VIII

1972:
A SEASON TO REMEMBER

W HEN STATE CALIBER FOOTBALL IS MENTIONED in Lewisville, recent history would direct us to Houston, Texas, on December 18, 1993, and the Farmers' 43–37 defeat of Aldine McArthur for the Division II 5A State Championship. For those who began following Farmer football in the past 20 years, there is a piece missing in the whole picture of the winning tradition, that being the dramatic 1972 "Cinderella" season, where the maroon and white finished 12–2 and runner-up in Class 3A to the Uvalde Coyotes, 33–28, in Austin's Memorial Stadium. Stories of this dream season emerged as fuel for the frenzy surrounding the week before the 1993 title game, but the particulars about the 1972 title quest were omitted, more due to the lack of time and space than apathy. Included in the omission is the origin of many of the traditions surrounding current Farmer football that exists today. For example, Big John, in either the familiar vamp from the band during anxious

Friday Night Farmers

moments in the game or prior to kickoffs, or the mascot who paces up and down the sidelines during the game, did not exist until the 1972 season. Nor did the concept of Farmer Quarter, the three-finger pitchfork, and other familiar traditions that characterize Farmer football. Prior to the 1972 season the Farmers finished 2–7–1, capping a six year drought of any hopes at winning. Needless to say, the team, school and community were receptive to new ideas and quickly embraced these things Coach Bill Shipman brought into the 1972 season. In turn, these concepts evolved into many of the traditions currently held at LHS.

After the 2–7–1 finish in 1971 the Fighting Farmer football program was in dire need of an overhaul. Coach Shipman had begun to implement some changes toward the end of the '71 season to begin the rebuilding process. The first step was in installing a two-platoon system, where players played only one position, allowing them to concentrate on one aspect of the game. Other changes occurred during the summer as the players assumed responsibility for the success and implemented a self-imposed training schedule of agility drills, weight training and conditioning in preparation for the '72 challenge. Since supervised workouts by the coaching staff are forbidden under UIL rules, the players were on their own. A core group, made up mostly of seniors, met together at the stadium to run stands, sprints and agility drills. They also developed drills to increase their reaction time, a vital skill to make a successful football player. Bill McLain, a banker at Lewisville State Bank in '72, donated his personal weight room for the eager players to lift weights, which they did each day, working out different muscles during each workout. After an intense weight workout the players concluded by running a relay from McLain's house to the corner stop sign. To end the daily workouts some of the players would go to either Grapevine Dam or Lewisville Dam and run up and down the steep incline, both strengthening their legs and increasing their lung capacity for better endurance. This, according to Farmer middle linebacker Jim Bragg, is where the 1972 district championship was won. Bragg, along with other seniors, had determined that 1972 was going to be different than the dismal 2–7–1 1971 finish, and getting in excellent condition was the first in a series of steps to accomplish this goal.

Bragg got his first taste of varsity competition in 1970 as a sophomore. It seems Head Coach Don Poe was displeased with the team's performance and threatened to make them run a lap for each point they lost by. This occurred after back-to-back losses to Plano and McKinney, 48–0 and 49–0 respectively, and the prospects of running 49 laps after a three hour workout did not bode well with some of the players. Many of them quit, leaving vacancies behind, resulting in Bragg and others being promoted from the junior varsity.

The morale was low in the Farmer field house after the '70 season. Bringing back Coach Shipman for the 1971 season helped increase interest in the waning program, but the absence of senior leadership contributed to the 2–7–1 finish. That's when Bragg, along with Steve Coker, Eddie Mullins, Tim

1972: A Season to Remember

Eshleman, Gary Autwell, Allen Fox, Randy Mayes and Jim Merritt decided to take matters into their own hands and train all summer. They recognized the caliber of football talent was on the increase and wanted to capitalize on it. They knew it was their last opportunity for a district title.

Others began to join in the summer as well, mostly juniors. John Anderson, Rusty Cade, Joe Martin and a few others followed the example set by the senior core group. The players often assembled at Anderson's house for breakfast or lunch before and after workouts. Don and Nancy Anderson often opened their home to the players at all hours of the day and night. Besides the players getting an early start on the '72 season, a closeness was beginning to develop, which Shipman, Bragg and Martin all agree was the main contributing factor in the team's success. Football was getting to be fun in Lewisville again.

Shipman and the other coaches were extremely optimistic about the 1972 season. After the 2–7–1 fiasco the season before, Shipman did not quite know what to expect but knew the Fighting Farmers would be competitive, primarily due to the leadership displayed by the players who had undergone the summer workouts. His main concern regarded the youth of the team as only a handful of seniors were returning, 18 to be exact. Of the 18, eight were starters, four each on offense and defense, with Eddie Mullins returning as the only two-way starter. That left many holes to fill, which kept things challenging during two-a-day workouts.

Preseason polls reflected the inexperience of the Farmers as well. Dave Campbell's Texas Football picked Lewisville to finish sixth out of seven teams in District 6-3A, selecting the Bonham Warriors to capture the crown. McKinney was predicted to finish as the runner-up. In fact, the only team the Farmers were expected to beat was the South Grand Prairie Warriors. So much for preseason polls.

As summer workouts progressed Shipman and company were impressed with the intensity and condition of the young Farmer team. The summer workouts had indeed paid off. A newcomer to the Farmer offense began catching everyone's attention in the backfield with his quickness, slashing running style and great hands. Mike Nichols was a junior starter slated to return as tailback for the '72 season. He and quarterback Randy Cade, both sophomores in '71, were returning with a season's varsity experience under their belts, and they looked forward to the new year. Nichols' quickness and Cade's combined rushing and passing strength would add potent weapons in the offensive attack that Farmer Offensive Coordinator Don Harvey would build upon with the emerging talent. The new faces in the offensive scheme were Joe Martin and Paul Rice.

Martin was a relative newcomer to Lewisville, having moved there the summer before his ninth grade season two years earlier. He came to Lewisville from Lockney, Texas, a smaller town than Lewisville, located approximately 50 miles northeast of Lubbock. His father was head coach at Lockney High School, but died of a heart attack in 1970. Martin's aunt lived in Lewisville so his mother moved him and his younger brother, Chuck, to the budding community. As a freshman he alternated at quarterback with Cade, but started the following year on the junior varsity when Cade was promoted to the varsity. A shoulder injury to his non-passing arm knocked him out during the season, but he recovered from surgery in time to vie for the quarterback job as the '72 season began.

Rice was a different story. He was not a newcomer to Lewisville, but a pleasant surprise to those who had casually followed Lewisville football through the newspapers. He was a longtime resident of Lewisville, attending elementary and junior high there. Rice made the eighth grade "A" team as a seventh grader, so he was no stranger to those who he would rejoin as teammates in 1972. As a runner, the Farmer coaches had witnessed him develop into an outstanding back with excellent speed, quickness and power as a freshman. Several players and coaches hinted to Head Coach Bill Shipman that they would like to have had him as a teammate on the varsity in 1971, but Shipman declined, allowing Rice a season to mature. During his freshman year he had some attendance trouble and was removed from the team a few times, but finished the year in good standing with the coaches; good enough to get an opportunity to play in 1972.

The Farmers ran a slot-I formation in 1972, which featured the fullback and tailback lined up directly behind the quarterback, and a slotback on the opposite side of the tight end, one yard behind the line of scrimmage.

Slot-I Formation

Originally Rice was placed at slotback due to his speed and good hands, with Mark McWhorter at fullback and Nichols at tailback. Shipman figured to open the offensive attack a bit more in '72 with Cade's developing passing arm, and with Rice at slotback, he would have another target to shoot at.

As workouts progressed, Shipman had what he called a "good" problem to have. He had two quarterbacks of high caliber in Randy Cade and Joe Martin, each with their own strengths. Cade was big and strong and was very effective in running the football. Martin, on the other hand, was a bit smaller, but possessed an accurate passing arm. With his shoulder completely healed, he felt he had a legitimate chance at winning the starting job and was working out with the determination to do so. Shipman knew he had a choice to make, but needed some help in making it. Cade was the starter from '71, but Shipman declared every position open going into the fall workouts. Apparently Martin took him seriously, throwing Shipman into a dilemma.

Things cleared up considerably during an intra-squad game one day, however. At the end of each week of two-a-days, it was customary to have an intrasquad game the following Saturday morning. To accomplish this the players would be divided into two teams; the first team offense and second team

1972: A Season to Remember

defense on one team, and the first team defense and second team offense on the other. This design was so that both first team units would be scrimmaging each other, providing a suitable test for one another. Rice was penciled in at slotback on the first team offense, but was substituted at tailback to give Nichols a breather. Indeed, Rice gave the first team defense a test, as defensive coordinator David Visentine recalls: "We couldn't stop him. As a pretty good defensive team with good players, we just could not stop him." Instead of scolding his defense for their inability to halt Rice, Visentine waited until after practice to have his say. The coaches met to evaluate the overall play of each unit and put their heads together on how they could improve the team. That's when Visentine suggested to Shipman and the other coaches that Paul Rice should be moved to the starting tailback position. As much trouble as the Farmer defense had with him, surely other teams would as well. That meant moving an established player, Mike Nichols, to make room for Rice, something Shipman had not contemplated having to do. But the decision was eminent, and Rice was named starting tailback for the 1972 season, making it the second consecutive season the Farmers started a sophomore at that position.

Moving Rice to tailback both left an opening at slotback, and had Farmer coaches searching for a spot to place the talented Nichols. That decision was the easiest. Nichols, with his speed and power, was moved to fullback to serve with Rice as a one-two offensive punch. As far as slotback was concerned, another situation developed. Shipman had, since the beginning, wanted to somehow get both Cade and Martin in the starting lineup, but the opportunity just wasn't there. At quarterback in 1971 Cade was used more as a runner than a passer, showing formidable skill in carrying the football. Because of his size and strength he could block as well, thus Shipman had the situation he had searched for. Cade was moved to slotback, and quickly adjusted, and Martin stepped into the starting quarterback spot. The odd man out due to the shuffle was senior fullback Mark McWhorter.

The starting backfield was set after all the shuffling was over, and there was not a senior in the quartet. Floyd Voss and Billy Graham alternated at split end, with Mark Angeli earning the tight end spot due to his reliable hands. Mark McCurley, Randy Mayes, Eddie Mullins and Niles Ladehoff were all returning seniors on the offensive line, and were joined by Rudy Durham as the only junior lineman.

Defensively the Farmers were anchored by four returning starters from the '71 roster, led by tackle Eddie Mullins. He was joined on the line by defensive ends Steve Coker and Gary Autwell, while Ray Bowden and Richard Tharp alternated at the other defensive tackle position. Jim Bragg anchored the defense from his middle linebacking position, along with Rusty Cade and John Anderson, to complete the trio of linebackers. Allen Fox and James Merritt returned in the defensive backfield as safeties, with James "Red" Bishop and Sammie Voss completing the backfield at the corners. With both lineups secure the Farmers were ready to open the 1972 season.

FRIDAY NIGHT FARMERS

Lewisville vs. Boswell — September 8, 1972
The young Farmers opened the season against the Eagle Mt.-Saginaw Boswell High School Pioneers, making the journey to the Tarrant County school. More accurately, the Farmers almost did not open against the Pioneers due to a one-and-a-half hour delay. It seems there was a scheduling mix up, not with the teams, but with the officials. The referees originally scheduled to oversee the contest mistakenly reported to another game, so a second crew had to be hurriedly assembled. The delay was tough on the young Farmers, especially Martin. The contest against Boswell being Martin's first start at quarterback on the varsity was nerve-racking enough, but the 90 minute delay made it even more so. Finally a referee crew arrived, and the 1972 Fighting Farmer football season got underway.

Their opponent, the Boswell Pioneers, had some big lads on the offensive line, giving the young Farmer defense a tough test early in the season. One side of the Pioneer offensive line averaged 225 pounds, and that was in 1972 when 200 pound players were considered huge. Comparing that with the 1993 Farmer offensive line, which averaged 238 pounds each player, the '72 Farmer defense would have their hands full, especially when the biggest starting defensive lineman was 208-pound Ray Bowden. They did not have a chance to test the waters; they were in over their heads.

Boswell scored first with just under a minute left in quarter number one, at a time when practically all other games being played that night had already ended. The bullish Pioneer offensive line pushed the Farmer defense down the field 75 yards, with halfback Pat Murphy doing the honors on a 1-yard plunge, giving Boswell a 7–0 lead. The Farmer offense, on the other hand, sputtered throughout the first quarter and most of the second. Finally things began to click, as Paul Rice scored from the 2-yard line with 3:01 left in the first half. Rice displayed his talents earlier in the scoring drive with runs of 43 and 26 yards, revealing to the Pioneers, and most of the Lewisville contingent, at least those who had waited out the delay, that he was for real.

As the first half came to a close, Boswell had mounted a drive and had the ball on the Farmer 20-yard line. On the half's final play the Pioneers tried to throw into Lewisville's end zone, but had a little difficulty doing so. As quarterback Gary Easley faded back in the pocket he spied no open receivers. As he scanned the secondary for anyone in a blue jersey, he felt the combined pressure of Farmer defenders Rusty Cade and Steve Coker converge on him, and retreated. First he back-peddled, then he turned and ran as the maroon and white duo gave chase. Finally, the two caught him at mid-field for a 30-yard loss, plus or minus a few yards. That play preserved the 7–7 tie and ended the first half.

The third quarter was less than spectacular as the teams obliged one another with fumbles. In fact, the entire period was marred with fumbles and penalties, preventing either team from adding to their point total.

The Farmers managed to put together a touchdown drive in the fourth

1972: A Season to Remember

Mike Nichols (top) and Paul Rice (bottom) see action against the Boswell Pioneers. The duo led the offensive charge of the Farmers throughout the 1972 season.

quarter, scoring on a screen pass from Martin to Rice that covered 25 yards. Cade split the uprights for his second extra point of the night, and the Farmers had their first lead of the young season. In an attempt to control their own destiny, the Farmers tried an on-side kick. They were unsuccessful, however, as Boswell recovered and began, what they hoped would be, a drive for a chance to either tie or win. They never had to make that decision, although they did get close. Facing a fourth down, the Pioneers found themselves at the Farmer 18-yard line, needing 5 yards to keep the drive, and their scoring opportunity, alive. Their chances fell to the turf as the fourth-down pass plummeted to the earth, turning the ball over to the Farmers with about 30 seconds left to go in the already late contest. Lewisville held onto the ball to end the game, securing its first win of the season.

The Farmers were fortunate to win the game, especially when reviewing the final statistics. The Pioneers out-rushed the Farmers with 239 yards to Lewisville's 196. Boswell had 17 first downs, while holding the Farmers to only eight. That's a little deceiving, however, as Rice had carries of 43 and 26 yards, as well as the 25-yard scoring pass. These three plays accounted for 94 of the 224 total Lewisville yards, indicating the Farmers' ability to cover much more territory per play. In fact, Lewisville ran only 31 plays all evening, compared to the Pioneers' 66. Rice had 142 of the 196 Farmer rushing yards with one touchdown. His 25-yard pass reception late in the game accounted for the other Farmer score.

Perhaps it was the hot weather, opening game jitters, or the delay caused by the tardy officials that was responsible for the sluggish performance. One thing was certain; the Farmers would have to improve if their success was to continue. Shipman promised to do just that.

Lewisville vs. Waxahachie — September 15, 1972
Week two had the Farmers scheduled to play the Waxahachie Indians in Lewisville. The Indians were drop-kicked in their opening contest by the powerful Brenham Cubs, 46–0, after finishing a dismal 1–8–1 in 1971. The Farmers were healthy after game one, suffering no injuries except for the usual bumps and bruises. Waxahachie would prove to be no match for the new and improved Lewisville Fighting Farmers.

Again the Farmers got a strong performance from Rice, as he added 166 yards to his two-game rushing total for the season. He scored two touchdowns, both on the ground, and had two others called back because of several ill-timed penalties. Rice had already rushed for 308 yards and scored four touchdowns in the young season in leading the offensive attack, and eyes were beginning to open around the metroplex in the direction of Lewisville.

Martin got the Farmers on the scoreboard first with a 10-yard touchdown run midway through the first quarter. Randy Cade's extra point attempt flew wide of the mark, but the Farmers were on top, 6–0. Actually, Lewisville would score in each of the four periods against Waxahachie in some form, while holding the Indians scoreless for the team's first shutout of the season.

After Martin's touchdown came Rice's first score in the second quarter. The play was an 18-yard run, set up by a 37-yard Mike Nichols carry to the Waxahachie 18-yard line. Rice had scored earlier, but the touchdown was called back on a holding penalty, pushing the ball back 15 yards. Several plays later the Farmers reached the 18-yard line again. That's when Rice scored the touchdown that counted. Cade successfully tacked on the extra point and Lewisville was snug with a 13–0 halftime lead.

The second quarter scoring drive was sparked by a Steve Coker punt block, giving the Farmers the ball in good field position. In fact, the defense had vastly improved over their performance in game one, allowing the Indians a meager 65 yards rushing; almost one-fourth of the total allowed against Boswell.

1972: A Season to Remember

Late in the second quarter cornerback Sammie Voss intercepted an Indian pass to stop their only real scoring threat of the evening. In the third quarter safety James Merritt pounced on the first of several Waxahachie fumbles. The recovery was made at the Farmer 35-yard line, preventing the Indians from scoring yet another time. Later in the game the other safety, Allen Fox, almost picked off a pass himself with an alert play in the secondary.

The offense showed vast improvement in the second week as well. Besides the 29 point total, the Farmers amassed 298 total yards—268 of them coming on the ground. Rice accounted for 63 of those yards on a touchdown run in the second quarter to complete his scoring for the evening. After Merritt recovered his fumble in the third quarter, Rice scored yet another touchdown, which was called back on offsetting penalties. The Farmers settled for a 27-yard Randy Cade field goal, as the drive was halted more by a sudden high wind storm than the Waxahachie rush. The stiff gale took both teams by surprise and shut down the passing game for the evening. The field goal made it 23–0 going into the final stanza.

Backup fullback Mark McWhorter shocked the Indians at the 2:33 mark into the final period with a 31-yard scoring play up the middle. McWhorter's run did not surprise Shipman, however.

He had been named the starting fullback, before the backfield was remodeled to include Rice, and was quite capable as a blocker and runner. Shipman told reporters that he "felt like McWhorter did a tremendous job, and that he would make lots of contributions to the Farmer offense as a backup to Nichols." Cade's extra point attempt into the stiff wind, still gusting at around 30 miles an hour, went astray, netting the final 29–0 score.

Shipman described the game as a tremendous team effort, borrowing a phrase from Joe Kapp, quarterback for the Minnesota Vikings in the pre-Fran Tarkenton era of the '70s, by saying it was "39 for one for 48. That is, 39 boys with one purpose for 48 minutes." That became a popular motivational phrase Shipman employed during the 1972 season, and the players responded to it, and others coined by the Farmer mentor. Another Shipman motto going into two-a-days indicated to players that things were going to be different in the Lewisville Fighting Farmer football program as well. He tagged it the 4-H's of football: Hang loose, hit hard, have fun and hustle.

Shipman installed other innovations to create an environment conducive for fun and productivity. Two or three times a week he led the team in a visualization exercise. This exercise was conducted in the dark, requiring the players to close their eyes and visualize themselves making great plays. The goal was to implant a positive image of individual play. Jim Brown, the great running back of the Cleveland Browns, often responded, when asked how he had made a great run, that he had seen himself make that run over and over in his mind. Apparently the method was working for Shipman's young crew.

The booster club had a stereo system installed in the field house during the summer, and the players' favorite music was emitted over the speakers before and after practice to help them relax and to create a fun environment. After some practices, or to relieve tensions brought on by intense preparation, Coach Shipman held a dance contest among any of the players willing to participate. Red Bishop usually won the impromptu competition, but others demonstrated moves that Shipman, Harvey and the other coaches would like to have seen on the field. All these tactics implemented by Shipman worked together to build a closeness between the players and coaches, which was reflected in the teamwork displayed on the field.

Lewisville vs. Grapevine — September 22, 1972
One of the most fierce foes in Farmer history was slated as Lewisville's third opponent of '72. The Farmers had a three-game win streak over the Mustangs before Grapevine was removed from District 6-3A after the 1970 season. The teams did not meet in 1971, so after a one year sabbatical the rivalry continued.

The Mustangs were winless going into the Farmer game, and proceeded to be no match for the developing Lewisville offense. Relying primarily on the run in the first two games, Grapevine was unprepared for the Farmers' game plan that evening. On Lewisville's first play of the contest Joe Martin hurled a pass to tight end Mark Angeli, covering 57 yards for an early score; this from an offense averaging 232 yards rushing. James Merritt, who handled kickoff duties for the Farmers all season, tried his hand, or rather his foot, at place-kicking. His PAT was good and Lewisville led 7–0 early in the game.

All in all, the game against Grapevine resembled the Waxahachie encounter in several ways. It was largely a display of the powerful Farmer rushing game, rolling up 329 yards rushing of their 383 total yards. It was also characterized by penalties and fumbles, costing the Farmers at least one other score. It was different in this aspect; Mike Nichols led the game in rushing instead of Paul Rice, revealing the truly balanced running game the Farmers mounted against their opponents. Lewisville's second score of the evening came on a Nichols 71-yard run, both the longest run of the evening and of the season to that point.

The Farmer defense held the Mustangs on their next series of downs, and Sammie Voss charged in to block the ensuing punt, with the Farmers recovering at the Grapevine 8-yard line. A 15-yard penalty pushed the Farmers back to the 23-yard line, but the infraction only delayed the inevitable. Two plays later found Nichols blasting over from the 3, set up by Randy Cade's 20-yard carry. The extra point was missed, but the Farmers set comfortably on top with a 20–0 lead; all this action coming in the initial period.

Perhaps the Farmers were a bit too comfortable. A Lewisville fumble deep inside their own territory practically handed the Mustangs their only score for the evening. The only thing the Farmers did not do was line it up and run it in for them. Grapevine's Stanley Skaggs carried it over from that point, cutting the Farmer lead to 20–6. It remained that way as the extra point was no good. The miscue more than likely cost Lewisville their second consecutive shutout, as the Mustang touchdown was not only the first score of the evening for them,

1972: A Season to Remember

but was also their first score of the season. They had been shut out in their first two contests, including a 21-0 loss to Richardson Berkner the previous week.

The Farmers took the opening kickoff of the second half and marched 62 yards for their fourth touchdown of the game. Again Nichols did the honors from the 5 for his third touchdown. Lewisville failed on the extra point attempt but regained their 20-point advantage over the Mustangs at 26–6. The score did not stay that way for long as Rice finally got loose on a 65-yard sprint to the end zone. After missing two extra points already, Lewisville elected to go for two to straighten out the score, but the attempt failed, leaving the score 32–6, the eventual final score. Lewisville dodged a bullet late in the contest, however, creating a little excitement for the home fans at Grapevine. The Farmers lined up to punt deep in their own territory with Allen Fox set to kick. The boring contest must not have been sufficient to hold his attention, as the ball slipped through his fingers, allowing the Mustangs a serious chance at doubling their point total for the year. They were well on their way with a quick 14-yard gain to the 4, but shot themselves in the hoof by fumbling on the subsequent play. Middle linebacker Jim Bragg fell on the ball before anyone else could, giving the visiting Farmers the ball inside their 5.

Only able to move the ball to their 27, the Farmers kicked to Grapevine. Sammie Voss nabbed a Mustang pass to add to the long list of alert defensive plays before a punting exhibition by both teams ended the game.

It pleased Shipman to see Nichols take up the slack with his 176 yards rushing on 20 carries, as the Mustangs hounded Rice all evening. No doubt scouts viewing the contest raised an eyebrow seeing Nichols step up to the challenge, throwing a wrench into the works on how to prevent the Farmers from getting into the end zone. Still another aspect of the Lewisville game plan proved effective with Angeli scoring on the opening pass play. In fact, in three games five different Farmers had hit paydirt indicating this Lewisville team was multidimensional.

Although the Farmer win against Grapevine was convincing, Coach Shipman was concerned about the mistakes his young team had made, especially the fumbles and penalties. It was a fumble that led to the Mustang score, and nearly allowed a second one. Had the game not been under control at the time of the mistakes it might well have turned out differently. Shipman pledged hard work on reducing the errors as district play was nearing.

Lewisville vs. Burleson — September 29, 1972
Week number four was homecoming for the Farmers, and the alumni had a treat to look forward to in returning to their home town. After all, their Farmers were 3–0 and emerging as a top team in the area. It was also an opportunity to examine this Paul Rice everyone was talking about. After three games he already had 417 yards rushing. Not only that, but Nichols, his counterpart, had 310 yards himself, so the prospect of a homecoming victory was all but in the bag.

The Farmers surrendered 221 total yards to their opponents, the Burleson Elks—more yardage than they had planned. Lewisville compiled 407 total yards themselves, jumping out to an early first quarter lead of 13–0. The Farmers' first score came courtesy of Nichols with a first quarter touchdown blast. Randy Cade's extra point conversion was good as Lewisville gained an early lead. Still in the first period the Farmers scored again, with Rice doing the honors. The point after was no good, but Lewisville had a 13–0 lead with 3:16 left in quarter number one.

The Elks came back, however, with a score of their own. Burleson engineered a 72-yard drive capped by a Mike Rubis 4-yard scoring play. They made good on their extra point attempt, drawing to within six with 9:41 left in the first half. That six point difference did not last long, however, as Rice struck again on the first play after the subsequent kickoff. On one of the longest Farmer runs of the season and, no doubt, their history, Rice raced 81 yards for the score, increasing the Farmer lead to 19–7. Cade's kick made the score 20–7, and the homecoming crowd was pleased with what they were seeing.

Rice put on another show just before the half, completing a scoring drive on a 12-yard dash to the end zone. Although the extra point failed, the Farmers had displayed a varied offensive scheme in the first half, demonstrating the ability to score quickly, or on a sustained drive. Rice's score put the maroon and white on top, 26–7, at the half.

The Farmer offense had not clocked out for the evening. They would add three more touchdowns before the night was over, including Nichols' third quarter score. Joe Martin connected with Mark Angeli for the two-point conversion, increasing the Farmer lead to 34–7. By this point it was all but over for the Elks. On a desperation attempt to make the game respectable Burleson tried to convert a fourth-and-two from their own 48-yard line, but were unable to do so. The Farmers took over at that point, and before long, the capacity crowd saw Nichols score the sixth Lewisville touchdown of the evening, and his third touchdown of the game. After Cade's successful conversion the score stood at 41–7.

Cade was in at quarterback to give Martin a breather late in the game. In fact, substitutions were shuttling in and out with regularity in order to allow more players the opportunity to gain experience as district play drew nigh. Cade demonstrated the passing arm that had earned him the Sophomore of the Year title the season before by tossing a 32-yard scoring strike to split end Floyd Voss. Merritt's extra point ended the scoring for the Farmers, no doubt pleasing the homecoming crowd with their 48 point accomplishment. The Farmer defense surrendered a token Burleson touchdown on a Harold Houston 17-yard reception with one-and-a-half minutes remaining, giving the Elks the final word. Burleson also made good on its two-point conversion, but proved to be no match for the mighty Farmer offensive machine.

The 48-point outburst, by far the best offensive output of the first four games, left little to concern the coaching staff. Sure, there were a few minor

1972: A Season to Remember

Joe Martin (8) prepares to hand the ball off behind Eddie Mullins (75), Rudy Durham (67) and Randy Mayes (65).

problems that needed attention, mainly fumbles, penalties and the kicking game, but these shortcomings had not cost the Farmers much, if anything. All in all, Shipman, et. al., was pleased with what he saw, as was the near capacity crowd. In fact, everyone was happy. The Sophomore float won, Rita "Skeeter" Proctor was named Homecoming Queen and the Lewisville Fighting Farmers had win number four.

Lewisville vs. South Grand Prairie — October 7, 1972

Regardless of what kind of non-conference results a team has, it seems that the level of competition increases when district play begins. For the Farmers' first district contest in '72, however, it was business as usual as Lewisville smothered the Warriors, 46–7, to notch their fifth win of the season. It was too soon for playoff talk, but no doubt the thought had crossed the minds of more than a few of the Farmers' fans, maybe even a coach or two, but nobody dared utter a sound. After all, it would take all the Farmers' might to plow through the remainder of the district schedule to even have a shot at the crown that had eluded them since 1957. But with a district record of 1–0 they were one step closer to considering themselves capable of taking the 6-3A title.

Lewisville had the ball five times in the first half, scoring on four of its possessions. More than likely they would have scored a fifth time, but time ran out on them as they held the ball until the clock struck zero. The Farmers borrowed a play they had used against Grapevine, as Martin found Angeli on a 15-yard pass early in the first quarter. Actually this was their second touchdown of the drive, but the first one they were able to keep — as a penalty negated the original score. The extra point attempt was no good, but as had happened the last three games, the Farmers jumped out to an early lead.

Friday Night Farmers

Playing on their home turf, the Warriors fought back on the ensuing drive, scoring a touchdown of their own. The successful PAT gave South Grand Prairie a 7–6 lead, something the Farmers had not experienced since Boswell bulldozed their way to the early lead in game one. Nevertheless, the Farmers trailed for their first time in 15 quarters.

Lewisville resolved the deficit on their next possession with Rice scoring on a 5-yard dash. Lewisville led 12–7. Their attempt for a two-point conversion failed, but the Farmers still led, 12–7, as the first quarter expired.

The Lewisville defense came to life on the next series of downs. Linebacker John Anderson struck first by recovering a Warrior fumble at the South Grand Prairie 33-yard line. The turnover set up an 8-yard touchdown run. Martin hit Angeli for the two-point conversion and a 20-7 lead. Anderson performed an encore by picking off a Warrior pass on their next drive, again setting up a Farmer score. This time Martin himself did the honors, slipping in just before the half. The score stood at 26–7 as the first half expired.

The third stanza was without any scoring, but not without any action from the Farmer defense. Sammie Voss nabbed the second Farmer interception of the contest, giving the offense an opportunity it could not cash in on. The drive ended on a missed field goal attempt. Lewisville got another chance in the third quarter but it, too, ended, this time with a failure to convert a fourth-down play.

The Farmer defense would intercept three passes on the evening, the final one coming by James Merritt. Merritt's interception followed the fifth Farmer touchdown drive of the evening as Rice stepped across the goal line from the 1. Randy Cade had done most of the work on the drive on a 30-yard run prior to Rice's score. Cade caught his wind in time to boot the pigskin through the uprights for the extra point, making the score 33–7 with the Farmers safely on top.

Merritt returned the interception from the 50-yard line to South Grand Prairie's 31, where the Farmers set up shop once again. Mike Nichols immediately covered the 31 yards of real estate, burying the Warriors under a 39–7 lead. Cade's extra point made it two in a row for him, increasing the lead to 40–7. The Farmers would add one more score, before boarding the bus to return to Lewisville, on a Joe Martin quarterback keeper from 2 yards away. Floyd Voss, normally the split end, came in to attempt what would be the final extra point of the game. The kick was blocked, however, leaving the final score at 46–7.

The victory over the Warriors was the fifth victory for Lewisville in 1972. Things were beginning to take shape for a valid run and the district crown. The offense continued to gain strength with their ball control style. The recent emergence of the passing game added another dimension to an already tough offense to defend. Nichols out-rushed Rice again in this contest, 155 yards to 152, on a 1,000-yard pace for the season. Rice's 152 yards gave him 787 halfway through the regular season, already making him one of the state's

1972: A Season to Remember

top rushers. About the only aspect of the Farmer attack lacking was the kicking game. After five games the Farmers had missed 11 opportunities at converting extra points. Randy Cade and James Merritt had split time in place-kicking and Cade seemed to have the edge, although neither of them had secured the job. Even Floyed Voss had a crack at it but was unsuccessful in his only attempt. As it stood the Farmers had converted only 66 percent of their extra point opportunities, which Shipman wanted improved. With the strength of District 6-3A, the difference between winning and losing could very well come down to an extra point.

Shipman employed some incentives at the beginning of the season to give the players something to shoot for in conjunction with the grading system used to evaluate the game. Each player had the potential to make three points per play, depending on how well his individual assignment was carried out. The offensive and defensive players scoring the highest were named players of the week on their respective sides of the ball. There was also a coveted award called the "Big Hit" award, based on the single play the coaches felt epitomized the toughness they desired, displayed by a vicious block or tackle. This was not restricted to defensive players either. A lineman could waylay some unsuspecting linebacker, who had been suckered in on a trap play, and earn the award. Also, pitchfork awards were awarded for specific plays. Touchdowns, fumble recoveries, key tackles or blocked punts; all of these were typical of efforts that were worthy of the pitchfork. The awards were clear, plastic circles, about the size of a fifty-cent piece, which adhered to the helmets of the recipients. The pitchfork was white, surrounded by a white circle which bordered the entire applique, causing it to stand out against the maroon background of the helmets. The awards were handed out after Thursday's practice as a weekly ritual. There was a friendly competition as to who received the most, but the pitchfork awards worked to create a competitive environment which brought the best out of the players.

Lewisville vs. Richardson Berkner — October 13, 1972
Bill Shipman is not a superstitious man, although this Friday the 13th could have almost persuaded him to be. The Farmers defeated Richardson Berkner 34–0 for their sixth win and second shutout of the season, but it could have been much more had it not been for a few "quirks" that occurred that night.

Once again Mike Nichols led the Farmers in rushing with 183 yards, while scoring twice on long runs. The first Farmer touchdown came on Lewisville's first possession as Nichols moved his 200-plus pound frame 47 yards for the score. It was Merritt's turn to kick, and he converted the extra point attempt giving the Farmers a 7–0 lead. Eddie Mullins recovered a Ram fumble at the Berkner 33-yard line, setting up the Farmers' next drive. That's when the sequence of "coincidences" occurred in that rather strange game.

The Lewisville drive stalled at the Berkner 13-yard line as the Farmers were unable to convert a fourth-down attempt. The Rams took over and began a futile drive, surrendering the ball to the Farmers who began what they hoped would be their second score of the contest. Once again the Farmers' drive reached the Ram 13-yard line, and again the Farmers lost the ball, this time fumbling to Berkner and losing a second opportunity to score. Strange.

The Rams were on the march before Allen Fox snatched a Berkner pass, or thought he did. A Farmer penalty erased the interception and sustained the Berkner drive. Unable to make a first down, the Rams lined up to punt, which they did successfully ... or unsuccessfully depending on how one looks at it. The punt traveled a mere 13 yards, (there's that number again) potentially working to the Farmers' advantage. Another Lewisville penalty, however, abolished the meager punt, allowing the Rams to retain the ball. An alert play at the goal line by Fox thwarted a Ram touchdown pass, giving Lewisville the ball at their own 30-yard line.

The Farmers escaped the twilight zone on the subsequent drive with Rice going over from the 4-yard line. Merritt's kick made it 14–0, which stood through the first half. Toward the end of that first half Berkner fumbled the ball at their own 12-yard line one (1 yard away from the 13) and Sammie Voss pounced on it, setting up a golden opportunity for Lewisville going into the locker room. But, alas, the Farmers fumbled back to the 14 (1 yard from the 13 the other way) leaving the score 14–0.

So with a jinx factor of plus or minus one yard, the Farmers stood on a 14–0 lead as the second half rolled around. Fox intercepted his second Ram pass and returned it to the Berkner 23-yard line. Later, Martin hit Randy Cade on a 19-yard scoring strike to get the Farmers rolling again. A successful Merritt kick extended the Farmer lead to 21–0, making it 3-for-3 in the kicking department.

Berkner threatened on their ensuing drive, marching to the Farmer 20-yard line, but Fox turned in a hat trick by picking off his third pass of the game in the end zone to personally stop the drive. Taking over at the 20-yard line, the Farmers drove to mid-field but fumbled the ball, proving the jinx was not restricted to the proximity of the 13-yard line of either end of the field. The Rams found out differently, however, as they charged with relative ease to the Farmer 14-yard line where, oddly enough, the Lewisville defense held on the fourth-down attempt.

The Farmers added two additional scores before the contest ended. Martin tossed a 6-yarder to Cade for his second touchdown of the night. The point-after was missed, ruining Merritt's perfect night. With just under a minute left Nichols went on a tear again, scoring his final touchdown of the eerie night from 75 yards away. This time Merritt converted, completing the final score of 34–0.

Shipman and Harvey attributed the missed scoring opportunities to a lack of concentration and less than perfect execution, rather than superstitions. Several bright spots, offensively, included Nichols' 183 yards and two touchdowns, and the effectiveness of the passing game. Despite the seven penal-

1972: A Season to Remember

ties and two lost fumbles, the Farmers rolled up 413 total yards. Had it not been for the 13-yard line, who knows what the total yardage might have been.

Defensively the Farmers shined. Defensive Coordinator David Visentine was more than pleased with the Farmer defense as they held the Rams to 139 total yards, citing the individual play of Fox, Mullins, J.K. Woods, Richard Hunter and Rusty Cade as exceptional on that Friday the 13th. After the convincing win over Berkner, the Farmers broke into the list of the top 25 in the state, landing at number 23.

Lewisville vs. North Garland — October 20, 1972
The Farmers had their hands full against the North Garland Raiders in week eight, at least for the first half. It appeared the defense had taken the night off, assuming the Farmer offense could just outscore their opponents with its potent combination of rushing and passing. On the night, the defense gave up 262 yards, the most they had surrendered since game one. The score reflected the Farmers' vulnerability as well, at least in the first half.

As for the offense, they had little trouble with the Raider defense, accruing their greatest total yardage, 462, and their largest single game point-total on the season. They outscored North Garland, 49–14, to remain unbeaten for the season.

The contest resembled a track meet more than a football game as Rice and Nichols raced up and down the field providing or setting up Farmer scores. Rice ended the night with over 250 rushing yards, going over the 1,000-yard mark and scoring five touchdowns; the most any Farmer would score in any game all season.

Rice primed the Farmer pump first by providing a 39-yard dash on the team's opening possession. Merritt booted the extra point for an early 7–0 lead . . . but not for long. After a series of exchanges, North Garland struck back on a 2-yard Billy Hooks touchdown run. Hooks turned around and smacked the extra point through the uprights, knotting the score at 7-7.

Hooks' touchdown run capped a 33-yard Raider drive that tied the score. After the Farmers took the following kickoff Rice sprinted 67 yards to the end zone for a quick 13–7 lead. Merritt made good on the extra point, making the score 14–7, still in the first quarter. The subsequent Raider possession began at their own 17-yard line and ended 83 yards later, climaxed by a Tim Griffin 1-yard plunge. The scoring play came on a fourth-and-goal gamble at the 1 which they were able to convert. Hooks kicked the extra point and the Raiders drew even with the previously invulnerable Fighting Farmers of Lewisville.

The '72 contest between Lewisville and North Garland was the second meeting between the two schools. 1971 was the first year for North Garland in District 6-3A, and the Raiders were the only team the Farmers defeated in district play that season, accounting for exactly one-half of the total Lewisville victories. It seems the Raiders remembered that in the '72 stanza, as they put up a pretty good fight.

The Mad Hogs swarm to stop a Boswell ball carrier (top), and a Waxahachie runner (bottom).

Some of the fight left, though, as Hooks fumbled a Farmer punt deep in the Raider end of the field. Billy Graham recovered the miscue, giving Lewisville the ball 11 yards away from the goal line. Rice ran it over from that point, giving the Farmers a 20–14 lead in the seesaw battle at Homer B. Johnson Stadium in Garland. Merritt was true on the conversion making it 21–14.

The "Mad Hog" Farmer defense began to come to, shaking the cobwebs out of their defensive scheme. Forcing a punt, Rice fielded it at the 27-yard

1972: A Season to Remember

line, darting down the field toward the goal line in an effort to make it in the end zone before time expired in the first half. He only made it to the 2-yard line before being brought down, but the Farmers had the ball well within reach. A score here would double, in only a few minutes, what had taken most of the first half to achieve. Martin sneaked the ball over from that spot, accomplishing that goal and stretching their lead to 27–14. Merritt came through again with a successful point-after conversion to increase the lead to 28–14. The score was done so quickly that the Farmers even had time to kick-off before the half ended. The Raiders fumbled on this kickoff, as they did on the previous one, and this time Mike Habern made the recovery for Lewisville at the Raider 11. Lewisville shot themselves in the foot by committing several penalties on the drive, spoiling the chance to add another score before the half.

The defense was tagged "Mad Hogs" early in the year, more of a name that described their style of play and what they accomplished on the field than anything else. It was adopted with a sense of pride that fit the collective personality of the scrappy defense, led by Jim Bragg and Eddie Mullins. The term accurately describes the reckless abandonment with which the defense carried out their task. Though slow to gel, the defense had developed into a strong unit during district competition, surrendering a mere seven points per game. The first half of the North Garland game caught the Mad Hogs a bit over confident as the Raiders moved the ball with relative ease—too much in fact. If not for the early Raider mistakes the Farmers may have found themselves playing tit-for-tat instead of being able to build a big lead and control the ball, which had been their primary game plan. With the offense being able to capitalize on the errors, it bought time for the Mad Hogs to regroup and revert to playing the kind of game that had characterized them in the first six contests.

And that they did. As for the Raiders, they were held to a negative 4 yards rushing in the third quarter, signaling to all that the defense was back from their first half vacation. After the Farmers had taken the second half kickoff in for the third unanswered touchdown on Rice's 6-yard bolt, the defense held the Raiders in check. Not only did they hold them, but they blocked the subsequent punt, once again allowing the offense to begin work inside Raider territory. Starting at the 27-yard marker, Rice ended a two-play drive from 10 yards out for his final touchdown of the evening. Merritt was six-for-six in extra points, making the score 42–14.

The defensive surge had indeed been effective. Actually, it appeared that the Farmers' fans had witnessed two different games. The first half was obviously played by some imposters, while the Farmers they had seen all season showed up in the second half. In fact, had it not been for the massive fourth quarter substitutions the defense might well have not allowed any positive yards in the second half.

All in all, the game served as a wake-up call to repair the chinks in the

Farmers' armor, just in the nick of time, too. Their next opponent would be the Bonham Warriors, who were much better than their 0-7 record led one to believe. They had played stout 4A teams in each of their four non-district games (Sherman, Denison, Paris and Plano), and drew two of the toughest District 6-3A teams in their first two conference games in Gainesville and McKinney. In fact, Dave Campbell's Texas Football thought so highly of the Purple Warriors that they picked them in their annual preseason poll to capture the 1972 6-3A district championship.

Needless to say, the scare by North Garland was a blessing in disguise, putting the Farmers in the proper frame of mind for what lay ahead.

Lewisville vs. Bonham — October 27, 1972
For a game that ended in a 26-0 decision in favor of the Farmers, it sure was a close contest; a lot closer than the 26-point shutout revealed. Readers of the newspaper the following Saturday morning who noticed the lopsided victory, more than likely thought that Lewisville had dominated yet another team, yawned and took another sip of their coffee before flipping to the comics.

The Farmers had a poor track record against the Bonham Purple Warriors. In fact, in the 14 games against them prior to the '72 season, the Farmers were 0–14, and had never beaten the Fannin County foe. Not only that, they had only been close twice, in back-to-back seasons of 1961–62, losing 13–12 in '61 and 2–0 in '62. Other than that, Bonham pretty much dominated Lewisville as well as being a dominant force in District 6-3A throughout the late '60s and early '70s.

So game eight was no easy contest for the Farmers. The Warriors contributed to their own demise by losing six—yes six—fumbles, several of which practically handed Lewisville touchdowns. True, it had rained all day, making the ball difficult to hang on to, but the Farmers had little trouble in doing so, fumbling only once. As far as yardage goes, the game was fairly even, with Lewisville gaining 290 total yards to Bonham's 246. Actually, Bonham out-rushed the Farmers 236 yards to 231. It would have been more, too, had not an 81-yard quarterback keeper on Bonham's first play been called back on a clipping penalty. The run had gone to the one-foot line before being called back, so the Farmers dodged a bullet early on in the contest.

That was pretty much it as far as the first quarter action was concerned. Both teams fumbled once apiece, and it began to look like neither one could get anything going. The Farmers found their footing in the second quarter as Rice hit paydirt, or rather mud, on a 4-yard slither, because one could not really scamper in the mud. Merritt's extra point caromed off one of the uprights and ricocheted through, giving Lewisville a 7–0 second quarter lead.

Bonham fumbled the ball in the Farmers' lap on the next series, hardly giving the offense a chance to rest. From the Warrior 28-yard line the Farmers began a two-play drive, climaxed by a 9-yarder from Nichols. The touchdown was set up by a 19-yard gain by Randy Cade. Merritt was true on the conver-

1972: A Season to Remember

The name of the game is defense. Ray Bowden (73) signals that the Mad Hogs stopped a Warrior fourth-down conversion, one of three on the night.

sion and the Farmers quickly doubled the score. Two other scoring opportunities were missed due to a missed field goal and a Joe Martin interception, ending the first half with the Farmers not so comfortably on top of a 14–0 lead.

The Mad Hog defense controlled much of the second half by stopping the Warriors from converting three fourth-down situations, including one with just inches to go. Conversely, the Farmer offense scored twice more after getting the ball on the drive stoppages. Mark Angeli made an acrobatic catch on a pass that had been batted around like a volleyball, grabbing the ball at around the 50-yard stripe. Unfortunately Lewisville was not able to sustain the drive, and Allen Fox got set to punt. The ball was downed by speedster Billy Graham, putting Bonham in the hole at their own 3. The Warriors never got out of the chute. On play one of the drive Bonham blundered again, fumbling to Lewisville at the 5-yard line. Rice ran it over from that point and the score stood 20–0. It remained that way as the conversion attempt failed.

The final score came on a 39-yard fourth quarter touchdown run by Mike Nichols. The Warriors slipped through to block the extra point attempt, ending the scoring at 26–0 in the Farmers' favor. A late Warrior drive was combatted by the Farmer defense, preserving the shutout and giving Lewisville the first victory over Bonham in 15 attempts.

Lewisville vs. Gainesville — November 3, 1972
The Farmers were 8–0 going into the final two weeks of district play with their two toughest opponents yet to face in the Gainesville Leopards and the McKinney Lions. Gainesville had already lost to McKinney and were in second place in District 6-3A with a 6–1 record. Lewisville and McKinney were

tied for first, both with perfect district records. The Farmers traveled north to Gainesville for the next-to-last regular season game, with hopes of maintaining their spotless record and setting up the showdown with McKinney for the final home game.

It had rained all day, which set the tone for the way things would go for the Farmers that night. Averaging well over 300 yards per game in total offense for the season, the Farmers could manage only 174 total yards and one Paul Rice touchdown, while giving up 259 total yards to the Leopards. The Farmers turned the ball over on three interceptions, one of which led to the second of Gainesville's three scores.

Rice scored the lone touchdown of the contest, however, as Gainesville's Larry Barnes came on to kick field goals of 20, 23 and 30 yards on the muddy turf to secure a 9–6 victory, darkening the Farmers' hopes of a district championship. A fourth field goal attempt by Barnes went wide in the second quarter.

Shipman assumed the blame for the Farmer defeat, attributing the loss to the jazzed-up game plan installed during the week specifically to handle the tough Gainesville front line. The Leopards' defensive front was anchored by George Lewis at noseguard and had played havoc with the running game of every opponent they had faced. McKinney squeaked by Gainesville the week earlier, 14-7, but Lewis turned in a strong performance in the losing cause. His presence in the middle of the line was intimidating, enough so to cause the Farmer coaching staff to revamp their offensive attack.

Lewis was a master at playing the run from the middle, which accounted for the bulk of the Farmer offense. Shipman and Harvey altered the game plan to double team Lewis, attempting to get outside of Lewis' grasp. They also inserted a more active set of pass plays to counter the presumed lack of running that they thought would be available.

As luck, or fortune, would have it, Lewis was moved to the defensive end position, throwing a wrench in the Farmer attack.

Hoping to get outside, they were now unable to do so with the presence of Lewis on the end. The passing did not work well either, since the Farmers had not been able to establish the run due to the slippery conditions. So, the shifting of Lewis, the muddy field and the errant passes worked together to mar the once perfect record of the Farmers.

As it stood the Farmers were tied for second place with Gainesville, with both having 4–1 district records. But Gainesville had the edge over Lewisville, with their upset victory over the Farmers, in the event of a tie. McKinney now stood alone on top, with a 5–0 record and in the driver's seat.

Lewisville vs. McKinney — November 10, 1972
Needless to say, things were a little bleak around the Farmer locker room after the Gainesville loss, which carried into the next week. The coaching staff knew that applying pressure would only worsen things with the upcoming game against McKinney, so they avoided doing that. A victory for the Farm-

ers would throw District 6-3A into a three-way tie, provided Gainesville won the remainder of their games. If that had occurred the crown would have been determined by the flip of a coin . . . which is not what the Farmers wanted. According to Coach David Visentine, "We wanted to control our own destiny. We didn't want it to come down to a coin flip." What they preferred was some assistance from either South Grand Prairie or Berkner, as they were slated to play Gainesville in the final two weeks.

But first, the Farmers had to do their part and take care of McKinney, or the rest would have been academic. No doubt their confidence was shaken a bit, but they had narrowly lost to a tough Gainesville team, not some scrubs. This was the same Gainesville team that was edged by McKinney, 14–7, in week seven of the season. So the Farmers had much to be hopeful for; they matched up well against the Lions.

Then there was the determination factor. Lewisville had not been in the playoffs since 1957, when all the '72 Farmers were just little tykes. During the summer workouts the seniors had determined that 1972 would be better than the 2–7–1 1971 finish, and it already had been. At 8–1 the Farmers were guaranteed their best finish since 1957, but apparently that was not good enough. Mullins, Bragg, Coker, Autwell and Fox, all seniors, were determined to do everything in their power to see that their football season did not end against McKinney the following Friday night. In fact, to reveal his intensity, while several of the players were assembled at the Old Town post office on Charles Street the Saturday morning following the bitter loss to Gainesville, Steve Coker, in a display of sheer determination, or toughness, or madness, or whatever, stuck one of his arms in a bed of fire ants, allowing them to climb up and down it, biting his flesh at will. While dozens of the insects were gnawing away, Coker just looked at the other players and said, "This is how sure I am that we will beat McKinney."

No one was quite sure how to interpret Coker's declaration, other than to take confidence from the display of toughness. A quiet confidence began to envelope the Farmers at that moment, at least the players who had seen Coker's arm eaten up by the fire ants. Some how, some way, the Farmers were going to find a way to win.

As the week of preparation unfolded, excitement began to build both in the school and in the community. The band competed in UIL Marching Contest on Tuesday of that week and won a first division in the contest held at Haltom City. After the band learned of their rating they cheered with glee, but their minds soon turned to other matters after the excitement died down. They formed a roman numeral one in the stands, not to signify their own success in achieving a one rating, but began chanting, "Who the hell's McKinney? We're number one!" That was in mid-afternoon. Upon returning to the school after contest, instead of getting in their cars and going home to reminisce about their day's success, they went to the practice field where they found the Farmers in the midst of preparation for their final regular season game. As the workout was concluding, the band formed a spirit line for the players to run through as they left the practice field.

Later in the week Lewisville Mayor Sam Houston signed a resolution declaring Friday, November 10, 1972, as "Beat McKinney Day." Merchants throughout the town hung signs, or had their windows painted, in support of the team they had grown so fond of.

Other things popped up to show support for the Farmers, too. Cars were plastered with shoe polish that read, "Beat McKinney" and "We're No. 1." Citizens purchased maroon tee-shirts with white letters and a message that simply read, "Beat McKinney," a slogan that reflected the feelings of the entire community.

In preparation for the game, to comply with the increased demand for tickets, the bands for both schools were relocated from the stands to folding chairs on the track, which as it turned out, were the best seats in the stadium. It would be a packed house for the biggest game of the season.

The weather was perfect for the game. It had not rained all week, and unlike the previous two weeks, the field was in excellent condition. It appeared Mother Nature did not want to be a factor in this all-important showdown, content to join the throng as a spectator rather than an active participant. That way each team would have the opportunity to display their strengths instead of altering their plan of attack for such factors as a muddy field or a wet football. So on that cool, fall night, a true district champion would be crowned.

The Farmers got on the scoreboard first in the second period after the first quarter ended in a 0–0 stalemate. The touchdown run came on a 2-yard Paul Rice dive up the middle, capping a seven-play 24-yard drive. Cade's extra point made it 7–0 with 10:57 left in the first half. That set the stage for an active second period of play.

Following the initial Farmer score, McKinney instantly marched down the field in a drive that ate up just under three minutes, with running back Tommy Parker taking it in 2 yards for the score. Jimmy Stewart tacked on the point-after, tying the score, 7–7, with time still available for a lot of action before the halftime show would begin.

On the ensuing drive the Farmers fumbled at their own 36-yard line and McKinney recovered at that point. They were able to capitalize on the opportunity as they moved in for their second score of the busy quarter, this time with quarterback Benji Smith sneaking over from the 4. Stewart added the extra point, and McKinney led 14–7 with 5:36 to go.

Lewisville began the next drive at its own 36-yard marker and quickly moved down the field. Rice rebutted the McKinney score on a touchdown run, this one from inside the 1-yard line. Cade dittoed his extra point efforts, and the Farmers kept pace with the much heralded Lions, 14–14. Rice's score came with 2:21 left in the first half of what was shaping up to be a seesaw match, with each team displaying their ability to score.

The Mad Hog Farmer defense had hoped to hold the Lions on what should

1972: A Season to Remember

have been the final drive of the first half, however McKinney quarterback Benji Smith engineered a scoring drive to end the first half as he carried it over from a yard away, his second touchdown of the quarter. Stewart kicked the extra point, already earning a hat trick in just the first half, as McKinney led going into intermission, 21–14.

At the half the Farmers made a few adjustments, but mostly the coaching staff spent the time trying to refocus on what had been successful for them all season. No doubt some of the players were still keyed-up, given the gravity of the game and what was at stake. So, after a coke and a pep talk by Shipman, the Farmers readied themselves for an action-packed second half.

Quarter number three resembled the first period as neither team was able to generate any offense, and the quarter ended as it began with the Lions still on top, 21–14. The Farmers were fortunate in the period as they fumbled twice, losing both to McKinney, but prevented the Lions from cashing in on the Lewisville errors. Unable to capitalize, McKinney still clung to that seven point lead going into the final period, the one which would produce the District 6-3A champion of 1972.

McKinney increased its 21–14 lead with 11:43 left in the game as Tommy Parker pounced in from the 4-yard line. Stewart did his thing again, and the Lions were comfortably on top of a 28–14 score... and the window was beginning to close on the "Cinderella" season of 1972 for Lewisville's Farmers.

An 8-2 season would have been exceptional for Lewisville, especially on the heels of the 2-7-1 finish in 1971. That's what McKinney Head Coach Ron Poe suggested to Shipman as the two exchanged game films, a display of the lack of respect he had for the Farmers. Surely with a win total four times that of the previous season, the Farmers could claim that they had revived a program that was all but dead, and reclaimed Lewisville's pride and respect. Oh well, good try boys. Better luck next year.

But the Farmers thoughts did not immediately turn that way. Lewisville answered the last McKinney score with a third Paul Rice touchdown run of 2 yards with 6:57 remaining. With the score 28–20, instead of routinely booting the extra point, Shipman elected to do something unexpected. Lewisville faked the extra point, with Martin rolling to his right with the option of either running or passing. As Martin ran the McKinney defenders reacted to the fake and headed in his direction. First one, then another Lion pursued, eventually depriving Martin of any running room the closer he got to the goal line. As the defenders converged, Martin tossed the ball over their outstretched hands into the waiting arms of Rice, who had slipped, undetected, into the back of the end zone, pulling the Farmers to within striking distance at 28–22. That is exactly what the Farmer coaching staff wanted; an opportunity to score one final time without the pressure of winning the game by having to complete a two-point conversion in an obvious situation. Offensive Coordinator Don Harvey recalled, "We didn't want to get into a situation where they (the McKinney coaching staff) knew we would have to go for two and defend against it. We knew we would need a two-point conversion if we were to win, and we knew we would have to make it. By choosing to do it on the third touchdown it caught them a little off guard and made it a bit easier to make it." Shipman added, "We accomplished what we wanted to do instead of the situation dictating to us what we would have to do. In a sense, we controlled our own destiny by going for, and making, the two-point conversion when we did. I think it took a lot of the pressure off our boys and gave them a lot of needed confidence." Regardless, the two-point conversion set off a sequence of events that will long be remembered by the thousands who were on hand to see them.

Following the third touchdown, the Farmers attempted an on-side kick but were unsuccessful. Farmer fans felt a bit uneasy as McKinney took possession of the ball at their own 46-yard line with barely six minutes left to play. The Farmers gambled once on the two-point play and succeeded; they gambled again on the on-side kick, but that one backfired, only in the sense that Lewisville was unable to come up with the football. The Mad Hog defense remedied that, however, by not allowing the Lions to advance the ball and forcing them to punt. The Lions lost a bit of their composure, too, as they drew a major penalty for a late hit, giving Lewisville a 15-yard bonus. After the dust had settled, Lewisville found itself at its own 43-yard line with 5:33 remaining in the contest, setting up, perhaps, their last chance to score. What happened from that point has gone down as one of, if not the most, memorable offensive possession in Lewisville Fighting Farmer history.

As the season began Shipman instituted several things to create enthusiasm and to help maintain a positive attitude, especially at times like these. Remember the 4 H's; hang loose, hit hard, have fun and hustle? That was just one example of the type of climate Shipman and the coaches had worked to create. Another tradition born in 1972 was called "Farmer Quarter." That was Shipman's designation of the fourth quarter of any football game his 1972 Farmers were involved in. In essence, the fourth quarter was claimed as the quarter in which anything the Farmers needed to accomplish would be taken care of at that time. It was a cleanup quarter; a time for the Farmers to take care of any unfinished business, so to speak. The *Lewisville News* Advertiser's Jim Burnett put it best: "Farmer Quarter. For all practical purposes, it's a period of time in which Lewisville's Farmers destroy everything in sight." It worked early in the season as Rice scored on the 25-yard screen pass against Boswell in the opening contest. However, it fell short the week before against Gainesville. The most pressing concern for Shipman, the Farmers and their fans was if it would work against McKinney.

As the Farmers lined up to begin the critical drive the fans from both sides stood on their feet. The bleachers cracked and swayed under the collective weight of the enthusiastic crowd. The Farmers began the drive with the ball perched at their own 43. Rice carried for 5 to the 48 and gained another 2 to the mid-field stripe. Facing third-and-two, Martin faded back to pass, in hopes

1972: A Season to Remember

of catching the Lions by surprise and covering a big chunk of yardage, if not the game tying touchdown itself. Instead, the McKinney front line pursued Martin, not allowing him to even look for a receiver, let alone find one. It was all he could do to avoid anything more than a 3-yard loss; it could have been worse. Martin retreated back to the original line of scrimmage at the 43-yard line. Upon seeing his options diminish, Martin immediately scrambled forward to salvage what yardage he could. He already knew the ensuing fourth-down play would be lengthy, and he was doing his best to shorten the yardage needed.

Martin lunged forward to the 47, losing 3 yards on the outstanding McKinney defensive surge. Now Lewisville faced a critical fourth-down situation, needing to reach the McKinney 48 to sustain the drive. This would be the first of three critical plays engineered by the collective minds of the Farmer coaching staff that would not go as designed.

The Farmers called time out, their third and final one of the half. After an involved discussion on the sideline between Shipman, Harvey and Martin, it was decided the play to run was a screen pass to the middle of the field with Rice as the primary receiver. This was the play that held their future. If they were not successful here, they would have to check it in for the season.

McKinney's defensive front had been fairly effective against the run and extremely effective against the pass. Rice had rushed for 115 yards to this point, on 35 carries, for a season low 3.3 yards-per-carry average. A routine play to Rice would more than likely be stopped short of the first down, as the Lion front and linebackers would be keying on him. On the other hand, a long pass downfield would be too obvious, so the choice was limited to a mixture of the two; a screen to Rice. Perfect call — if everything worked properly and the McKinney defense cooperated. The Farmers did have one concern, however.

Most defenses are fairly predictable, not so much in their formation as for their reaction. For example, it is almost guaranteed in running a play action pass that, if the fake to the running back is carried out skillfully, almost always will the linemen and linebackers freeze in order to play the run. That momentary hesitation allows the receiver to get by the coverage in order for the quarterback to deliver the ball, provided the play is properly executed. With the design of the screen play the Farmers called, the defensive line is lulled into thinking they're putting a heavy rush on the quarterback. Just before the defense moves in for the kill, the quarterback is to toss the ball to either a back or receiver, nestled securely behind the offensive line, which had successfully suckered the defense into thinking they had beaten their blocks. The concern Shipman and offensive line coach Tommy Shields had was with the McKinney noseguard, not so much for his athletic ability, although he was quick, but rather for his unpredictability.

The noseguard for McKinney was small and quick athletically, but he was "slow" mentally and did not behave normally, which might be good if trying to con some money out of him, but not so good when trying to defend against him . . . which is what made him valuable to the Lions. While running throughout the game the Farmers had been able to control him fairly well, but the screen play required that he be snookered into going after Martin, something they really could not control.

Nor did they. Instead of rushing Martin like all the other Lion front line had done, he stayed back, right in the middle of the works. He was where Rice needed to be—not ideal for the situation.

Martin, in rapid retreat, finally had no choice but to throw it in the area assigned to Rice and hope for the best. As the ball drifted toward the line, the noseguard muscled his way in between the ball and Rice and barely, but surely, tipped it, altering the throw, Martin described, "from a semi-wobbly pass to an end over end pass," unable to be caught. The noseguard had made an outstanding play and saved the day for the Lions, at least for a split second. The batted ball was deflected away from Rice but into the hands of startled offensive tackle Niles Ladehoff. Alertly, he held on to the ball and ran in the right direction, gaining 9 yards, two more than necessary. This gave the Farmers the much needed first down. After that bizarre play, Martin thought, "we're gonna score."

The McKinney coaches vehemently disputed the call, stating that an offensive lineman is an ineligible receiver. The officials explained that after a defender touches a forward pass it is a "live" ball, meaning anyone is eligible to catch it, thus Ladehoff's play stood. The outburst by the McKinney coaches worked to their disadvantage, and the Lions never really recovered from the shock of it all.

The Farmers had new life at the McKinney 46-yard line with time rapidly dissolving off the clock, as it always seems to do in these situations. From there it was Rice for 3, then for 2 . . . the clock still ticking. Martin kept on the next play with a great run for 7—first down! Again it was Rice, this time for 3. He followed that with a 9-yarder . . . first down again, approaching the final minute. A quick 10 yards gave the Farmers their third first down of the drive, still 7 yards from the potential winning score, and the Farmers could smell the end zone. They could also see the clock ticking away.

Rice carried it for 3 yards down to the 4, and again for 1 to the 3. On third down the McKinney front finally stopped Rice for no gain leaving the Farmers only 21 seconds to get the ball in the end zone. It was fourth-down-and-goal as well, so the Farmers were almost out of cards. They had used their last time-out to set up the screen pass, so whatever play selected would have to be sent in from the sideline.

The procedure for calling plays by the Farmers in 1972 was to shuttle them in with the wide receivers, in this case Floyd Voss and Billy Graham, unless a time-out or a play near the Farmer sideline allowed Martin and the coaches to confer directly. The formation and play was given to the receiver, and he carried it into the huddle and delivered the play verbally to the entire team.

1972: A Season to Remember

In actuality, the receiver called the formation, then the play, and Martin called the snap count. After calling the play the receiver then left the huddle to line up, then Martin himself repeated the entire sequence so that everybody was certain what to do. It was Floyd's turn to shuttle the play in, so he brought it in from Shipman on the sideline.

The play the Farmers were supposed to have run was a "split left, slotback reverse pass option," meaning Voss would line up wide on the left side of the field, with Randy Cade at slotback, also on the left side. By design Martin was to have turned to his right, after taking the snap, and pivot around completely to fake a handoff to Rice, who was diving into the left side of the line, following Nichols. This would have Martin going to his left in the opposite direction he initially turned. Meanwhile, Cade was to have taken one step toward the line, then reversed back behind Martin in the opposite direction where Martin would secretly hand him the ball. Cade then had the option of running into the end zone or throwing to either tight end Mark Angeli, or Voss or Rice, or whoever the heck was open—so long as it wasn't a lineman. It resembled a scene from "A Chorus Line," the choreography was that complex. Regardless, it was supposed to have worked. But Voss, excited, did not speak clearly upon entering the huddle, so the formation was not fully understood, and to compound matters, when Martin repeated the play he called the right play, but the wrong formation. Fortunately for the Farmers the snap count was right both times.

When the offense left the huddle none of the key personnel to carry out the play called were in the right place, except for Martin, Nichols and Rice. The situation was intensified as there was but seven seconds and counting as the team lined up. The play appeared to be headed for failure. The trouble continued. When the ball was snapped the clock showed :01 . . . just in the nick of time. Martin, however, instead of turning right, turned left, putting him in the wrong direction to continue the play as it was designed. Martin made the fake to Rice, but missed Cade altogether, as by now they were both going in the same direction. Rather than panic, Martin had the presence of mind to assume the path Cade would have taken if all had gone correctly, and proceeded to his right. The fake to Rice, although unorthodox, was effective, as the entire defensive front froze. This allowed Martin to get around the defensive end and linebacker, who eventually reacted to the action and started to pursue. Martin had the same pass/run option as Cade would have if he'd gotten the ball, but it was clear that he had only one thing in mind; get across the goal line, somehow, regardless of the wide open Angeli in the back of the end zone.

Still running to his right, Martin did the only thing he could do; he selected a spot just inside the end zone flag and headed toward it. As he neared, so did the McKinney defenders—ever so close. He could feel their Lion breath as he ran. It evolved into a race to the end zone. As Martin neared, he realized he had only one option if he were to be successful. Still a yard away, Martin

Farmer quarterback Joe Martin running . . . and diving . . . and scoring the final touchdown to defeat McKinney, 29–28.

dove as the final second ticked off the clock, and landed . . . just inside the flag at the spot he aimed at. There were no penalty flags, and as the referee's arms went up, the fans, players, band, everyone erupted after witnessing the unbelievable event unfold before their eyes.

This tied the game at 28-all. Having gone for two on the previous score, all the Farmers had to do was boot the extra point and go celebrate, at least a district co-championship, and maybe the chance to enter the playoffs. Due to the excitement generated by Martin's score, the Farmers were penalized for delay of game as the celebration on the field lasted a bit longer than the officials felt necessary, making the extra point try more than routine with the additional 5 yards. Eventually the Farmers lined up for the point-after, with the game and district championship on the line.

All fans who witnessed the game no doubt saw the alert play by Ladehoff that kept the drive alive. Most learned, also, that the play that Martin scored on was a broken play. But only a handful know what happened on the extra point attempt that almost cost the Farmers a victory.

Center Mark McCurley lined up over the ball and readied himself for the snap. Martin and the others got set as Cade was prepared to kick the ever-so-important extra point. As the snap came back, Martin handled the ball and placed it on the tee, awaiting Cade's foot. As Martin placed the ball down, however, he put it down on the front right corner of the tee, considerably off-center. Not only that, he placed it in a way such that the downward pressure of

Postgame celebration — Sammie Wilson gives Red Bishop (40) a ride on his shoulders after the dramatic come-from-behind victory over the McKinney Lions in 1972.

1972: A Season to Remember

the ball caused the tee to flip up, almost interfering with Cade's oncoming shoe. Instead he missed it—the tee that is—but not the ball, as he nailed it squarely, sending it through the uprights for the much needed point which gave the Farmers the upset victory.

Needless to say the crowd was jubilant, so much so that they ignored the UIL rule prohibiting fans from coming onto the playing field, and poured onto Farmer Field by the hundreds. The band had the best seats as they were set up at the south goal line, the one in which Martin crossed for the winning score. They, too, ran onto the field in droves. And no one stopped them either. After all, it had been 13 years since the Farmers had been in the playoffs, and even then, it was not achieved against so many odds. Incidentally, in the midst of the noise the announcement came across the public address system that the Farmers had received the assistance they needed.

South Grand Prairie had beaten Gainesville, giving the Farmers the right to advance into the playoffs.

Lewisville vs. Boswell — November 24, 1972
As the Farmers were securing the opportunity to represent District 6-3A in the playoffs, the Boswell Pioneers captured the 5-3A crown, making them Lewisville's opponent in the opening round of the playoffs. This would be their second meeting of the season with the Farmers taking game one in the come-from-behind 14–7 victory. No doubt Boswell, and their head coach, a young Neal Wilson, would be out to settle the score against the Farmers, who had spoiled their perfect season hopes in week one.

The rematch was scheduled to be played at Haltom City's Birdville Stadium. With their first game a close one, everyone was set for a thriller in the bi-district contest, but it did not turn out that way. The Farmers scored early . . . and often. Rice scored twice in the first quarter on touchdown runs of 4 and 10 yards, his 26th and 27th touchdowns of the year, while the Mad Hog defense denied the Pioneers any offense at all. The second quarter was a duplication of the first with the Farmers scoring twice again, this time Martin taking it in from 6 yards out, and later tossing 8 yards to Randy Cade. Cade was four-for-four in extra point attempts, giving the Farmers a 28–0 halftime lead, and the game was in the bag.

The Farmers scored once more in the contest on a 5-yard Paul Rice run to close out the scoring, both for the Farmers and the game. Cade made it a perfect evening with his final extra point, wrapping up an impressive 35–0 bi-district championship.

Along with the nickname of "Mad Hogs" for the defense, the offense earned the tag "Mad Dogs," with the offensive line called the "Blasters." That's exactly what characterized the play of the six-man front as they blasted the defensive front off the line of scrimmage repeatedly, wearing them down and allowing Nichols and Rice to run at will. Anchored by center Mark McCurley and coached by Tommy Shields, the Blasters' combined efforts led the way for Nichols and

FRIDAY NIGHT FARMERS

The Mad Hog defense stops a Boswell ball carrier in the 1972 Bi-District contest. Lewisville dominated in a 35–0 win.

Rice to gain over 3,700 yards rushing in 1972. Guards Randy Mayes and Rudy Durham, tackles Eddie Mullins and Niles Ladehoff and tight end Mark Angeli worked in unison to compile one of the most forceful offensive lines in Farmer history. In fact, four of the six were named to the 6-3A All-District team, with Rudy Durham making the second team. Niles Ladehoff was the only Farmer offensive lineman overlooked to receive post-season honors.

And the 35–0 blasting of Boswell thrust the Farmers into the second round of the playoffs.

Lewisville vs. Mt. Pleasant — November 30, 1972
The Farmers, with their 35–0 bi-district victory, earned the right to play the Mt. Pleasant Tigers in the quarter finals at Mesquite's Forrestor Field. This stadium would be the first stadium the Farmers would play in that had astroturf. In preparation for this the Farmer coaches arranged for the team to work out at various surrounding stadiums supplied with the synthetic surface. The team was extremely surprised on Thursday of that week when the buses stopped at Texas Stadium for their final workout before the quarter final contest. This marks the first appearance by a Farmer football team in Texas Stadium, but certainly not the last.

Mt. Pleasant won the District 7-3A title with an undefeated record and

1972: A Season to Remember

Billy Graham (21) gains good yardage as Mark McWhorter (43), Niles Ladehoff (74) and Mike Nichols (35) lend support.

edged Wilmer-Hutchins, 14–13, for their bi-district crown, compiling a perfect 11–0 record. Going into the game the Tigers were picked as a one-point favorite by the Harris Rating System as both teams possessed potent offenses. Lewisville had scored 343 points through 11 games, while Mt. Pleasant produced an impressive 407. Both teams had allowed fewer than 100 points each, with Mt. Pleasant giving up 71 and the Farmers 86. Although District 7-3A was not as strong as 6-3A, the game was shaping up as one of the potentially best of the season, but then again, the Boswell game was expected to have been also.

The game was so evenly matched that neither team was able to score in the first half, although the Farmers did get close. Rice took a Martin handoff and darted to his left for, what appeared to be, a short gain. Upon seeing no running room he then turned 90 degrees up field into the line again, apparently on his way down. On his way to the turf he stuck his hand down, stabbing the turf to maintain his balance, then shot out of the gang of would-be tacklers and into the end zone for one of the most incredible individual efforts displayed by a Farmer running back. Unfortunately the officials whistled the play dead when Rice ran into the line, claiming that he had touched his knee to the playing surface. A replay of the game films clearly shows that Rice had, indeed, avoided touching his knee to the turf. Regardless, that was the only real threat by either team in the first half as the score stood at a 0–0 deadlock at the half.

Rice's near touchdown run was not the only bright spot for Lewisville in the first half. From their own 32-yard line, one of the Farmers' first half drive stalled, forcing Lewisville to punt into a strong wind. The Tigers anticipated getting the ball with good field position, that is, before Allen Fox's 50-yard spiral pinned them back at their 22-yard line.

Opening the second half with a 73-yard scoring drive, the Tigers took a 7–0 third quarter lead on a Freddie Lewis 28-yard touchdown reception. The pass from quarterback Craig Carney came with 7:54 left in the period, putting the Tigers one notch up.

The score apparently snapped the Farmers out of their quarter final daze as they took the following kickoff and powered their way down the field 69 yards to offset the Tiger score. Martin did the honors on a quarterback keeper around the left side from 2 yards out. The scoring play was set up by Rice carrying on eight of the 13 plays, accounting for 57 yards in the drive. Cade booted the ball through the uprights to tie the score, 7–7, leaving 2:12 in the third quarter.

Mt. Pleasant was unable to move the ball on their next possession, largely due to a huge third down tackle for no gain by Sammie Voss. The alert tackle set up a fourth-and-16 situation. With Mt. Pleasant punting into the wind, the Farmers took the ball with excellent field position at the Tiger 39. From there Rice did the work on eight consecutive carries, the final one good for 4 yards and the go-ahead score. The touchdown came on a 4-yard dive with 8:42 left in the contest. Cade's extra point attempt was thwarted by a high snap, making the Farmer lead only 13–7.

Mt. Pleasant began their next drive at their own 33-yard line and immediately went to the air. Carney had been successful in connecting with his favorite receiver, Freddie Lewis, who hauled in 136 yards worth of passes on the evening. With the ball at the Farmer 46-yard line, Carney attempted yet another of his 11 total passes of the evening, but was sacked for a 9-yard loss. With third-and-long Carney tossed another pass toward Lewis, who was fleeting through the Farmer secondary. Farmer linebacker John Anderson slipped in front of Lewis, however, and picked off the pass at the Lewisville 23-yard line, bringing a screeching halt to the Tiger scoring threat.

As it turned out, Anderson's interception may have been the turning point in the game. Not only did it prevent a potential go-ahead touchdown/extra point combination, but it set up the Farmers for their final score of the night. To cap the drive Rice scored from 9 yards out, putting the Farmers securely on top at 20–7, with Cade's successful extra point, leaving the Tigers a meager 1:27 to play catch up ball.

It was a good thing there was little time left, too, as the Tigers roared back in the short span to score a desperation touchdown. A big chunk came on a 52-yard pass to Lewis. Two plays later running back Vincent Green ran it in from 3 yards out to pull the Tigers to within seven, at 20–13. A two-point conversion attempt failed and that's the way the game ended, giving the Farmers the quarter final trophy.

Lewisville vs. Burkburnett — December 7, 1972
After 12 games the Farmers had achieved an 11–1 record and found themselves in the state semifinal round of the Texas high school playoffs; a place no Lewisville team had been before. The 13–0 record in 1947, and 11-0 record in 1950, had been the best finishes for the Farmers until the 1972 season, with both teams capturing regional championships. This was the closest Lewisville came to a state final appearance.

But they would have to go through Burkburnett's Bulldogs to get there. Burkburnett had captured the District 4-3A championship, and squeezed out bi-district and quarter final victories over LaMesa, 19–16, and Dumas, 7–6. The Bulldogs had not displayed near as potent an offense as the Farmers, scoring only 253 points in comparison to Lewisville's 363. Defensively they had surrendered 141, while the Farmers had given up only 99. Both of these indicators would dictate the Farmers to be favored, but the Harris Poll had

1972: A Season to Remember

them dead even. Not only that, but the Bulldogs were ranked number six in the state while the Farmers had finally broken the top 10 going into the bi-district game. And one by one teams had been knocked off, leaving Brenham as the top ranked team, followed by Uvalde and Burkburnett, with Lewisville close behind.

Offensively the Farmers had already combined to form the most lethal attack as Rice neared the 2,000-yard rushing mark with 1,958 to date, while scoring 30 touchdowns. Nichols, overshadowed by Rice's efforts, had 1,153 yards himself with 12 touchdowns, and these were just two of a number of offensive weapons in the Farmer arsenal. Cade had proven himself both an effective runner and receiver, and occasionally tossed a pass or two, complicating things a bit for the opposing defenses. A pleasant surprise was the reliable combination that tight end Mark Angeli's hands and speed provided, a dependable outlet if needed, as he had snared two touchdown passes during the season.

In fact, it was Angeli's efforts in the first quarter that garnered Lewisville's first score as he was on the receiving end of a 19-yard Joe Martin pass. Burkburnett charged in and blocked the extra point attempt, giving the Farmers a 6–0 lead at the four-minute mark.

Burkburnett's highly proclaimed quarterback Sam Hancock found out what a Mad Hog was on the following drive as the Farmer defense crushed him, forcing him to fumble. Sammie Voss was outside the barrage of defenders and recovered the ball for Lewisville, and Hancock learned then that it was to be a long evening.

After the fumble recovery Rice went to work and did not stop until he had added 176 yards rushing to his season's total, giving him 2,134 yards on the season. His three touchdowns increased his season total to 33. Rice's touchdowns came on runs of 2, 37 and 1 yard as he led the Farmer offensive attack. His first score came in the first quarter on the 2-yard punch, followed by a successful two-point conversion. The Farmers almost had an additional touchdown in the second quarter as defensive back James Merritt picked off a Sam Hancock pass and returned it 95 yards for an apparent touchdown. A clipping penalty negated the score, but the Farmers retained possession at Burkburnett's 37-yard line.

Rice's next score came on an impressive 37-yarder in the third quarter. Burkburnett again blocked the extra point, but the Farmers remained well in front at 20–0 . . . and they never looked back. Lewisville added two more scores in the fourth quarter to tidy things up, including Rice's final score from 1 yard out. The other touchdown came on a 10-yard strike from Martin to split end Billy Graham. Successful extra points after both scores completed the scoring for Lewisville for a 34–0 thumping of Burkburnett's usually powerful (but not that night) Bulldogs. The semifinal victory stunned observers of Texas high school football across the state, relaying the message that, although new to the playoff scene, the Lewisville Fighting Farmers were no fluke. The win earned the Farmers their first state championship appearance in the school's 69-year history.

Perhaps no one was more surprised at the outcome than Farmer Head Coach Bill Shipman. Although he expected to win, he did not expect a blowout such as the one he witnessed. He explained that it was just a matter of the Farmers taking control early and knocking the Bulldogs off their game-plan, not allowing them to do the things they had been successful in doing all year. The quick 14–0 Farmer lead forced Burkburnett into altering their plan of attack, but not succeeding. The Farmers then piled it on once they discovered the chink in the Bulldog armor, icing the game well before the final gun sounded, allowing them to face the Uvalde Coyotes in the state championship contest the following week.

On a side note, the Farmer-Bulldog match was played at Texas Christian University's Amon G. Carter Stadium. The contest, played on a combination of natural grass and dirt, was the final game played there before grass was substituted with artificial turf the following season. In fact, the Farmers have closed down several stadiums in winning fashion. In 1981 the Farmers traveled to Odessa to do battle with the Permian Panthers for the bi-district crown. The contest scheduled at Odessa High ended up being the final game played there as the Panthers were due a new stadium for the following year. Indeed, they would like to have gone out on a winning note, but the Farmers denied them that privilege by advancing to the next round of the playoffs with a 19–15 edge in first downs, giving Lewisville the nod in the 14–14 tie. So, in the stadium where the haunting chant of "Mojo" was born, the Farmers had the final word.

Lewisville vs. Uvalde — December 15, 1972
The early scouting report on the Uvalde Coyotes raised a concern with Coach Shipman as it revealed the use of less than conventional plays in achieving the opportunity to vie for the 3A state title. In fact, they had defeated Brenham the week earlier for the chance at the crown, and Gregory-Portland the week before that for the quarter final championship—both victories coming on trick plays in the fourth period. The Coyotes were talented enough to win without trick plays; the shenanigans only added to the difficulty in defending against them. Uvalde coach Marvin Gufstason, brother of the legendary University of Texas Longhorn baseball coach Cliff Gufstason, was the architect of a potent offense with the likes of quarterback Lynn Leonard. Leonard had thrown for 1,800 yards on the season at a 64 percent clip. Running back Oscar Mirelez and Mike Paradeaux led the ground attack, with Paradeaux's 700 yards leading the team. The play that defeated Gregory-Portland was a pass from the wide receiver to the tight end for a fourth quarter score. The play was set up by a lateral from Leonard. The trick used against Brenham was a bit more shrewd. As Leonard took the snap from center he faked to both backs charging through both sides of the center. While doing so he crouched, securing

1972: A Season to Remember

the ball snugly between his thighs and stomach, which allowed him to make the fakes with his hands free. After faking he then took the ball and placed it on the ground next to guard Richard Sanchez's foot, where it lay awaiting the proper moment. After the area was clear, Sanchez picked up the "hidden" ball and ran 68 yards for the score that sent the Coyotes into the state finals.

Needless to say, the trickery concerned the Farmer coaching staff somewhat. In addition to normal preparation they added other schemes to recognize and defend against the confounded gimmicks.

Of course, the Farmers were also worthy of respect, given the combined rushing talents of the dynamic duo—Paul Rice and Mike Nichols. The two had gained 3,434 yards in 13 games as probably the most productive backfield in the state. Certainly they were the youngest, which could have been a factor in the nerve category since no Farmer had seen the playoffs since 1957. Conversely, Uvalde had lost to Gregory-Portland in 1971 in the playoffs but had beaten them for the quarter final championship en route to an undefeated season. Their 24–1 two-season total may have been intimidating to the young Farmers under normal conditions, but Rice, Nichols and company were not considered normal.

The Farmers boarded the buses early in Lewisville on that December 15 and headed south toward Austin's Memorial Stadium in time for the 7:30 p.m. kickoff. Shipman, concerned that the routine game day schedule would be disrupted, attempted to simulate a normal school day and had the buses stop every hour. He then instructed the players to get off and walk south for five minutes, as if they were in between periods when changing classes. Shipman felt that the four-hour trip might add to the potentially nervous conditions, so he broke the monotony by having the players walk as they normally would when in school. This is indicative of the innovations Shipman would use to create conditions favorable for winning. Whether it had anything to do with the outcome of the game is unknown, but the message it sent to the players revealed the care and concern Shipman and the other coaches felt for their players.

The unique mixture of athletes that made up the 1972 Fighting Farmer roster could be described in several ways. First, they were a disciplined group of young men, indicated by the willingness of many of the players to give up their summer and work on their agility, strength and conditioning, especially since the prospects for the upcoming season were dim, having just completed the dreaded 2–7–1 record. Second, they were a diverse blend of personalities, from the jocular and outspoken likes of Rusty Cade and Randy Mayes to the soft spoken images of strength projected by Mike Nichols and Mark McCurley. There was the ever present intensity of Steve Coker, along with the inner strength displayed by Eddie Mullins. And many, many more, all blended together and complemented each other to accomplish the very thing that each player dreams of when reporting for two-a-days on those hot August mornings and afternoons . . . to play in a state championship contest.

Farmer fans demonstrate their enthusiasm during the pep rally before the championship game.

Perhaps the one word that describes the 1972 Farmers better than any other is unity. The 39 or so players had grown close during the '72 campaign, which developed into a "sixth sense" in working with one another. Each coach would meet with the players under their charge and opened their home to the dozen or so he was responsible to for communicating the ins and outs of the intricate offensive and defensive schemes designed by the coaches. One common event occurred with regularity on Saturday mornings after the ball games. Many of the players reported to the training room for treatment of the bumps and bruises acquired the night before, watching cartoons and reading the newspaper's account of the ball game while being treated. Then the group would migrate to the film room to watch films of the game, hoping to eliminate any mistakes made after evaluating their performance. This all took place before 10:00 a.m., at which time the players would assemble at the home of Defensive Coordinator David Visentine and his wife Beth, and proceed to help themselves to any foodstuff suitable for breakfast. And not once did the generous coach and his wife complain.

In fact, they relished it. Once, after one of the playoff wins, the Lewisville Booster Club sponsored a celebration of the victory at the Visentine home and served an enormous cake in honor of the win. Instead of ingesting the cake, however, some of the players decided it made pretty good ammunition, at which time a cake fight erupted, with Visentine and his wife as the instigators.

1972: A Season to Remember

Soon cake was everywhere, with all attendants beside themselves with laughter. And what did Visentine and his wife do about it? They cleaned it up without a word; a clear indication of what having the players and other coaches around meant to the morale of the team.

This type of unity was reflected in the community. It was proud of its Farmers, indeed, pledging allegiance to the Maroon and White as hoards made their way down the Interstate to witness the biggest game of the year.

Uvalde got things started in the scoring department on a 1-yard run by Mike Paradeaux, a play which climaxed an impressive eight-play, 68-yard drive of basic football with no monkey business.

The extra point by quarterback Lynn Leonard was good, giving the Coyotes a 7-0 advantage with 7:20 remaining in the opening quarter.

Following the score the Farmers came to life on a 63-yard drive of their own, comprised of a mere two plays set up by Gary Autwell's fumble recovery. The highlight was a 58-yard dive off tackle by Rice, which had Farmer fans on their feet in order to catch a glimpse of the speedy sophomore who would set new rushing records in Class 3A that would take 13 years to break. Cade converted the extra point and all of a sudden the game was tied, 7–7.

Announcers speculated that the '72 state championship game would be determined by whoever got the ball last. Fans were glued to their seats for fear they would miss a scoring play. Those going out for a coke and a hot dog just missed out all together. Less than a minute after the Farmers scored, Uvalde's Paradeaux bulled over for his second 1-yard touchdown of the evening. The scoring play was set up by a 41-yard pass from Leonard to running back Oscar Mirelez. Leonard's extra point was successful and the race was on, with the contest not yet a quarter old.

Although it took until the 6:48 mark, Lewisville countered the Uvalde score with a 1-yard plunge, again by Rice, followed by Cade's second extra point. The Farmers drew even at 14–14 with under seven minutes to play in the fast paced first half.

Striking quickly as coyotes do, Uvalde scored again, this time with Steve Strong hitting paydirt on a 25-yard run with 5:42 left in the half—plenty of time for the lead to change several times if the first 18 minutes and 18 seconds were any indication. Leonard's extra point was successful, and the Farmers saw themselves playing catch up ball again as Uvalde held a 21-14 lead.

The Farmers returned the favor on the ensuing drive, covering 66 yards, with Nichols taking it in from 15 yards out. Cade made it three-for-three on the conversion and the game was deadlocked once again, 21–21, with 1:57 remaining in the first half. It was apparent that nobody had taken the night off. Even the scoreboard operator was overworked in keeping up with the frequent score changes.

Uvalde answered the bell once again with a late half score on a 10-yard strike to tight end Randy Gerdes, giving the Farmers something to think about during half time. This time Leonard's kick was no good, and the Farmers

Rice crosses the goal line for a Farmer touchdown against Uvalde.

finally had some room to work as the Coyote lead remained at six, 27–21, going into the locker room.

The first half had been an action packed thriller, producing 48 points and very little defense. The Coyotes had their hands full with Rice, allowing him to score twice. Likewise, the Farmer defense was troubled by the Uvalde attack as three different Coyotes scored touchdowns, setting up a fight to the finish in the second half. Part of the Farmer defensive troubles were attributed to the Uvalde reputation for trick plays—no doubt the Mad Hogs were off balance a bit with their eye out for the unusual. This took away their aggressiveness, allowing the Coyotes to move down the field more freely than usual. At the half Visentine and Shipman decided to abandon the lookout for trick plays and resume the style of play that had allowed just over seven points per game.

The defensive adjustment worked, too. Had it not been for the Farmers suffering an interception at their own 9, the now stingy defense would likely have shut out the Coyotes in the second half completely. As it stood Uvalde cashed in on the golden opportunity on an ugly score. After losing a yard to the 10, Leonard fired a slant pass to Gerdes, who caught the ball at about the Farmer 2 and was greeted by a swarm of maroon jerseys. The impact forced the ball free as Gerdes was falling over the goal line, and it lay on the turf until split end Kim Sobieski alertly fell on it and was credited with the score. A two-point conversion failed, and the Farmers trailed by their widest margin of the night, at 33–21, still early in the second half.

The Blasters regrouped on their next possession, showing no signs of calling it quits. At this point in the game there were no secrets remaining and everyone knew what Lewisville would do on their next drive. The Farmers called Rice's number on seven of the next nine plays, the final one being a 14-yard touchdown romp for his third score of the game. Cade connected on the extra point and the Farmers were within striking distance at 33–28, as the pace picked up where it left off in the first half.

The pace altered, however, as the Farmer defense made its presence known, completely dismantling the Coyote attack. In fact, it looked like a totally different ball game as the contest progressed. Apparently Uvalde threw out the trick plays, allowing the Farmer defense to stick to their regular game plan. In doing so Lewisville corralled the Uvalde running backs and receivers, while supplying the offense with several opportunities to add the winning score.

The best opportunity the Farmers had came toward the end of the third period as Allen Fox intercepted the first of two he would pilfer that evening. He returned the ball to the Coyote 23-yard line, where Lewisville set up shop.

1972: A Season to Remember

Allen Fox intercepts a Lynn Leonard pass in the second half of the state championship game.

The Farmers marched to the seven setting up a first-and-goal from that point. The third quarter came to an end, giving the Farmers a brief pause before continuing, what they hoped would be, a touchdown drive to give them the lead for the first time in the game.

On the first play Martin carried to the 5 for a pickup of 2. It was Rice on the next play for a gain inside the 2-yard line, bringing up third-and-goal, about a yard-and-a-half away from the much needed score. Rice carried on the third-down play but was dropped for a half-yard loss back to the 2, and everyone became anxious. This could well have turned out to be the Farmers' last opportunity to score, and with fourth-and-goal at the 2, they didn't want to blow it. The last three plays had been to the right side of the field, but with no success, with Rice doing the chores on two of the three. Lewisville still had many weapons remaining in their arsenal, ready, willing and able to be utilized in this situation. There would be no field goal; that was out of the question.

There was little doubt as to who would do the work on the final play. They could have called upon Randy Cade from his slotback position to try and garner the score on a trip up the middle, a play which had been successful all year. Or they could even try a reverse run/pass option like the one that was supposed to have been used against McKinney before Martin lost his sense of direction. But that may have taken too long to develop, and with so little field to work with, it was too risky a play. They could have hit Angeli on a corner route in the end zone; perhaps he'd have been open, perhaps not. The Farmers had only completed one pass in the game thus far, so the possibility of an air strike at such a critical time was unlikely. Then, too, they could have opted for Nichols on a dive up the middle. After all, with his power he averaged about 4 yards a carry—twice the yards needed. He already had a 15-yard touchdown run earlier in the contest. Surely he could score. Instead, however, they may rather have used him to block as they had throughout the year, leading the way for Rice to race up and down opponents' sidelines. No, Nichols would do the job he was suited for. There is a saying, a cliche, that goes, "You gotta dance with the one that brung ya!," which is a less than sophisticated way of saying that in critical situations it is wisest to go with what worked best, and for the 1972 Fighting Farmers, Paul Rice behind Mike Nichols is what worked best. Rice was their money man, and they would need all his talent if they were to cash in.

The play called was a sweep to Rice around the left side, away from the Lewisville sideline. In actuality, the Farmers were taking everything they had and throwing it against the Coyotes, but not out of desperation; hardly any time had passed in the fourth quarter. It was from a position of strength. By design, Joe Martin would turn and pitch to a moving Rice while Mayes, Nichols, Durham and Martin would lead the charge, allowing Rice to pick an opening and tiptoe into the end zone and the Farmers to go ahead for the first time in the battle. After all, the Farmers expected to win, not just show up.

Uvalde utilized an eight-man front with three defensive backs. The ends played up in a two-point stance; that is, they stood on both feet instead of on all fours like most defensive linemen. Instead of playing it as a normal line position, they played off the line of scrimmage much like a cornerback would. The advantage to this is that it forces the offense to alter their normal blocking scheme, especially with the running game, which comprised about 95 percent of the Farmer game plan. The disadvantage to that style of defensive formation is that once a back breaks through the line of scrimmage there are only three other defenders for him to beat, which Lewisville had great success in doing in scoring four touchdowns. In fact, they had already amassed a yard shy of 300 rushing yards, with Rice accounting for 205 of them. The likelihood of him gaining the 2 yards necessary was good; the odds were in his favor.

He would not have to do it alone either. The entire offensive line had controlled the line of scrimmage much of the night, allowing Rice to accumulate his yardage, the fifth highest in Texas high school playoff history at that time. In fact Rice alone bettered the Uvalde rushing total by more than 50 yards, not to mention the combined contribution of Nichols, Cade and Martin. This, indeed, was the Farmers' strength.

As the play developed the line charged, virtually destroying the Coyote front. Uvalde had 10 men up on the line, with a lone safety out wide to cover the split end should the Farmers have any aspirations of going to the air. As Rice caught the pitch from Martin, already the Blaster machine was at work. Mullins annihilated the man over him, driving him to the ground. McCurley, after centering the ball, charged the noseguard, pushing him back and anything or anyone else who got in the way. Durham, from the left guard position, blocked the safety, who had cheated up just behind the center of the line as would a middle linebacker, and drove him back, much like his father had done some 22 years earlier as a guard for the 1950 regional championship Farmer team. The safety was no contest for Durham. Ladehoff and Cade "blocked down"; that is, they allowed their man to charge past them into the backfield away from the play as they went in search of other Coyotes to skin. Meanwhile, Mayes had pulled from his right guard position and blind-sided the defensive right tackle, taking him completely out of the play and earning a pitchfork, for what it was worth. As Mayes cleared the gap, Nichols and Martin lead the way through the gaping hole in search of a defender, and not finding one until they were 4 or 5 yards deep into the end zone. "Paul should be able to slip across the goal line," they must have thought separately, together, "with a hole this huge."

1972: A Season to Remember

And it appeared he would, too, except for one minor detail. The Uvalde left end, Osburn, lined up on the off side, or opposite side, where the action was headed, and did not charge immediately into the backfield. Instead, he "stayed at home"; that is, he remained in his position until getting an accurate read as to where the ball was, and who had it, and determining what, if anything, he could do about it. When he sniffed out the play he came, undetected, from the opposite side and caught Rice by surprise just before he crossed the goal line, denying the Farmers the go-ahead touchdown. With Rice's momentum one would think he could still have gotten in, however, it looked as if he had not foreseen any contact and was not prepared for the impact, making him an easier target for Osburn to corral. Regardless, the outstanding play on fourth-and-goal cost the Farmers the score.

It cost them the game, too, as it turned out. The Farmers never got any closer to getting into the end zone, even though they had two additional possessions in the remainder of the contest. Since then some fans may have second-guessed Shipman and crew, a thing always easier to do from the bleachers, questioning the decision in giving the ball to Rice when the Coyotes would surely be looking for him to get it. "He should have given it to Nichols," said many. "He would have scored." The truth is, it will never be known if Nichols would have scored, or Cade or Martin for that matter. As surely as it was meant to be for the Farmers to defeat McKinney for the district title to even get an opportunity at the state crown, it was not meant for them to beat Uvalde for whatever reason, and Lewisville would have to look to another season to reach that final goal in obtaining a state championship.

As the clock slowly ticked away, tears began to fall down the cheeks of many of the Farmer faithful. A band member screamed, "No!" in defiance of the inevitable, while mothers and dads gathered their belongings in preparing to make the dreadful exit; it was to be a long drive home. As exhilarating as it was to have beaten McKinney for the district crown, that win was overshadowed by the loss of the state championship game, especially when victory was so close at hand. Joe Martin captured the sentiment of the players and fans 22 years later. When asked how long it took him to get over it, he calmly replied, "I didn't"—which is what you would expect from those 1972 Farmers.

TRADITIONS

Although the 1972 Fighting Farmer football season ended on a sour note, there was much more to be enthused about regarding the Lewisville High School football program. In a single season the Farmers had gone from "worst to first," and with a backfield of underclassmen, the future was bright. Rice had set a new 3A rushing record with 2,359 yards, not to mention Mike Nichols' 1,400-plus yards. Adding that to third year player Randy Cade, Martin, with a year of varsity competition under his belt, and experienced receivers Billy Graham and Mark Angeli, the Farmers had much to build on for the 1973 season. Regardless of the impact the loss to Uvalde had on the players, as well as the community, it would be difficult to mourn the loss in light of the many positive things born out of that season.

Many traditions evolved from the spirit demonstrated during the drive to the championship. After the 2–7–1 finish in 1971, the Farmers and their fans were receptive to any changes that would boost spirit, especially in a program that had been dead for so long. The concept of "Farmer Quarter" was created by Shipman to motivate his players to be conditioned in order to achieve whatever was necessary in that final period. It worked 12 times during the season, failing only twice, but from that year the attitude that the Farmers "owned" the fourth quarter began and is captured in the rhythmic chant of "Far-mer Quar-ter, Far-mer Quar-ter" from the throngs of Farmer fans.

The three-fingered pitch fork was demonstrated by Shipman during one of the pep rallies, and it stuck, remaining as a gesture which demonstrates, "Farmer Power." Most teams indicate their allegiance with the "we're number one!" signal; the index finger pointed upward. Instead, Shipman chose a rather unique way to show spirit by holding the index, middle and ring fingers up, as if ordering three hot dogs from a vendor at a baseball game. The symbol resembles a pitchfork, and became a sign of allegiance to the Maroon and White. When fully engaged, it is displayed by raising both arms straight up into the air like a referee signaling a touchdown. With the pitchforks displayed, the arms begin swaying back and forth to the rhythm of the song, "Big John" played by the band; an impressive sight when viewed from the opposing side.

Several phrases were adopted during that season, serving as a focal point when repeated; sort of a rally cry. Shipman's 4 H's; hang loose, hit hard, have fun and hustle, was the favorite of the head coach's mottos. Then there was 39 for 48 for one; 39 boys, for 48 minutes, for one purpose. This phrase described the unity which characterized the Farmers of '72 who were able to accomplish so much. Offensive line coach Tommy Shields originated a phrase to dispel uncertainties regarding less than perfect weather conditions. A cold or rainy night has often hampered players mentally before a game began, causing a team to lose its focus. Shields coined a phrase that offset the fear by saying, "All weather is Fighting Farmer weather." The coaches taught that, too. In fact, Shipman told the *Lewisville Leader*, "We are developing a mental toughness so that no matter what the weather is like it will be just right as far as the team is concerned." All of the sayings became rally cries of the Farmers to motivate the players to a higher level of achievement.

The Legend of Big John
Of all the traditions begun in 1972, none has played a bigger part of the traditions of Lewisville High School than the creation of Big John. The spirit of Big John is depicted in the Farmer mascot who parades up and down the sideline at Farmer football games but goes deeper than that. For something that be-

1972: A Season to Remember

gan as a motivational anecdote, it quickly developed into the symbol, not only of the team it represented, but also the community from which it evolved.

Shipman, an English teacher as well as coach, was creative, and drew upon his creativity to bring to life a concept born in his mind. What began as a play, a gimmick, soon evolved into a weekly feature the players eagerly anticipated after each Thursday practice. It was the last thing they did on Thursdays. The original story went like this:

> Years ago, Lewisville was a small town, not even a spot on the map. Primarily a farming community, all the roads leading to and from the tiny downtown strip of merchants located there were dirt. Concrete and asphalt had not even been thought about yet, much less invented. Among the stores which dotted the road now called Main Street sat the town's lone saloon, at the end of the dusty trail on the way out of town, which provides the setting for this story.
>
> One day a commotion stirred in the usually quiet town. A farmer, fresh from the field, hopped off the horse he'd ridden into town and went into the saloon. He ordered a drink and gulped it down hurriedly, apparently in some kind of rush. The bartender asked, "What's your hurry, fella?" "Ain't you heard? He's coming!" said the farmer as he left through the swinging doors. The bartender gave him a look of confusion, then shrugged his shoulders and dismissed it.
>
> A bit later a family drove their covered wagon packed with all their belongings through town, stopping at the saloon for a quick drink before making their exit. The father ordered a beer, the mother and children ordered something much softer. After finishing their beverages the mother scooted the kids out the door while dad paid the tab. "Where are ya'll headed?" inquired the barkeep. "Out of town," replied the man. "Gotta get out of town. We're from the east and we're leaving. A guy named Big John's comin'!" Now the bartender was curious. "Who is this Big John character?" he thought out loud. He went outside and looked up and down the street. All he saw was the family's lone wagon headed west. He laughed and ventured back into the saloon to resume his duties, which consisted of little more than waiting for the next customer to come in. After a while other farmers came into the bar one by one for drinks and supplies, all making the same claim about Big John's threatened arrival, all with fear in their eyes. Each farmer that came in was more scared than the one before about the character he had only recently heard of. Regardless of who this Big John was, the bartender didn't mind. Everybody stopped at his saloon on their way out of town and it was good for business.
>
> This had gone on all day, and each time the bartender ignored the warnings of his concerned customers. As the sun was setting some cowboys came riding in from the east, about eight in all. They came through town warning what few citizens remained that they had better leave because Big John was on his way. They stopped at the saloon and notified the bartender about Big John's impending presence, pointing to a huge cloud of dust off to the east. "That's Big John," said one of the cowboys with a lump in his throat, visibly shaken, as a bead of sweat rolled down his face. Upon finally seeing some physical evidence of what was previously believed to be a mythical character, he boarded up all the entrances to the saloon and prepared to evacuate. But before he could get out of the door he heard a big sound of rushing wind, like a tornado, in front of his saloon. Then he heard it stop. It was useless to try to leave. Whatever was out there, he couldn't outrun it. He

peaked through a space between some boards he had loosely hammered into place, to get a glimpse at this figure. What he saw was frightening.

A man—no, a giant—got down off the buffalo he'd ridden into town. When he dismounted he kicked the buffalo and it whimpered off behind the saloon, and he hurled the wildcat he used as a whip into a heap by the front porch. The bartender could tell the man was about 12 feet tall as he stood upright before entering the saloon.

The saloon owner gulped. The mountain-of-a-man moved toward the saloon; no doubt this was Big John.

When he entered the bar he knocked the hinges off the swinging doors. As he walked the earth shook, accompanied by a clap of thunder. The glasses rattled with each step. The bartender, his knees shaking, made his way to the bar as the creature approached. He sat at the bar and swept it clear with his arm, sweeping it first with his left arm then with his right. The timid bartender, his voice shaking, asked, "What c-c-c-can I g-g-get y-y-you, s-s-s-sir?" "Gimme a gallon of whiskey and eight loaves of bread," which he drank with one gulp and ate in one bite each. As he finished, he rose from the crumbling bar stool to go. Before he passed through the door, he turned to the bartender and gruffed, "Don't you think you better leave? Big John's coming, don't you know," and he left. He whistled for his buffalo and it came running. He snapped his fingers and the wildcat jumped to its feet, and soon the giant was on his way.

The saloon owner sat among the ruins of his once profitable saloon. Dejected and frightened, he hardly noticed the meek, but rugged, gentleman enter. He asked the bartender, "Excuse me I can't seem to find anybody around. Where is everybody?" The bartender responded, "They're all gone. Everybody left. Some guy named 'Big John' was coming and nobody wanted to be around when he got here. By the way, I haven't seen you around these parts before. Who are you?" "Why, my name's John. Big John."

The bartender went on to learn that Big John was not the kind of man everyone made him out to be. In fact, he was quite the opposite. Big John, himself, was a farmer who lived on the outskirts of the small town of Lewisville. He rarely came to town except to get supplies; mostly he just stayed to himself. He was always ready and willing to help anyone needing a hand.

Shipman used this side of Big John's personality to motivate his players from week to week. The first week of the 1972 season he told his players that one day, over in Tarrant County, Big John was called over to help some people there. They were having trouble with a guy named "Bully Boswell." Each week Shipman would recite a story about how Big John was needed to defend the honor of some neighboring community, using the mascot of their opponent as the object of his wrath. The concept caught on and Big John is now affixed to the spirit that characterizes the Lewisville Fighting Farmers.

The legend of Big John has been a part of Lewisville football since 1972, being adapted year after year to fit the need of the Farmers' situation. The legend reemerged in 1993 as Lewisville made its drive to the state title.

Farmerette varsity soccer coach Jim Bragg, a member of the 1972 team, was on hand to spin the Big John yarn throughout the year, as well as before

1972: A Season to Remember

the state championship contest. He modified the legend to fit the game against Marcus. Bragg's version went like this:

> Big John is a good guy, who helps all farmers in the area with a magic ax. He uses it to protect the farmers. Big John is the personification of all that is wholesome.
>
> Apparently there were some people in town that were prejudiced against the farmers; they didn't like the way they lived. They were well-to-do, and flaunted it by snubbing their noses at the farmers. They didn't like the farmers, and decided to move west to rid themselves of the backward hicks. They moved west to Flower Mound, but were still close enough to Lewisville to ride in and harass the honest citizens there. Finally, they carried it too far, and began pillaging and stealing from the farmers, so much so that the farmers had to call Big John for help.
>
> The farmers from Lewisville told Big John about these marauders from the west, especially the ring leader, a guy named Marcus. It was his scheme to lure Big John off his farm so that he could take his magic ax. Marcus swore to Big John he would leave the farmers alone, the only catch was that he would have to fight him, with the prize being the ax. If Big John won, then Marcus would go back west and never bother the farmers again. However, if Marcus won he would take the ax and be free to roam the countryside of Lewisville and hound its citizens.
>
> Big John agreed and said he knew a man named Goldsmith who had some land where they could do battle for the ax. Big John was able to defeat Marcus, keeping the ax and the farmers safe from the marauders. Each year they came back to try to get the ax, and sometimes they would take it, but Big John finally threw Marcus Marauder to Copper Canyon and settled the dispute once and for all.

Bragg visited with the team each week in the playoffs of 1993 and told them of some other communities that needed help. Some folks in Burleson had an infestation of Elks that needed removing. Some folks in the southern part of Grand Prairie had constant attacks from a band of Warriors and needed Big John's assistance. Even as far west as Midland folks would call on Big John; something about an insurgence of Rebels.

Others needed help, too. There was a pack of Cougars in Abilene that had to be disposed of, and Big John did the job. There were some Wildcats down in the Temple area that had gotten the best of Big John once, about 14 years earlier, but he skinned them this time. He had been in so many battles, and each time delivered those needing assistance, although he was barely able to get away from those Cougars out The Colony way.

Soon his reputation spread all across Texas, and Big John was called upon by the governor to defend the whole state. The battle was for military control, and their opponent was General MacArthur. That would be the final battle of the year.

Bragg told the Farmers of a time before, when Big John had a chance to defend the state against a pack of Coyotes, but he was unable to do so, coming up a yard short of victory. Bragg assured them that Big John would not come up short again.

Much of what was achieved and originated in 1972 still remains with the

Friday Night Farmers

Lewisville Fighting Farmer football program today. From Farmer Quarter and the three fingered pitchfork, to Big John, all are part of a rich tradition and spirit that is reflected in a winning program. Bill Shipman, after the thrilling come-from-behind victory over the McKinney Lions, captured the essence of Lewisville Fighting Farmer football in a poem called "Friday's Game" published in the *Lewisville Leader* the following Sunday:

> We've played it like it's meant to be
> With all our hearts and souls,
> We've given everything we've had
> And tried to reach our goals
>
> We've had our trials and troubles,
> We've also had our fun,
> We've gutted through the rainy days
> And sweated in the sun.
>
> We've laughed a lot together,
> And together, once, we cried;
> But there never was a single time
> We couldn't say, "We tried!"
>
> And trying, men, is really
> What the game is all about.
> Giving everything you've got
> And always putting out.
>
> Let's play as we have always played;
> Up high, but not uptight,
> Let's take it to them all the way.
> Let's win our biggest fight.
>
> And now it's come to this one game;
> One single Friday night.
> The crown is there for us to wear,
> If we can win the fight.
>
> We know that you can do it, men,
> We love you, every one,
> And we'll rejoice together
> When Friday's game is won.
>
> — Bill Shipman 1972

. . .

CHAPTER

IX

GROWING UP—
MOVING UP TO 4A

THE FARMERS ENJOYED incredible success in the 1972 and '73 seasons with a remarkable 21–3 two year total, including their first ever state final appearance. Nestled in district 6-3A, the Farmers had finally gotten a handle on how to compete at this level, with a combination of broad talent and improvement to the football program, however, the growing population forced LHS upward the following season into the Class 4A division.

The challenge encountered in 4A competition proved to be severe as the Farmers were met with stiff competition in their first year in District 13-4A. New foes were introduced with the 1974 schedule, such as Euless Trinity, Ft. Worth Northside, Denison, Sherman, Denton and Paris, as well as the rekindling of some old rivalries with teams that had been bumped up to 4A several years earlier. Irving, who the Farmers had not played since 1927, and more recently, R.L. Turner (formerly Carrollton), continued a series that had been discontinued after the 1963 season, with Carrollton's realignment. Greenville and Lewisville last met in 1967 and would be matched against one another in the seventh game of 1974, while the contest drawing the most interest for Farmer fans was game number four on the Farmer schedule, featuring the first Lewisville-Plano encounter since the Wildcats defeated the Farmers, 49–0, in 1971.

The schedule was not the only change the Farmer football program would encounter in 1974. With his final two seasons at Lewisville fostering a combined 21–3 record and a state final appearance, Coach Bill Shipman resigned as head coach in 1974 to go to Abilene, Texas, as head coach of Abilene High School. Defensive Coordinator David Visentine, from the 1971, '72 and '73 coaching staff, got the nod as head coach for the Farmers' first year in 4A competition.

Visentine joined the Farmer staff originally in 1971, when Shipman resumed as head coach after a two year administrative stint as an elementary principal. Shipman brought up Tommy Shields from the Lewisville Junior High staff, and added Don Harvey as the offensive back and receiver coach to complete the four-man staff. Although this newly assembled crew could muster only a 2–7–1 record, with the addition of three more coaches the Farmers were able to work through the poor finish in '71 and turn the Lewisville Farmer football program around the following two seasons. With the introduction of the two-platoon system, a system where few players, if any, played both offense and defense, the players were allowed to concentrate on one area of the game, thus maximizing practice time and utilizing more players. Theoretically, this allowed for increased development of highly skilled players to specialize on a small aspect of the game and play only half the time, ensuring they were fresh by not having to be on the field the entire ball game. With the talent pool increasing each year due to the Farmers '72 success, participation appeared to be on the increase with the shift to 4A.

Visentine was a prodigy of the two-platoon system implemented by Shipman and continued its use in 1974. Prior to coming to Lewisville, Visentine spent one year as defensive coordinator and head track coach at San Antonio McCollum High School. Although a pleasant spot, San Antonio was not home for Visentine and his wife, Beth, who were both products of Mineral Wells—located west of Ft. Worth—and he began inquiring about coaching positions in the Metroplex. James Francis, of James McGill Sports Center in Denton, was a mutual friend of both Visentine and Shipman, and he put Visentine on the trail of the opening at Lewisville. He accepted the position offered to him as defensive coordinator, where he served from 1971–73 before accepting the head coaching position made available with Shipman's resignation.

This was not Visentine's first experience as head coach, although it was his first at the 4A level. Prior to his tenure at McCollum High, Visentine spent five years at Keller High School, with the final two as head coach. Keller made playoff appearances in each of Visentine's five seasons, with the deepest penetration to the semifinal round, so winning was not unfamiliar to him. With this background, Visentine had hoped of continuing the success experienced during the Shipman reign.

Growing Up—Moving Up to 4A

The competition at the 4A level proved to be a bit much for the Farmers under Visentine, however, as Lewisville finished 5–5, 4–4–2, 4–6 and 2–8 during the next four seasons. In 1974 the Farmers opened with back-to-back losses to Euless Trinity and Irving, 21–7 and 28–14, and narrowly escaped a third straight loss by defeating Ft. Worth Northside, 14–13, in a last second come-from-behind victory. The Farmers would lose to Plano, R.L. Turner and Denton in the remainder of the '74 schedule, and gain victories over Denison, Greenville, Sherman and Paris to complete the respectable 5–5 season and 3–3 district record.

Besides moving up to 4A competition in 1974, the Farmers' woes were compounded due to a heavy loss of personnel to graduation. The only talent the Farmers had to build upon was two-time All-American tailback Paul Rice, who was returning for his final year of high school competition, along with a handful of players from the '73 team. Of those returning in 1974, only Rice, Wesley Winget and Billy Graham were starters; the rest spent time on special teams and in relief situations when the games were well in hand. So the experience level was minimal going into the '74 season.

The 1975 season brought less success than in '74, with the Farmers finishing 4–4–2 to maintain a .500 clip for Visentine's first two seasons. The year got started off a bit rocky before the first game was played, as the lineup was shuffled during preseason to make up for the apparent loss of the starting fullback to medical complications. The starting backfield had been set in spring training with Bo Stewart at quarterback, Gary Kerbow at fullback and Art Longshore at tailback. All three were seniors set to play in their final season, with Stewart and Longshore returning from the '74 squad. All three had outstanding spring workouts and it appeared the backfield was secure going into the '75 stanza. However, during mandatory team physicals prior to the beginning of fall workouts, it was discovered that Kerbow had developed a hernia and would not be permitted to participate in any athletics without corrective surgery. The only option for Kerbow, who was also starting catcher for the Farmer baseball team, was to undergo surgery three days into the '75–76 school year, anticipating that he would be ready for baseball season the following spring. Any hopes for him playing football were gone. With Kerbow out for the season, Visentine and backfield coach Don Harvey were scrambling to find a replacement.

Stewart, who had been a member of the varsity since his sophomore year, was set to start for the second consecutive season at quarterback. Prior to his sophomore year he had been a strong running back, much like his father, Reveau, had been from 1935–37. Reluctant to change to fullback, Stewart agreed to give it a try for the sake of the team, opening the door for backup quarterback Jeff Eschleman to move into the starting job. Meanwhile, backup fullback Greg Bernard, a junior, had seen the opportunity to both grab the starting job and allow Stewart to remain at quarterback. Bernard met the challenge and started at fullback, allowing Visentine and the Farmers to remain

One of the few reasons to celebrate in 1975—a first quarter touchdown against Plano.

in tact and avoid the severe offensive realignment of personnel. In the background, Kerbow was recovering from his recent surgery.

With the offensive lineup now secure, the Farmers began the season with a convincing 14–0 shutout victory over Euless Trinity, the only victory over the Trojans the Farmers would record in their four meetings since 1974. The following week Lewisville tied a tough Jesuit Ranger team, 7–7. The Ranger offensive and defensive lines were anchored by All-American Bill DeLoach, who stood 6 feet 6 inches, and weighed 275 pounds. Farmer defensive tackle Vernon Brown handled DeLoach defensively, but the bulky defensive tackle thwarted the Farmers offensive efforts, resulting in the 7–7 stalemate. Lewisville handled Ft. Worth Northside in game three with a 30–0 homecoming victory. Where a year earlier the Farmers were 1–2 after three games, the 1975 season found them 2–0–1 going into district play, and, with an open date scheduled the next week, it would give Visentine and his staff extra time to prepare for their first district opponent—the Plano Wildcats.

It appeared the extra time was well spent as the Farmers shocked the Wildcats in the first quarter. A long pass from Stewart to tight end Ken Barr resulted in an early first quarter touchdown. The impact of the score was intensified as an offside penalty called on the play against Plano was refused by Lewisville, allowing the 7–0 score to stand through the first period of play.

Growing Up—Moving Up to 4A

It appeared the Farmers were not a fluke with their 2–0–1 record coming into the Plano contest, however that would soon come to an end. Wildcat quarterback Sammy Bickham warmed up in the second quarter and promptly tossed two of his four touchdown passes he would throw that October 3 evening, leading Plano to a 42-7 victory over the Farmers.

That first quarter against Plano would be one of the few remaining bright spots in the season for the '75 Farmers. The following week would see Lewisville come from a 13–0 deficit to tie Denison's Yellow Jackets, 13–13, and lose the next two games against R.L. Turner and Greenville by a combined score of seven points. The Farmers offensive difficulties continued as Bernard, who arose to fill the fullback spot vacated by the ailing Kerbow, sprained an ankle against Greenville and was listed as doubtful for the eighth game of the year against Denton. Quietly in the wings, however, Kerbow had returned to the roster by game four, seeing minimum playing time against Plano, Denison and Greenville. It was uncertain what he would be able to do in an extended role, but with no options available, Kerbow was slated to start against the Broncos.

The Farmers responded to the adversity and recent tough losses by defeating Denton 28–6, with all the Farmers' points coming in the first half. Lewisville displayed a balanced offensive punch that evening with Kerbow providing 80 yards on 14 carries to lead all rushers.

The Farmers split the final two games of the season, losing to a powerful and quick Sherman team, 28–14, the eventual district winner, and defeating Paris 13–7, to finish 4–4–2. Given the adversity at the outset, the Farmers wound up the season on a positive note.

The 1976 Farmers would win only four games as well, losing six, after district realignment. Lewisville and Denton remained in District 13-4A, but Paris, Sherman, Greenville, Denison and Plano were all dispersed into other districts, while Euless Trinity and Hurst L.D. Bell, along with the three Wichita Falls teams (Rider, Hirschi and Wichita Falls High), were combined to construct the new 13-4A district beginning in 1976. Two of those four victories for Lewisville came against Wichita Falls teams, Hirschi and High, accounting for half of the Farmers' wins, with the other two victories coming against Ft. Worth Western Hills and Denton. Still, disappointing losses to Duncanville, 21–12, to open the season, and Hurst L.D. Bell in game eight, 14–10, and blowout victories over the Farmers by Richardson Berkner, 37–14, R.L. Turner, 31–19, Euless Trinity, 47–7, Wichita Falls Rider, 23–6, and Denton, 17–0, marked the inconsistencies which plagued Lewisville throughout the Visentine empire.

The following season saw the Farmers assigned to a new district, that being District 6-4A. Although it was a new district assignment for Lewisville, the grouping was identical to 1976's 13-4A, retaining its members from the previous two seasons. In fact, Lewisville played the exact same schedule it did the year before, but with less success. The Farmers got but one district victory—two less than they had gotten in '76—and one win outside district, for a 2–8 overall record. The Farmers repeated the non-district win against Western Hills, as they had done in 1976, this time exploding past the Cougars, 41–9, for their second loss against Lewisville in as many years. The Farmers defeated Wichita Falls Hirschi, duplicating the '76 match-up, with a 20–13 margin in game eight. Aside from these two victories, the Farmers' scrapbook was thin for the '77 season.

Lewisville was 1–3 in non-district contests, with the lone win against Western Hills, while being completely dominated by Duncanville and R.L. Turner, 31–16 and 49–21, and played Richardson Berkner relatively close, losing by a 10-point margin, 23–13. District play opened against Euless Trinity, with the Trojans showing no mercy on Lewisville by racking up 50 points, while surrendering only 10. The following three games, all district contests, are what sunk the Farmers' ship in '77, as they dropped three straight contests by a total of 11 points. Lewisville lost to Wichita Falls High in Wichita Falls, 14–7, before surrendering a disappointing homecoming loss to Wichita Falls Rider, 20–17. The final loss of this three-game stretch came on the road against Hurst L.D. Bell. The Farmers' 21–20 defeat was a bitter pill to swallow, leaving them little to play for during the remainder of the season. Lewisville mustered enough pride to capture their only district victory over Wichita Falls Hirschi, 20–13, before ending the season on a sour note, losing a 55–25 free-for-all against Denton.

Visentine had inherited a difficult situation when he took over the reins from Bill Shipman in 1974. With a 21–3 record in 1972 and '73 to finish their stay in 3A competition, the Farmers were thrown into the 4A fire with few weapons to defend themselves. Though Paul Rice was clearly a viable talent at any level of competition, he was not enough. There were few who complemented Rice, such as Bo Stewart, Shawn Wood, Wesley Winget and Billy Graham on offense, and Terry Cade, Steve Beggs and LeRoy Deaver on defense, but there just simply was not enough talent to be competitive in 4A ball at the level those in Lewisville had been accustomed.

And there are those who would argue, legitimately so, that Shipman, upon seeing the talent pool rapidly depleting, decided to get while the gettin' was good, leaving his successor, in this case Visentine, holding the proverbial bag like an innocent man who had foolishly picked up a smoking gun at the scene of a crime—not guilty, but the prime suspect responsible for the death of a successful program.

Regardless of who, if anybody, was solely responsible for the demise, it was apparent that Shipman's successor would have some work to do. The blame, if any, could have just as well been placed on the growth of the community, forcing the Farmers into a new level they were not ready for. Whether he knew it or not, Visentine was raising an awkward child, forced to master a body he was yet ready to occupy.

Some citizens in the community conducted a witch hunt of sorts, circulating several petitions which insisted on Visentine's ousting. Others silently

Growing Up—Moving Up to 4A

felt sympathy and understanding. Most Farmer faithfuls realized the changes Visentine and the Farmers were experiencing and held an optimistic hope in their hearts; others complained and criticized the Farmers and their coaching staff. The truth was, simply, there were not enough talented bodies to go around, thus contributing to the plummeting of the Farmer football program in similar fashion to the way it did from 1958–71.

Regardless of the sentiment of the community toward the football program, Visentine felt responsible for the demise of a program that many felt was in perfect working order when he took it over and managed to dismantle it somehow, as a spoiled child would do with a new toy received at Christmas. Visentine had already proven himself capable as a head coach while at Keller, capturing district titles in both of his seasons as head coach. He had been valuable as an assistant in contributing defensive schemes in three separate programs that had accounted for five district crowns in eight seasons as a defensive coordinator, with one of those seasons a second place final and a 9–1 record. It was evident that Visentine was not afraid of success, he just could not make it work in Lewisville at a time when the Farmers had come off, perhaps, the best two-year period in their history. The pressure was complicated by two factors; taking the place of the popular Shipman, and coaching the All-American Paul Rice in his final season, where, Visentine feared, much of Rice's future success might depend on his senior year. With this combination of pressure, Visentine resigned after the four-year stint as head coach of the Lewisville Fighting Farmers to make way for his successor, who would have the challenging task of rebuilding a program which had been shaken off course, somehow, from the winning foundation it had been built upon.

. . .

CHAPTER

THE WILSON YEARS

BY THE END OF THE 1977 SEASON the Farmer football program was in need of a shot in the arm. Lewisville had finished a combined 15–23–2 from 1974–77 under the direction of David Visentine, and he was not retained after the '77 season, by mutual agreement between himself, Athletic Director Max Goldsmith and Superintendent Leo C. Stuver. With the resignation final, Visentine rejoined Bill Shipman in Andrews, Texas, as an assistant, leaving Goldsmith and company with the task of finding a successor that would turn the program around that had dipped below the .500 mark the previous four years.

Goldsmith began the process in December 1977 by advertising for and interviewing prospective candidates for the Farmer head coaching spot. He received much interest in the position, being bombarded with inquiries from across the state, from the Gulf Coast to the panhandle, and it was his responsibility to select three finalists. After weeding through the papermill of hopefuls and conducting the necessary interviews, Goldsmith narrowed the field

The Wilson Years

to three prime choices, each with a history of running competitive programs. The three finalists would then appear before a committee of four school officials: Dr. Weldon Parks, School Board Member; Mr. Ben Harmon, former head coach and LHS principal; Clayton Downing, Personnel Director; and Goldsmith. Doyle Parker from Bellville High School, James Hyden from the Arlington School District and Neal Wilson from Eagle Mountain-Saginaw's Boswell High School were the ones selected by Goldsmith to appear before the committee. All three applicants were given careful consideration, but ultimately, by unanimous consent of the committee members, Neal Wilson was named as Visentine's successor as head coach of the Lewisville Fighting Farmers. As for Parker and Hyden, each went on to productive careers in athletics. Currently, both hold athletic director positions. Parker is an assistant athletic director at Texas Tech University in Lubbock, Texas, and Hyden is the Athletic Director of the Arlington Independent School District.

Wilson, although new to the Farmer football program, was not new the Lewisville, as he began his coaching career in 1965 as the eighth grade football and basketball coach at Lewisville Junior High, where he stayed for one year. In 1966 he went to Decatur as an assistant for two seasons before becoming head coach in 1968. He remained at Decatur through 1970, then landed the head coaching position at Boswell, where he remained until the conclusion of the 1977 season. The job at Lewisville High School was his third, and last, head coaching job. Wilson reported to work on February 1, 1978, and began the task of rebuilding the waning Farmer program.

The first step in this process was to assemble a coaching staff, as those left from the Visentine era vanished one by one to either other jobs or other coaching opportunities elsewhere. Of the six assistants under Visentine in 1977, his final year, two are still employed in the Lewisville I.S.D. Tom Kupper, then offensive line coach, is currently the Director of Maintenance. Prior to this position he was Director of Transportation from 1978–1982. Don Harvey, offensive coordinator under both Shipman and Visentine, was a counselor and Assistant Principal at Lewisville High School after the '77 season, before becoming Principal at Timbercreek Elementary. The other four coaches each went their own way leaving a vacant coaching staff waiting on Wilson when he arrived.

After Wilson assembled his staff they began the chore of evaluating the talent and putting together an offensive and defensive scheme the Farmers would employ in the Fall of 1978. The combination of talent and coaching under Wilson's leadership turned out to be the right one, as the Farmers posted a 9–1 record in the new head coach's inaugural season. The Farmers lost their bi-district bid against Odessa Permian, 17–7, in Abilene's Shotwell Stadium. This was a game the young, rejuvenated Farmers had a chance to win, according to Wilson. Lewisville led 7–6 going into the fourth quarter, but the Farmers were facing a stiff wind, as well as a stiff Panther team. With the wind, Permian kicked a field goal to go ahead 9–7, and later scored a touchdown and two

FRIDAY NIGHT FARMERS

The 1978 Fighting Farmers — Champions of District 6-4A

point conversion for the final 17–7 margin. Though a disappointing loss, Wilson, the Farmers and the fans were ecstatic over the turn around from the 2–8 finish in 1977 to the 9–2 finish in 1978.

A key to the success in 1978 was the starting backfield for Lewisville. The wishbone backfield featured Dale Brown, Eddie Tillman and Freddie Wells, with Dwayne Wilson and Jeff Shoemake alternating at quarterback. This was, perhaps, the most talented trio of running backs featured in a Farmer backfield. Each one of the three possessed both power and speed, and were a threat to score from anywhere on the field, making them difficult to defend against. Shoemake had exceptional speed as well, and added a fourth dimension to the wishbone offense Coach Wilson installed in the spring of '78. Brown, Tillman, Shoemake and Dwayne Wilson (no relation to the coach), had taken their lumps in 1977 during the 2–8 drought, but gained valuable experience in varsity competition in '78. Shoemake, a member of the Farmers since his sophomore year in 1976, returned for his third year of varsity competition. The addition of Wells completed an already set backfield which proved formidable during the '78 stanza. Had it not been for an injury to Tillman at mid-season the Farmers may have scooted past Odessa Permian and penetrated deep into the playoffs. Besides the loss to the Panthers, the only other loss the Farmers encountered was to the Arlington High Colts, 31–14, in week four of '78. Regardless, the Farmers outscored their opponents in Coach Neal Wilson's first season 354–142, including a 68–15 thumping of R.L. Turner.

The win against Turner was the first victory over the Lions since the Farmers moved into 4A in 1974. In fact, prior to 1978 the Lions had owned the Farmers, defeating them 10 straight times, and 14 times since the two teams first met in 1937. Lewisville defeated Carrollton in the first meeting between the two schools in 1937, 18–2, under coach R.E. Mattingly. In 1962 Carrollton

High School was renamed R.L. Turner High School, and sported powerful teams during the mid-to-late '60s. With blue-chip players like Bill Montgomery and Clifford Hodge, a lethal quarterback-to-wide receiver combination, the Lion offensive attack yielded many long scoring plays. Montgomery went on to quarterback at the University of Arkansas, and Hodge played at both Oklahoma University and North Texas State University after graduating from Turner High. Hodge also played in the Oil Bowl, the annual All-Star game between Texas and Oklahoma All-Stars. He was also voted to the All-Texas team of the '60s and named Best Receiver in Texas of that decade.

Two of Hodge's three brothers also played at Carrollton High/ R.L. Turner. His oldest brother, Kenneth, was a wide receiver like Clifford, and was a two-time All-American, first at Carrollton, then at Baylor University where he played his college ball. In one college all-star game he received passes from notable quarterbacks Jerry Rhome and Roger Staubach. He played one year for the Houston Oilers before a leg injury ended his short professional career.

The youngest of the Hodge brothers was Bill Hodge. He played wide receiver in the late '60s and went on to play at Trinity University in San Antonio. There he set many scoring and receiving records and was named All-American in 1973.

Since Neal Wilson became head coach of the Farmers, however, Lewisville holds a 6–2 advantage through the 1993 season, so the Carrollton/R.L. Turner jinx seems to have dissipated. Besides breaking the 10 game losing streak to the Lions with the 68–15 win, this game was also the fourth highest scoring game in Farmer history.

The splendid play of the Farmers in Wilson's first season as head coach landed many Farmers on the all-district teams, including the 6-4A Sophomore of the Year, Offensive Player of the Year and the Coach of the Year. Two out of the trio of running backs, Dale Brown and Freddie Wells, were named to the first team All-District team, with Brown named as Offensive Player of the Year. Jeff Shoemake, one of the alternating quarterbacks, also made the first team. Linemen Scott Marshall, Tim Webb and Edward Murphy, along with place-kicker Jesse Garcia, completed the first team selections for the '78 season, while Wilson was a unanimous selection for Coach of the Year of District 6-4A. Brown and Garcia were also named to the first team the previous season. Mike Burt, now a coach at Flower Mound Marcus High School, was named Sophomore of the Year. The Farmers also had 12 members named to the second team, including Dwayne Wilson, the other quarterback in the Farmers' rotation of signal callers, and Rory Durham, another current member of the Marauder coaching staff.

1979

The 1979 Farmer football season brought more success than the previous one, resulting in a semifinal playoff appearance and Neal Wilson's best career finish as a head coach. The Farmers went 12–1–1 on the year, tying the 1972 state final team for most wins in a season by a Farmer team. The addition of the regional playoff round allowed the '79 Farmers the opportunity to win the same number of games without reaching the state finals. The extra round was necessary to accommodate the expanding number of teams in 4A competition.

The Farmers played a tough pre-district schedule, opening with a 14–9 victory over the Duncanville Panthers. Lewisville had beaten the Panthers for the second straight year, but prior to the '78 season the Farmers were 0–4 against them. Lewisville and Duncanville had played six times from the season the teams first met in 1966, until 1979, and each time it was the opening game of the year. The Farmers would tie the Panthers in 1980, 21–21, and beat them again in 1981, 32–18, giving the series edge to Duncanville 4–3–1. These two teams have never met in either a district contest or post-season play.

With the narrow victory over Duncanville, and victories over Richardson Berkner and Arlington Bowie, 16–7 and 14–7, and a tie in week four against Arlington High School, 14–14, there was a question mark as to the offensive ability of the 32-plus point scoring average displayed in 1978. Even a 19–10 homecoming win over the Bishop Lynch Friars was nothing to jump up and down about, aside from the fact that the Farmers were still undefeated at 4–0–1 entering district play.

However, the tough non-district portion of the schedule allowed the Farmers' offense, seasoned with veterans from the 1978 playoff team, to develop as they rolled up 196 points in the five remaining contests in regular season, averaging 39.2 points per game. At the same time, the stingy Farmers defense surrendered a mere 26 points in district play, indicating that Lewisville was peaking at the proper time on both sides of the football.

With a 9–0–1 regular season record, Wilson and his Farmers were set for the bi-district round of the playoffs for the second consecutive year. After losing the bi-district contest against Odessa Permian in 1978, the Farmers would open playoff competition by facing another stiff West Texas foe. The opponent slated for the Farmers was the highly touted Abilene Cooper Cougars, well stocked with first class athletes and a ranking as both the state's and nation's number one high school football team. The powerful Cooper offense centered around their prominent fullback Terry Orr, along with tailback Keith Pantalion. Each had 700 or more yards rushing for the season to compliment the passing talents of quarterback John Slaughter, rounding out the balanced Cougar offensive attack. Overall, Cooper pounded out 341 yards per game, 200 by land and 141 by air, behind the massive offensive line, which averaged 200 pounds per man. The Cougars had another 700-yard producer in Slaughter as a passer, throwing primarily to his favorite receiver, David Williams, who netted 22.5 yards per catch.

Slaughter, Orr and Pantalion combined to account for 2,100-plus of Cooper's 3,410 regular season total yards, so the Farmers would have their hands full in their bi-district playoff tilt as they had against Odessa Permian the year before.

The Wilson Years

Farmer Coach Neal Wilson passes out bumper stickers that read "Beat Cooper," after the 1979 victory over Denton. The win wrapped up the District title and earned Lewisville the right to play the Cougars.

To indicate the level of talent on the highly touted Cooper team who was to square off against the Farmers, Orr, the big fullback, after completing his final season as a Cougar in 1979, attended the University of Texas at Austin in the fall of 1980. Orr eventually was shifted to the tight end position, where he finished his career as a Longhorn. The move proved fruitful for him as he was selected in the 1983 NFL draft by the Washington Redskins.

Neither Wilson nor Cooper head coach Ray Overton expected a high scoring contest, as each had lavished the other's accomplishments of the regular season with accolades and respect, the way coaches are supposed to do so as not to give the opposing team an unnecessary reason to get fired up. Wilson played the part of the underdog as Ronald Reagan had done in the Knute Rockne story, but without the drama. He was confident in his Farmers, especially with the experience his young team had gained from the previous year's thumping by Odessa Permian. Although a loss, it was not for naught as the Farmer coach would record it in a mental file to draw upon at the next opportune time. That time would come just 12 months later where he, and the Farmers, found themselves up against yet another West Texas challenger.

Overton, on the other hand, was busy trying to play down his team's number one ranking, counting it more of a curse than a blessing. He felt the number one spot actually hurt the Cougars instead of helping them, although their 10–0 regular season mark did not reveal it, which included victories over Wichita Falls High, Midland Lee and Odessa Permian, as well as powerful 3A perennial state contender Brownwood. Even the media had the Farmers picked as a 17 point underdog. Regardless of the reputation of either team, Lewisville and Abilene Cooper would have to shed themselves of their regular season accomplishments and get set to take on each other in the "second season" of the year.

So the powerful Cougars came to town to meet Lewisville at Texas Stadium on November 23, 1979. Undoubtedly this would be the biggest game of the year for the Farmers, and Wilson as well, in just his second year as the Lewisville mentor. The Farmers' potent running attack, featuring Freddie Wells and Greg Jenkins, and quarterbacks Rex Cole and Hal Stewart, provided a steady diet of wishbone for the Cougars, but oddly enough, it was the passing game which would provide the key play of the contest.

Wilson's prophesy came true in regard to the defensive nature of the game. The first half ended in a 0–0 stalemate. In fact, each team played the majority of the first half in their own end of the field, with each team crossing the midfield stripe only once. The deepest penetration by either team was by Cooper, as they infiltrated the Farmer turf to the 42-yard line. The Farmers could only manage to reach the Cooper 48. Freddie Wells did have the longest gain of the half for Lewisville with a 12-yard first quarter run, but all in all it was a defensive chess match which Wilson felt played into the Farmer game plan.

Although they had not scored, Lewisville counted the first half as theirs with the success of shutting down the two-edged running attack and highly touted aerial game, that had averaged 341 yards and nearly 38 points per game. With the score knotted at zero, and neither team having a penetration inside their opponent's 20-yard line, the attention began to turn to the next tie breaker under the University Interscholastic League rules—the total number of first downs—should the game remain deadlocked. Cooper had the edge in this category, 3–2, so the objective observer might have given the Cougars the edge for the first half, but those present could see the Farmers were poised for an upset given their first half defensive accomplishments. The first half resembled the notorious international chess match between America's Bobby Fischer and the Soviet Union's Boris Spassky in 1972. Each spent the first day or so feeling each other out, waiting for the other to make a costly mistake of which he could take advantage. That was how Wilson and Overton had spent the opening half.

The Farmers got the first break of the game as Lewisville's Sam Shost pounced on a loose football at Abilene Cooper's 31-yard line to open the second half. Forty-three seconds later, Farmer fullback Greg Jenkins stormed over from 4 yards out for the first score of the intense contest. The play had been set up by a 27-yard gain by Wells on the first play after the fumble recovery. The point-after attempt failed due to a high snap, but the Farmers had stung a stunning blow quickly in the second half in a manner like Muhammed Ali would lull Joe Frazier or Larry Holmes through six rounds before delivering a sharp jab to gain control of a fight. In the words of Bobby Fischer during that infamous chess match, "check."

The blow served more as a wake-up call as the Cougars regrouped on the next drive and marched 69 yards for the go-ahead score. Orr carried it over from the 1, followed by a Kyle Stuard extra-point to give Cooper a narrow 7–6 lead.

"Check," muttered the Russian.

After a Farmer punt the Cougars added another three points on a 30-yard Stuard field goal, capping off a nine-play, 54-yard drive. The score stood 10–6 in favor of Cooper, and although not pressing, time was beginning to run out for Lewisville. In a game such as this, Wilson knew his Farmers wouldn't get many more chances to capture the lead.

"Your move," said Spassky, with a slight grin.

It appeared the Farmers would go ahead early in the fourth quarter as Lewisville got a much needed break. Defensive end Jeff Kammerer sneaked through the Abilene Cooper offensive line to partially block a Cougar punt on a third-down quick kick from inside their own end zone. The Farmers recovered the ball and set up shop 21 yards from the Cooper goal line and, hopefully, the go ahead score. Wilson licked his lips while Overton sweated a little.

Fisher contemplated his next move as Spassky squirmed in his chair.

Lewisville's ensuing drive reached the Cooper 1-yard line where the Farmers and Wilson faced a dilemma. Although the stiff Lewisville defense had given up little to the Cougars on the day, likewise, the Farmers had not set any offensive records themselves, evidenced by the six lone points scored by them thus far in the contest. The Farmers faced a fourth-down-and-one situation, needing to push the ball, somehow, across the goal line and into the end zone. A field goal was out of the question, Wilson knew, so the problem was how to get the ball across. Wells was having a decent game, so it was no surprise that the coaching staff would call his number. That they did, on a plunge up the middle. Overton and his staff figured Wells would get the handoff as well, and the Cougar defense stacked him up at the line for no gain, thus dodging a Farmer bullet with the clock still ticking away.

Wilson had considered going wide on that critical fourth down, but success up the middle throughout the evening persuaded him to hand it off to Wells behind the highly talented offensive line, anchored by center Rory Durham. The play backfired, not so much because of the failure of the Farmer offense, but rather due to an outstanding effort by the Cougar defense. *Tick, tick, tick . . .*

So, with the unsuccessful fourth-down attempt, the Farmers turned the ball over on downs to the West Texas foe at their 1-yard line. "Fine," thought Overton and company. "A nice, long, game-ending drive, get back on the bus and beat the sun back to Abilene." *Control the ball, control the ball . . .*

Cooper did control the ball, but only for a while, as the Cougars' drive stalled at the same 21-yard line where Lewisville took over just a possession earlier. Facing fourth-and-long, a punt was in order. After a 43-yard kick the Farmers began their biggest drive of the season thus far from their own 36-yard line with 3:26 remaining; still enough time to salvage the bi-district title.

Lewisville had depended on the run throughout the season and continued to do so against Cooper, but with time dwindling and the Cougar defense finally getting a handle on the Farmer running attack, Wilson thought it might be time to mix things up a bit, not waiting for desperation to tip his hand. From their 36-yard line, the Farmers began a calculated effort of simultaneously moving the ball into the end zone and erasing the clock. A first-down running play was accomplishing one-half of their plan in chewing up time, however the ball wasn't any closer to the end zone. With second-and-long, on perhaps their last drive, the Farmers lined up, still at their own 36. Hal Stewart, in at quarterback, faded back and hurled one of the few passes the Farmers had thrown all season, and one of eight they would throw that night. On the other end of that pass attempt, down the left sideline, sprinted Eugene Corbin, who somehow got behind his two defenders, leaped in the air and snagged his only pass reception of the year to date. After making the catch Corbin fell to the turf of Texas Stadium 28 yards downfield, to keep the drive, and the Farmers' bi-district hopes, alive.

The run had indeed set up the pass, even though it was such an obvious passing down. The Farmers suddenly found themselves on the Cooper 36-yard line with new life and a fresh set of downs. *Tick, tick, tick . . .* No need to panic; still enough time. After the Farmers regrouped Wells gobbled up a quick 11 yards, then Stewart tossed another strike to the 12, this time to the other wide receiver, Eric Ferris. The completion to Ferris set up the go-ahead touchdown on the Farmers' next play. Stewart optioned to his right, making a last second pitch to Wells, who tiptoed down the sideline past the Cougar defenders and in for the score. He was close to stepping out of bounds as he struggled to maintain his balance after turning upfield on the option run. Wilson, Wells and the entire Lewisville entourage held their collective breaths awaiting the referee's call. No out of bounds signal . . . no yellow flag. Touchdown! The sidelines, along with the south side of Texas Stadium, erupted with the call. Steve Bernhard's extra point attempt split the uprights and the Farmers, again striking quickly, were nestled atop a 13-10 lead with little time remaining.

"Check!" uttered Fischer, with an assuring smile on his face.

The go-ahead touchdown drive covered 64 yards on seven plays but chewed up only 2:02 of the 3:36 remaining when the drive began. This left

The Wilson Years

Cooper with 1:34 to work with before the ensuing kickoff, and with their prolific passing game the Cougars were far from calling it a night. From their own 43-yard line Cooper attempted four straight passes, each one falling incomplete and with it, easing a bit of the anxiety felt by the Farmers and their fans. As the final pass plummeted to the tartan turf, where Clint Longley had engineered a thrilling comeback for the Cowboys on Thanksgiving Day of 1974 filling in for the dazed Roger Staubach, it appeared Stewart and the Farmers had done likewise, and two thirds of the 15,760 fans let out a collective sigh of relief that had weathermen and women in the metroplex scrambling to find out from where the newly formed high pressure system originated. With 1:01 left on the clock, the Farmers again took over, with no time outs remaining in the Cougars account. All the Farmers had to do was run three plays and it would be over. *Check . . . and, mate.*

Oh no, not so fast. At this point in the game a strange thing occurred that confused the players and fans equally. The Farmers were penalized three straight times for illegal procedure, marching them backward from the Cougar 43 into their own territory. The combination of the lost yardage and the inability to devour the remaining time on the clock forced the Farmers to punt with just under a minute remaining. Enter Dallas Wotlin.

Although the running of Wells and passing of Stewart were big factors in this contest, perhaps equally so was the punting of Dallas Wotlin. Averaging a respectable 36.6 yards per punt, Wotlin had pinned the Cougars inside their own 10-yard line most of the night with accurate kicks angled for the corner. The poor field position virtually removed the passing attack from the Cooper game plan, allowing the Farmers to concentrate on halting the fierce running game, which they did. And when the Cougars did pass, they simply weren't affective as they had been throughout the regular season, averaging just shy of 4 yards per catch. So from his 42-yard line Wotlin performed his magic once again, kicking the ball out of bounds at Cooper's 9-yard line, both preventing a possible runback and leaving the Cougars to travel 91 yards in the 48 remaining seconds. *Check mate at last.*

No yet. Lanny Dycus had replaced John Slaughter at quarterback for the Cougars and immediately stung the Farmer prevent defense for a 52-yard completion to David Williams. As quickly as the Farmer faithful had relaxed, they were back on the edge of those blue stadium seats with twice the anxiety as before, as Cooper began the next series at the Lewisville 39. Only 10 to 15 more yards would put them in field goal range, enough to tie and let them slip out of town with a 13–13 tie, but be able to advance due to an edge in penetrations. They got 9 of those yards on the next play with another completion from Dycus to Williams, but had only five seconds remaining. It all boiled down to this final play.

Spassky downed a shot of vodka and lit up another cigarette while Fischer extended his hand.

Overton felt that a 40-yard field goal attempt was too risky, so he elected to

FRIDAY NIGHT FARMERS

Farmer running back Freddie Wells eludes an Abilene Cooper tackler at midfield during the 1979 Bi-District contest. Wells scored the go-ahead touchdown late in the game to secure the win.

go for all the marbles on a final pass attempt. The Farmers, in their prevent defense, never had to worry about the pass, as noseguard Edward Murphy sacked Dycus, who had rolled left looking, no doubt, for Williams in the end zone. The sack ended the game and gave the Farmers the bi-district crown. *Check, and mate . . . finally.* The fat lady had sung, and Big John was pleased.

Wells finished the game as the night's leading rusher with 121 yards on 23 carries, going over the 1,000-yard barrier with 1,010 total yards on 143 carries and 16 touchdowns on the season. All in all, the game's final totals told the story. Cooper actually had more total yards than Lewisville, with 238 to the Farmers' 226, however a good bit of that came on the 52-yard Williams completion on the final drive. Aside from that play, the Farmer defense held the Cougars to 186 yards, 155 yards below their season average. The Farmers edged Cooper in first downs, 13–12, and rushing yardage 165 to 118. Cooper had the edge in passing yardage with 120 to Lewisville's 60, including the 52-yarder late in the game. Aside from that single play, the game was extremely even down the line.

There was an explanation for the rash of procedure penalties against the Farmers while trying to run out the clock. It seems, in a desperate measure, some of the Cougar defenders were simulating Stewart's signal calling, causing some offensive players to jump. This tactic, against the rules and worth a 15-yard unsportsmanlike conduct penalty, somehow went undetected by the officials, thus allowing Cooper that final opportunity to evade defeat. This tactic was not a new experience for the Farmers, however. Odessa Permian had done that the previous year when they defeated Lewisville in the 1978

The Wilson Years

Lewisville v. Abilene Cooper
Bi-District Championship: November 23, 1979
Texas Stadium — Irving, Texas
Game at a Glance

Lewisville		Abilene Cooper
13	First Downs	12
47–165 (3.5)	Yards Rusing	38–118 (3.11)
60	Passing	120
7–36.6	Punts	7–36
8–50	Penalties	4–30
–0–	Fumbles Lost	1
226	Total Yards	238

bi-district game, 17–7. Regardless of their motivation, the efforts of the Abilene Cooper Cougars just simply weren't enough for the 1979 Lewisville Fighting Farmers, who were focused and well prepared for one of the biggest wins in Farmer history.

Clearly, the bi-district win was the highlight of the 1979 season. Regional and quarter final victories over Ft. Worth Arlington Heights, 28–12, and El Paso Coronado, 15–7, both played at Texas Stadium, set up the semifinal showdown with the Temple Wildcats, also at Texas Stadium. The Wildcats were 13–0 and had been ranked number one since the Farmers knocked off Cooper in the bi-district game three weeks earlier. Lewisville, too, was undefeated with a 12–0–1 record and ranked as the number three team in the state. The stage was set for a potentially thrilling state semifinal contest.

Farmer fullback Greg Jenkins fumbles into the end zone against Coronado. Jenkins recovered the fumble for a Farmer score in their 15–7 win.

Both teams were capable of breaking a game wide open as Temple averaged 34 points per game, while the Farmers averaged 26. Though both offenses were potent, they were as different as night and day. The Wildcats featured a wide open offensive attack to take advantage of their team speed, while the Farmers preferred a grind-it-out type of ball control offense. Again, Wilson predicted the possibility of a defensive battle, much like the Cooper game had been, and hinted that if it was the Farmers would have the advantage, citing the need to control the line of scrimmage. "If we control the line of scrimmage, we win. If we don't control it, we're in trouble," Wilson confided to *Daily Leader* Sports Editor Dudley Green.

Though successful in controlling the line of scrimmage, the Farmers neglected an essential element for victory; the elimination of mistakes. On the opening drive Lewisville, under Stewart's direction, drove to the Temple 7-yard line with their patented ball control offense, only to fumble it away back at the Wildcat 11. That was as close as either team came to getting the ball in the end zone, as Temple experienced trouble against the finely tuned Farmer defense. Late in the second quarter, just before the end of the first half, a shanked Dallas Woltin punt fluttered only 14 yards, going out of bounds at the Farmer 41 and giving Temple a golden opportunity. They set up shop at the 41, driving to the Farmer 9 before the defense stiffened, disallowing the Wildcats entrance to the end zone. Temple elected to attempt a field goal in hopes of stealing three points before slipping into the locker room for a coke and a rework of their game plan. Kevin Korompoi booted the ball the necessary 27 yards for the score, and Temple led 3–0 at the half.

The first half had been a classic defensive high school football game, marred only by the early first quarter Farmer fumble. Aside from a few routine offensive adjustments, there would be no major changes made at the half. No X's and O's drawn on the board or remodeled defensive schemes. There would be encouraging words from the coaches and between the players themselves. The fact was, it was anybody's ball game to win.

It appeared the Farmers would get that opportunity early in the second half, as an alert Steve Hunter recovered a Temple fumble at the Wildcat 39 at the 10:50 mark in the third period. At worst, the Farmers should come away with a 3–3 tie, which would tip things in the favor of Lewisville, having a 2–1 advantage in penetrations. Actually, the worst scenario would be that Wilson and company would come away empty-handed, which is what happened. The Farmers drove to the Wildcat 8-yard line before suffering an ill-timed illegal motion penalty which stalled the drive. No problem—just kick a field goal, which is what the Farmers did, or attempted to do. A bad snap eliminated the field goal possibility, and the Farmers began to get dejected. Wilson knew that opportunities like this were precious and his crew couldn't afford to let any more pass by without cashing in. The game was growing older and older.

Lewisville began another possession early in the final quarter and it ap-

The Wilson Years

peared that they had figured out how to move the ball against the Temple defense. The drive went 14 plays before fizzling out with the nose of the ball between the Wildcat 19 and 20-yard line. Although not entirely across the 20, it was good enough for another penetration, giving the Farmers a 3–1 lead in that category, but still behind on the scoreboard 3–0. Now the Farmers faced a fourth-down-and-three situation at that spot, and Wilson decided to play the percentages by settling for a field goal. A tie score at this point in the game would most likely hold up and the Farmers would advance on the merit of the 3–1 advantage in penetrations inside the opponent's 20-yard line; the first tie breaker under the playoff format derived by the UIL.

The field goal attempt would come from the Wildcat 27-yard line, making it a 37-yard effort for sophomore kicker Steve Bernhard to convert. Bernhard had been successful on several field goals during the season, and the 37-yarder was definitely within his range. As the Farmers lined up, Temple, in a strategic move to distract Bernhard, called time out. Apparently the move worked, as Bernhard's kick had plenty of range but missed outside the right upright. Wilson had contemplated going for the first down instead of the field goal but felt his Farmers might not get another chance to score. They had to come away with some points from the 14-play drive, so the Farmer head coach decided to go for the tie. The defense had held Temple in check all evening, so the decision to settle for a tie was a pretty safe bet, had Lewisville been able to score.

But that wasn't the case and Temple took over on the missed field goal attempt at their own 20, with little time remaining. The Farmers got one last chance deep inside their own territory with 57 seconds left, but a Stewart pass was intercepted at the Lewisville 8, ending their last opportunity, and with it, the 1979 "Cinderella" season. Had Lewisville defeated Temple in the

The 1979 State Semi-Finalists

semifinal game they would have had a strong chance at a state championship, as the Wildcats went on to beat Spring Branch Memorial the following week for the state title, 28–6. No doubt the Farmers were the toughest foe of the season for the Wildcats.

The 12-1-1 finish of 1979 was Wilson's best finish as the head coach of the Lewisville Fighting Farmers, and the post-season honors reflected the success achieved from the semifinal finish. Lewisville landed 13 players on the first team All-District team, including Freddie Wells as Offensive Player of the Year and Edward Murphy as Defensive Player of the Year. Neal Wilson was named Coach of the Year for the second consecutive season as well. Fourteen Farmers also made the second team. Rory Durham and Wells were named to the All-State first team, the first Farmers selected since 1973. Dallas Wotlin, Edward Murphy and Rod Fearnside were named to the All-State's second team.

1980 to 1985

Going into the 1980 season there were a lot of expectations of the Farmers, based on the 1979 semifinal playoff appearance. The University Interscholastic League revised the classifications by eliminating the Class B division and renaming it the "A" division. Consequently, each division ahead was changed with 1A becoming 2A, 2A becoming 3A, and so on, making the highest classification 5A, which was formerly 4A. The enrollment requirements did not change, just the nomenclature, so the Farmers competed at the 5A level for the first time in 1980, along with the rest of the former 4A teams.

Also, going into the 1980 season the Farmers were ranked number one in the state despite losing skill players like Wells, Stewart and Jenkins to graduation. Going into his third season, Neal Wilson, with a 21-3-1 two-season record, had hopes of leading the Farmers to that elusive first state championship. Along with that number one ranking came the accompanying pressure, much like the pressure Bill Shipman and company felt after their 1972 state final appearance. They, too, were ranked number one the following year.

Wilson had an indication during a preseason scrimmage against the Richland Rebels that things would not fare as well as the predictors forcasted. A team the Farmers of 1979 would have easily walked on, the Rebels were extremely tough for the 1980 version of the maroon and white. Wilson cited a lack of quickness in the Farmer backfield as to why they could not get things rolling as they had the year before, and the regular season hadn't even started.

The Farmers opened the 1980 schedule against Duncanville, with the Panthers shocking Lewisville in a 21-21 tie, and the season unraveled from there. Plano defeated Lewisville 28-7 in week two, falling well away from that preseason number one ranking they had lost after the tie against Duncanville. The first win of the season came in game three, as the Farmers showed the first signs of offensive life with a 28-17 victory over Arlington Bowie, and they doubled their win total for the season the following week with a 13-0 win over the Arlington High Colts, a traditional playoff team. Things were

The Wilson Years

looking up for the Farmers with a 2–1–1 record and a two-game winning streak, providing momentum for district play just two weeks away. Wilson felt his team resurging and had plans of salvaging the season in spite of the early trouble.

The Jesuit Rangers would interfere with that plan, however, as they handed the Farmers a tough 7–3 homecoming loss, which hamstrung them going into district play. The next week the Farmers opened the district schedule against Wichita Falls High, losing again, 13–0. The loss was deceiving, however, as Lewisville had 19 first downs to the Coyotes' two. In fact, Wichita Falls only crossed the 50-yard line two times all evening, both resulting in touchdowns, including a 65-yard reverse pass. On the other hand, Lewisville was unable to get the ball into the end zone, thus the Farmers suffered their third loss in the first six games of the 1980 season.

With the Farmers 0–1 in district play, Lewisville appeased its woes somewhat the following week with a 45–0 thumping of Denison. Things were still hopeful for a district crown, but quickly diminished as Lewisville fell to Sherman, 10–6, to all but shut the door on their title hopes. After a much needed open week, the Farmers defeated Wichita Falls Rider, 20–0, for only their second district win, and just their fourth of the year, before losing a heartbreaker to Denton, 13–12, to wrap up the dismal season. Overall the Farmers were 4–5–1 and finished nowhere near the number one ranking predicted before the season began. This was Neal Wilson's only losing record as head coach of the Farmers in his eight years in command.

The burden of a number one ranking contributed to the rocky season, as each team had no trouble getting motivated to play the Farmers. Add to that the revenge factor brought on by the 12–1–1 wake left in 1979, and Lewisville had its hands full going into the 1980 stanza, taking the best shots from those teams who had been destroyed by the Farmers a year earlier. So Wilson and his staff retreated and regrouped in the spring of 1981 with the intention of improving their level of play the following fall.

And improve they did, as Lewisville reeled off 10 straight victories in 1981 in the regular season, including a perfect 5–0 district mark, and captured their third district title in four chances with Wilson at the helm, proving that 1980 was the fluke season. The momentum propelled Lewisville right into the playoffs to face the defending state champions—the Odessa Permian Panthers.

Permian defeated Port Arthur Jefferson, 28–19, in 1980 to capture their third state championship since their first appearance in the title game of 1965. With the 1980 crown the Panthers were 3–3 in state championship games and had aspirations of adding the 1981 title to its resume, but had to contend with the Lewisville Fighting Farmers to accomplish this task. Lewisville lost the coin toss for the home field advantage and had to travel to Odessa for the bi-district contest.

The Farmers traveled to Odessa to meet Permian one other time, that being 1978 in Wilson's first year as head coach. They met for the bi-district contest,

FRIDAY NIGHT FARMERS

The 1981 Lewisville Fighting Farmers

with the Farmers losing by a slim 17–7 margin. 1981 was different, however, as Lewisville jumped out to a 14–0 lead and never trailed. Permian fought back to tie, largely due to a Farmer turnover, but Lewisville held an edge in first downs, 19–15, and held on to win the contest. The victory was doubly sweet as the Panthers were scheduled to construct a new football stadium in the off-season, so the loss to Lewisville was Permian's last contest in the stadium in which so many traditions were built, and where the fear of "Mojo," the Permian battle cry, was born.

With the bi-district crown in hand, the Farmers met Fort Worth Eastern Hills for the area championship. The Highlanders, led by running back Jeff Atkins, featured a potent offensive attack. According to Wilson, Eastern Hills was a good football team and could score as needed. The analysis proved true as Eastern Hills defeated Lewisville 15–7 at Texas Stadium for the area title. Although the Farmers only went two rounds in the playoffs, Wilson got the football program back on track before it had a chance to veer very far from the path for success he and his staff carved three years earlier.

Eastern Hills proved to be a nemesis for Lewisville in 1982 as well, as they defeated the Farmers 19–6 in the second week of the season. This was the only regular season loss for Lewisville as they went on to a near perfect district record and a fourth district title for Wilson. The only blemish during the remainder of the regular season was a 0–0 tie against the Plano Wildcats. Although a tie, the contest was awarded to Lewisville on the basis of penetrations, giving the Farmers a 6–0–1 district record and yet another Wilson-engineered district crown.

The Wilson Years

The 1982 District Champions of 12–5A.

With their victory over Lewisville, Eastern Hills had captured their second consecutive win over the Farmers. From 1981, when the two teams first met, the Farmers and Highlanders have played nine times. The Eastern Hills victory in 1982 was their last victory over the Farmers, however, with Lewisville firing off seven consecutive victories over the Ft. Worth school to complete the nine game series. Aside from the 1981 playoff faceoff, the Farmers and Highlanders met regularly in the second week of each season during the non-district portion of the schedule, with the last contest between the two area teams coming in 1991, resulting in a 56–14 Farmer win.

After wrapping up the 1982 district crown, the Farmers hosted the Carter Cowboys of Dallas at Farmer Field in the first round of the playoffs. The playoff format was changed for the 1982 season, which allowed the top two finishers of each district to qualify for post-season play. The format allowed for the top two teams from two districts to meet at the bi-district level, with the winner playing the runner-up of the opposing district. This allowed the Farmers to meet the runner-up of District 11-5A, Dallas Carter. Interestingly, the game against Carter was the first and only post season contest involving the Farmers at Farmer Field, although Lewisville had hosted several playoff games as a neutral site for area teams, including a thrilling 0–0 tie between the Bowie Jack Rabbits and Wylie Pirates in 1981, which Wylie won on penetrations. In fact, the Farmers have participated in 40 playoff games from 1932–93, with only the 1982 bi-district game played at Lewisville.

Playing at Lewisville did not bring the Farmers any luck, however, as Carter won 9–7 in a rather sloppy game. Lewisville lead throughout most of the contest, 7–3, and it appeared the Farmers would win had they been able to control the ball, however they fumbled late in the game, giving the Cowboys a chance to win. The Farmer defense held, forcing Carter to punt, and Lewisville took possession deep in their own territory, clinging to that stingy 7–3 lead which they would proudly take. But the Farmers fumbled again, surrendering the ball to the opportunistic Cowboys, who put the ball in the end zone for the 9–7 final. Carter advanced to the semifinal round before losing to Hurst L.D. Bell to end their season.

1983 and '84 would be lackluster seasons according to the standard Wilson had established in his first five years as the head coach of the Lewisville Fighting Farmers. In 1983 Lewisville finished 8–2, normally enough to make the playoffs, but with back-to-back district losses to Plano and Richardson, 7–6 and 28–21 respectively, the Farmers could sew up only the third place spot. It appeared that Lewisville was off and running as they won the first five district contests, but the five-game win streak was followed by the two losses, eliminating the Farmers from the playoffs with the third place finish.

The talent level plummeted yet further in 1984, as the Farmers finished 6–3–1, well out of contention for the district crown. As they had done in '83, Lewisville rifled off sizeable victories in the first five games over Arlington High, Eastern Hills, Jesuit, Greenville and Berkner, outscoring their opponents 157–27 to open the season. The Farmers displayed their first signs of mortality in game six, surrendering a 7–7 tie to the Lake Highlands Wildcats. The following week the Farmers got revenge against the Richardson Eagles for the loss in '83 with a 35–17 victory, making them 6–0–1 and in the driver's seat on the road to the district title. Unfortunately, that would be the final victory of the season for the Farmers as they gave up three straight losses to J.J. Pearce, Plano and Plano East to end both the season and the Farmers' attempt at another playoff appearance.

The failure to maintain an offensive punch through the season cost Lewisville the final three games as they dropped the contests by a combined 14 points. Pearce dealt the most painful blow with an 8–7 victory, while Plano and Plano East downed the Farmers 20–14 and 14–7. Going into the final game Lewisville still had a chance at the playoffs as the district runner-up. Had they turned the tables on Plano East's Panthers they would have earned that spot. Instead the Panthers won, giving them the district title with Plano grabbing the runner-up spot. The Farmer loss to J.J. Pearce proved to be a fluke.

Max Goldsmith retired as athletic director for Lewisville I.S.D., a position he held since 1970, and Wilson assumed those duties in the spring of 1983. He had coached in '83 and '84 while serving as athletic director, and the pressure began to take its toll on him. LISD had been expanding rapidly each year, largely due to the opening of the D/FW International Airport just a few miles southwest of the city. The new airport created the usual influx of employment opportunities and the subsequent need of peaceful suburban communities as a retreat from the bustle of the mercantilism of Dallas and Fort Worth.

The Wilson Years

LISD had built a new high school in Flower Mound, Edward S. Marcus High School, to accomodate the expansion to the west, and had began construction on a high school in The Colony to house the growing student populations in The Colony and north Carrollton, both components of the widespread Lewisville Independent School District. Soon—in 1986—both schools would enter varsity competition, and the responsibilities of the athletic director would triple, so Wilson had announced that he would surrender his duties as head coach of the Lewisville Farmers after the 1985 season. With the combination of a two year playoff drought and Wilson's finale, the Farmers wanted to extend his final season as far as possible.

Lewisville began the '85 season in normal Wilson fashion, winning the first eight games. The least number of points the Farmers scored was 24, in a 24–0 shutout over Lake Highlands. The closest game was the eighth game of the season, as Lewisville beat J.J. Pearce's Mustangs in a 35–28 free-for-all. The season almost fell through the cracks following the victory over Pearce, as Lewisville dropped the final two regular season contests to Plano and Plano East by scores of 22–7 and 24–23.

Plano East secured the district championship by virtue of their win over both the Farmers and Plano High earlier in the season, forcing a three-way tie for the second place spot between Lewisville, Plano and Berkner. Lady luck was with the Farmers as Wilson won the coin toss, allowing them to make one final appearance in the playoffs with him as their head coach.

The Farmers faced the Kimball Knights for bi-district, defeating them 41–7 in a less than challenging contest. Next, Lewisville won the area championship with a 20–14 victory over the North Mesquite Stallions in a solid high school football game, setting up the regional showdown against Cypress-Fairbanks High School, located in a suburb near Houston, to be played at Floyd Casey Stadium on the Baylor University campus in Waco. The Farmers, fortunate to have made the playoffs, now found themselves against one of the state's toughest teams.

Although Lewisville had been able to make things work in their favor offensively through most of the season and in the first two playoff contests, they were not able to get things going against Cy-Fair. The Farmers dropped that contest, 35–7, to end the season and Wilson's career as the Farmer chief. He would now slip into his role as athletic director and the challenges that went with overseeing the scheduling, staffing and budgeting of the rapidly growing LISD Athletic Department.

As the Farmer head coach from 1978–1985, Neal Wilson compiled a combined 67–19–5 record, with four district championships and five playoff appearances. He was named Coach of the Year in '78, '79, '81 and '85, and Metro Coach of the Year in 1979 to go along with that same honor he had won as head coach at Eagle Mountain-Saginaw's Boswell High School in 1977. The key to Wilson's success has been in constructing teams that have been competitive at all levels of competition. He believes that in high school football you cannot

The 1985 Lewisville Fighting Farmers — Neal Wilson's final team finished with a 10–3 record and reached the regional round of the playoffs.

have simply winning a district title as a goal, but rather being competitive, stating that, "As long as a team is competitive it has a chance to win."

And Wilson should know. His high school coaching career as a head coach, spanning 18 years, has resulted in a 153–39–6 career mark. Wilson had built upon the winning Farmer tradition that had begun in the early '30s under R.O. Davis, and continued under R.E. Mattingly, Lewis McReynolds and Bill Shipman, elevating the Fighting Farmer football program to a higher level of excellence and competitiveness.

. . .

CHAPTER

XI

BIG PLAYS

EVERY CHAMPIONSHIP TEAM can turn to particular plays that were pivotal in the outcome of that season. Perhaps the most widely known one is the "immaculate reception" in 1972 by Franco Harris of the Pittsburg Steelers, as they defeated the then Oakland Raiders by him grabbing a deflected pass at his shoelaces and rambling 60 yards (with 5 seconds left) down the field for the game winning touchdown. The Raiders were stunned, as were the millions who watched the play nationwide. Or one may recall the famous "Hail Mary" pass from Roger Staubach to Drew Pearson against Minnesota in 1975 for a last second, game-winning score. Staubach performed many miracles during his career at Dallas, but none were as memorable. Franchises and teams with traditions of winning have similar stories in their history that fans have recalled time and again, and the Farmers are no different in this regard. Though many plays stand out in the minds of those who made them, or watched them gleefully from the grandstands, there are six specific plays that were directly responsible for enabling the Farmers to snatch victory from the jaws of defeat.

Three of the six plays occurred over a three-year period and served as bright spots during an otherwise dismal time in Fighting Farmer history. Not only did the first three plays come in three consecutive years, they were made by the same player. As a sophomore John Garrison started at quarterback for the Farmers in 1968, and he continued to do so through his senior year. Playing in the shadows of his older brother, Walt Garrison, at that time an established member of the Dallas Cowboys, and his father, W.L. "Mutt" Garrison, a star with the Farmers in the late 1930s, he had a strong athletic heritage to draw upon. Garrison won the starting job from senior Pat Boyd, primarily on the strength of his passing arm. He shined in preseason scrimmages against Seagoville and Sulphur Springs, and it appeared he would help turn the Farmers around from their 1–9 record the season before. He lead the young Farmers to victory over the Boswell Pioneers, 31–0, to open the season, including two touchdown passes and one 11-yard touchdown run himself. It appeared Garrison had set a tremendous pace for himself and the Farmers in that initial contest with his 123 passing yards.

In the second contest, the first home game in 1968 in Lewisville's new stadium, Garrison hurled a 35-yard touchdown strike to flanker Lawrence Johnson on the Farmers' first play from scrimmage. Although the Farmers eventually lost the game to the Waxahachie Indians, Garrison himself was off to a good start for the young season. Even though he accomplished much as a sophomore quarterback, especially in directing the Farmer passing attack, it would be another aspect of his game that would account for three of the most exciting plays in Farmer history.

On October 11, 1968 the Farmers were 3–1 going into district play. Lewisville, aligned in the ever-so-tough district 6-3A, drew a difficult match for the conference opener, as the McKinney Lions came roaring into town, not having lost a district contest in some 10 seasons. The Farmers did not roll over and play dead, however. In fact, after two first-quarter McKinney fumbles, Lewisville took advantage of the miscues and took an early 14–0 lead only 5:15 into the contest. This shocked the once feared Lions, and it took them two-and-a-half quarters to recover. They finally did snap out of it with 4:06 left in the contest, scoring two touchdowns within that time frame, largely on the strength of two key passes. All of a sudden the Farmers found themselves tied at 14–14 with 1:50 left on the clock. The upset victory seemed to be slipping away; that is, before Garrison and company had their final say.

McKinney tried an onside kick, but the alert Gary Goldsmith fell on the ball, giving the Farmers good field position at the Lions' 48-yard marker. A quick pass by Garrison to Curtis Bishop put Lewisville 19 yards closer to the winning score, however two consecutive incompletions left the Farmers with fourth-and-long and, more critically, only three seconds on the game clock. Their only hope was either a long pass or a field goal. They elected for the field goal attempt, coming 44 yards away. As the ball flew through the air the time evaporated from the clock, with the attempt coming up short. The Farmer placekicker got another shot, however, as one of the Lions was somewhat anxious in his attempt to block the kick and jumped offside a wee bit soon.

Big Plays

The penalty moved the ball 5 yards closer for the second chance. This time the ball reached the goal post, hit the crossbar, bounced up and hovered in the air for what seemed like an eternity, but was in reality only a few seconds. It came back down, again striking the crossbar and falling through on the back side of the goal post to complete the 39-yard field goal. The three points gave the Farmers a thrilling last second 17–14 victory, as fans ran on the field mobbing the players, including the placekicker, remembered more for his exploits as a passer than for his placekicking. You see, along with his job as quarterback, John Garrison—sophomore John Garrison—handled duties as punter and placekicker, and kicked the last-second field goal on that mid-October evening at Farmer field.

The Farmers finished 6–4 that season, but three district losses allowed them only to finish somewhere in the middle of the pack. The last second victory over McKinney, however, lasted in the hearts and minds of the Farmers and their fans, giving them a satisfying feeling for the '68 season.

In equally dramatic fashion, the Farmers defeated Plano in 1969, 7–6. Rather than a come-from-behind victory, the Farmers secured their lead early on a 16-yard touchdown pass from John Garrison to wide receiver Robbie Messinger with 2:59 left in the opening quarter. Garrison performed an encore by converting the extra point for the early 7–0 lead. That would close the scoring for the Farmers that Halloween night in 1969, but that would not end the action, including a stunning collective performance by the Farmer defense.

There were a lot of stars for Lewisville that evening. Six times the Wildcats had the ball deep inside Farmer territory, including four in the fourth quarter, and each time the pesky Farmer defense made a big play to suppress the Plano attack. Another big play on a Wildcat field goal return appeared to be headed for a touchdown, but speedy tailback Joe Bishop nabbed the swift Wildcat returner from behind as the first half clock ran out.

In the second quarter Plano looked to be on their way to their first score of the evening, facing a fourth-and-one situation at the Farmer 33-yard line—too close to the goal line to punt, but too far to attempt a field goal. That's what is considered four-down territory; that is, the area between the opponent's 30 and 40-yard line where the chances of converting on a fourth-and-short situation are better than kicking a field goal or punting the ball inside the 10-yard line. After all, there's handling the snap, getting off a good kick, preventing a blocked kick -all things that could go wrong. With fourth-and-one, Plano elected to go for it. One would figure on a safe plunge up the middle, or perhaps a quarterback sneak to pick up the needed yard. Plano had something else in mind, however.

Hoping to catch the Farmers looking for the run, Plano quarterback Patrick Thomas faded back to go for all the marbles, or at least make the first down. Farmer defensive tackle Fred Sullivan sniffed out the play, however, smashing through the line and into Thomas for a 7-yard loss.

That was early in the second quarter. Later that same period Plano had the ball at the Farmer 28, again facing a fourth down. This time Lewisville's Ronnie Cummings provided the big play by knocking down a Wildcat pass to halt the drive. The Farmers evaded disaster yet another time in the first half with three seconds remaining. Garrison attempted a rather long field goal, but the kick fell considerably short of the mark. So short, in fact, that Plano's Ralph Williams, defending the goal, was able to field the ball at the 15, returning it through the middle of the field. Williams avoided tacklers along the way and appeared to be heading to paydirt. That's when Joe Bishop sped through the barrage of Wildcat blockers to prevent the score, preserving the 7–0 lead at the half.

Plano finally got on the board late in the third quarter. The Wildcats' Tommy Propes provided the opportunity with a nifty 24-yard punt return. Three plays later the Wildcats had covered 38 yards with relative ease, capped off by a 2-yard touchdown run by Tommy Carroll. What turned out to be the biggest play of the game occurred on the extra point attempt. Instead of routinely smacking the ball through the uprights, Plano kicker Gary Owens' effort drifted wide of the mark, leaving the Farmers with a one-point advantage.

Not much happened after that until the fourth quarter, which found the Farmers backed up near their own goal line for virtually the entire final period. Early on the Wildcats were knocking on the door at the 20-yard line, only to have fullback Mitchell Paxton fumble that opportunity away to Lewisville's Gene Keith. One hundred eighty seconds later found the Farmers defending their goal again, this time at the 15-yard line. On fourth-down-and-one Farmer tackle George Puls led the defensive charge in stopping Plano's Paxton from gaining the first down. Two great defensive stands, but alas, the Farmer defense was not through for the night.

A 41-yard pass play by Plano's quarterback Glen Hansen to Roger McEntire gave the Wildcats their best opportunity to snatch the lead. The play ended at the Farmers' 6 giving Plano first-and-goal at that point. The first two plays of the drive netted a mere 2 yards to the 4—the Farmer defense still sharp—setting up a critical third down. Paxton, Plano's goat for the night, fumbled after being demolished by the brutal Farmer defensive line, and Lewisville's Mark Sandlin pounced on the ball averting still another Plano threat.

Even with the outstanding Farmer defense, the offensive unit had not been overly productive. After taking over at their own 4, Lewisville had no success in moving the ball and was forced to punt. After the kick, Plano set up shop at the Farmer 33 to mount their final drive with under two minutes remaining. The Wildcats moved to the 26-yard line, setting up third-and-three. Consecutive pass attempts on third and fourth downs were unsuccessful and the Farmers took over on downs. The Wildcats, fresh out of time-outs, were unable to stop the clock, allowing Garrison to hold the ball and gobble up the remainder of the clock on the final two plays, while the defense let out a sigh of relief on the west sidelines

The 7–6 victory over Plano knocked the Wildcats out of contention for the

Big Plays

6-3A title race, giving them their second district loss. The Farmer victory cleared the way for Bonham to eventually win the crown.

At the time it did not seem as vital as it turned out to be, but the extra point by John Garrison, which incidentally, looked ugly as it traveled over the goal post, secured the Farmer upset victory over Plano early in the contest.

The following season, 1970, would provide Farmer fans with another nail-biter in the ninth game of the year. Lewisville had a 4-4 record going into the contest with no chance at the district title. Their opponent, the Gainesville Leopards, still had a shot at the championship, needing wins both against Lewisville and the powerful Plano Wildcats to end the season and secure the title. Lewisville, at 3-3 in district, could only hope to play the role of spoiler.

The Gainsville game was fairly sloppy, as high school football goes. Much of the poor play was largely due to the muddy conditions caused by the heavy rains experienced in the Gainesville area that day. The elements contributed to seven fumbles altogether, six of those miscues by the Leopards, which gave the Farmers the opportunity to win the contest.

For three quarters the scoreboard read 0-0, as neither team could either generate enough traction to move the ball, or hold on to the pigskin long enough to produce any points. Gainesville lost four of its fumbles during the first three periods, disallowing themselves any chance at scoring. The Farmers had two cracks at scoring themselves, but fumbled away a golden opportunity after a 38-yard completion from Garrison to speedster Ronnie Cummings. The other opportunity looked promising, featuring Garrison's 27-yard pass to Robbie Messinger, followed by a 30-yard gain by running back Joe Bishop. The drive stalled, however, but left the Farmers well within field goal range, although a bit risky due to the faulty footing. Garrison's kick drifted wide, leaving the Farmers and the Leopards unproductive—that is until the fourth quarter arrived.

Things changed on the first play of the final period. Gainesville had managed to hold onto the ball long enough to sustain a drive toward the third quarter's end, and the ball was resting on the Farmer 4-yard line when the whistle blew ending the period. The Leopards had renewed their strength during the quarter change, and Dennis Bingham ran the ball in on the first play of the final stanza. Instead of risking a missed extra point due to the wet field, the Leopards elected to go for two. After all, they had seen the slippery turf cause Garrison to miss his field goal attempt in the first half and concluded that their chances of converting were better by land rather than air. Allan Newton ran the ball in for the two points and the 8-0 Gainesville lead, hoping that score would be sufficient to secure a victory.

It was not meant to be, however, as Lewisville recovered the fifth Gainesville fumble of the night at the Leopard 6-yard line with just under five minutes left on the scoreboard. A few plays later Ronnie Cummings scooted across the goal line from a yard out to pull within two. A tie certainly was better than a loss at this point in the season, especially if it spoiled someone's plans of making the playoffs. Besides, it made no difference to lose 8–7 or 8–6. It would still be a loss. The situation dictated that the Farmers go for two like Gainesville had done, which they did. The play to Cummings for the touchdown worked so well that Head Coach Don Poe decided to use it again. It worked equally well the second time, as Cummings invaded the end zone for the two points, and more importantly, the tie.

Now Gainesville was playing, not to win, but rather not to lose. On the following kickoff the Leopards began a conservative drive at their own 28-yard line in hopes of holding onto the ball and securing the tie. No doubt the five fumbles had the Leopard coaching staff concerned on how to do just that. Attempting to score was out of the question given the 72 yards needed. The dividend of trying to move the ball into scoring position from their own end of the field was a gamble the Leopards did not want to take, given the possible risk of a turnover. So they elected to run the clock out and settle for the 8–8 tie.

Even the simplest plans can go wrong, however, as Gainesville discovered trying to run out the clock. Farmer linebacker Mark Reynolds slammed into a Gainesville running back with 30 seconds still on the clock, separating him from the ball for the sixth, and final Leopard fumble of the night. Noseguard Dennis Vorin made the fumble recovery at the Gainesville 28-yard line, giving the Farmers a chance at victory.

Lewisville drove to the Leopard 11-yard line with five seconds remaining, forcing them to attempt what measured to be a 28-yard field goal. With only time for one play, that had to be it, so the Farmers again called upon John Garrison and his golden toe. Garrison had missed the earlier attempt and was no doubt eager to get a shot at redeeming himself.

And that he did. As Doyle Williams placed the ball on the tee, the clock began ticking off what few seconds remained. As was the case in the last-second victory against McKinney two seasons earlier, there would be no second chance at another field goal because of an offside penalty. This time Garrison only got one chance, which was all he needed, as simultaneously the ball traveled through the uprights and the clock struck zero, giving the Farmers a thrilling 11–8 victory. Although Garrison led the Farmers to 17 victories during his tenure as quarterback, none were more memorable or exciting as the three achieved on the merits of his place kicking.

In 1972 Lewisville quarterback Joe Martin dove into the southwest corner of the end zone, as the final six seconds ticked off, to defeat the heavily favored McKinney Lions for the District 6-3A championship. That contest was at Farmer Field, where the Farmers have been dominant since its construction in 1968. What permitted Martin the opportunity to score the winning touchdown came earlier in the drive on a fluke play, allowing the Farmers to sustain the game winning drive.

The Farmers began the fourth quarter down 28–14, and it was beginning to look like their dream season was coming to a close. Midway through the period Lewisville's Paul Rice scored, and turned around in time to catch the two-point conversion pass on the next play, making the score 28–22. On their final drive Lewisville began moving the ball, headed for what would be the winning score. Along the way the drive almost stalled, however, as the Farmers faced a fourth-and-seven situation.

Lewisville had run the ball most of the season and continued to do so against the Lions. With a strong offensive line and a backfield with the likes of Paul Rice and Mike Nichols, they would have been foolish to do anything else. Their combined 3,756 total yards rushing for the year was reflective of the one-sided offensive attack. However, even with the best of backs, on a fourth-and-seven on what could be the final drive of the season, a pass was in order. The Farmers had only thrown three in the game to that point, one to Rice on the two-point conversion after the previous touchdown drive, one other completion for 44 yards, and one incompletion, accounting for all of the Farmer passing attack in the game.

The obvious pass would be either a drop-back pass to a wide receiver on an out pattern, just enough to pick up the first down, or a quick look-in pass over the middle to tight end Mark Angeli, who had reliable hands. Instead, the Farmers chose to somehow get the ball in the hands of Paul Rice, on who's strength had gotten them this far, with as much running room as possible. Coach Bill Shipman figured a back with that much talent could carve out enough yardage to garner the first down.

The play called was a middle screen to Rice. By design the offensive line was to block for one second, then allow their assigned man to slip by them to rush quarterback Joe Martin, who was simultaneously back-peddling 10–15 yards. The scheme was to convince the defense that they had beaten their blocker and were about to converge on the quarterback for a huge loss, all the while the offensive line was reassembling at the line of scrimmage, with a back or receiver slipping behind them in time to catch the pass the quarterback had lofted over the outstretched arms of the onslaught of linemen. Why, the back may even make a feeble attempt to block in order to pull off the charade. Anyway, with a wall of blockers ahead of him, surely Rice could gain the needed 7 yards and keep the drive alive.

Everything worked as designed; everything that is, except McKinney's noseguard didn't cooperate with the Farmers' plan. At first sight it appeared he read the play and stayed in the middle of the line in order to foil things. In actuality, he reacted, or rather didn't react to the play, and was left behind at the critical point of attack. In short, he was in the wrong place at the wrong time as far as the Farmers were concerned. Regardless of how or why he was there, the fact is, he was there and Lewisville had to deal with it. Martin released the ball as scheduled, and it headed toward the line and the waiting hands of Paul Rice, who no doubt would snatch it from the air and gallop behind his blockers into the end zone, and the Farmers would live happily ever after. That's where the confounded McKinney noseguard intervened.

Instead of Rice nabbing the pass, the noseguard jumped up and batted the ball away from him in an outstanding defensive play. That was the bad news. The good news was he batted it in the direction of offensive right tackle Niles Ladehoff, who alertly caught the ball, and, in a fashion much different than Rice, lumbered down the field for the much needed first down. In fact, Ladehoff got 2 extra yards, gaining 9 on the play instead of the 7 needed.

Normally, an offensive lineman not lined up at the tight end position is ineligible to receive a pass. Doing so constitutes an illegal reception and is accompanied by both a 5-yard penalty and a loss of down. However, these were not normal circumstances. When the McKinney lineman touched the ball all the restrictions were removed, allowing anyone on the field, including Ladehoff, the right to receive the pass.

The reception was Ladehoff's only one of the season, making him the 12th leading receiver for the Farmers in 1972, but none were more important, as Lewisville sustained the drive and eventually scored the magical touchdown leading to the pot of gold at the end of the District 6-3A rainbow.

In 1979 the Farmers lost to the Temple Wildcats 3–0 in the state semifinals. In order to reach the semifinals the Farmers had to first play the number one ranked Abilene Cooper Cougars. The Cougars had a three-pronged attack equally divided between quarterback John Slaughter, and running backs Terry Orr and Keith Pantalion. Between the three they had 2,100 yards of the 3,140 team total. The Farmers would have their toughest game of the season.

It was a close game as both defenses held the two powerful offenses in check. The Farmers had the upper hand with a defensive mastery of the first half, especially by shutting down the potent Cougar passing attack. The first half ended 0–0, and Lewisville scored first in the second half for a 7–0 lead, but Abilene bounced back, eventually taking the lead 10–7. Late in the game the Farmers began the winning touchdown drive, capped by a 13-yard Freddie Wells touchdown, giving the Farmers a dramatic come-from-behind victory.

That winning drive began at the Farmer 36-yard line with little time on the clock. Although Lewisville relied heavily on the run with a high magnitude of success, it was necessary to go to the air to cover the ground needed. After a first down incompletion the Farmers faced a second-and-long situation, not quite a desperation attempt, but the pressure was starting to build. After receiving the play from the sideline, Hal Stewart, quarterback of the Farmers, extended a marginal fake to the fullback then dropped back behind a wall of protection.

Specifically, the play called was a "34–15 split end post, tailback banana." Although this sounds like a breakfast menu, in reality it was a designed play-action pass where the quarterback faked to the fullback two steps down the line, while the split end and tailbacks ran their assigned pass patterns. The split end was to run a post pattern, which is a path straight down the field 10 yards, then breaking inside toward the goal post. He would either be open or have drawn enough coverage to leave the other route open. The other route, the banana, was run by the tailback from his position out of the backfield.

Big Plays

The path was to run from the tailback spot up the left sidelines into the area cleared out by the wide receiver. The shape of the pattern was curved like a banana, hence the name—banana. The tailback was the secondary receiver, depending on who the cornerback covered. If the cornerback went with the wide receiver, the tailback would be wide open. If the cornerback covered the tailback, then the wide receiver would be open. It was the quarterback's responsibility to read the coverage and find the open receiver. Either way, the Farmers hoped this play would get them out of the hole they were in at that critical time in the game.

As Stewart dropped back in the pocket the wide receiver that was lined up wide on the left side headed straight down the field as fast as possible. He broke inside on the post pattern as scheduled, drawing the defender with him, then adjusted slightly as the ball was in the air. His adjustment drew additional coverage from another defender, increasing the difficulty of completing the pass. As the ball approached, the receiver was sandwiched between the second defender and the original one, who had turned around and caught up with the action. As the trio converged it was apparent the ball was slightly overthrown. Noticing this, the Farmer wide receiver leaped in the air and caught the pass, falling to the turf at the Cougar 36-yard line. Six plays later Wells took the option pitch from Stewart and raced 13 yards for the game-winning touchdown.

The Farmers ran the wishbone formation, geared more for running than for passing—which they rarely needed as they were able to run at will. The receiver had not had many opportunities to catch any passes, but was used more as a decoy or blocker than a receiver. In fact, the dramatic catch to set up the winning score was his first reception of the season, and for Eugene Corbin, the timing could not have been better, as the catch he made was one of the greatest ones in Lewisville Farmer history.

What made the play even more spectacular was learned after the game was over. Corbin and the other wide receiver, Eric Ferris, were used to shuttle the plays in from Head Coach Neal Wilson. It was Corbin's turn to relay the play in, which he did . . . along with an additional message from Wilson. "Tell Hal to hit Freddie (Wells) on the banana route," meaning, don't even look for another receiver. The Farmers had run that identical play earlier in the game with Wells catching the ball for a sizeable gain, so Wilson figured on similar results, or at least he hoped so. Corbin ran the post with no prospect of catching the ball; his only objective was to draw enough coverage to get Wells open. No one was more surprised to see the ball headed in his direction than he was.

Stewart recalled, "The corner took Freddie out of the play, so I had to throw it to Eugene. I knew it wouldn't be intercepted but knew Eugene would have to make the catch of his life." And that he did, although he didn't expect to have to.

"If I did my job the cornerback would go with me," Corbin explained, "leaving Freddie open in the flats. When I cut I felt the safety in front of me and the cornerback on my heels. I thought, 'Great, Freddie will be open.' I was startled to see the ball coming to me. When I saw it I stretched out and caught it, and the force of the ball pulled me down." When he got back to the huddle he inquired as to what happened to Wells. It was explained to him that the cornerback had taken him out of the play, leaving Corbin as the only hope for the Farmers on that play. After the catch there was a feeling of increased confidence in the huddle, giving the Farmers hope that they just might pull off the biggest upset of the season. And it may not have happened without the key pass reception by Eugene Corbin.

The 1993 bid for the state championship came 21 years after the Farmers first state final appearance, and the Farmer program and fans were hungry for a title. When Dwayne Brazzell romped over from the 10-yard line to regain the lead, Head Coach Ronnie Gage jumped up and down as the Lewisville fans almost blew the roof off the Astrodome with their cheering—truly the most exciting moment in Farmer history. However, the play proceeding the touchdown run was the key one of the drive, allowing Lewisville the chance to win.

The final drive began at the Lewisville 43-yard line with 3:10 to go. Aldine MacArthur had just scored to go ahead 37–36 for their second lead of the game. Lewisville began driving the ball, gaining 3 to 4 yards per carry, but came up against a fourth-and-one. Chad Nelson, Farmer quarterback, picked up the needed yard and Lewisville had a new set of downs. This time the Farmers faced a third-and-eight situation. Nelson and Brazzell had provided much of the ground attack, but had been held in check on that series. The Farmers had only thrown one other pass that day, a touchdown pass to Byron Mitchell, and it was time for another one.

Lewisville lined up in the regular wishbone formation, and after snapping the ball Nelson faked a handoff to Brazzell, who attracted a few defenders up the middle, then dropped back to attempt a pass. Running a post pattern down field was LaDarrin McLane, who had broken over the middle and gotten in front of his defender. As McLane broke, Nelson delivered the ball with pinpoint accuracy, and McLane made the catch at the 12-yard line. He was tackled immediately at the 10 and all the fans on the Farmer side awaited to see the referee's signal. The play was away from the Lewisville stands, so the fans could not tell immediately if the pass had actually been caught. When the official signaled the pass complete, pandemonium broke out as strangers were hugging and high-fiving each other in jubilation. The follow-up touchdown run by Brazzell was almost anticlimactic.

So, the Lewisville Fighting Farmers have many big plays to their credit, both offensively and defensively. This collection of plays stand out as pivotal ones, allowing Lewisville to eventually develop as a contender year in and year out, and to remain a favorite in the hearts of the citizens of Lewisville.

. . .

CHAPTER

A Dream Realized

1986–90

AFTER NEAL WILSON'S RETIREMENT as head coach of the Farmers at the conclusion of the 1985 season Chuck Mills assumed the duties as head coach, while Wilson concentrated on his new position as athletic director. Mills experienced considerable success as mentor of the Farmers, with his best finish in 1987 as area finalists. In 1986, Mills' first season, the Farmers finished 6–4 overall and 4–3 in district. A close 17–6 loss to Denton, and consecutive losses to Wichita Falls Rider and Wichita Falls High marred a promising season for the first year coach.

The 1987 season got off to a bumpy start, with a 1–3 record, including back-to-back losses to Jesuit and Denton. The record would have been 2–2, although the use of an ineligible player under the much cursed House Bill 72 negated what would have been a 34–7 victory over Ft. Worth Western Hills in game one. After the loss to Denton, Lewisville rifled off six straight victories to secure the runner-up spot in District 5-5A, allowing them to reach the playoffs in Mills' sophomore season as head coach. The Farmers defeated Ft. Worth Trimble Tech in the bi-district round, 41–20, but lost the area championship game to Arlington High, 21–3. Despite the loss the Farmers turned in a strong performance on the season with 15 players named to the All-District team, including two All-Staters. Noel Crum and David Burns earned both first team All-District and All-State honors, with Burns grabbing the Co-Defensive Player of the Year award in District 5-5A. Charlie Ford, Scott Stout, Chuck Bambridge, Brian Nickelson, Jeff Cox, Ted Banks and Chris Ogburn were named to the second team, while Mike Eiffert, George Martinez, Lee English, Jeff Price, Jason Downing and Gaylon Van Zandt received honorable mention. To round out the post-season honors, Coach Chuck Mills was named District 5-5A Co-Coach of the Year.

The Farmers posted eight wins in 1988 but were unable to make it to the playoff round due to a season-ending tie against Marcus. The game was awarded to the Marauders on the merit of a 17–15 edge in first downs, the second tie-breaking component under the Texas High School playoff format. The first tie-breaker is total number of penetrations inside the opponent's 20-yard line. Each team had three, forcing the outcome of the game to be based on first down totals. With the contest technically awarded to Marcus, for play-off purposes, the Farmers were forced to surrender the "Ax," the object captured by the victor in the annual contest between the two neighboring schools.

The game was tagged, "The Battle for the Ax," and was the brainchild of a local business man who suggested the idea to LHS Principal Doug Killough. "Jesse Jones, who was president of the North Texas Bank at the time, approached me with the idea. He was from Sherman, and their [Sherman's] rivalry with nearby Denison is called 'The Battle for the Ax.' He asked if we could do the same thing here, so Larry [Sigler, principal at Marcus High School] and I met, and agreed it would be a good thing. Mr. Jones had the ax made and donated it for the trophy," explained the LHS chief administrator. Killough had a plaque made on which to mount the prize that accompanies the ax to the victor's campus, and on it are metal plates where the latest score and date are engraved.

Fueling the idea was then *Lewisville Leader* Sports Editor Art Stricklin, who also hailed from the Sherman-Denison area and helped project the intensity of the rivalry on the Lewisville-Marcus annual meeting. Although the concept was not promoted by the athletic department (that was fostered by the media), it was not discouraged either, and has now grown into one of the most eagerly anticipated games on both schools' schedules.

The Farmers would much rather have surrendered the Ax than the playoff opportunity in 1988. Being tied by Marcus was bad enough, but it costing them a spot in the playoffs was worse, especially to a team in only its third year of varsity competition. Lewisville manhandled Marcus in their first meeting in 1986, 42–0, with LHS's Craig Guillen scoring on touchdown runs of 3

A Dream Realized

and 30 yards to lead all ball carriers. Marcus, finishing 2–8 for the season, had virtually no chance to beat Lewisville, largely due to their inexperience than anything else. The Farmers compiled 401 total yards, with Guillen supplying 123 of them, holding Marcus to 177 total yards. Lewisville defensive back Richard Allen snared two Glenn Buck passes on the night, half of the Farmer total number of interceptions that night, and took away one of the few real Marauder weapons of the young team.

In 1987 the Farmers retained the Ax, but not after a first half scare from the much improved Marcus team. The Marauders scored two unanswered touchdowns in the first quarter, one by Marty Kidd and the other by Marty Garrison, and it appeared a major upset was in the works at Goldsmith Stadium. They had already won six games on the year, assuring themselves of a winning season regardless of the outcome of the game with Lewisville, and they would not have minded adding a seventh win to their season total. The Farmers bounced back in the second quarter with two scores of their own, a Scott Stout 8-yard touchdown run, along with a 36-yard Preston Pomykal field goal, but still trailed 14–10 at the half.

Lewisville's powerful offense cranked out two more touchdowns in the third quarter, including a rare touchdown pass of 39 yards from quarterback Mike Eiffert to Al Meyers. The other score was a 17-yard Lee English gallop into the end zone. Defensive end David Burns added a safety in the game's final period to ice the win, 26–14, putting off the upset for at least another season.

The key to the Farmer victory was the way the defense hounded Marcus' lethal passer, Glenn Buck. He was sacked five times and could manage only five completions in 14 attempts for a mere 59 yards. Conversely, Lewisville's Eiffert threw for a whopping 104 yards (rare for a Farmer quarterback), completing six of eight passes and the 39-yard touchdown to Meyers. Actually Eiffert completed seven passes, but one was to Marauder defensive back Scott Basham to stop a Farmer drive. The Farmer win gave them a 2–0 advantage in the newly created series, and the Ax hung on the wall in the office at LHS until Marcus' 1988 tie/win.

The first four weeks of the 1989 season was a nightmare for Chuck Mills and the Farmers, as they lost three of four games to begin the season. Even their win, a 10–7 decision over a hapless Richland Rebel team, was not impressive, at least not compared to what the Farmer fans had been accustomed to. Lewisville dropped the first two contests to their neighbors to the south, R.L. Turner and Newman Smith, teams they had beaten soundly the year before. The losses, 21–7 and 14–0, put the Farmers in a hole early in the season as the offense sputtered, scoring just 17 points in three games. Although Lewisville lost to Sherman 49–24, in week four to open district play, the offense started showing signs of life. Sophomore Andre Brown was an integral part of that offensive unit which went on to gain consecutive victories over Wichita Falls Rider, Denton, Weatherford, Wichita Falls High and Keller before losing to Marcus outright, 23–15, to end the regular season.

Friday Night Farmers

The '89 Battle for the Ax was one of the sloppiest games by the Farmers in the history of the Lewisville-Marcus rivalry. The Farmers jumped out to an early 6–0 lead on a 1-yard plunge by Brown early in the battle. The big play of the Farmer drive was furnished by Brown's counterpart, junior running back Howard Hancox, with a nifty 50-yard dash on the game's second play, reaching the Marauder 16. From there the Farmers bulled to the 1, setting up the Andre Brown score. Tommy Grace's extra point was missed leaving the Farmers a point shy of perfection.

The 6–0 Farmer lead lasted about a nanosecond, as Marcus' Mark Weir caught a Ryan Cross screen pass and rambled 51 yards to draw even at 6–6. Shawn Smith booted the extra point, giving the Marauders a lead they would never relinquish.

Marcus scored again in the second quarter on another touchdown pass by Cross, with Darren Standifer on the receiving end of the 12-yard strike. Smith was perfect on his point-after attempt, upping the Marcus advantage to 14–6.

The Farmers finished the evening with a mere 144 total yards, less than half that of Marcus' total. The big spark for Lewisville, which kept them in the contest, was a 73-yard third quarter punt return for a touchdown by Tim Moody. Again, the conversion attempt failed but left the Farmers still within striking distance, 17–12.

Moody's touchdown came after a Shawn Smith 23-yard field goal earlier in the second half that stretched the Marauder lead to 17–6. The punt return made it 17–12, and the Farmers came to within two points of at least a tie after a Tommy Grace field goal from 26 yards out. That came with 6:26 left to play, and the Farmers hoped to get the ball back for another chance to score and steal the game in the final moments. Miracles have happened, and Lewisville hoped to pull one off against their crosstown rivals.

The Marauders never gave them a chance. Taking the ball at their own 24-yard line, Marcus coolly drove it down the field the entire 76 yards in 14 plays, with Mark Weir carrying it the final 10 for an in-your-face score as time ran out, leaving the Farmers on the short end of a 23–15 score. To add insult to injury, Marcus didn't even bother to kick the extra point.

Although Marcus defeated Lewisville, the Farmers' 4–2 district record was good enough for a second place finish in District 5-5A behind Sherman, setting up a bi-district showdown against Ft. Worth Trimble Tech. The Farmers lost, 18–13, at Pennington Field in Bedford, ending their season with a 6–5, ho-hum, finish.

The UIL instituted a new rule in 1990 which created a two-tiered playoff format in the Class 5A division. The format allowed for a third team to enter the playoffs, with the largest enrollment of the top three finishers competing in, what was termed, the "Big School" division, or Division I. The remaining two teams would compete in Division II, the smaller division, permitting more teams to make the playoffs. The extra spot in the playoffs provided for a team that, perhaps, had experienced some injuries, overcome eligibility require-

A Dream Realized

ments, or simply took a bit longer to get things together as a team, and gave them an opportunity to extend their season. Under the pre-1982 format only one team from each district made the playoffs. There was little margin for error with this design. In 1982 the district winner and runner-up entered post-season play. With the new rule in 1990 a team could stand a few losses and still make the playoffs, which is what happened to several teams who went deep into the playoffs, most notably the Aldine MacArthur Generals in 1993. MacArthur had overcome three regular season losses, two of those in district play, and narrowly missed another loss to its crosstown rival, Aldine High School, to get the opportunity to enter the playoffs in '93. They took full advantage of the chance by making it to the state finals. If not for the expanded playoff format, the Generals could have gotten their Christmas shopping finished much earlier.

The Farmers opened the 1990 campaign by shutting out their first three opponents by a total score of 86–0. They defeated R.L. Turner, 24–0, in the first game, trounced Ft. Worth Eastern Hills, 45–0, and defeated the Grand Prairie Gophers with a solid 17–0 victory. It was not until week four that the stingy Farmer defense allowed any points, surrendering nine to Denton. Lewisville defeated them 17–9 to open district play, and they were poised to take a shot at the district crown.

Lewisville soundly defeated Sherman, 34–10, to avenge the loss in the previous season, and put themselves on top in the district standings at 2–0. The Farmers won a close one against Wichita Falls Rider the following week, 23–21, but came back the next week to scalp Keller's Indians, 35–9, and the Farmers appeared invincible. The next game the Farmers would play would be against the Marcus Marauders . . . and another Battle for the Ax.

The 1990 contest between Marcus and Lewisville produced over 650 combined yards, and 66 points, in the most exciting game of the eight total match ups between the inter-district rivals from 1986–93. Lewisville broke the ice by scoring first on a 5-yard Colby Wilson touchdown run. Mark Potter kicked the extra point, and Lewisville owned a 7–0 early first quarter lead. More accurately, they rented the lead, as Marcus answered the Farmer score with one of their own on a 4-yard pass from Marcus quarterback Ryan Cross to Darren Standifer, still in the first period. The Cross-to-Standifer combination had connected in 1989 for a 12-yard touchdown to contribute to Marcus' first defeat of the Farmers.

Cross' first period touchdown pass was one of four he would toss that night, by far the most in any Marcus-Lewisville game. Besides the scoring strike to Standifer, Cross hit Carl Alvord for a 24-yard score, sandwiched by touchdown tosses to Brian Smith of 27 and 9 yards. On the night, Cross completed 18 of 26 passes for 274 yards, eight shy of the entire Farmer total offense for the game.

Meanwhile for the Farmers, fullback Andre Brown was turning in a stellar performance himself. After Marcus had stolen a 14–7 second quarter lead,

Friday Night Farmers

Brown supplied a 3-yard scoring run to knot the game at 14 with Potter's extra point. Lewisville hardly had time to catch its breath before Cross struck again with the 24-yard touchdown pass to Alvord. The extra point attempt by Michael Finidori was blocked, giving the Marauders a 20–14 lead. The Farmers closed the gap, pulling to within three points, as Potter kicked a 28-yard field goal before the half. The Farmers were still behind at 20–17, but closing fast.

In the third quarter Brown scored his second touchdown on a 26-yard run to put Lewisville on top again, 24–20, for the only scoring by both teams in that period. Brown's final score came after a sustained Farmer drive that ended the third quarter and continued 30 seconds into the fourth quarter, padding the Farmer lead on a 3-yard plunge. The score stood 31–20 and the Farmers could breath, finally, boasting a defense that had given up only 49 points in the previous seven games. Surely they could hold the Marauders and snatch the Ax away from their firm grip in the 11:30 that remained on the clock.

The Marauders began the season with a four game losing streak, but had revived in time to take a legitimate stab at a spot in the playoffs. They had a two game win streak going into the Farmer game and owned a 2–2 district record, identical to Wichita Falls Rider and Sherman, with all three tied for third. Meanwhile, the Farmers sat on top with a 4–0 record, closely followed by Haltom at 3–1. With three games remaining Lewisville was in control of its destiny, while Marcus was fighting to survive . . . which may have prompted the fourth period outcome. After Lewisville went up 31–20 the Marauders zipped down the field 76 yards in only four plays. The drive was climaxed by a 9-yard touchdown reception by Smith on a fade route. A two-point conversion attempt was successful, and the Marauders were breathing down the Farmers' necks, 31–28, with plenty of time left. All they had to do was keep the ball away from the quick-striking Marauder offense and maybe even score one more time for emphasis. After all, the Farmers had been reasonably successful in moving the ball throughout the contest, converting several critical third down situations . . . which is where they found themselves at their own 39-yard line with nine minutes left in the final quarter. Instead of playing it safe with a sure hand-off up the middle, the Farmers elected to go for all the marbles with a long pass attempt. Unfortunately, they outwitted themselves. Colby Wilson's pass attempt to Bryan Brown was completed, but not to Brown. Marcus' Mike Autry stepped in front of Brown and picked off Wilson's pass at his own 41, and the momentum began to shift the Marauders' way.

From that point Marcus reached midfield, still a yard short of the first down. Rather than concede, Head Coach Que Brittain and company decided to do a little gambling themselves by handing off to running back Reyn (pronounced "rain") Cloud up the middle. Cloud picked up the first down with 2 yards to spare, and the Marauders were still in business. Carl Alvord had caught a touchdown pass earlier in the game and had two key receptions in the final scoring drive. He gained 13 yards on a crucial third-and-six play with an outstanding effort, and snared a 28-yard bullet to give the Marauders a first-and-goal at the Farmer 7. From there Marcus' Cloud took a screen pass to the 1-yard line and carried over on the next play for the go-ahead score. Michael Finidori's kick was good and the Marauders regained the lead they had relinquished early in the third quarter.

The Farmers had two other opportunities to score, but both drives ended in interceptions as Marcus held on to capture the Ax for the third consecutive year with a 35–31 thriller. No doubt this has been the most exciting contest of the Farmer-Marauder series through 1993, as well as one of the most exciting football games in the metroplex in 1990. KRLD radio station, which broadcasts a metroplex high school football game as a weekly feature, selected to air the Battle for the Ax, and was pleased they had opted to visit Goldsmith Stadium that Friday night. Craig Way, announcer with KRLD, told reporters that the Lewisville-Marcus game was the most exciting game, and certainly the best one they had covered to that point in the season. Anyone witnessing that game would agree.

After losing to Marcus, the Farmers went on to lose the final two contests of 1990 to a tough Haltom team, 10–9, and a mediocre Richland Rebel team to finish a disappointing 7–3. Meanwhile, Marcus completed the remainder of their schedule undefeated, tying the Farmers's 4–3 district record; good for a third place finish. By virtue of the victory over Lewisville they qualified for the playoffs as the third team to represent District 5-5A, forcing the Farmers to stay home and sharpen their pitchforks.

1991

The 1991 season brought a change which would have a big impact on the Lewisville Fighting Farmer football program as LISD Athletic Director Neal Wilson recommended that the coach from Northwest High School in Justin, Texas, be named the new Farmer head coach. Chuck Mills had resigned to accept a position on the football staff of the University of North Texas in Denton, Texas, creating a vacancy in his wake. The replacement, although new, was no stranger to Lewisville as he had been a member of the Farmer coaching staff under both Wilson and Mills from 1978–86 before departing to achieve a lifelong goal of becoming a head coach. The opportunity at Lewisville allowed Ronnie Gage the chance to rejoin Wilson for the third time in their coinciding careers, this time with Gage on the sidelines as head coach and Wilson in the athletic director's chair.

Wilson and Gage first connected, not in 1978 with Gage as an underling on the Farmer coaching staff, but much earlier when Gage was a junior at Decatur High School. Neal Wilson was in his second season as head coach there, and Gage played center and defensive back for two seasons under him, with the Eagles winning the district championship in 1970. Wilson described Gage as, "an average athlete that worked hard," a combination that appealed to Wilson, eventually influencing him to extend the offer to Gage for the number one Farmer job. Gage gladly accepted it, after a four year stint as the head coach of the Northwest Texans in Justin.

1991 was a season of uncertainties, as the Farmers carried a three-game losing streak from 1990 into the season. With a new head coach, the Farmers and their fans did not quite know what to expect from the young Ronnie Gage. Most knew that he had spent a few years at Lewisville but didn't know how that would translate into productivity on the field. All they cared about was that the Farmers had not claimed a district championship since 1982, and they were hungry for one. An opening season 16–9 loss to Turner hinted that the Farmers would struggle under the new head man, while everyone adjusted to each other and the new schemes Gage installed.

The Farmers held a noble goal for the 1991 season, which was to win district and make the playoffs. They had the desire to accomplish that goal, and certainly had the talent. Andre Brown had already proven himself a valuable commodity the past two seasons as a running back and had aspirations of leading the Farmers down the playoff trail. Bryan Brown returned at quarterback with a season of varsity competition under his belt, as well as key players like Lamont Turner, Josh Parker, P.J. Shields and a seasoned Metrick McHenry. As a junior in 1991 McHenry had demonstrated glimpses of his rich talent as running back in the same backfield with Andre Brown and Duane Allen, who also returned from the 1990 roster. Newcomers like Buddy Phillips, Dwayne Brazzell, Pete Bonenberger, Mike Frazier and Chad Nelson—all sophomores—added to an already competitive team but still needed refining, as their 2–3 record over the first five games would reveal.

Lewisville resembled Dr. Jekyl and Mr. Hyde through the first half of the season. After losing to Turner in game one, the Farmers bounced back to humiliate Ft. Worth Eastern Hills, 56–14, and Grand Prairie, 21–0, the next two weeks to head into district with a 2–1 record. It looked as if the mixture of young and old Farmers had straightened out the opening game miscues and readied themselves to walk through District 5-5A, snatch the crown and dance all the way to the state championship, high-fiving each other all the way. A painful 28–25 loss to Denton to open district play caused the Farmers to drop their dance card, however, and Sherman stomped all over it a week later with a 26–7 victory over Lewisville. That's when Gage had a heart-to-heart chat with his emerging team in hopes of dispelling any losing habits developed during the slump. According to the Farmer mentor, "After we lost the first two district games to Denton and Sherman we quit talking about the playoffs and started talking about putting ourselves in a position to have a winning season." That was important to Gage and his staff as the last time Lewisville recorded a losing record was in 1980, over a decade earlier. He, too, wanted to get his players to focus on the immediate games rather than the playoffs, so by removing the lofty goal of winning the district title the pressure disappeared, allowing his young team to develop at its own pace.

A Dream Realized

The plan worked, if it could be called a plan, as Lewisville downed Wichita Falls Rider, Keller and Marcus in consecutive district wins like Fred Flinstone downs bowling pins, and Lewisville had worked themselves back into the playoff hunt. Although each win was vital, none was more satisfying than the thumping they gave the Marauders. It had been four years since the Farmers had beaten them, the closest being the 20–20 tie in 1988, and they had almost forgotten what the Ax looked like, much less how it felt. None of the '91 Farmers were on the last team to have beaten Marcus, and it was with great pride that they retrieved the Ax, by their victorious effort, and brought it back to LHS where they felt it belonged.

Against Marcus, Andre Brown had his most productive game as a Farmer, rushing for 300 yards and scoring four touchdowns to add to his three the year before. Altogether Brown has scored eight touchdowns in the Battle for the Ax, the most of any player from either team by far. Metrick McHenry's four touchdowns are a distant second, although his 88-yard run to open the scoring for both teams is the longest in the series' short history, and one of the longest in Farmer history.

Besides McHenry's record-setting run and Brown's four touchdowns, the 1991 Battle for the Ax produced several impressive series' records. The Farmers rolled up a powerful 481 rushing yards and 495 total yards, both Battle for the Ax records. In the '91 contest the two teams combined for 886 total yards of offense, with players and footballs flying all over Goldsmith Stadium that night. The 10,000 or so fans indeed witnessed an offensive battle. Despite the free-wheeling offensive output, Marcus punted five times, the most since the duel began, and both teams together punted eight times—a series record. Lewisville's 45 points are the most by either team and the 71 combined points scored that evening also set a Battle for the Ax record.

Although the game ended with a 45–26 lopsided score, the first half was not indicative of the eventual outcome. The Farmers jumped to a quick 14–0 lead midway through the first quarter on just two offensive plays. The first score was the 88-yard run by McHenry. Farmer defensive back Mark King set up the second touchdown by intercepting the first of three Marauder passes that would be pilfered that night. That came at the Marcus 48. Duane Allen got the call for the Farmers on the subsequent play, covering the entire 48 yards and doubling Lewisville's score. The Marauders did get on the board in the first quarter, however, on a 5-yard run by Jeff Boyd. Michael Finidori added the extra point and the Farmer lead was trimmed to 14–7. Lewisville's Mark Potter made good on a 46-yard field goal to end the exhausting first quarter and extend the Farmer lead to 17–7. The 46-yarder by Potter is the longest field goal in the Lewisville-Marcus rivalry.

The Marauders weren't intimidated by the fierce Farmer output of the first period. They had guns of their own and they brought them all, fully loaded. Three plays after Potter's field goal, Marcus quarterback Jason Franz hit Carl Alvord for a 32-yard scoring play. Alvord snared the pass in the flat and rambled down the field through Lewisville's Chad Cummings and Lamont Turner, both All-District candidates, to complete the 32-yard scoring play, making the score Lewisville 17, Marcus 14. That's how the first half ended before the real shootout began.

In the second half it was all Farmers. Rather, it was all Andre Brown, as he alone supplied all the scoring for Lewisville. In the third quarter he had half of his 300 yards on two touchdown runs of 76 and 75 yards. Potter converted on both extra point attempts, and the Marauders suddenly found themselves down by a 17-point deficit. Using their fire power, they answered Brown's touchdowns with a 32-yard field goal by Finidori, followed by a 43-yard touchdown pass from Franz to Jeff Boyd to keep pace with Lewisville. It was Boyd's second score of the night, putting Marcus within striking distance at 31–24. With the arm of Franz, and the collective speed of the Marauder backs and receivers, anywhere Marcus got the ball they were in scoring position.

Brown added his third and fourth touchdowns on runs of 55 and 31 yards to bury the Marauders, who could not manage to produce any effective offense to match Brown and the Farmers. A token safety due to a bad snap on a punt attempt by Lewisville accounted for the only scoring by Marcus in the final period, making the final score 45–26. The victory over Marcus accomplished two things for the Farmers; one, it improved their district record to 3–2 after the 0–2 start, and two, it handed the Marauders their first loss of the season.

Following the game with Marcus the Farmers lost a tough contest to Haltom City, 27–20, in bitter cold weather. Sherman was the district front runner with an undefeated record, followed by a pack contending for the second and third spots, including the Farmers with their 3–3 record. Going into the final week of the season the Farmers still had a mathematical chance at a tie for a playoff berth—if everything went just right, and they didn't step on any cracks, walk under any ladders, or if no black cats crossed their paths and they held their mouths right. Actually, what did have to happen was they had to beat Richland in their final game, and Marcus had to lose to Wichita Falls Rider on the following Saturday, which would throw four teams into a tie for second place . . . which is exactly what happened. Lewisville defeated Richland in a 31–28 shootout at Goldsmith Stadium, and Gage and staff traveled to Wichita Falls the next day to witness the Marauders fall prey to merciless Wichita Falls Rider, creating the log jam for second place. The scenario resembled Norm, Cliff, Woody and Sam, the four Cheers regulars, all trying to get out of the same door at the same time, with the first two out making the playoffs. It wasn't comical, though. It was serious, especially for a young Ronnie Gage in his first season as head coach of the Lewisville Fighting Farmers.

The four-way tie was decided by something just a bit more sophisticated than the paper/rock/scissors game. The standard, but reliable, coin flip would decide which two of the four teams would play at least one more week. Lewisville, Wichita Falls Rider, Marcus and Haltom City, by virtue of their identical

A Dream Realized

4–3 district records, were the teams vying for the second and third playoff spots. Representatives from each team met and began flipping coins like school yard boys until only one had a result different than the others. Rider was the first to win and secured the first of the remaining playoff spots. Their coach, Wayne LeBleu, put his quarter in his pocket and watched the other three flip for the last one. Gage's skill (or luck) proved superior, as the Farmers won the final coin toss to earn a playoff spot, and the three representatives from District 5-5A for 1991 were Sherman, the champions, then Rider and Lewisville.

Lewisville had the largest enrollment of the three and competed in the big school division. That matched them against the L.D. Bell Blue Raiders, with the game scheduled to be played at Texas Stadium. Bell was 10–0 and picked as an early favorite over the Farmers. The Farmers, who had steadily improved each week, were not intimidated by Bell's perfect record and apparent confidence. Consequently, Lewisville knocked them off, 30–17, to extend their season one more week, which lined them up against Arlington Sam Houston for the area championship.

Sam Houston had a talent laden team, proving to be more than a handful for Lewisville. The Farmers tried, but could not keep pace with the Arlington school, losing 46–27, which brought the 1991 campaign to a close, but not without corresponding honors. The Farmers had three players named as first team All-District members: Josh Parker, Andre Brown and Lamont Turner. Matt Yost, P.J. Shields, Metrick McHenry and Duane Allen made the second team, with McHenry being named the district's Co-Offensive Player of the Year. Seven Farmers received Honorable Mention, including Chad Cummings, Mark Potter, Bobby Krastin, Rusty Buschow, Mark King, Mark Bisson and Bryan Brown. In retrospect, Gage named the victories over L.D. Bell and Marcus as highlights of his inaugural season as the Farmers' main man.

1992

The 1992 season would bring added success to the already revitalized program in Gage's second year. First, the Farmers improved their regular season record from 6–4 the previous year, to 8–1–1. Second, Lewisville won the District 6-5A championship outright—no ties, coin flips or shared title—the first since 1982. And third, they made it three rounds deep into the playoffs before bowing out. Most importantly, however, Gage and company noticed a hunger in their young players that would not be fulfilled without a state title. Unfortunately for the Farmers, they did not get a shot at a state championship as they fell to the powerful Odessa Permian Panthers, 28–0, in the regional round of the state playoffs.

To open the '92 season Lewisville avenged their loss to R.L. Turner from the year before by waxing them 31–7. The Farmers tied a tough Plano East team in week two, 14–14, but bounced back to defeat Carrollton Newman Smith, 24–9, for a 2–0–1 record going into district play, which opened against an emerging Grapevine Mustang program, newly aligned in District 6-5A. By Gage's own confession, the Farmers did not play well against the Mustangs who, incidentally, are one of the Farmers' oldest rivals. They were last aligned in the same district in 1970 but were pre-district foes in 1972 and '73, which was the last meeting for the two neighboring towns prior to the 1992 showdown.

Since 1920 the Farmers and Mustangs have played 46 times with Lewisville having a slight advantage with a 23–20–3 overall record. In the early days the rivalry was traditionally played on Thanksgiving Day, obviously before television and the Dallas Cowboys drew the attention of most sports fans in the metroplex. From about 1925 until 1938 the two teams engaged in the Turkey Day battle until they were separated from the same district, forcing the game to an earlier date on the schedule in subsequent years. But in 1992 the Farmers were sluggish and dropped the game to the Mustangs, 28–14, for their first, and only, regular season loss of the year. Lewisville went on to win the remainder of their scheduled games, resulting in the first district championship for Head Coach Ronnie Gage.

Gage described his still young 1992 team as one that, "struggled against mediocre teams, but played well against tough teams." Near losses to The Colony High School and Allen, 28–21 and 35–28 respectively, raised questions as to which Farmers would show up from week to week. Sound victories over Sherman, 41–21, Wichita Falls Rider, 21–0, Denton, 17–7, and Marcus, 35–10, revealed the inconsistencies of a Farmer team that played well at times, and just well enough to win at other times, reminiscent of the Dallas Cowboys in the mid to late '70s under Tom Landry.

Regardless, the win over Marcus wrapped up the district championship for the first time in a decade for the Lewisville Fighting Farmers. In the contest Lewisville rolled over the Marauders, amassing 381 total yards in the victorious effort. The Farmers garnered the first three scores of the game, jumping out to a 21–0 lead, and Marcus was never really in the ball game. Lewisville quarterback Chad Nelson and Metrick McHenry, in his senior year, took turns scoring, with Nelson's getting the first and third touchdowns on runs of 33 and 15 yards, sandwiched by a 9-yard McHenry gallop. Topher Roach was successful on all three extra point attempts, completing the 21-point exhibition, and Coach Gage and his staff put it on automatic pilot to play out the remainder of the game. A Michael Finidori 32-yard field goal provided the only score for Marcus in the first half, giving Lewisville a 21–3 halftime lead.

The Farmers scored in each of the final two quarters, with McHenry supplying both touchdowns to close out the Farmer scoring for the game and the regular season. McHenry scored on a 3-yard run in the third quarter, and followed that with an incredible 28-yard dart, featuring inside and outside moves that left a trail of Marauders behind wondering which way he went. According to Gage, "It was probably the greatest run I've witnessed while at

A Dream Realized

LHS." That perspective includes the 300-yard performance by Andre Brown the season before. On the run McHenry took a Chad Nelson handoff at the 28 and darted into the middle of the line, breaking a tackle in the backfield, but moved to his left after finding no running room. At the 25 he met a Marcus defender and disposed of him with a lateral move as the would-be tackler came up empty-handed. Eight yards later he met two more defenders, but they collapsed as McHenry took a step inside, then back outside, leaving them in his maroon and white wake. The last man who had a chance at him was pursuing full blast from the opposite side of the field. McHenry saw him out of the corner of his eye and countered with a 90 degree move back inside, and it was clear sailing for the remaining 10 yards for his final run, and touchdown, as a Farmer at Goldsmith Stadium.

McHenry did lead all ball carriers with 145 yards on 18 carries, followed closely by Dwayne Brazzell's 139 yards. Much of the running success can be attributed to the underrated, but talented, offensive line, coached by Offensive Coordinator Bill Pietrosky. Four of the five starters received post-season honors, making the offensive line one of the strongest units on the team. Center Jason Golden, guards Jason Ulichnie and Buddy Phillips, and tackles Matt Yost and Jesus Ambriz made up the "Steamrollers," a fraternal unit within the Farmers exclusive to the offensive line.

The group was originated by Pietrosky in his first season as the offensive line coach in 1986. "There is no tangible gauge to measure the individual efforts of the offensive line," according to Mike Anderson, 1993 Farmer right tackle, "so the 'Steamrollers' serves to unify the line. The backs have their yardage, which we take pleasure in providing, and the defensive players have their tackles and opportunities to hit people, but for the offensive line the only way you get noticed is if you miss a block, or have a holding penalty called against you. With the Steamrollers, Coach 'P' gives awards for crushing blocks and keeps them on a chart in the field house. That's his way of recognizing our efforts." It is with extreme pride that the offensive line fights its battle in the trenches. Coach Pietrosky used the Steamrollers to, indeed, unify the linemen, describing their duty as crushing the defensive line in a methodical manner. "They may not be fast, but they're reliable," remembers Pietrosky. The purpose in unifying the line by means of the Steamrollers was to create an, "us against the world," mentality, but not to the extent that it overshadows the overall team goal. Instead, Pietrosky used the Steamrollers as a motivator for his offensive line to rally around. It paralleled the "Blasters" of the 1972 state final team, and for all practical purposes, the objective was the same for both groups. Before the 1973 season offensive line coach Tommy Shields took the entire line to the Gulf Coast for a week to form a unity he knew they would need when the going got tough during the regular season. Coach Pietrosky unwittingly adopted the same philosophy with the creation of the Streamrollers.

As a subgroup of the Steamrollers, the Steamroller Hall of Fame followed, with its membership composed of all offensive linemen recognized in the All-District selection. Gary Camp was the first inductee in 1986, followed by Noel Crum, an All-Stater in 1987, and Chuck Bambridge and Carlton Brown in 1988. In 1989 Mike Danielson and Arthur Godinez made the select group, with Godinez repeating in 1990, the first to do so, along with Shane Vigue. Josh Parker was the lone inductee in 1991, but in 1992 Pietrosky placed five Steamrollers in the Hall of Fame based on their 1992 performance. Yost, Golden, Phillips, Ulichnie, along with sophomore tight end Martin Simmons, were all added to the prestigious group, which reflected the success of the powerful Farmer offense.

Regardless of the reason for creating the Steamrollers, it worked, as both McHenry and Brazzell rushed for over 1,000 yards apiece, allowing the Farmers to capture the 1992 district crown and enter the playoffs. The Farmers' bi-district contest was scheduled for Texas Stadium against the Burleson Elks, in which the offensive line played a vital role. The Farmers amassed 519 total yards and scored 48 points, the most they had accomplished in either category all season. Burleson scored seven inconsequential points to avoid the shutout, but the Farmer offense turned in its best performance of the year. The game was KRLD's featured game of the week, but the sportscasters could not decide who to name as its offensive player of the week. Due to the difficulty of deciding, the entire Farmer backfield was selected, a tribute to the talented offensive line.

In round two of the playoffs the Farmers faced the South Grand Prairie Warriors for the area championship, again at Texas Stadium. The two teams had not met since 1973, when they were both aligned in District 6-3A 21 years earlier. The Farmers defeated them 38–19 in '73 to cap a two game winning streak over the Warriors. The two teams only played each other four times prior to the '92 encounter, with the series even at 2–2.

The Farmers duplicated their scoring efforts from the week before totaling 48 points and tying their season high. Chad Nelson rushed for over 200 yards, the first time in his career, and the Farmers totaled 552 yards, including 80 yards in passing. Two third quarter scores by the Warriors made the game close for a while, but Nelson supplied touchdown runs of 81 and 69 yards to negate the South Grand Prairie scores and secure a 48–28 victory. The win enabled the Farmers to overcome the hurdle they had hit two previous times and participate in the regional round, something they had not done since Neal Wilson's last season as the Farmer head coach. Lewisville would have to head out west to take on the Odessa Permian Panthers for the third time in their history.

Lewisville actually had a pretty good record against Permian. In the two previous meetings the Farmers were 0–1–1, with the tie being awarded to Lewisville on a 19–15 first-down advantage—a technical victory. Essentially, the Farmers were .500 against "Mojo," and felt their chances were pretty good for the '92 regional match-up. The Farmers and their entourage made a two-

A Dream Realized

day trip out of it. They departed at noon the day before, got a hotel and took in an afternoon's practice in preparation for the next day's contest. Included in the throng of Lewisville fans were the media, moms and dads, long lost aunts and uncles, and girlfriends, all who were welcome and had a right to be there, but which unintentionally served to distract the football team from its intended goal—beating Permian. That was a mistake that Gage admits was made, "more due to inexperience than anything else. I learned a lot about traveling from that game, and I promised if we got in that situation again I would do things differently."

Unfortunately, the distractions took their toll out on the young Farmer team, contributing to their loss to the confounded Panthers, 28–0. Nelson confessed, "the travel revolving around the game was more impressive than the game itself. Personally, I made some bad reads, but as a team we just didn't really play." Gage felt the defense performed well, but his Farmers were a bit intimidated by the "Mojo" cloud that seemed to hang overhead. Lewisville trailed only 7–0 near the end of the first half, but Permian scored on a trick play as the half ended and carried a 14–0 lead into the locker room. However, the lack of Farmer offense throughout the remainder of the game could not keep the defense off the field, and the Farmers eventually surrendered 28 points and a regional round defeat.

With the loss to Odessa Permian the Farmers finished 10–2–1 and gained a ton of experience. They earned their share of post-season honors as well, including Coach of the Year in Ronnie Gage, Offensive Player of the Year in Metrick McHenry, and Martin Simmons as Sophomore of the Year. Lewisville had six players named to the first team All-District team, and four to the second team. Of the 10 players selected three would return as starters in the 1993 season.

1993

Going into the 1993 season the Farmers had high hopes, especially with three out of four of the potent backfield returning. Quarterback Chad Nelson, fullback Dwayne Brazzell and half back Byron Mitchell would be joined by Waylon Holland in the backfield to give Lewisville experience at the so-called skill positions. The real question mark was the offensive line, which had lost four of its five members to graduation. Only guard Buddy Phillips was returning as a starter, challenging both Pietrosky and Gage to find suitable replacements. Simmons was returning as tight end for just his junior season, but the head coach's main concern was the tackle and center positions.

Thirteen players would battle it out for the four open slots, and Pietrosky would make the selections. Most had seen playing time as backups on the varsity or starters on the junior varsity, so the choices Pietrosky had to select from were good ones. Due to the experience, or lack of it, Gage and Pietrosky considered dipping into the defensive line for possible candidates to fill the vacancies, and listed defensive tackles Dan Merritt, noseguard Pete Bonenberger and defensive end Mike Frazier among those who would be considered. Gage's philosophy for football is, "players win football games, and in critical situations we want players on the field." Not that any of the offensive line hopefuls were not players, it's just that Merritt, Bonenberger and Frazier were proven commodities, "players," if you will, and would be dependable in the clutch, which is why they received consideration.

As it stood, the others got the message and responded to the challenge. Victor Zeliff joined Phillips to secure the left side of the line as tackle, and Mika Clark and Mike Anderson won the guard and tackle positions on the right side. Chad Dawson and Bret Johnson would battle it out in the early part of the season for the center spot. As the season progressed the 1993 version of the Steamrollers developed into one of the best offensive lines in Farmer history, answering the biggest question about the 1993 Farmers.

As for the defense the Farmers were extremely sound, losing only three starters to graduation. The 1993 version would feature a solid front line and secondary, along with the returning duo of linebackers in Zack Welton and Shannon Brazzell. Brazzel, only a sophomore, had started five games as a freshman filling in for the injured Lance Aldridge. He performed so well that the job was his at the outset of the '93 season, forcing Aldridge into a backup role. The secondary also featured a sophomore who had seen playing time as a freshman in Reggie Crawford. Crawford took Metrick McHenry's place as free safety, joining Blaine Herring, Mike Frazier and Dwight Hunter, all returning starters. Defensive Coordinator Terry Goode's job was made much easier with the plethora of defensive talent returning for the Farmers.

On opening day Lewisville was ranked to finish first in District 6-5A and fifth in the area behind Kimball, Arlington Lamar, DeSoto and Dallas Carter. They had been placed above traditional powerhouses like Plano, Arlington High and Euless Trinity, indicating that expectations of the Farmers were high from more than just the folks in Lewisville. The Farmer secret had gotten out, and Gage was making sure his team would not get lost in the ratings and would respond to the challenge placed before them. Clearly, their goals as a team were to make the playoffs, win district and be more competitive than the previous year should they reach the regional round of the playoffs again and have to face one of those traditionally tough West Texas foes. An underlying goal was to gain respect from the state of Texas, in general, and the 5A division specifically for the football program at Lewisville that had been on the verge of breaking through as a 5A power to be contended with and not just one that periodically makes a good showing.

Lewisville vs. R.L. Turner — September 3, 1993
If they did not believe the preseason rankings before the game, the R.L. Turner Lions certainly did after, as the Farmers powered over them, 30–9, to win the opening contest of 1993.

A Dream Realized

The offense displayed the level of play they had mastered in '92, pounding out 293 rushing yards once they got on track. A 7–6 Farmer lead at the half had the coaches a bit concerned as Lewisville suffered from opening night jitters. Nelson had trouble with the defensive schemes the Lions were throwing at him and had it not been for a Zeb Cornist interception, which he returned to the Turner 18, the Farmers might not have scored at all in the first half. Running back Waylon Holland did, though, on a 6-yard run, and Lewisville held a slim 7–0 lead after Topher Roach's extra point kick. Turner followed with a touchdown of their own on a 2-yard run by Brandon Hoffard before the half. The extra point failed, giving the Farmers the slight edge going into the locker room.

Once in the locker room Gage was thankful for the mere one point advantage. With the nervousness his anxious team displayed it could have been worse. Instead of changing schemes and making adjustments, he spent the time getting his players to relax and have fun. Knowing they had the talent to win was one thing; getting them to be able to display it was another. Cornist's interception was the catalyst to get the maroon machine rolling. He had a banner night showing his experience as a junior starter. Cornist had six tackles, two quarterback sacks and forced two fumbles in addition to the interception which set up the first score.

On the other side of the ball three different Farmers provided all the scoring once the offense found its bearing. Holland scored a second touchdown in period three on a 22-yard run. The Roach kick made it 14–6, but Turner narrowed the lead to 14–9 on an Ivan Luna 50-yard field goal, which closed the Lions scoring for the night. In the fourth quarter Dwayne Brazzell, who was the game's leading rusher with 79 yards on 14 carries, scored on a 2-yard run, and the Farmers surprised everyone by running a reverse to Reggie Crawford. Crawford netted 49 yards on the play and the final Farmer touchdown on the night. A token safety due to an errant Lion snap ended the Lewisville scoring, securing the opening game victory at 30–9. It would be a victory the Farmer coaches could savor and build upon.

Lewisville vs. Plano East — September 10, 1993
Lewisville was on the road again for the second contest, which came against Plano East at Clark Field and would no doubt be a more formidable opponent than Turner proved to be. On a mission to overcome the 14–14 tie the year before, the Farmers knew they would be facing their toughest non-district opponent on their schedule. Sandwiched between Turner and Newman Smith, both Carrollton schools with subpar talent, the Panthers were clearly an early test for the still maturing Farmers.

Plano East utilized the trendy run-and-shoot offense with nearly half their plays as passes, which would be an early test for the seasoned secondary of the Farmers. Lewisville, normally aligned in a 5–2 defense (that is, five down linemen and two linebackers), would institute a fifth defensive back—commonly known as either a nickel back, or nickel package—to combat the passing frequency of Panther quarterback Jeff Whitley. Two premier running backs would also pose a challenge for the Farmers. Alfonso Pinto and Marcus Williams alternated as the lone running back in the pro-style set, with Williams possessing the ability to score from anywhere on the field with his speed. This would be a different ball game than the Turner contest.

As expected, the game was a closely fought defensive battle laced with big plays, which spelled the difference. Dwight Hunter leveled Plano East's Marcus Williams on the opening kickoff, tackling him at the Panthers' 14-yard line where they began their initial possession, and Plano East never overcame the deficit. The most they gained in the series was 2 yards, forcing them to punt to the Farmers. Lewisville took over at Plano East's 40-yard line, and five plays later Chad Nelson raced 18 yards for an early touchdown. After a Topher Roach kick Lewisville held a 7–0 lead which remained until just under six minutes in the third period. That's when the Farmers would add to that lead, on a 37-yard gallop by Byron Mitchell straight up the middle of the field. That occurred at the 5:46 mark in the third quarter and it appeared, due to some outstanding defense, that the 14–0 score would be enough to gain the Farmers the second win, proving they could go up against the "big boys" on the road with their wishbone attack.

The Panthers followed the Farmer score with a touchdown drive of their own, a 69-yard, 10-play drive engineered by Aaron Easterling, who had replaced starter Jeff Whitley. Easterling provided key plays to sustain the drive, notably an 11-yard gain on a third-and-10 situation. Two key pass completions for more than 20 yards each allowed Plano East to get into the end zone on a 1-yard Easterling run. The score came late in the third quarter with still enough time to score again and avoid a loss to the Farmers. Panther coach Mike Bailey had already decided what he would do if faced with the choice of settling for a tie, like the season before, or going for a win. "No question," he said, "we would have gone for two."

The Panthers never had to make that choice. They did get close, however, on a bizarre play following an outstanding defensive stand. A Panther drive, starting at their own 22-yard line with 7:52 remaining in the contest, was stuffed by the Farmer defense, forcing Plano East to punt from their own 33-yard line. On the coverage the ball bounced off the back of an unsuspecting Farmer, and an alert Chris Eddins recovered the ball for the Panthers at Lewisville's 43-yard line. "Uh-oh," thought Coach Gage and the contingent of the Farmer fans on hand to hopefully watch their beloved boys go 2–0 in the young season. The turnover shifted the momentum in favor of the Panthers, and Gage got a lump in his throat. His defense had just staved off a Panther drive; now, it had to do an encore with no break.

Plano East drove from the Farmer 43 to the Farmer 7, threatening to score. They faced a critical third-and-one situation, with essentially two chances to gain the first down and get the ball into the end zone. They did get the ball

A Dream Realized

into the end zone, but not with the results they had expected. On the third-down play the Panthers had hoped to catch Lewisville looking for the run and attempted a pass into the end zone for all the marbles. They lost those marbles, however, as the Farmers' Dwight Hunter stepped in and picked off Easterling's pass 2 yards deep, returning it to the Farmer 16. That huge play ended the Panthers' hopes of winning their second game of the year. It also demonstrated the type of play the Farmers would consistently turn in during the season. According to Chad Nelson, the Plano East game was indicative of the teamwork that the young Farmers possessed. "Both units complemented each other. If the offense was struggling, the defense would come through and give us a chance to win. If the defense didn't play well, the offense would take control of the game. It wasn't anything we planned, it just worked out that way. The game against Plano East showed how well both units worked together. Offensively we did as much as we could. The defense really came through," Nelson recalled.

Gage felt fortunate to come out of Plano alive. "We were very fortunate to come out of a great game like this with a win. It was a great defensive high school ball game." Indeed it was.

Lewisville vs. Newman Smith — September 17, 1993
Lewisville's Homecoming was scheduled for the third game of the season, a bit earlier than usual. The toughest contest of the evening was not on the field, but rather in deciding who was to be Homecoming Queen, as the Farmers scored at will and defeated the dismal Trojans, 51–7. In a contest in which six different Farmers scored touchdowns—four of them sophomores—Lewisville was able to allow their backup players to get some varsity experience and the veterans to get a rest. It was a good thing, too, as quarterback Chad Nelson was named as LHS's first Homecoming King at the halftime ceremony. With the Farmers safely atop a 31–0 lead at intermission Nelson would not have to worry about tarnishing his crown; he was through for the night. After all, he'd had a busy first half, which included a 40-yard bomb to senior split end Erik Otsuji for the Farmers' first score. After that the sophomores took over to show that they could play football, too. Fullback Jason Voss scored a 4-yard touchdown to complete the first quarter scoring, and Reggie Crawford had a second quarter 7-yard run to extend the Farmer lead to 21–0. Topher Roach was perfect for the night on each of his three extra point attempts, as he had been all year, and later added a 41-yard field goal before the half ended. Prior to that, Shannon Brazzell stepped in front of a Mike Mussett pass and sprinted 28 yards to score, still in the first half.

In the second half the "Young Guns" came out shooting again, first on a 34-yard LaDarrin McLane touchdown run for the only third quarter score for either team. Alan Blacketer, in relief for Roach, did the honors with a successful extra point, and the Farmers led 38–0. Newman Smith's only score came next as quarterback Mike Mussett let loose with a 78-yard bomb to Phillip

Hayes early in the fourth quarter.

Lewisville scored the final two touchdowns of the game, both coming from a Farmer who had seen little playing time during the 1993 season. Freddy Wilson scored on both of his rushing attempts on the night, with runs of 2 and 65 yards, to close out the scoring on that busy Farmer night. Lewisville proved that it was not a one-dimensional team. The fact that six different Farmers scored, including a rare touchdown pass, revealed the depth of talent that would carry Lewisville far.

Lewisville vs. Grapevine — September 24, 1993
Week four ushered in district play, and the Farmers would face a young, but lethal, Grapevine Mustang team. The Mustangs had been picked to finish dead last in District 6-5A in 1993, and their 1–2 pre-district record seemed to prove the pollsters true on the prediction. Junior Mustang quarterback Sam Johnson was getting his bumps and bruises early as Grapevine lost to Richardson Berkner and Keller, but they defeated Weatherford the week before district play opened to record their only victory. Mustang Head Coach Mike Sneed hoped his young team had gained enough experience in the first three weeks of the season to be competitive in the traditionally tough District 6-5A.

Although Johnson, the district leader in passing through three games, junior receiver Jodfrey Fails and senior defensive tackle Chris Ruzic were bright spots for Grapevine, they simply weren't bright enough. The Farmers soundly defeated the Ponies, 42–8, to remain unbeaten, sharing the district lead with Denton, Wichita Falls Rider and Marcus after the first week. It was not without a fight, however.

Lewisville scored six times with Nelson, Dwayne Brazzell and Voss each scoring twice, however there was some concern about Nelson's ability to perform that night. Gage was worried because Nelson's father had suffered a slight heart attack earlier in the week and wondered if that might be a distraction to the star quarterback. Nelson and his father were very close, and Chad was visibly affected by his father's condition, so much so that Gage accompanied him to the hospital the Thursday evening before the opening district contest. After the visit the younger Nelson was comforted, and his play reflected it. He gained 105 yards rushing and was 4–6 in passing for 73 yards. That's not all, either. He scored on touchdown runs of 43 and 60 yards for 103 of his 105 total yards. A Dwayne Brazzell touchdown gave the Farmers a 21-2 halftime lead, with the two Mustang points coming on a bad snap on a Topher Roach punt attempt at the Farmer 16. Roach recovered the ball in the end zone, but the Mustangs were there to make sure he didn't get out, giving Grapevine a safety.

In the second half Sneed knew he would have to use some unconventional measures if his young Mustangs were going to get into the ball game. As the second half opened Grapevine both kicked and recovered an onside kick, a shrewd move on the Grapevine head coach's part. Recovering at the Farmer

A Dream Realized

40-yard line, Johnson led the Mustang stampede and found one of his frequent targets, wide receiver Damien Chambers, open on a 39-yard slant pattern, to draw them six points closer to the Farmers at 21–8, with most of the third quarter remaining. After a Farmer punt Grapevine charged right back, threatening to get the ball across the goal line. The Mustang drive penetrated deep into Lewisville territory but fell short on a tremendous defensive stand, mere inches from a second Grapevine score. The Mustangs had to surrender the ball to the stingy Farmers at that point. What the near capacity crowd at Goldsmith Stadium witnessed on the ensuing drive was rare and spectacular. Coach Ronnie Gage, figuring to move the ball out and get some breathing room, never really figured his offense would do what it did. From inside the 1-yard line Lewisville and its Steamrollers did just that, steamrolled the entire 99-plus yards, climaxed by a 7-yard Dwayne Brazzell touchdown to complete the near 100-yard mission. In actuality it was a 14 point swing. Not only did the Farmers prevent the Mustangs from scoring, but they were able to garner a score themselves, giving them a 28–8 advantage. That drive did the Mustangs in. Besides the score, the drive erased 7:30 minutes from the clock, leaving Sneed and company little time to overcome the deficit. At that point the game was practically over.

That's not what reserve fullback Jason Voss thought. He came in to relieve Dwayne Brazzell, the workhorse on the 99-yard drive, and finished the night with a marginal 9 yards on four carries, barely averaging 2 yards a carry. However, two of those runs resulted in touchdowns, one from 4 yards out and the other from 1. The final one came with 1:24 to play and completed the Farmer scoring for a 42–8 district win.

Lewisville vs. Sherman — October 1, 1993

The Sherman Bearcats were on tap for the next Farmer contest, with Lewisville traveling to Sherman for the second week of district play. The Bearcats went into district play ranked number 10 in the Dallas/Ft. Worth area by the *Dallas Morning News,* but slipped to 16 after a loss to Wichita Falls Rider in week four. Sherman Coach John Outlaw had picked the Farmers to dominate District 6-5A before the season began and alluded to the fact that his Bearcat team had no talent at all, down-playing his team's decisive victories in the first three weeks prior to losing to Rider. His alibi, that the teams his Bearcats had beaten were mediocre 4A teams, gave the allusion that Sherman could barely tie their shoes, much less compete in the district they had been a dominant force in throughout the past four seasons. The truth is, they had an explosive offense and one of the top passers in the area in quarterback Quinton Pelley. Pelley was third in the district in passing, completing 63 percent of his passes for 596 yards. Grapevine's Johnson led with 682 yards, closely followed by Marcus' Matt Tittle with 672 yards.

The Farmers, on the other hand, were 4–0 and had broken into the Associated Press top 10 list at number 10 by virtue of their 42–8 shellacking of Grape-

The Farmers break through the spirit sign before the Sherman game.

vine in week four. But in Sherman Lewisville had experienced trouble in past years and all indications were that they would again in 1993. Rather than being suckered into Outlaw's verbal antics, Gage saw past that and prepared his Farmers for a tough District 6-5A battle, the most important one of the season.

Lewisville began the scoring, as it had the four previous games, on a first quarter 10-yard run by Chad Nelson. The keeper capped a 75-yard trademark Farmer/Steamroller drive that chewed up 7:22 of the first quarter. To control the ball was important for the Farmers as they knew it would accomplish two goals: first, it almost always ended in a Farmer score, and second, it kept the ball out of the hands of Sherman's prolific passer, Quinton Pelley. Sherman did score on the subsequent drive on a David Deel field goal from 26 yards out, with Lewisville considering itself lucky to hold the Bearcats to a field goal. On the kickoff to start the field goal drive, Sherman's Marcus Kemp ran through the Farmer coverage and would have scored, had it not been for Topher Roach's touchdown-saving tackle at the Farmer 40-yard line.

Lewisville answered the call on their next possession, scoring their second touchdown in period two, this one coming via the pass. Martin Simmons snared a Nelson pass and carried it into the end zone, covering 48 yards for the score. Topher Roach, already busier than usual with the first quarter tackle, converted the extra point, extending Lewisville's lead to 14–3. That's when the game opened up, and what unfurled was one of the most exhaustive high school football games played in 1993. It would be inaccurate to say there was

A Dream Realized

no defense. It is incomprehensible to imagine what would have transpired had the defenses not played as well as they did. The fact is, there were two high powered offenses at work, and defending them would pose a great challenge, to say the least.

After the Farmers went up 14–3 they surrendered 21 straight points, including a 17–14 deficit at the half. It was the first time Lewisville had trailed at any time in 1993, and Coach Gage and his staff were concerned. This was the Sherman team that had beaten three so-so 4A teams and lost to Wichita Falls Rider the week before. They were without their leading rushers, and according to Bearcat Coach John Outlaw, really had no right to be on the same field with the Farmers. Something or someone had lit a fire under this stubborn Sherman team, and by golly, they actually believed they could beat those Farmers. Gage's staff had to find a way to extinguish that fire, even if it meant calling Red Adair to do it.

Sherman's Jerwayne Parker offered up the first of the three touchdowns on a 21-yard dash, seeing his first action in varsity competition as a freshman against the Farmers. Hunter Smith, the fleet-footed Bearcat receiver, scored the first of three touchdowns he would score that night on a 54-yard reception from Pelley just before halftime. That made the score 17–14 for the Bearcat halftime lead, and had the Farmer coaches scratching their heads to come up with a plan to ward off the Sherman attack.

They didn't. At least not immediately. Pelley and Smith connected again to begin the scoring in the third quarter, this time covering 81 yards and taking a 24–14 lead. With the Farmers' style of ball control offense it was essential for them to score soon to ensure themselves plenty of time to produce enough offense sufficient for a win. The Farmers rallied for the next two touchdowns, both supplied by Byron Mitchell in the fast-paced third quarter. The first, a 37-yard run up the middle, came with 7:59 in the third period to cut the Bearcat lead to three. The second, a 7-yard run put the Farmers on top once again. Topher Roach supplied the extra points after both scores, giving Lewisville a 28–24 lead.

Unlike Perry Mason or F. Lee Bailey, the defense could not rest. Sherman was bound and determined to upset Lewisville. After losing their opening district game, they were on the verge of being knocked out of the district race with a loss to the Farmers, and they did all they could to prevent that. David Deel kicked a 22-yard field goal to pull within one at 28–27, and the show wasn't over yet. Lewisville's Dwayne Brazzell, one of four Farmer backs that combined for 406 rushing yards, hit paydirt from 15 yards out to put the game out of reach, 35–27, with 1:24 left on the clock . . . at last.

Or so they thought. With the precision of a skilled surgeon, Pelley and Smith quickly covered the 76 yards required in only 1:07 in contrast to the Farmer offense. That was basically the difference between the two teams. Lewisville preferred to grind the ball out, as evident by the 32:06 time of possession. After all, there were only 48 minutes to go around, and the Bearcats made good use of the balance of time remaining as they almost matched the Farmers score for score. The final 1:07 seconds seemed to tick off at a two-for-one pace, with two actual seconds available for every clock second. It didn't move fast enough for Gage, Goode and the Farmer defense; something about a watched pot never boiling. Anyway, with twelve seconds remaining, Hunter Smith caught his third, and last, touchdown pass of the night (thank goodness), to pull the Bearcats to within two at 35–33. There was no doubt in anyone's mind what Sherman would do with the extra point attempt. Obviously John Outlaw and his Bearcats would go for two, especially with the loss to Rider a week ago. 0–1–1 looked better than 0–2 any day, especially if it brought the mighty Farmers down with them.

Sherman lined up at the Farmer 3 for the coveted two-point conversion. Pelley sent everyone out in hopes of finding someone open. With Smith and his counterpart, Andy Russell, flooding the right side, Farmer defensive backs Mike Frazier and Jason Cotten were Johnny-on-the-spot, with tight coverage. Pelley hurled the ball toward Russell, hoping he could make some kind of "immaculate reception," kind of like Dwight Clark did against Dallas to begin the San Francisco 49er's dynasty of the '80s, but Cotten spoiled that hope by stepping in front of him for an interception—thank you very much. After the Farmers recovered an unsuccessful onside kick attempt, the game was finally at a manageable level; 47 minutes and 53 seconds deep into the contest. Gage finally breathed. He had been holding his breath throughout the final drive, but with Cotten's pick he could exhale. After the clock read 0:00, he began to get his color back. Sherman had taken its best shot and it wasn't quite enough.

It was a fun game to watch regardless of which team you supported. It was reminiscent of game six of the 1975 World Series between the Cincinnati Reds and the Boston Red Sox. The Red Sox were down 6–3 in the bottom of the sixth inning when pinch hitter Bernie Carbo was summoned from the bench. All he did was slap a three-run home run 420 feet to straight away center field and tied the score. The game went to 12 innings when Boston's Carlton Fisk hit the dramatic home run to break the deadlock and send the Series to a seventh game . . . truly one of the most memorable games in sports, and the Farmer-Bearcat game was from the same mold. Lewisville received an aerial baptism unlike they had received in the first four weeks, and they felt fortunate to escape as the victors.

Lewisville vs. Wichita Falls Rider — October 8, 1993
The Farmers remained at home against their next foe, the Wichita Falls Rider Raiders, for the third conference game. Rider was 1–1 in district play, beating Sherman, 17–10, and losing to Denton, 10–0. Both contests were low-scoring ones, indicating the style of play the Raiders and Coach Wayne LeBleu preferred to employ. Rider liked to duke it out defensively and slowly crank it out offensively, hoping to have the edge with low scoring games. It worked against Sherman; it did not against Denton.

A Dream Realized

The Raiders had the district's second leading running back in Kevin Wagner. Wagner had 565 yards on 135 carries; only Denton's Deon Green had more (593 yards on 86 carries). The closest Farmer was Dwayne Brazzell, 113 yards behind. But the Raider offense proved to be vulnerable as Denton held Wagner to a mere 44 yards. Once the running game was shut down, having to rely on the pass was distasteful, according to LeBleu. "We can't throw feed to starving birds," was his response to his team's lack of a formative passing attack; an honest, but comical evaluation of the Raiders' necessary reliance on defense and the running game. A strong showing by the Farmer offense could have made it a long ride home for the Wichita Falls team.

Gage cited the combination of the physical Raider defense and the bumps and bruises his Farmers suffered in the shootout in Sherman as potential detriments to a Farmer victory over Rider. A handful of Farmers had experienced injuries against the Bearcats, ranging from guard Buddy Phillips' foot injury to corner back Mike Frazier's sprained ankle. Nelson, Dwayne Brazzell and Waylon Holland, three-fourths of the Lewisville wishbone attack, were beat up a little, but each would be listed as a starter against Rider. Only Phillips would see no action.

The Lewisville defense had developed into one of the premier defensive units in the state. Through five weeks no back had gained 100 yards against the pesky Farmers. In fact, R.L. Turner's Jose Rodriguez's 76-yards in game one was the most surrendered by the Farmers all year, not good news for the incoming Raiders. By all counts, the game measured to be a close one in contrast to the Sherman game a week earlier.

The Farmers dodged a bullet early as Rider's Jonathan Hawkins almost provided the Raiders with a touchdown to open the game. He returned the initial kickoff some 64 yards, and Rider set up shop in Farmer territory early in the contest at Lewisville's 31. Unable to mount a drive, however LeBleu and company were forced to settle for a 30-yard field goal attempt. Jason Cotten, the Farmer who made the game-saving interception against Sherman, broke through to block the attempt, and the Raiders blew a chance to get ahead quickly against what would be a tough Farmer defensive effort.

Lewisville shot itself in the foot on the ensuing drive as Chad Nelson fumbled, one of only a handful in his two-year career as the Farmer quarterback, giving Rider the ball in Lewisville territory at the 27. The Raiders capitalized on the Farmer miscue, with Tavares Hansboro carrying it in 9 yards with exactly four minutes remaining in the opening quarter. The extra point attempt failed, but the Raiders jumped out first for a 6–0 lead. It looked as if the lead might hold, too, as the Raider defense stopped the Farmers, forcing them to punt. But things can turn bad quickly and did so for the Raiders, as Jayme Carr muffed a booming Topher Roach punt at around his own 15-yard line. The result was an alert Byron Mitchell recovery for Lewisville at that point, and Nelson made up for his earlier mistake by scoring on the first play of the drive—a 15-yard keeper. Roach kicked the extra point, and the Farmers held a 7–6 lead.

No one scored again until midway through the third quarter, but there was plenty of action—all defensively. Both defenses held their respective opponents to season lows. Rider could only manage 108 total yards on the night, 68 of those rushing. The Farmers gained just 239 themselves, including a season low for its leading rusher, Dwayne Brazzell. The powerful Farmer fullback totaled a mere 42 yards on 11 carries, a tribute to the well coached Raider defense. The option was all but eliminated, forcing Lewisville to punt five times; the most they would have to in any single game all season. Topher Roach, the Farmer kicker, was a key element in the game. Averaging 40 yards a kick, Roach pinned the Raiders in their own territory all evening, allowing the Farmer defense to tee-off on the Rider backfield. Roach added an impressive 41-yard field goal against the wind in the third period to finish with a full night's work.

Lewisville did manage to mount some resemblance of its familiar offensive output. A 70-yard eight-play drive in the fourth period was capped by a 7-yard Nelson run to close the Farmers scoring for the night. Nelson completed his only pass of the night on a critical third-and-long play at the Farmer 31-yard line. The pass, a 34-yarder to Martin Simmons, was the fifth completion from Nelson to the bulky tight end on the year, and the combination was becoming a key weapon for Lewisville in critical situations.

The Rider defense held the usually potent Lewisville offense to a mere 239 total yards, a far cry from their season average of 394. Nelson led all rushers with 72 yards, and Brazzell was a distant second with 42. The Raiders were even less prolific with 108 — yes only 108 total yards; usually a quarter's work for the Farmers. The stingy Lewisville defense rendered the Raiders inept, shutting down Wagner, Hansboro, and whoever Rider threw into the mix, securing the 17–6 Farmer win.

Lewisville vs. Denton — October 15, 1993
With things rolling right along for the Farmers at 6–0, they would face their toughest challenge of the season against Denton's Broncos in game seven . . . or at least they were supposed to have. Denton, at 5–1, had experienced their only loss of the season to the Marcus Marauders a week earlier, 41–26, showing the first signs of vulnerability.

During that contest the Broncos' sophomore sensational running back, Derrick Peoples, suffered a hip pointer and left the game shortly before the first half ended, eliminating one-half of the district's leading rushers. He had 95 yards at the time of his departure. The other half of the district's top runners, also a Bronco, was Deon Green. In fact, Green and Peoples were the number one and two leaders in rushing with 782 and 652 yards respectively; Dwayne Brazzell was well behind with 494. But Peoples would not play against Lewisville, allowing the dominant Farmer front line to concentrate solely on stopping Green and keeping quarterback Shane Hardin busy in the backfield. Hardin started in place of Bronco regular Ross Appleton, hopefully to counter

A Dream Realized

the loss of Peoples and add another dimension the Farmers would have to contend with. Hardin had been impressive late in the contest against Marcus in engineering two late touchdown drives, while Appleton was unsuccessful on all five of his pass attempts, suffering two interceptions. Head Coach Jim Bateman thought Hardin might be the change his Broncos needed after the disappointing loss.

For Lewisville, Brazzell looked doubtful for the contest due to a chipped bone in his ankle suffered during the game against Rider. Though not serious, Coach Gage did not want to take any chances of further injury to the Farmers' leading ball carrier. Byron Mitchell would slip into the fullback spot to fill in for Brazzell, and sophomore Jason Voss rotated in for Mitchell at the halfback position. The depth factor was definitely in favor of Lewisville, especially in the running back department, as the Farmers had a stable full of thoroughbreds ready to go at a moment's notice.

The Lewisville-Denton series began in 1974, the first season of 4A competition for the Farmers, and continued through the 1981 season. The Farmers and Broncos were separated due to district realignments, but the competition resumed in 1986 when the two teams became members of District 5-5A and has continued since. Although a natural rivalry because of their geographical proximity, the series has never reached the level of intensity everyone expected it to. When the teams first met in '74 the media called it, "the Denton County Showdown," offering to supply a trophy that would go to the victor each year, but the athletic departments of both districts objected to the idea, preferring the rivalry to be friendly rather than hostile.

Of course, the Denton game is an important one each season but just does not have the emotion of the Lewisville-Grapevine series of old, or the always entertaining Lewisville-Plano rivalry. Only the fairly recent Lewisville-Marcus annual battle parallels the intensity of the early Grapevine and current Plano contests. The 1993 Lewisville-Denton game would be a key District 6-5A contest. The Farmers were confidently rolling through the tough district, having already defeated two of the favored teams in Sherman and Wichita Falls Rider. The biggest test of the season would come against the Broncos, but the Farmers had an advantage with a one game lead. Neither team could afford a loss if they were to control their destiny

The key for a Farmer victory over Denton would be the defense, specifically the defensive line. Noseguard Pete Bonenberger and tackles Todd Landrum and Dan Merritt would have to turn in a combined championship effort if they were to stop the explosive Denton offensive attack and keep Deon Green in check. If Lewisville was successful there the Broncos would be forced to go to the air, a part of their game plan they hadn't mastered.

The Farmers had a 7–0 lead early in the game and had not even taken a snap from center. After stopping the opening Bronco drive, Lewisville's Dwight Hunter returned a Shane Hardin punt 53 yards through several would-be tacklers, and sailed down the west sideline for the first Farmer score. Topher

Roach added the extra point for the 7–0 lead, and the Farmers had shocked the Broncos in the early going.

Lewisville added another touchdown in the first period on a 58-yard run by reserve running back Jason Voss. Voss was in at halfback for Mitchell, who had replaced the ailing Brazzell at fullback. For the first time of the season Roach missed an extra point, and the first quarter Farmer lead stood at 13–0.

Lewisville did not let up in the second quarter, either. While the defensive front line was controlling the scrimmage line, the Farmers were supplying offensive support. A 1-yard touchdown run by Dwayne Brazzell, who had entered the game briefly to test the sore ankle, climaxed a 10-play, 66-yard drive to increase the Farmer lead to 19–0. The Farmers attempted a two-point conversion to catch up in scoring but failed to get the ball in the end zone, giving Denton only a 19-point deficit to overcome. A Lewisville fumble helped the Broncos make up part of that. Denton's Mike Kinslow pounced on the first of three Farmer fumbles at the Lewisville 24-yard line to set up the first, and only, Denton score of the game. It took the Broncos 10 plays to cover the 24 yards, but they did, with Deon Green going over from the 1. James Schuessler kicked the extra point, and the Broncos had a glimmer of hope going in at halftime.

The Broncos had virtually no offense in the second half, and Lewisville had little more . . . but then again, they didn't need it, as the stiff Farmer defense refused to allow Denton to cross the 50-yard line in the second half. The only time they entered Farmer territory was after blocking a Topher Roach punt at the Farmer 39. The possession was short lived, however, as Dwight Hunter intercepted Ross Appleton's pass on the first play of the drive. Appleton had replaced Hardin at quarterback for the second half, but with no more success than Hardin. In fact, wingback Mike Neely was the Broncos leading passer with one completion for 30 yards. He was the only Bronco not to suffer an interception to Hunter. Both Hardin and Appleton fell victim to the Farmer free safety's prey, with each serving up two interceptions to Hunter for a game-high of four picks for any Farmer all season. The final one was for a 26-yard touchdown in the fourth quarter, killing any chance the Broncos had at coming back.

Before Hunter scored his second touchdown, Chad Nelson extended the Farmer lead to 25–7 on a 25-yard third quarter run. Nelson connected on the two-point attempt, making the score 27–7 before Hunter did his thing to bump the lead up to 34–7. The final touchdown of the game came on a 1-yard run by Lee Stewart to complete the Farmer scoring at 41–7.

As far as numbers are concerned, neither team rewrote any school records. Denton, which had averaged 327 yards of offense coming into the game, was restricted to a meager 151, a tribute to the Farmer front line, coupled with the injury to Peoples. The Farmers, on the other hand, had only 203 total yards themselves, 58 of them coming on Voss' first quarter touchdown run. The real story of the game was Dwight Hunter's four interceptions and two touch-

A Dream Realized

Captains Buddy Phillips (71), Chad Nelson (11) and Dan Merritt (61) meet with Dustin Ptak (17) and Mark Cusano (32) of The Colony to determine the first half kickoff.

downs; one from an interception return and the other from a punt return. His play insured the Farmer offense good field position all evening, part of the reason why the Farmer total was so low. Regardless, Lewisville found themselves at 7–0, and 4–0 in district, and out front in the District 6-5A race.

Lewisville vs. The Colony — October 22, 1993
With a 7–0 record and a 4–0 district record all the Farmers had to do was tie The Colony to assure themselves a playoff berth. The Cougars were 1–3 in district but were just under the Farmers in defense, allowing 213.6 yards per game, and might prove to be a problem for Lewisville, which relied heavily on its offense. The Colony had never beaten Lewisville, having only played once before, but gave the Farmers a good scare in 1992, losing 28–21, at Goldsmith Stadium. This game would be played at the Cougars lair, however, where they had been successful.

Even though The Colony was 1–3 in district play, the losses were not blowouts, and the Cougars were no pushovers. The Colony recorded losses to Marcus, 17–3, Grapevine, 21–14 and Sherman, 20–17, before soundly defeating Wichita Falls Rider, 27–6. The close games demonstrated that The Colony could not be taken lightly, nor would Gage allow them to be. This was one contest he did not look forward to. "I dreaded the game against The Colony all year, especially after how 1992's game turned out. The rivalry had been building up over the past several seasons, once they learned they would be

It's good! Topher Roach's only extra point against The Colony ended the Farmer scoring that night. Josh Altom held, while Byron Mitchell (22) kept the Cougars from blocking the kick.

in our district. I just had a gut feeling going into this year's game," remembered Gage.

The Farmer head coach's intuition was accurate, as The Colony gave the Farmers fits all night. Besides the pesky Cougar defense, Lewisville committed three costly turnovers at critical times in the contest to set the tone for the way things would go for the Farmers that evening—or rather, not go. A Farmer fumble at their own 13-yard line led to the Cougars' only score, which came in the third period. The Colony's Mike Henefer recovered the costly miscue that eventually led to a John Stefaniak touchdown plunge from a yard out. Eddie Elrod kicked the extra point which tied the two strong defensive teams at 7–7.

The Farmers' score came in the second quarter on a 9-yard keeper by Chad Nelson. Nelson had a 75-yard run for an apparent touchdown in the final period, but the officials ruled he had stepped out of bounds at the 49, nullifying the potential winning touchdown. Another Farmer touchdown was erased by a (ahem!) penalty, and Lewisville could not seem to do anything to please the Zebras. "There were some controversial calls; some tough calls," according to Gage, but he admits it was The Colony's preparation and well coached defense that prevented them from winning.

The Cougars were not without misfortune of their own. Late in the contest The Colony had the ball at the Farmer 4-yard line. Quarterback Aaron Brown ran it in from that point for a short-lived 13–7 lead, but only for a moment, as the play was called back on a holding penalty. Following the infraction the Farmers held the Cougars, forcing a 28-yard field goal attempt. Pete

A Dream Realized

Dan Merritt (61) and Zeb Cornist (99) pressure Cougar quarterback Aaron Brown (10) while attempting to pass.

Bonenberger broke through the line to block Elrod's kick, and that was as close as the Farmers came to losing.

The Farmers had a final chance to score on the drive which ended the game. Lewisville drove into Cougar territory and tried to get in field goal position. They could only manage to reach the 38-yard line with a half a minute or so to play. Instead of attempting what would have been a 55-yard field goal, Gage elected to run the clock down to a few remaining seconds, time enough for a single play, which drew criticism from the crowd. Gage didn't care. He knew a tie would clinch a playoff spot, and that was his team's first goal for the 1993 season. The final play, a long pass to defensive back Reggie Crawford, who had lined up as wide receiver, fell incomplete, and the clock ran out—and with it, the first team to secure a playoff berth from District 6-5A was named. "We were lucky to get out of there with a tie," Gage said, citing the mistakes his team had made as the primary reason, especially some missed blocking assignments. "We made some changes to the offensive line, more to keep people fresh than anything else," explained the third year Farmer coach. "Mika Clark was moved from guard to center, and we inserted Pete (Bonenberger) and Dan (Merritt) in as guard and tackle because of their experience." During the contest, Farmer left guard Buddy Phillips, the lone returning starter on the offensive line, re-injured his left shoulder on the scoring touchdown drive, an injury that kept him out of spring drills in '93. Clark, Bonenberger and Merritt, along with Mike Anderson, Victor Zeliff, Chad Dawson and Phillips, alternated during the remainder of the season to ensure the Farmers a fresh offensive line to head up their wishbone attack. In short, Gage explained, "We used four people to play two positions."

Despite all the negative things that came out of the game against The Colony, several good things happened. Dwayne Brazzell had returned full-time in the backfield and appeared to be at full strength. The injury to Phillips did not end his season, and he was able to return to the line-up the following week. The Farmers secured a playoff spot for themselves regardless of what happened throughout the remainder of the regular season. But most importantly, the 7–7 tie against The Colony served as a wake-up call for Lewisville, which forced them to refocus on the chink in their armor and make sure no other team penetrated that weakness again.

The Farmers slipped in both the area and state rankings as a result of the tie against The Colony. Both lists had them at number eight, dropping five spots in the *Dallas Morning News'* area poll and only one spot in the Associated Press' state poll. Although the slippage was a bit disappointing, the fact that they secured for themselves a spot in post-season play was a plus, even though their winning streak had come to an end. In fact, going back to the 1992 season, the Farmers' regular season win streak reached 13 games before coming to a halt in The Colony.

Lewisville vs. Allen — October 29, 1993
Lewisville still had a test in the final game against the Marcus Marauders, but they had to contend with the Allen Eagles prior to that contest. It could not have come at a better time of the year either, as the Eagles were in the cellar at 0–5 in district play. It would be a bit of a break for the Farmers, even though the Eagles played them close the year before, losing only 35–28 in a game that wasn't even supposed to be close. Like the game against The Colony in '92, the Farmers committed key turnovers against Allen which led to scores, forcing Lewisville's Metrick McHenry to knock down a last-second Mel Johnson pass, intended for Cedric Redwine, to prevent a tie or possible win.

The 1993 game would be different, however. The Farmers were well seasoned with many players returning from the '92 squad, although Allen returned a good number of veterans as well. Quarterback Mel Johnson was back, but his favorite target, Redwine, was gone, and their starting lineup was dotted with youth and inexperience. They had 11 seniors, four juniors and seven sophomores returning from a 5–5 team that finished with a 2–5 district record in '92. The key to the Farmers' future success was defense, and with a playoff spot secure the pressure was somewhat relaxed . . . and the fiery Farmers were ready to have fun against the Eagles.

And fun they had, too. In one of the coldest games—if not the coldest—played at Goldsmith Stadium, six Farmers shared in the scoring, while shutting out Allen en route to a 52–0 lashing of the team that had played them so close the season before. The temperature was cold; 20 degrees, after a norther had blown in earlier that afternoon. The wind chill factor was eight degrees, but the Eagles offense was even colder as the Farmer defense held them to 149 total yards in a game that got out of hand early. By the end of the first

A Dream Realized

Zeb Cornist hog ties an Allen ball carrier as Dan Merritt (61) moves in to assist.

quarter the score was 27–0, with the only Farmer mistake coming on a missed extra point on their second score. That touchdown was a 3-yard Dwayne Brazzell run, the first of two he would score that blustery night.

Byron Mitchell starting the scoring with a 19-yard run to give the Farmers an early lead. The Farmers won the toss and elected to have the 30 mile-an-hour wind at their backs, a strategy that worked in favor of Lewisville. The Farmers got the ball in Eagle territory after a wind-thwarted punt, which set up a four-play scoring drive, capped by Byron Mitchell's 19-yard touchdown run. Topher Roach kicked the wind-aided extra point, which must have landed somewhere in the vicinity of the D/FW International Airport, and the Farmers never looked back. Two other touchdowns were supplied by Reggie Crawford's 38-yard run and Brett Cox's 20-yard return of a fumble recovery. Crawford scored a two-point conversion after his touchdown, but Roach's extra point after Cox's fumble return failed—his second miss of the game. No doubt it was affected by the stiff wind.

Roach missed five extra points on the night, none of which were entirely his fault, nor were they critical to the outcome of the contest. To indicate the type of game it was for Lewisville, Lee Stewart, the Farmers' third-string fullback, was the games' leading rusher, with 75 yards on nine carries. He also scored the final two touchdowns on runs of 1 and 56 yards, accounting for all the points scored in the fourth period. Waylon Holland and Brazzell scored one touchdown apiece in the second and third quarters in the Farmers' rout of the Eagles. The Eagles were just happy for the game to be over and to get on those warm buses so they could nurse their wounds on the way home.

The victory over Allen upped the Farmers' playoff situation by securing at least the runner-up spot in District 6-5A; Grapevine was close behind after overcoming an 0–3 start. The Mustangs had achieved a 5–1 district record, one-half game behind the Farmers' 5-0-1 district mark, and both teams had assured themselves a place in the playoffs, but the third spot was still up for grabs. Marcus, Rider and Denton all had outside chances, with Marcus in the best position of the three. The Marauders had two chances to be assured of a playoff berth. First, all they had to do was defeat the Farmers, a task that seemed possible after the Farmers' game against The Colony, but grew less likely after the momentum gained from Lewisville's stomping of Allen. Second, even if the Marauders lost to Lewisville, a Grapevine victory over Wichita Falls Rider would give Marcus the final spot from District 6-5A. Either way they would have to contend with a renewed Fighting Farmer team in the 1993 Battle for the Ax.

Reserve quarterback LaDarrin McLane (12) fires a pass into the Eagle secondary.

Lewisville vs. Marcus — November 5, 1993

Even though the Farmers plucked the Eagles, 52–0, they managed to slip in the AP poll to the number 10 slot, the spot they occupied when first breaking into the state's top ten after pounding Grapevine in week four.

Marcus never made it to the state poll, although they made it to the number 16 spot in the area rankings, largely on the arm of the area's second leading passer, Matt Tittle. Tittle had amassed 1,875 yards while completing 55 percent of his passes. Only nine of his 229 attempts had been intercepted, and he tossed nine scoring strikes thus far, mainly to his favorite receiver, Jeff Briggs; the area's third leading receiver. The prolific Marauder passing attack could have been a problem for Lewisville: one only had to turn back to the Sherman game to see the damage done in that contest. The Farmer defensive backs were burned for 284 yards and three touchdown passes against the Bearcats. Since then, however, Farmer defensive backs shored up their coverage and pass rush, with Dwight Hunter leading the way with his four interceptions against Denton. Since the Sherman near-massacre, the Farmers allowed a combined 119 passing yards in four games, picked off six passes and allowed no touchdowns through the air. Whatever lesson they learned against Sherman, it stuck, which prepared them for the showdown with Marcus.

Besides the aspect of an outright district championship, the Farmers had plenty to motivate them. No doubt they would be playing in front of a full

A Dream Realized

house at Max Goldsmith Stadium, with a capacity of 10,000. They were playing their crosstown rivals, who had a knack for getting under their skin. Marcus Head Coach Que Brittain liked to make it sound as though his team was nothing but an assembly of scrubs, and that the Farmers had all the talent in the Lewisville I.S.D.—conveniently forgetting the likes of Matt Tittle, the district's leading quarterback and area's second rated passer, Chad Row, a blue-chip offensive lineman, Travis Loughmiller, a hard hitting linebacker, and Shawn Merchant, the district's fifth leading rusher. They had plenty of weapons themselves but mostly preferred an aerial attack. As far as offense went, both teams were about dead even, with Lewisville owning a slight edge in total offense with 3,079 combined yards to Marcus' 3,027. The real difference between the two teams was defense.

The Farmer defense was ranked ninth in the area, allowing just over 200 yards of offense per game. Aside from the 359 yards allowed to Sherman, the most yardage the Farmers gave up was to Newman Smith's 283 in the homecoming game, a contest which featured a host of reserves getting playing time because of the 51–7 score. The combination of the powerful Farmer offense and stingy defense made Lewisville a unanimous favorite, but Gage knew it would be a tough contest. "There was a lot of pressure to win. A victory would guarantee us the championship; a loss would give us the runner-up spot. Of course, I preferred a win so that we could control our destiny," remembered the Farmer head coach.

There was no doubt Lewisville would be motivated, with as much on the line as there was. "The kids motivated themselves. As coaches, our job was to keep their focus on the game rather than the hype that surrounded it. But we also tried to make it a fun game, the way high school football is supposed to be," detailed Coach Gage on the approach his staff took in preparing his team for the final regular season game. "Although there is a lot of hype surrounding the game with the ax and all, the administrators pretty well keep it in check so as not to take away from the fun of it." That's the tone the game had taken the previous seven years; a good, clean, friendly rivalry played with a lot of pride and intensity.

The 1993 contest would be no different. In fact, it embodied the sum total of what the rivalry had become, with both programs evolving into top area football teams, climaxed by playoff spots decided on the outcome of their annual encounter. It was, and is, a tribute to the legacy of Lewisville football to produce not one, but two teams as consistently competitive as Lewisville and Marcus have become, with a third one on the horizon in The Colony. That the district race, or at least some part of it, would be decided at Max Goldsmith Stadium would be fitting for a community and school which had all too often been overlooked when the topic of high school powerhouses was brought up. That was fine, though, as it often worked to the Farmers' advantage.

The first half of the Battle for the Ax was dominated by an outstanding defensive effort on the part of the Marauders, and it was evident that they were in a must-win situation. Their play certainly indicated it. Defensively they held the Farmers' sluggish offense to a season low 77 yards in the first half, accomplishing one-half of their game plan. On offense they were successful in moving up and down the field, but could not get the ball across the goal line. The only thing they had to show for their efforts was a 22-yard Matt Baldock field goal, good enough for a halftime lead in the all-important game.

Upon reflection, Gage had a reasonable explanation for his team's uncharacteristic dismal performance. "Going into the game, we as coaches felt like we had to do something different against Marcus because they knew our offense and personnel so well. We prepared differently, thinking we could get ourselves in some situations or some early reads at the line of scrimmage and get an advantage, but all we did was take away from our strengths. We outcoached ourselves, something every coach is guilty of at one time," admitted Gage. That explanation parallels the mistake Coach Bill Shipman confessed to in 1972 by altering a similar offensive scheme going into the ninth regular season game against the Gainsville Leopards. The Farmers lost, largely due to the alienation from their strength of straight-ahead running. The "new" game plan backfired on them, much the same way Gage's new scheme produced less-than desired results in the first half. That caused the Farmer coaching staff to go back to the proverbial drawing board at intermission.

"In the locker room at the half we (the coaches) scrambled around trying to decide what we could do to get things going. What we had done hadn't worked so we were looking for something that we thought would," the almost desperate but still calm head coach recalled. "Coach Mike Campbell spoke up and said, 'Coach, can I say something?' I said, 'Sure,' and looked around, not knowing what to expect. He suggested, 'Let's cut the crap and get back playing our ball game.' We all kind of got quiet for a few moments, and it finally dawned on the rest of us that he was right. That's when we brought all the players together and decided to go to our old game plan." The coaches had indeed overlooked the obvious, that being the strength of their powerful ball control offense. After Campbell's timely prompting, they reduced their second half game plan to about five or six plays for the final 24 minutes of the game. "We withstood their drives," Gage told his Farmers before reemerging from the locker room, "and we've overcome some mistakes, but we're only down 3–0. We've taken their best shot." And with those words, a rejuvenated Farmer team, excited with enthusiasm, was ready to take control of the second half.

And control they did. The Farmers scored on their first possession of the second half on a 42-yard drive that looked like the Lewisville offense of old. Dwayne Brazzell carried it over from the 1, and the Farmers had their first lead of the game. Topher Roach, under better weather conditions than the week earlier, kicked the extra point, and Lewisville led 7–3 at the 8:13 mark in the third quarter.

After Brazzell's score the Farmers gained a lead they would never relin-

A Dream Realized

quish, although it would come in jeopardy a time or two before the night was over. Marcus drove the ball like a team on a mission on their subsequent drive, reaching the Farmer 8-yard line before stalling out. Brittain had no choice but to attempt a field goal; after all, their was still plenty of time in the game. Marcus' Matt Baldock booted his second field goal of the game, this coming from 26 yards, and the Farmer lead narrowed to 7–6.

The Farmers, back to their familiar ball control offense, constructed a 60-yard scoring drive to counter Baldock's field goal. Waylon Holland's 2-yard jolt on the drive's 12th play stole the rising momentum away from Marcus, and Lewisville led 13–6 early in the fourth quarter. Roach missed on the extra point attempt. The Marauders had been overcome by the spirit of Big John, and fallen prey to "Farmer Quarter," the familiar battle cry—a holdover from 1972. Or at least it looked that way until Tittle sparked the red and silver with a quick drive down the field with under three minutes remaining. The prolific Marauder passer coolly rifled off completions of 12, 21 and 32 yards, before the Farmers knew what hit them. By the time their collective heads quit spinning they were able to watch Tittle carry it over from the 5, pulling Marcus to within seven at 20–13. The multitude of Marauder fans who had filed out after Lewisville's final score began scrambling back to their seats. This one wasn't over yet.

To make matters tense for the Farmers, they fumbled the predictable on-side kick, which Marcus recovered at their own 49, giving Tittle and company a final shot at winning back the Ax and assuring themselves a playoff spot, regardless of the outcome of the Rider-Grapevine game. With 1:06 on the clock, Tittle fired off two completions inside Farmer territory, including a 27-yarder to Jeff Briggs. The Farmer fans were getting uneasy, but their anxiety was eased when Dan Merritt and Zeb Cornist combined to sack Tittle for a loss on third down, setting up a final fourth-and-19 play. Tittle dropped back to attempt his 40th pass in the game, a Battle for the Ax record for attempts through the '93 game, and threw in the direction of Briggs. Instead of a Briggs reception, however, Lewisville's Reggie Crawford leaped up, making what may have been a game-saving interception at the Farmer 7 to preserve the win, retain the Ax and, most importantly, capture the second straight District 6-5A crown.

The 20–13 Lewisville victory over Marcus was their third consecutive win against them, giving the Farmers the series edge at 5–2–1. They had faced one of the best passing attacks in the state and survived, giving up 237 passing yards to Tittle. It was unlikely the Farmers would see anything remotely similar to the Marcus aerial attack in the playoffs, at least not anytime soon.

Lewisville vs. Burleson — November 12, 1993
Lewisville's bi-district round featured the identical match-up of 1992, facing off against the District 5-5A third place representative, the Burleson Elks. Lewisville crushed the Elks in the '92 round, 48–7, and the prospects were

Friday Night Farmers

(Left) Dan Merritt comes over the top to put pressure on Marcus' Matt Tittle (15). Lewisville won the eighth Battle for the Ax, 20–13. (Right) Erik Otsuji (88) and Carlos Cherigo (80) hold up the Ax after the Farmer victory.

favorable for the Farmers again in '93. Burleson lost their bid for the runner-up spot the week before, being blown out against district rival Cleburne, losing 41–0. Needless to say, the Farmers were heavily favored. After all, the '93 version of the Farmers had more tools than did the '92 squad, and the first round playoff game for Lewisville appeared to be a cake walk.

And it was. The Farmers again demolished Burleson, 43–7, for the bi-district championship in the second game of a first round playoff doubleheader. The Farmers struck quickly and often in a game that unfolded much like the one against Allen two weeks earlier, scoring 28 unanswered points in the first period, with over half of those coming from better than 40 yards away. Waylon Holland sped 55 yards up the field for the first Farmer score. After two unsuccessful Burleson possessions Dwight Hunter returned an Elk punt 47 yards—his second punt return for a touchdown in the season—and increased the Farmer first quarter lead to 14–0; but they weren't through yet. On Lewisville's next drive Chad Nelson dashed 43 yards for the third Farmer touchdown of the opening quarter. He also scored later in the period on a 4-yard keeper to round out the scoring in the opening quarter. Topher Roach was successful on each of his four extra point attempts to account for the 28–0 advantage, and there were still three quarters left to be played.

Burleson managed to hold the Farmers to a single score in the second quarter on a 6-yard Dwayne Brazzell burst for a 34–0 advantage. A mishandled

A Dream Realized

snap on the point-after attempt forced holder Josh Altom to run it in, and this effort turned to gold, too. Altom's two-point conversion increased the Lewisville lead to 36–0, with the Farmers barely even breaking a sweat. By this time most of the starters were replaced by reserves for a golden opportunity to gain playoff experience.

It was against the second and third teams that Burleson generated the bulk of its 149 yards and lone touchdown, which came on a 22-yard pass to Lerone Jordan from the beaten and bruised Elk quarterback Steve Kelley. The kick was successful, enabling the Elks to avoid the embarrassment of a shutout. The Farmers had the last word, however, on an 8-yard pass from Nelson to Martin Simmons. It was Nelson's third touchdown pass of the season, with the lopsided score allowing the Lewisville offense to brush up on its passing attack, which was the only reason Nelson was in the game in the second half. He had been relieved in the second quarter by LaDarrin McLane before returning in the third period.

Simmons' touchdown reception was his second one of the season, making him the Farmers' leading receiver of the year, but that's like being the Maytag repairman, with the ground-oriented wishbone running attack of Lewisville. The massive Farmer tight end had just eight receptions for 197 yards and the two touchdowns, but was a key element of the offensive line with his blocking ability. His efforts earned him Sophomore of the Year honors in District 6-5A the year before, and he had developed into a blue-chipper in just his junior year. But then, with 243 pounds distributed over his 6-foot-4-inch frame, it was no surprise.

Dwight Hunter added two more interceptions to his credit, giving him eight for the season. Three other Farmers intercepted one apiece; Blaine Herring, Lance Aldridge and Freddie Wilson. Holland was the game's leading ball carrier with 87 yards on just four carries, the bulk of that coming on the 55-yard touchdown run. Altogether the Farmer offense amassed 297 total yards, not much when compared to the 330-yard season average. They only made eight first downs, primarily because most of the Farmer scores covered big yardage. All in all it was a complete game on both sides of the ball. The defense continually gave the ball to the offense in great field position, via the five interceptions, and the Farmers did not have that much ground to cover for each of their scores, which was the reason for the relatively low yardage. By the game's end there was no doubt the Farmers were peaking at the proper time.

Lewisville vs. South Grand Prairie — November 19, 1993
Lewisville would face another familiar foe in the area round of the playoffs for the second straight week, again at Texas Stadium. In 1992 Lewisville defeated the South Grand Prairie Warriors, 48–28, and the Farmers hoped for similar results in '93. Rather, they planned for them. The Warriors did not appreciate the scalping they received the year before and vowed not to fall prey to

Lewisville a second time. Coach Gage knew this game would be different than his team's most recent victory and prepared his team appropriately.

South Grand Prairie had to take a portion of the credit for motivating the Farmers, though. It seems wingback Anthony Bookman rattled to the press something about a rematch against the Farmers being the Warriors' sole purpose for suiting up in '93. The talk alluded to just shy of guaranteeing an upset of the state's ninth ranked team, and Gage, Pietrosky, Goode and the other coaches put the verbal assault to good use. The report was prominently displayed on the field house wall as a constant reminder all week to the Farmers that someone was taking pot shots at them; and it wasn't even on the field.

The confusing thing about Bookman's comments was that his team finished a mere 5–5, barely making the playoffs. They beat a mediocre Ft. Worth Dunbar, 31–13, in their bi-district match, a long way from declaring themselves King of the World, and threatening virtually the same team that thumped them out of Texas Stadium the year before. There was one major difference between the '92 and '93 Farmers; the '93 version was better, which was why Bookman's comments backfired.

As an athlete, Anthony Brookman had the raw talent to single-handedly dismantle a team. His 4.3 speed in the 40-yard dash demonstrated that. He had returned two kickoffs for touchdowns already, and had a combined 1,576 yards (922 rushing, 654 receiving) from his wingback position, proving to be a dual weapon of the Warrior offense. His running buddy, tailback Joe Young, led the team in rushing with 1,042 yards, and the tandem did pose a serious threat to the ordinary team. But then again, the Farmers were no ordinary team.

Lewisville held the duo in check in '92, with 66 yards between the two, a mere pittance compared to what the Farmers had seen throughout the '93 season. Denton's Deon Green and Rider's Kevin Wagner were at least as good, if not better. Against South Grand Prairie in 1992 Dwayne Brazzell alone had 156, and he wasn't even the Farmers' leading rusher. Chad Nelson cashed in 193 yards and presented a greater problem for the Warriors. South Grand Prairie's concern going into the '93 game had more to do with combatting the quick-striking Lewisville offense than any points they could score themselves.

Ronnie Gage called it, "the best game we played all year. A real solid performance," referring to the Farmers' 24–0 elimination of the Warriors. Lewisville rolled up 406 total yards, 340 rushing and 66 passing, while restricting the Warriors to 172. Lewisville methodically scored in each quarter to slowly mesmerize the much maligned Warriors, dominating practically every aspect of the game. The only category the Farmers fell behind in was passing, gaining 66 yards to the Warriors' 85. But then, with Lewisville's 340 rushing yards, they did not need to throw, except for practice.

The Warriors did have some success in moving the ball early in the contest. On their initial drive they managed to reach the Farmer 20, but could get

A Dream Realized

Behind sound blocking, Chad Nelson (11) sets up to pass against South Grand Prairie.

Running wild—Dwayne Brazzell penetrates the Warrior secondary for major yardage at Texas Stadium. Brazzell rushed for 145 yards in the area contest.

Getting Set—Zack Welton (42) calls the defensive formation for the Farmer defense.

no further and settled for a 37-yard field goal attempt. It could have gone differently, though. On second-and-nine from the Farmer 20, Warrior wide receiver Brian Parker could not manage to hold on to quarterback Ricky Thompson's pinpoint pass in the end zone, and South Grand Prairie Head Coach David Thompson got that "uh-oh" look on his face. Things worsened as the field goal attempt went awry, and the Warriors went away from their first opportunity to score empty-handed.

The Farmers didn't, though. Lewisville mounted consecutive drives of 80 and 85 yards, largely behind the straight ahead running of fullback Dwayne Brazzell. Brazzell, who finished the contest with 145 yards on 24 carries, almost matched his totals of 156 yards and 29 carries of the previous year, and ran with a noticeable determination fueled by Bookman's comments earlier that week. Except for a fumble at the 1 on the first drive, Brazzell turned in a stellar performance behind the powerful offensive surge. Chad Nelson was the benefactor of Brazzell's fumble as he scooped it up and carried it in for the first score. Roach split the uprights for the 7–0 first quarter lead on a night for Lewisville where, even when things went wrong, they went right.

Lewisville scored in similar fashion in the second period on an 85-yard drive. That time Brazzell didn't fumble away his chance to score as he plunged in from the 2 to double the Farmer lead. Roach was successful on the point after, and with the Farmer lead increased to 14–0, it was time for the defense to respond.

Two times the Warriors penetrated into Farmer territory, and two times the defense responded, turning South Grand Prairie away at the 34 and 15-yard lines. At both spots the Warriors opted to attempt to convert the drive on fourth down instead of punting, with the Farmers denying each attempt. The successful stands took the wind out of the Warriors' sail, and Lewisville had them right where they wanted them.

In the midst of the war, Bookman did have his say, though . . . about 68 yards worth, which was all the Farmers allowed him. And while the Lewisville defense was containing him, and the rest of the Warriors, the offense was grinding out their final two scores; a 26-yard Topher Roach field goal, and a 1-yard Reggie Crawford touchdown run. Crawford, a sophomore, was in relief for a slightly injured Waylon Holland and gained 91 yards, while the Warrior defense was busy keying on Brazzell and Nelson. On the evening the Farmer offense controlled the ball while picking up 22 first downs, the most since the Sherman game in week five, en route to their regional encounter out west the following week.

Lewisville vs. Midland Lee — November 27, 1993

Coach Ronnie Gage's Lewisville Fighting Farmers set three specific goals for 1993 football, and two of those goals had already been accomplished. The first was to make the playoffs; they achieved that with the tie against The Colony.

Second on the list was to win the District 6-5A championship, and that was

A Dream Realized

realized with the 20–13 victory over the Marcus Marauders in the final regular season; retaining the Ax was icing on the cake. Their third objective was to advance to the regional round of the playoffs, not just make an appearance, but to be competitive with the intention of winning. The Farmers had reached the same round in 1992, having had to play the Odessa Permian Panthers at Odessa's Ratliff Stadium. The young Farmers stumbled in that contest, losing 28–0, but more critically, did not make a respectable showing ... which is why they wanted a chance to redeem themselves. It was not enough just to go to Odessa, Abilene, or Midland (which is where they ultimately traveled) but to earn some respect in the ranks of Texas high school football by getting over that West Texas hump. They could only accomplish that with a victory.

On a few occasions they had gotten over the hurdle that West Texas teams had represented but had fallen victim in recent history more often than not. Going back to 1955, '56 and '57, the Farmers lost consecutive bi-district contests to West Texas teams; Chilicothe, 20–7 in 1957, Burkburnett, 28–19 in 1958, and Electra, 32–7 in 1959. Had Lewisville defeated Chilicothe in '57, it's likely they might have claimed their first state championship that season. They were the state's leading scorer that year, with 522 points, but an injury to eventual All-American running back Gordon Salsman early in the game virtually eliminated their chances. The Farmers finally cleared the West Texas hurdle in 1972 when Lewisville pummeled the Burkburnett Bulldogs, 34–0, at Amon Carter Stadium in Ft. Worth.

Lewisville shocked not only the state but the nation as well, by knocking off the highly touted Abilene Cooper Cougars in dramatic fashion in 1979, 13–10, on their way to a semifinal appearance in Coach Neal Wilson's second season as the Farmers' head man. Wilson led his team to victory over Odessa Permian in 1981, sort of, as a 14–14 tie fell the Farmers' way on a 19–15 edge in first downs, a measure used to break ties in playoff games and district contests when necessary. It would be 11 years before the Farmers would have to line up against a West Texas opponent, although they made the playoffs four time during that span. The farthest level they reached was the regional round in 1985, but were forced south to play Cypress-Fairbanks instead of heading west.

But the most recent encounter against those mystical West Texas nemeses was against Permian in '92, and the experience surrounding that game left a bitter taste in the Farmers' mouths, especially mentor Ronnie Gage. There were some mistakes on the field; the 28–0 score reflects that. The most damaging mistakes, however, came before and up until game time. The first mistake was in traveling to Odessa the day before. The team missed school and chartered a bus, arriving amidst an entourage of family, friends and media, too much to suit Coach Gage. "That year against Odessa we learned a lot about traveling, organizing and dealing with the hype surrounding a playoff game of that caliber. Besides the presence of the media, there were moms, dads, aunts, uncles and girlfriends that were a distraction to what we needed to accomplish. It wasn't anything intentional, it was just that we didn't know how to handle that attention, and it took away from our performance. It got out of hand. That's my fault and I wasn't going to let it happen in '93," admitted Gage.

Nor did he. The first step Gage and Athletic Director Neal Wilson took was to make the trip in one day instead of two, which meant a plane ride and no overnight stay. With the game scheduled at 2:00 p.m. that was a workable plan, with plenty of time to board a Southwest Airline plane at Love Field, fly to Midland in time and play the game, making it back at about sunset. Not a bad trip if all went as designed. The second, and probably most critical step, was to isolate the team from the fans, relatives and media until after the contest was over. By doing this Gage and staff were able to treat it like an ordinary game, maintaining their focus on the task at hand. This formula instilled greater confidence in a more mature Fighting Farmer team, combating any intimidation which may have crept into the team's psyche in conjunction with traveling to a territory where, only a year earlier, they had not been able to work their game plan. Things would be different in '93.

The similarities between the Lewisville Farmers and the Midland Lee Rebels were ironic and numerous. Both teams wore maroon and white, with the Farmers dressed in their visiting white jerseys. Both teams ran the wishbone offense, amassing approximately the same total yards on the season, give or take a turkey leg. And both teams' quarterbacks wore number 11. Defensively, they both crammed the line of scrimmage with a lot of people, taking the running game away from their opponents. It would be a test for both teams, no doubt.

Although the Farmers owned one of the best, if not the best, wishbone offenses in the state, they had never had to defend against it except, perhaps, in spring training, a setting more conducive for earning a spot on the regular season roster than preparing for an opponent's attack. The one major difference between Lewisville and Midland was that the Rebels utilized the passing game more often, to the tune of just under 1,000 yards, but not really anything the Farmers couldn't handle. Shoot, they survived against Quinton Pelley, Sam Johnson and Matt Tittle within their own district. Midland Lee's passing threat would be of no consequence to them; they'd seen it before.

Offensive Coordinator and line coach Bill Pietrosky, in his colorful way, instrumented a motto for the week to make certain the Farmers were properly motivated. Once they heard of the traveling arrangements, Pietrosky fired the players up by saying, "Boys, we're gonna fly in, kick ass, and fly out!" which brought a ring of enthusiastic cheers. The phrase was abbreviated to "FIKAFO" (pronounced fie-kuh-foe) and became a rally cry to use as a focal point for the team's mission at hand. Pietrosky remembered what it was like losing to Permian; he did not want it to happen again.

To prepare for the regional battle Coach Gage took the Farmers to Northwest High School in Justin, Texas, where he spent the four years prior to coming to Lewisville. This was to allow his team to familiarize themselves with

A Dream Realized

Zeb Cornist holds on to Midland Lee quarterback Courtney Turner (11) until the reinforcements arrive. Dan Merritt (61), Pete Bonenberger (55) and Ben Collinsworth (76) are in hot pursuit.

natural turf, the type of surface at Midland's complex. It also gave them a chance to get used to an unfamiliar site. It was Thanksgiving week, but the team eagerly worked out in the gym for about an hour on Thanksgiving Day, as well as the following Friday. The coaches did not want the holiday to distract from their preparation.

It was likely Midland Lee would not, either. The Rebels had shattered El Paso Bowie, 79–14, and had tied Odessa Permian during the regular season, the team Lewisville lost to in this same game the year before, so they could not afford to take any time off. The Cowboy game would have to wait for another Thanksgiving Day.

Nobody expected a game like the one witnessed that November 27 afternoon. With both teams being ball-control oriented, it figured to be a low-scoring game, similar to the 17–6 game against Rider. And the Farmers would have been satisfied with that. Instead, they got much more than they hoped for, triggered by several untimely Rebel turnovers and some big plays by a few Farmers. Midland Lee received the opening kickoff and began a drive at their own 30-yard line. After netting zero yards on the first two plays, halfback Marlon Henry fumbled on the third-and-10 play into the waiting hands of Lewisville's sophomore standout Shannon Brazzell, giving the Farmers an early break in the contest. An early gamble on fourth-and-one kept the drive alive, with quarterback Chad Nelson scoring on an 18-yard keeper. Topher

Erik Otsuji (88) prepares to block Midland Lee's Dedrick Adams (12) to allow Byron Mitchell (22) to pick up good yardage.

Roach, unaffected by the natural turf, kicked the extra point, and before the Rebels could break a sweat, Lewisville owned a 7–0 lead.

Things got worse for Midland Lee before they got better, too. Farmer defensive back Mike Frazier intercepted Courtney Turner's first pass attempt, and the Farmers found themselves surprisingly near another score, one that only took two plays to complete. Byron Mitchell took the ball and, like he had done five times during the season, scored while the Rebel defense had its hands full with Nelson and fullback Dwayne Brazzell. Mitchell's score came from 24 yards out, giving Lewisville a 13–0 lead with less than 100 yards of total offense and lots of time still in the opening period. The point-after attempt was no good, but the Farmers were where they liked to be, well out in front of an early lead.

The Rebels, along with Head Coach Earl Miller, knew they could not allow any more turnovers against the opportunistic Farmers if they had any hopes of extending their season. Their real desire was to be able to play Abilene Cooper in the next round in a rematch of their final regular season game. Both teams were members of District 4-5A, and the area was buzzing with glee at the aspect of a quarter-final rematch, but Midland Lee would have to dispose of Lewisville's Farmers first, something they weren't doing in the early going. Henry redeemed himself for his early miscue by taking the Farmer kickoff 102 yards for the Rebels' first score of the afternoon. Steve Williams converted the extra point, and instantly the Farmer lead was cut to six at 13–7. The turnovers in the opening moments hadn't been an element in Lewisville's game plan, although the Farmers were thankful for them. Now it was time to get down to business.

The Farmers began the following possession at their own 28-yard line with

A Dream Realized

Zack Welton (42) receives the signal from Coach Terry Goode on the sideline as to what formation to run. It worked most of the day.

Nelson dropping back to attempt his first pass of the game. It would be his only completion in three attempts on the day, but it was a big one. The pass only covered a dozen or so yards to tight end Martin Simmons, but the junior All-District selection turned up the field and turned it into a 72-yard score. It looked like Simmons would be brought down at the Midland 20, but a vicious comeback block by wide receiver Carlos Cherigo wiped out not one hopeful tackler, but two, in one fell swoop, enabling Simmons to reach the end zone. Dwayne Brazzell carried the ball over on the extra point attempt, extending the Farmer lead to 21–7; all that action and still 2:03 remained in the first period. It was beginning to look like the Sherman game again.

Things settled down a bit in the second period, with both teams unable to match the pace of the first quarter. Aside from a 20-yard Topher Roach field goal, there wasn't much action, and the Farmers were thrilled to be leading 24–7 at the half. They were finally doing to others what had been done to them a year ago.

The Rebels opened the second half scoring after a Nelson fumble deep in Farmer territory, allowing Midland Lee to climb right back into the thick of things. The fumble came at Lewisville's 14, providing the opportunity for Henry's second touchdown run, a 12-yarder around left end. The kick was good and the Rebels had closed the gap to 24–14. A few more breaks like that and the Rebels could start thinking about playing Cooper after all.

The Farmers, specifically Shannon Brazzell, turned the tables on the Rebels, however, as he recovered a fumble, this one by quarterback Courtney Turner, and returned it 14 yards for another Farmer score, thanks to a recent rule change at the high school level which allowed fumbles to be returned. Brazzell, who played more like a senior than a sophomore, had already logged a first quarter fumble recovery to set up the Farmers' first score. That would not finish his contribution to the Farmer defensive efforts, either. Brazzell also nabbed a Courtney Turner pass in the final quarter, returning it 52 yards to stop a late threat by the Rebels.

Brazzell's fumble recovery for the touchdown came in the third quarter, the only score for the Farmers in that period. Lewisville scored the next touchdown as well, on a 1-yard run by Nelson. The extra point attempt failed, making the score theoretically out of reach at 37–14. Turner led the Rebels back for a touchdown at the 6:24 mark in the fourth period, and Midland Lee was mathematically in range of a least tying Lewisville, if not defeating them, had the Farmers somehow forgotten how to play the game of football, or if the Rebels were able to pull off a miracle. Turner's added two-point conversion afforded the Rebels at least an outside chance at claiming the regional crown by narrowing the Farmer lead to 37–22.

Lewisville countered the Midland touchdown, but not without a brief scare. The Rebels attempted, and were successful on, an onside kick in Farmer territory at the 45. A touchdown and two-point conversion here would have made the score 37–29 and they would have been right back in the game. That's when the younger Brazzell made his critical interception, returning it to the Rebel 13-yard line. In a tag-team effort resembling the heroics of the late Von Erich brothers of wrestling fame, the elder Brazzell carried the ball on the first play of the drive the entire 13 yards for the final Farmer score of the day. Roach's routine extra point widened the score to 44–22 in what was turning out to be the best Farmer performance of the season. They had scored more points in this game than either of the two previous playoff games, and aside from the 51 and 52 outputs against lackluster Newman Smith and Allen, it was the most the Farmers had scored all season. They had also earned some respect, one of the things that was on the Farmer quarterback's mind in traveling out west. "Our first goal was to make it farther than we did last year (in 1992). Our second goal was to earn some respect," reminisced Nelson, the smooth engineer of the Farmers' Wishbone Express. The 44 points garnered by the day's efforts surely accomplished that.

The Rebels did get another touchdown—a token 12-yard pass from Turner to Undra Graves. But by that time the fat lady had already sung, packed her bags and was heading back to Texas Stadium, where she would sing her song the following week to one team's pleasure, and the other's dismay. FIKAFO. The game was over when Brazzell, the Shannon version, made his interception in the fourth quarter. The action that filled the final six minutes or so was just to give the reporters material for Sunday's sports page. It was over, and Lewisville had vaulted over that hurdle which had tripped them up so many

A Dream Realized

times before, and had done it in a convincing manner. Turner's two-point conversion did little more than make the game appear closer than it actually was. FIKAFO, indeed.

Coach Gage knew for his team to be successful against the Rebels they would have to be properly motivated. Pietrosky had supplied a good bit of that spark with his clever motto. But Gage put things in a different perspective to his players than had been implied after the Farmers first learned they were to play a team that had scored 79 points in their previous contest.

Chad Nelson runs through the Rebel defense for good yardage. Nelson rushed for 70 yards and two touchdowns against Midland Lee.

The natural question was, "could the Farmers beat them, or even play with them?" According to tackle Mike Anderson, Gage exuded confidence in his improving team that spilled over during the week of preparation. "It's not a matter of if we can beat them," he told us, "it's a matter of whether they can beat us," . . . which is how the Farmers played that day.

Lewisville vs. Abilene Cooper — December 4, 1993
Abilene Cooper kept up their end of the bargain in the hope for an interdistrict battle for the quarter final championship against Midland Lee, but Lewisville interfered with those plans rather decisively. The Farmers were no strangers to the Cougars, either, but it had been some time since their last meeting. Lewisville and Abilene Cooper met only once before, and that was in 1979 for the bi-district championship which the Farmers won, 13–10, in a come-from-behind effort. The Cougars had defeated Haltom, 41–6, to earn the chance to revisit Texas Stadium and try to avenge the loss handed to their ancestors by the Farmers 14 years earlier.

Lewisville had faced a number of formidable offenses through the regional game and, aside from the Sherman encounter, had been less than generous in yardage allowed. They had bent at times on pass defense, but had never broken; they had thoroughly eliminated the run altogether. The Farmers had been challenged by some pretty good running backs; Kevin Wagner from Wichita Falls Rider, Deon Green from Denton, South Grand Prairies' Anthony Bookman and Joe Young, and Courtney Turner of Midland Lee, but none of these talented runners had gained 100 yards against the defensive front of the Farmers. In fact, the most yardage surrendered to any one back by Lewisville came in game one when R.L. Turner's Jose Rodriguez picked up 76 yards. The more proven backs like Green, Wagner, Bookman and Turner, averaged just over 50 yards rushing against the likes of Pete Bonenberger, Dan Merritt,

Ben Collinsworth, Jeff Branch, Zeb Cornist, Zack Welton and Shannon Brazzell, the heart of the Farmer defense.

The Farmer secondary had fallen victim to Sherman's Quinton Pelley and Marcus' Matt Tittle but, in recent contests, kept their opponents in check. Overall, the Farmers entered the playoffs with the area's ninth rated defense, holding their opponents to 210 yards per game. Through the playoff games that average dropped to just under 196 yards, an indication that the defense was still improving that late in the season. And they would have to, because they were about to face one of Texas high school football's most lethal offensive attacks in the Abilene Cooper Cougars.

Cooper's dual offensive attack would certainly be the biggest test for the Farmers, but not one they hadn't seen before. The Cougars ran a formation with a single running back and multiple receivers, something close to what Marcus had thrown at them a month earlier. Their leading ball carrier was a bruiser, who had accumulated 2,330 yards rushing, and the Farmer defense would have its hands full with him. At 6 feet and 210 pounds, Mike Rose was the size of a fullback but possessed the speed of a tailback, having scored 20 touchdowns on the season. On the other hand, the Cooper quarterback, Zac Allen, had passed for 2,095 yards and 21 touchdowns, giving new meaning to the phrase "balanced attack." Concentrating too much on either aspect of the Cougar game plan could open the other up, and the game could get out of hand in a hurry. Conversely, by taking away one weapon in the Cougar arsenal, in essence, both would be gone. In either case, Gage, Goode and company were preparing for the biggest game of the season.

At 13 wins the 1993 Farmers had tied a record with the 1947 Farmers for the most wins by a Lewisville team. The '47 team, coached by J.K. Delay, went 13–0 in winning the regional championship that season, which was as far as Class B teams played until the B classification was eliminated in 1980. Although one of the victories in '47 was a forfeit by the flu-ridden Boyd Yellow Jackets, it still counted as a win, and the 13–0 record stood for 46 years before the '93 Farmers tied it with the victory over Midland Lee. They had hopes of extending that number against Cooper with a win at Texas Stadium.

The Cougars took the opening kickoff and Allen began his surgical air strike on the Farmer defense, leading his team 62 yards in their opening drive. The Farmer fans were worried with the ease at which the Cougars were able to move the ball, something few teams had done throughout the season. Just when things appeared to get uncomfortable for Lewisville, Farmer defensive tackle Ben Collinsworth broke through to drop Allen for a loss back to the Farmer 10-yard line on a critical third down play, forcing the Cougars to attempt a field goal.

Holding the Cougars to three points after the early surge would have given the Farmers a boost, no doubt, especially after they had whisked down the field with ease. They went one better than that. Jason Cotten forged through to block David Anderson's 27-yard field goal attempt, and that's where the

A Dream Realized

Byron Mitchell (22) eludes a Cougar tackle and races for 19 yards and the second Farmer touchdown.

game ended for Cooper, at least psychologically. From the 26-yard line the Farmers methodically marched the other way in 11 plays with Byron Mitchell scoring on a 4-yard run for Lewisville's first score. Topher Roach routinely booted the extra point giving the Farmers a 7–0 lead.

On the Cougars' next possession the Farmer defense began to interfere with their combined pass/run attack, a holdover from the blocked field goal and subsequent touchdown after their earlier drive. After the Farmers successfully shut them down the Cougars were forced to punt, and Lewisville was off to the races once again. A 10-play Farmer drive was climaxed by Mitchell's second touchdown of the first half, this one coming from 19 yards away off a Chad Nelson pitch. Mitchell had to work for the score, breaking several tackles along the way en route to the Farmers' second touchdown. Roach added the extra point for a 14–0 Farmer lead.

The Cougars settled down after spotting Lewisville 14 points and engineered a second quarter touchdown drive, capped by a 12-yard pass from Allen to Bob Berg. Anderson recovered from the first period blocked field goal and converted the extra point, cutting the Farmer lead in half at 14–7. Just like that the Cougars were back in the game, gaining some momentum from their potent passing game. They got a break, too, on the Farmers' next possession. Abilene Cooper had not been successful in stopping the Farmers in the first half, and it was likely they would not have, had not Lewisville tried to surprise the Cougar defenders with a reverse-option pass by Reggie Crawford. Crawford's pass was picked off at Cooper's 33-yard line by Ben Munoz and returned into Farmer territory at the 47, with about five minutes remaining in the first half, and the Cougars were on the move. Threatening the end zone, Cooper's Allen hurled a pass in that direction, hoping to even the score and overcome the early mistakes. Instead, Mike Frazier stepped in front of the would-be receiver and intercepted the ball, cancelling the Cougar

Lewisville's Jason Cotten (23) lines up against Cooper's Jason King (28). The Farmer defender had a big day against the Cougars, blocking a field goal attempt and intercepting a pass.

threat. He returned it to the Farmer 7 with 2:12 remaining in the first half.

The Farmers were content to run the clock out, figuring they had dodged an Abilene bullet by preventing the score. Coach Gage changed his mind, however, after a 31-yard burst up the middle by fullback Dwayne Brazzell. Gage's thoughts immediately turned to "field goal," and he and his staff attempted to get his team into position. A 22-yard pass from Nelson to Martin Simmons accomplished just that, reaching the Cougar 27-yard line with two seconds remaining. In came Topher Roach and his dependable toe. A field goal attempt at this point in the contest was no gamble. Roach had kicked only two field goals all season, the longest one from 26 yards out. This one, from 43 yards away, would not have hurt the Farmers had they not made it; it would have been a bonus. Roach faced a strong rush as the snap came from center. The kick was high, and long . . . and right through the uprights, giving the Farmers a 17–7 halftime lead and momentum going into the locker room.

Although the Farmers led on the scoreboard at the half, they had not been able to shut down Cooper's passing attack. The two turnovers, along with the blocked kick, helped the Farmers get the advantage. For all practical purposes Cooper was still in the game with the score at 17–7, although the Farmers had the upper hand by being able to make the big plays. What transpired when the second half opened up, however, removed any chances the Cougars had at getting even for the '79 loss to the Farmers.

Lewisville began the second half with a 57-yard scoring drive, with Dwayne Brazzell doing the honors on a 5-yard run. After Roach's conversion the Farmer lead stretched to 24–7 early in the third period. On the ensuing kickoff Cooper's Jason King took a vicious hit from Shannon Brazzell and fumbled, and the Farmers found themselves in scoring position after Zack Welton recovered at the Cougars' 17-yard line. Lewisville upped their lead on a 1-yard run by Brazzell to complete the three-play drive. Roach made it four-for-four with another successful extra point, and the Farmers began to distance themselves from the Cougars with a 31–7 lead. And they weren't finished yet.

The Cougars were able to hang onto the ball and mount a drive on their next possession . . . sort of. Behind by 24 points, the Cougars were forced to go to the air in order to play catchup, but the Farmer defense never let up. On the sixth play of the drive a Farmer defensive tackle hit the Cooper quarterback, Zac Allen, forcing him to cough it up. Blaine Herring recovered for Lewisville to halt the Cougar drive at the Lewisville 34-yard line. The Farmers

A Dream Realized

Unity — the Farmer defense displays its unity in the defensive huddle.

covered the 66 yards in precision manner, capped by an 18-yard touchdown pass from Nelson to Marcel Battle, and the game had gotten completely out of hand, still in the third quarter. It was a dream for the Lewisville fans and a nightmare for the Cougars. Roach's extra point increased the Farmer lead to 38–7, and the Abilene fans began to file out of the stadium to get an early start home. They had seen enough of Lewisville, and they were getting sick of hearing the Farmer fight song echo off the semi-roof of Texas Stadium.

Altogether, the Cougars controlled the ball for exactly 1:38 of the 12-minute third period, while the Farmers were busy crossing their goal line at will. The Farmer defense had not logged much time in the second half, and frankly that was fine with Coach Gage. As the third quarter was coming to a close, the Farmers kicked off to Cooper for the seventh time in the contest, but things continued in the same vane for the Cougars. Kobie Johnson fielded the ball for Cooper and had a pretty decent run-back, but the effort was marred as he fumbled at the 36-yard line, and the Farmers had yet another opportunity to score. The defense would have to wait a little longer to see some action.

The opportunistic Farmers took advantage of the Cougar fumble, their third of the day, and scored early in the fourth quarter, with Reggie Crawford doing the honors on a 2-yard run. The lead now stood at 45–9, and the Cougars hadn't really gotten their hands on the ball in the second half. By the time they did the game was well out of reach. They did assemble two scoring drives before the game was over, both ending on touchdown passes from Zac Allen.

Farmer defensive end Jeff Branch (86) forces Cougar quarterback Zac Allen out of the pocket. Allen finished with 220 yards passing, but suffered a costly first half interception against a stiff rush that was present all day.

One was to Jason King, a 7-yarder, and the other to Berg covering 30 yards, but it was too little, too late. The two Cougar scores surrounded Mitchell's third touchdown of the game for the Farmers, but Cooper was in no position to trade touchdowns with Lewisville. After all the extra points were attempted and the scoring was completed, Lewisville was soaring with a 52–21 victory. They could have gone into the locker room midway in the final period, and it was likely the Cougars would not have caught up with the Farmers the way things had transpired for them that day. Allen, son of Cooper Head Coach Randy Allen, had a decent day passing with 220 yards, but with the Farmers in the prevent defense most of afternoon, that was no major chore. Rose, the heralded Cougar running back, was no factor at all, restricted to 69 yards rushing, a season low for him, and the Farmer defense had not surrendered 100 yards to any back for the 14th time of the season.

For Lewisville, Brazzell led the offensive charge with 168 yards on 20 carries. They also had key contributions from Mitchell and Battle, scoring four touchdowns between them, but the real story of the lopsided contest was the big plays and what the Farmers did with them. After each Cooper turnover Lewisville scored—four of those being touchdowns, along with the 43-yard field goal by Roach—and everything went right for Coach Gage, the Farmers and the town of Lewisville that day. Later that evening, after the game was a good six hours old, the Farmers won again, this time on a coin flip against their next opponent, which assured them home field advantage in the semifinal round the following week.

Lewisville vs. Temple — December 11, 1993
While the Farmers were busy dismantling the twofold attack of the Abilene Cooper Cougars, their next opponent, the Temple Wildcats, was shutting out district rival Killeen, 42–0, to ease into the semifinal round.

Temple was the defending State Champion of 5A Division II, but many considered them to be better than Converse Judson, the 1992 Division I Champion. The Wildcats bolstered that argument by beating Judson, 37–21, in the fourth game of the season as each team went on to win the state title in their respective divisions in '92. For Temple, that was their second championship under their legendary Head Coach Bob McQueen, with the last one coming in 1979. Interestingly, it was Lewisville that Temple defeated in the '79 semifi-

A Dream Realized

nal, 3–0, at Texas Stadium, en route to the championship over Spring Branch (Houston) Memorial, 28–6. Lewisville had not been as fortunate. Instead, the Farmers had to wait 14 years for the opportunity to contend for a state title again. That they had to play Temple was the result of the Wildcats' decisive win over Killeen; that they played at Texas Stadium was a different story altogether.

There are various methods for determining the site for a playoff game. The two coaches and/or athletic directors can meet and agree on a neutral location, such as the case when Burleson and South Grand Prairie played Lewisville. Both of them were eager to play at Texas Stadium against the Farmers in their respective playoff games. Or the zip-code method can be used, which requires the assistance of an official from the Texas High School Coaches Association (THSCA). In a conference call with the official, one coach would be allowed to select either odd or even, while the other coach would call out the name of a school in Texas. The official would then turn to the page where that school was listed in the Annual Texas Sports Guide, a comprehensive listing of all high schools in Texas, and find the zip code of the city where that school was located to see whether it was odd or even. The site of the game would be determined depending on what the first coach called. This method was used when the coaches could not meet face-to-face. In essence, the results were the same as a coin flip, which is what decided the site for the Temple-Lewisville game.

Coach Ronnie Gage, Assistant Superintendent Marshall Durham and Assistant Athletic Director Rody Durham agreed to meet Temple Coach Bob McQueen, along with Temple High School Principal Bill Lawson, and too many others to name, to select the battlefield for the upcoming semifinal war in which their two teams would engage. Gage was somewhat intimidated by the presence of the Wildcat coach, who was in his 22nd season at Temple and boasting a 202–52–5 overall record at the Central Texas school. "I felt like a small fish in a big pond," the third-year head coach of the Farmers recalled. But a glimpse at McQueen's state championship ring from the 1992 season brought the first realization of just how close he and his team were to playing for a state title. "When I saw his ring, that's when it first sank in that we had a shot at the championship," Gage reflected. But his Farmers would have to go through the Wildcats first, with the location to be decided in their meeting.

The two coaches and their contingents met at the Golden Corral Restaurant located on Corsicana Highway just off Interstate Highway 35 East in Hillsboro, Texas. The site was just minutes from Waco's Floyd Casey Stadium, where Temple had destroyed Killeen earlier that afternoon. After a brief, but cordial discussion about their mutual successes that day, the two coaches, and the rest, stepped outside to conduct the coin toss. What is normally a simple procedure turned out to be rather complex, at least in Gage's mind. "We went over all the possibilities regarding the coin toss, and it got kind of ridiculous. He (McQueen) came up with all kinds of situations that I never considered, and it was kind of intimidating. He said things like, 'if it hits the sidewalk and rolls off into the street then let's do it over,' or 'if it hits a car and goes across the street then we do it over;' all possibilities that I thought would never happen. I guess when you reach that level and have been involved in as many playoff games as he has, experience teaches you to cover all the bases," chuckled Gage. McQueen did the right thing and let Gage make the call, while he provided the coin. As he flipped, Gage said, "heads." That way his team's fate would be of his own doing, as much as can be with a coin toss. Either way, he would be responsible for the call he made, not someone else. The coin landed on the sidewalk, and it was clearly visible that it was heads, at least to the Farmer coach and his two comrades. Mr. Lawson also verified the results, almost from his hands and knees. It appeared that he was in disbelief at first glance and thought he could somehow change the outcome by staring it down. But it was not to be, and the Farmers had already decided the semifinal encounter against the Temple Wildcats would be at Texas Stadium, as was their last encounter 14 years ago.

Going into the game the Farmers would prepare themselves for a duo of runners unlike they had seen all season. They had faced teams with one outstanding back, such as Wichita Falls Rider, South Grand Prairie, Midland Lee, and most recently, Abilene Cooper, but neither of these teams' outstanding runners had been able to run wild against the Farmers. The closest they had come to seeing a tandem of backs akin to Temple's was against Denton, with Deon Green and Derrick Peoples, but an injury to Peoples prevented that match-up, and the Farmers simply shut Green down. Temple would be different, though.

The combination of Gerald Watson and Delarrius Wilson had been prolific for the Wildcats, with the pair accounting for 2,968 yards rushing between them through 14 weeks. Wilson was the rushing leader with 1,559 yards, but Watson was close behind with 1,409. Both possessed the ability to break away and score from anywhere on the field; their combined 28 touchdown total was an indication of that. Wilson had a greater motivation to do well against the Farmers. He was 35 yards away from breaking the school's all-time rushing record held by former TCU great Kenneth Davis, who now plays for the Buffalo Bills of the National Football League. Breaking Davis' record would be a nice thing to have on his resume. Why, he could stumble all day long and get the yards he needed. It was too much to ask the Farmer defense to hold him under the 35 yard mark. Besides, their main concern was winning a ball game, the biggest one of their lives, not preventing some kid from breaking a record.

The first half of the game was a pretty tight one, as both teams played like the champions they were. The Farmers opened up the scoring in trademark fashion with an 89-yard drive that the Wildcats just could not stop. The pounding covered nine plays and erased 6:04 from the clock with Dwayne Brazzell scoring from 3 yards out. Nelson's 36-yard run from the Farmer 16-yard line

A Dream Realized

Chad Nelson gets set at the line of scrimmage against Temple. He led all rushers with 135 yards and a touchdown in the semifinal game.

sparked the drive, enabling Lewisville to take a 7–0 lead against the defending state champions. By striking first the Farmers sent a signal to Temple that they had come to play. They had thrown down the gauntlet.

The Wildcats met the challenge on the next possession, proving why they were the defending champs, with a nifty little drive of their own. They weren't going to take the Farmer score lying down and proceeded to engineer a 40-yard drive for their first score. The drive was set up by a 38-yard kickoff return by Temple's Derick Bates, providing excellent field position and not allowing the Farmers the chance to relax. A 3-yard touchdown run by Watson put the Wildcats back in the game early in the second period with the score tied, 7–7.

The Farmers countered Watson's touchdown run on their next possession with Brazzell again going over, this time from the 2-yard line, to climax a 10-play, 67-yard drive midway through the second period. Topher Roach booted his second extra point and Lewisville led again, 14–7. Temple's Tracey Baugh ended the first half scoring for both teams with a 32-yard field goal, making the score 14–10 at the half. This game had been all that it was cracked up to be, with two powerful offenses putting on a good show, and yet Wilson had not gained his 35 yards needed to break Davis' record. Oh well, the second half was still to be played; surely he would do it then.

A pattern developed in the Abilene Cooper game and emerged once again

FRIDAY NIGHT FARMERS

Dwayne Brazzell carries the ball over from 2 yards out to score the second Lewisville touchdown. He safely, but surely gets the ball over the goal line on a dive up the middle behind Bret Johnson (52) and Buddy Phillips (71).

against Temple at the start of the second half. The Farmers won the opening flip, as they had done against Cooper, but elected to defer their decision until the second half, which put them on defense first; somewhat of a risky move when facing a duo as talented as Wilson and Watson. But Gage believed in his defensive unit, thinking they could turn away a team on its first possession and give the ball to its powerful offense to do some damage. The move to defer their decision was made so that the Farmers could have the ball first in the second half and come out of the locker room and score. It worked against Abilene Cooper the week before, and it would work against Temple in the semifinal game.

Lewisville took that second half kickoff and routinely marched down the field 69 yards for their third score of the afternoon, a 14-yard keeper by Nelson. The Farmers had extended their lead to 21–10, and Temple was unable to stop it. From that point on the game took on a different tone, one that spelled doom for the Wildcats. The pesky Farmer defense closed down the Temple attack, including the running game of Wilson and Watson. Down by 11 points, the Wildcats were forced to go to the air, something that delighted Farmer free safety Dwight Hunter. He picked off two passes from Temple quarterback Justin Lee, and the Farmer offense converted each one into points, the first a 1-yard touchdown by Brazzell, and the other a 32-yard field goal by Roach. By third quarter's end Lewisville had upped its lead to 31–7, and Wilson still

A Dream Realized

Dwayne Brazzell (32) gains a few of his 86 yards against Temple. He also scored three touchdowns to help secure a Farmer victory.

Byron Mitchell (22) prepares to take on Cooper's Patrick Stanford (14) and James Wright (23). Mitchell supplemented the Farmer attack with 62 yards and a touchdown.

Lewisville Head Coach Ronnie Gage looks on as his Farmers defeat the defending state champion Temple Wildcats, 40–16, to earn a chance at a state title.

hadn't gotten his 35 yards. It looked like the Abilene Cooper massacre all over again.

In the final period things got worse instead of better for the Wildcats, who were turning out not to be so wild. Lee retreated into his own end zone in an attempt to escape a Farmer rush, but he met the Farmers' Zeb Cornist instead, who tackled the weary quarterback for a safety, pushing the Lewisville lead to 33–7. Besides the two points, Lewisville got the ball back as a result of the safety. The Farmers promptly drove down the field for another score, the last of the evening, as Byron Mitchell galloped in from 15 yards away, and finally, the Lewisville wishbone attack was finished for the day.

The second half onslaught had featured the Farmers scoring 26 unanswered points, a situation the Wildcats could not overcome, not even with Delarrius Wilson and Gerald Watson. Temple managed to have the final say with a 9-yard touchdown pass from relief quarterback Scott Yepma to Derick Bates, but the failed conversion was reflective of the kind of day Temple had. Midway through the third quarter you could have put a pitchfork in this one; it was done.

The Farmers out-produced the Wildcats on the scoreboard, collecting 40 points to Temple's 16. They held the ball for 30:51 to Temple's mere 17:09, leaving the Cougars little time to get anything accomplished offensively. The Farmers did not turn the ball over at all, nor did they make any critical mistakes. They amassed 414 total yards, compared to Temple's 209, and they made the most of every scoring opportunity. But the most remarkable thing about the Farmer effort that day was that they held Delarrius Wilson and Gerald Watson to just 77 combined yards; two game-breakers that averaged 119 and 108 yards a game, respectively. And Wilson never got his 35 yards needed to break Kenneth Davis' school rushing record. He picked up only 22 yards on seven carries with no touchdowns, to end an otherwise brilliant high school career on a negative note.

With their victory the Farmers were one step away from making the dream come true, a dream that had been 21 years in the making. While Lewisville was declawing the Wildcats, a relatively unknown team, the Aldine MacArthur Generals, had undone Victoria's perfect season, handing them a 20–7 loss. The Generals, 12–3 on the season, would make their first trip to the state finals against the Farmers, who had not seen the championship game since losing to the Uvalde Coyotes, 33–28, in 1972.

A Dream Realized

Lewisville vs. Aldine MacArthur — December 18, 1993
The community of Lewisville had changed considerably since 1972. A car ride down Main Street revealed a move westward, from Mill Street and the old part of the heart of Lewisville east of IH-35E to the west, nearer to the Flower Mound border. The population had quadrupled in the 21-year span, and the town that once had only a single traffic light now had dozens, which lit up like Christmas lights up and down the now modern Main Street. A few remnants from 1972 remained: the string of businesses along Old Town located on the stretch of Main Street between Charles and Mill streets, the "round" bank, a building that housed what was once the Lewisville National Bank but which had changed ownership and names a half-dozen times or so since, the McDonalds at the corner of Main Street and IH-35E where the old Piggly Wiggly used to be and the familiar water tower just north of it that had the unmistakable three words painted for passersby to see: "LEWISVILLE FIGHTING FARMERS." The Farmer logo was also featured on the tower but had undergone a facelift of sorts. The faceless farmer, from 1972, clad in a football uniform, helmet, and brogans, with pitchfork in hand, had been replaced by a lean and mean mascot. This change occurred in 1987 to represent all sports and activities of Lewisville High School, not just football.

Much had changed, but one thing that remained was the love this city had for its football team, the Lewisville Fighting Farmers, and like 1972, the town was buzzing with excitement over the news that "their boys" would be playing for the state championship the following Saturday. And they had much to be excited about. Lewisville's Farmers had just convincingly dethroned the defending state champions, the Temple Wildcats, and frankly, there did not seem to be any possible way of stopping them. At once, the spirit of those who had been around since the last state final appearance began to be rekindled, and their minds pictured images of the '72 team, with players named Mullins, Bragg, Fox, Nichols, Martin, Mayes, Cade and Rice, and the dream that had been dormant for 21 years was resurrected. Those names would be replaced by other names, new names like Nelson, Branch, Brazzell, Merritt, Collinsworth, Simmons, Anderson, Cornist, Welton and Bonenberger, but the feeling of pride was the same. The Farmers were back.

Although the external signs were not as visible as in '72 (a sign of the influx of citizens and their diverse interests), there was an internal feeling of uncontrollable excitement that was very evident. People who did not know each other would strike up a conversation about the upcoming game and conclude that the Farmers were a shoe-in for the title. Of course, they were bias; their maroon and white attire gave them away. Debbie Fetterman of the *Dallas Morning News* reported that there were more "help wanted" signs than ones that read "Go Farmers" plastered in the windows of businesses down the west side of Main Street, but that was more from the rapid increase of commerce than the lack of support. It was clear this town could hardly wait for the game and eagerly anticipated it like a five-year-old awaited the annual

December 16, 1993

CONGRATULATIONS!

Lewisville High School
1993 Fighting Farmers

As you take the field in Houston this Saturday to win the State Championship, the spirit of the 1972 Farmer Football team will be with you. We came up a yard short for our State Championship and have been waiting twenty years for BIG JOHN to go back and win the biggest game of all.

Out of hundreds of thousands of high school football players in Texas, only a very few ever have a chance to play for a State Championship. We, the 1972 team, now share that with you. Fewer players win the Championship and that's something you will do this Saturday.

We are grown men now in our late-30s, but we'll always be Fighting Farmers with BIG JOHN spirit.

Among the thousands of fans cheering for you this weekend will be 48 of us that want you to get that one yard that we didn't.

HANG LOOSE — HIT HARD — HUSTLE — HAVE FUN

Win The Championship

The 1972 Fighting Farmers

This letter anonymously appeared in Ronnie Gage's mailbox at LHS. The sentiment reflected in the content reveals the support the 1972 Fighting Farmers gave to their successors.

A Dream Realized

arrival of Santa Claus, who, incidentally, was scheduled to arrive the week after. But for the time being all this community wanted for Christmas was a state championship.

Although the attention was overwhelming, the coaches wanted to make the game out to be just another game, a difficult task to pull off. They solicited the assistance of LHS Principal Doug Killough in this matter, and he suggested no spirit signs or posters be placed in the hallways of the school until Thursday of that week, which had been the normal routine throughout the season. On the other side of the preparation efforts, Coach Gage had found a success formula for travel, and he utilized it again, with a minor modification. Since the game was scheduled to be played at 12:07 p.m. on Saturday it would be necessary to travel to the game site the day before. It would also allow the players the opportunity to become familiar with the next day's battlefield. That meant a plane ride, which also meant a send off, and boy did the Farmers get one. The entire student body and half the community arrived to send off the Farmers, an overwhelming sign of support the players did not even realize they had. Noseguard Pete Bonenberger could not believe the support. "I was surprised. I knew support was there, but didn't realize how much. I came to Lewisville from California, and the spirit level there is just not the same. We were amazed," remembered the anchor of the Farmer defensive line.

The media was out in force all week, sometimes interfering with the preparation. But Coach Gage and his players were as accommodating in fielding their questions, from the sublime to the ridiculous. Chad Nelson recalled the strangest question asked him by a female reporter: "When you were small did you grow up on a farm?" Smiling at the absurdity of the query, Nelson politely said, "No, I lived in the city, just like everyone else on the team." All in all, the media did not prohibit the Farmers from getting ready for their most important game of the season; Gage would not allow it.

The pressure during the championship drive had taken its toll out on the young head coach, something he hadn't realized until after the Temple game. Gage explained, "I remember me and Stephanie (Gage's wife) going to a faculty Christmas party at Mecardo Juarez after the Temple game. I was so tired from the game and Stephanie was driving. She looked over at me and I was crying; tears streaming down my face. She asked me, 'Why are you crying? You're supposed to be happy.' I said, 'I am.' It was the release of all the emotions pent up during the playoff drive."

The stress of 16 weeks of football started showing up in the players, too. The fatigue factor started setting in, so the coaches did not require much in the way of physical preparation. At this point in the season it was more important to rest and not run the risk of an unnecessary injury than to have bodies flying around on the practice field. The coaches knew what their team was capable of; they would let them prove it against the Generals.

Of the hundreds of thoughts that raced in and out of Gage's mind during the preparation for the championship, one overwhelming thought remained

FRIDAY NIGHT FARMERS

The waiting game—LISD Athletic Director Neal Wilson (left) and LHS Principal Doug Killough (right) flank Farmer Head Coach Ronnie Gage at the Astrodome the day before the championship game.

as a focal point. "If you could just get to play in a championship in your career, that would be icing on the cake," Gage explained, recalling all the outstanding coaches, including Neal Wilson, who never got the opportunity to play for a title. He realized that this might be his only shot at a state championship, which made him feel a bit nervous, although he tried to conceal if from the players and coaches. Instead, he busied himself in preparing his team for the task at hand rather than dwelling on the things that could go wrong.

The championship game was to be played at the Astrodome in Houston, Texas, the very site where the likes of George Blanda, Dan Pastorini and Warren Moon had engineered memorable Houston Oiler offensive attacks in the early days of the old American Football League and, more recently, the American Football Conference. The site was determined before the semifinal contest with Temple. Prior to that contest, the coaches of the four potential state finalists, Lewisville, Temple, Aldine MacArthur and Victoria, were contacted and underwent a round-robin selection process of sorts, covering all the possible combinations for the state finals match-up. Texas High School Coaches Association Executive Director Eddie Joseph had Coach Gage and Aldine MacArthur Head Coach Bob Alpert on the phone to mediate the site selection. Initially they had attempted to use the zip code method, but that did not work out. They could not seem to come to an acceptable agreement, which is what prompted the involvement of Mr. Joseph. The director flipped the coin and Coach Gage was allowed to make the call. He called, "heads," the same

A Dream Realized

Ready or not; here we come! The Farmers charge onto the field to take on MacArthur in the title contest at the Astrodome.

call that had brought both Abilene Cooper and Temple to Texas Stadium, and he hoped it would do the same for Aldine MacArthur. There was a momentary silence, then Joseph's voice broke the silence as he asked, "Coach Gage, have you ever played in the Astrodome?" "No sir," Gage answered. "Well you will if you win. Good luck." They then exchanged a few pleasantries and hung up. Gage knew that his Farmers would not have the home field advantage, something they had in four out of the five playoff games thus far. Once Temple was disposed of, the plans were initiated to make the trip to the Astrodome, the Eighth Wonder of the World.

The journey to Midland had gone so well that a similar itinerary was made for the state trip. In conjunction with the airline and hotel arrangements, Gage met with the parents and asked them to leave the players alone until after the game in an effort to provide an environment conducive for optimal preparation. Every minute of the players' time was planned, which provided a minimum amount of free time so that the pressure would not overtake them. Every measure he and his staff took was toward keeping the team focused on their task.

On game day the Farmers boarded their buses at the Sheraton Hotel nearby the Astrodome and traveled to the stadium, arriving at around 10:15 or 10:30 a.m., although they were a bit premature in their departure; they left minus a few players and their defensive coordinator. The team trainer, David Ortmeier, was normally the last one to board the bus when the Farmers traveled. When he got on the bus that day everyone thought it was time to leave, so they left, leaving behind Coach Terry Goode and several players. Their absence went unnoticed, too, forcing them to find alternate transportation. Fortunately a few parents had remained behind and offered their services. It was a good thing they were only five minutes from the Astrodome.

Friday Night Farmers

Their early arrival allowed ample time for pregame activities; getting taped, walking the field and finding some remote place to capture a few moments of silence to concentrate on their assignment. Perhaps some reflected back on the past 15 weeks. It had been a long time since the kickoff of the season opener at R.L. Turner, and all that work throughout the season would culminate in the following three hours. Or maybe some were thinking about their specific assignments and envisioning how to carry them out. No doubt the 1972 team that came up a yard short against Uvalde 21 years earlier had at least crossed the minds of more than a few, but it all boiled down to one thing—beating Adline MacArthur.

There was a bit of excitement on the field before the game got underway, a precursor to the intensity of the contest. As the captains for both teams met at mid field for the coin toss, the 46 or so remaining Farmers stretched out almost the length of the field and, in a show of unity, joined hands and followed their captains on the field, stopping at the numbers. It was an impressive sight seeing all those white jerseys and maroon helmets aligned in a row, something they had done since the Marcus game. The Adline players misunderstood the show of unity, however, and interpreted it as an attempt at intimidating them. They went berserk and swaggered out on the field as well. They started talking trash, too, similar to the antics of Ricky Henderson of the Oakland Athletics. Armin Love, the Generals' strong safety, had to be restrained by one of the assistant coaches. Apparently the display had gotten to him. Gage insists the demonstration was innocent. "I really don't know why they reacted the way they did. That was something the kids had done on their own since the Marcus game. Surely their scouts saw it," explained Gage.

The adverse reaction to the Farmers' pregame activities may have had an effect on the opening drive of the game. The reaction worsened as the Farmers won the coin toss and, as they had done throughout the playoffs, deferred their choice until the second half. The Generals received the opening kickoff, with MacArthur's David Patterson returning Topher Roach's kick to their own 29, and the 1993 5A Division II State Championship was underway.

The Generals were a young but improving team, having made the playoffs courtesy of the forfeit by crosstown rival Aldine High School due to the use of an academically ineligible player. The win received via the forfeit improved their regular season record to 4–2, on their way to a 7–3 finish, with three of those losses coming in district play. The 4–3 district record was good enough to reach the playoffs, and the Generals had gotten better each week. Playoff wins over Port Arthur Jefferson, Galveston Ball, Lamar Consolidated, LaPorte and Victoria earned them their first championship appearance in the school's history. They outscored their playoff opponents 133–52, an indication that Alpert's young Generals were peaking at the right time, as were the Farmers.

MacArthur was led by sophomore quarterback Odell James, with his 6-feet-3-inches and 195 pounds. His leadership on the field had taken the full

A Dream Realized

Farmer fans celebrate Lewisville's first score.

season to develop but was very much in place by the time the title contest took place. Joined in the backfield by the explosive Delbert Garner, the Generals had averaged almost 400 yards in total offense per game, very similar to Lewisville, which would make for a close match-up for the '93 state title.

The Generals began the opening drive at their own 29 with Odell James picking up 2 yards on a quarterback draw, and the Farmer fans erupted at the short yardage allowed by their stiff defense. The following play had James attempting his first pass to running back Johnnie Roberts, which fell incomplete, bringing an even louder roar from the Farmer faithful, setting up the game's first third-and-long situation. The Generals' ace running back, Delbert Garner, carried on the third-down play for 7 yards, 1 yard shy of the first down. With MacArthur having lost their kicker and punter a week earlier against Victoria, Coach Alpert felt their chances of getting off a successful punt were worse than in gaining the needed yard, so they elected to gamble and go for it on fourth-and-one. Besides, a conversion here could give his young team a much needed lift early

Dwight Hunter (3) looks for a block after his first quarter interception to stop a MacArthur drive. Jeff Branch (86) and Todd Landrum (67) escort the All-State junior to the Farmer 39-yard line.

on in this important contest. So on fourth down they handed the ball off to Garner, their leading rusher. He had averaged over 7 yards a carry on the year and they figured he could get the job done. But Lewisville's defensive tackle Dan Merritt met Garner at the line of scrimmage and brought him to a screeching halt for no gain. This time the Lewisville fans almost blew the roof off of the famed Astrodome. The stop came at the 10:28 mark in the first period, and the Farmers had a prime opportunity at the General 38-yard line to begin their first drive.

On Lewisville's first play Chad Nelson gave the ball to the dependable Dwayne Brazzell, but Brazzell was tackled in the backfield for a yard loss. This time the MacArthur crowd went wild, quieting the Farmer fans a bit. The question came to the minds of many of the Lewisville folks as to whether the Farmers were going to be able to run on this team. If MacArthur could successfully remove the running game from the Farmer attack, they could beat them.

But the question as to whether the Farmers could run against them or not was answered on Lewisville's second-down play as Nelson faked to Brazzell on the option and raced around the right end, untouched, for 39 yards and the first score of the game. The quick score sent a message to all on hand that the Farmers were, indeed, ready. Topher Roach's extra point was good, and the Farmers held a 7–0 lead with 9:39 left in the first period.

The Generals started their first scoring threat from their own 9-yard line midway through the first quarter. The drive featured a combination of running plays by James and Garner that reached the Farmer 46 in nine plays. On the 10th play of the drive James attempted his third pass of the game. The first two had fallen incomplete, but this one was caught . . . but not by a General receiver. Farmer defensive back Dwight Hunter, as he had done 10 times on the journey to the title game, stepped in front of the would-be receiver and picked off James' pass, returning it 22 yards to the MacArthur 39-yard line, the exact spot where Nelson made his touchdown run on the Farmers opening drive. Gage was hopeful the results would be the same.

Lewisville appeared to be on the march as they chipped away at the MacArthur defense; first a 6-yard run by Waylon Holland, followed by a Byron Mitchell 2-yard run. It did not appear the General five-man front could stop the Farmers, but they got the break they needed on the third play of the drive. Nelson optioned to his left and, after a 6-yard gain, pitched to Mitchell who was trailing behind him. The pitch was slightly behind him, and he didn't handle it. The ball hit the turf and MacArthur quickly recovered it to both stop the Farmer drive and begin their first touchdown march.

The Generals settled down after the turnover and began a seven-play scoring drive from their own 24. The drive was highlighted by a pass completed to Ramond Robinson, good for 44 yards, that reached the Farmer 19. James then carried on three consecutive plays with the last one getting in the end zone for an 8-yard touchdown. Shannon Brazzell rushed in to block the extra

A Dream Realized

point, preserving the Farmer lead at 7–6, but the Generals had new life, and what had first appeared to be a long day for them was shaping up to be an interesting game.

The MacArthur score knocked the lid off of the defensive encounter that characterized the first period, and from then on it was an all-out offensive assault. James' touchdown run came at the 10:04 mark in the second quarter, and that score stood until the Farmers got the ball with 6:22 left in the first half. Beginning at their own 29-yard line, Lewisville marched 71 yards in six plays, using 3:11 to garner their next score. The drive was kept alive on a fourth-and-one situation with Topher Roach lined up in punt formation at the Farmer 38-yard line. As Roach received the snap from center he noticed an opening on the left side and decided to run for the needed yard rather than kick. He got 2, and the Farmer drive remained alive. Two plays later Nelson ran the same play he scored on earlier, this time for 55 yards and the second Farmer touchdown. Roach kicked the extra point and the Farmer lead stretched to 14–6.

Lewisville had worked on the fake punt during the week, and Roach specifically looked for an opportunity to utilize it. It could not have come at a better time. Since their score on the first possession the Farmers had gone punt/fumble/punt on their three following possessions with no first downs. That drive was critical to opening up the game, and Roach's successful execution of it was the charge Lewisville needed, just in the nick of time, too. Following Roach's ensuing kickoff the Generals came right back for their second score, a two-play drive, capped by a wobbly 55-yard pass from James to Robinson on a post pattern. With their kicking woes present, the Generals decided to go for the two-point conversion. James hit Garner in the end zone for the conversion, pulling the Generals even with the Farmers, 14–14, and leaving Lewisville under three minutes to do something with the ball before the half's end.

A run-back to their own 38 would have set the Farmers in favorable field goal position, but a major penalty nullified that, pushing them back to their 23, where the Farmers set up shop with 2:24 remaining before intermission. A pass from Nelson to LaDarrin McLane fell incomplete, but two consecutive 23-yard gains, the first by Nelson and the second by Brazzell, had the Farmers suddenly sitting on the MacArthur 31, and Gage and Pietrosky, instead of being content to run out the clock, had serious thoughts of stealing a touchdown before the clock struck zero—or at least a field goal.

While the two offensive minds were scheming, Roach was waiting in the wings, his leg already warm from kicking into the practice net under the watchful eye of kicking coach Gino Ristevski. The plan was to run the time down as close to zero as possible, to either score a touchdown or send Roach in for the three points. The Steamrollers chiseled away at the Generals' defense, first for 5 yards, then for 4 and so on, until they moved to the Aldine 9-yard line with still plenty of time to come away with some points. On the next play

Nelson faked to Brazzell to freeze the defense, allowing Byron Mitchell to get open in the flats from his running back position. Nelson hit him at about the 5-yard line, and he did the rest of the work himself, carrying it in for the last-minute score. Roach's point-after was perfect, as was the touchdown drive, and Lewisville was firmly atop a 21–14 halftime score.

The score just before halftime fit well in the Farmer scheme and followed the pattern that carried over from the Cooper and Temple games. With Lewisville scheduled to receive the second half kickoff, it would give them a chance to go ahead by a pair of touchdowns, something they might need with the ability James had displayed in leading the Generals down the field to score.

No doubt the coaches were encouraged about their team's first half performance. Offensively, except for the time they stopped themselves with the fumble, they had only minor problems driving the ball against MacArthur's defense. Of the six first-half possessions, the Farmers scored on three of them. They likely would have scored another had they not fumbled at the MacArthur 24-yard line.

During the halftime chat the coaches diagrammed plays with chalk on the cement floor of the Astrodome locker room. They discussed coverages and defensive reads, in particular on how to detect the quarterback draw MacArthur's James had been so effective with in the first half. All in all Lewisville was pleased with its performance, with their most important 24 minutes left to play.

Gage spent a portion of the halftime break lying on a training table, half from worn nerves and half from thinking of the right thing to say that, somehow, would inspire his players to expend all their efforts efficiently and effectively in the final two quarters. As was the custom, the players gathered around their head coach before departing the confines of the locker room for the playing field and listened eagerly to the words of their beloved mentor:

> "We've played fifteen-and-a-half weeks and nobody's beat you yet. We've got a seven point lead, and we're fixin' to get the second half kickoff. Okay? Now . . . the thing we've got to do . . . is, we've got to play the best half we've played this year. Now, let's go get the ball and shove it up their butt!"

That motivational speech brought a cheer from the team that had overcome the adversity of the tie against The Colony in week seven, avoided the Marcus attack, and knocked off two West Texas powerhouses and the defending state champions. They were focused and prepared and knew what it would take to win. They had experienced it 14 times already that season, a school record, and would do anything in their power to make it 15.

All eyes throughout the state were on them, at least those who had an interest in Texas high school football. The game was broadcast live on the Home Sports Entertainment cable channel in Texas and some surrounding states, and with the 5A Division I champion crowned the week before, this

A Dream Realized

was the biggest of the five championship games played that day. The Generals had barely out gained the Farmers in total yards in the first half—217 yards to Lewisville's 213—so the stage was set for an action packed second half of championship football.

The Farmers received the opening kickoff of the second half, once it finally got underway. The Generals had emerged from the locker room and were ready to go, but there was no sign of the Farmers. They had already ticked MacArthur off earlier when they stretched the length of the field for the coin toss; making them wait to start the second half would surely anger them. In fact, it did upset Coach Alpert. He gestured to the referees to throw a penalty flag for delay of game. His team had been waiting for five minutes and they were ready to play . . . right then.

Eventually the Farmers made their way down the tunnel to the field and got set to receive the kickoff, after having made the Generals wait. That tactic had been used against the Farmers the week before by Temple Head Coach Bob McQueen at the start of the game. The Lewisville players had filed out of the dressing room and were waiting on the Wildcats for a long time, much longer than the Generals had waited for the Farmers. Finally, Gage took his team back in the locker room until Temple actually showed up. Gage returned McQueen the favor in the second half, but he insists making MacArthur wait was unintentional. "We came out when they told us to. They told us we would start the half at a certain time because of television. I didn't see any need to get out there any sooner," explained the Farmer head coach.

When things finally got settled, Reggie Crawford returned the kickoff to the Lewisville 25 for the Farmers, and the hunt was on. It was standard Steamroller football for 11 plays with Brazzell, Mitchell and Nelson splitting time in sharing the load behind Bret Johnson, Pete Bonenberger, Mika Clark, Dan Merritt, Mike Anderson and Martin Simmons. Bonenberger replaced Buddy Phillips after Phillips was injured in the first half, but the offensive line did not miss a beat. The Farmers converted on two third-down plays in the drive as the surge of the offensive line pushed the General front five helplessly backward. Two 15-yard runs highlighted the possession, one by Brazzell and one by Mitchell, and Mitchell got the touchdown on an 11-yard run. Roach converted the point-after and the Farmers had, for the third consecutive week, taken the second half kickoff and driven down to score. That touchdown, along with Mitchell's late score in the first half, gave Lewisville a 28–14 lead.

Delbert Garner sparked the Generals on the following kickoff with a 38-yard return to the MacArthur 42-yard line. The Farmers were in position to ice the game right then as Cornist dropped David Patterson for a 4-yard loss on an attempted reverse. An Odell James pass fell incomplete, and the Generals faced a third-and-14 situation at their own 38. Had the Farmers held them on that play they could have marched down for a third unanswered touchdown and put the game away. Instead, Garner got the call on a draw play and carried for 15 yards, one more than necessary, and the Farmers missed a

FRIDAY NIGHT FARMERS

Zack Welton (42) buries the Generals' Delbert Garner at the MacArthur 42-yard line in the second half, as Mike Frazier (82) watches closely. The Generals went on to score, making the score 28–22 in the third period.

golden opportunity to shut the General offense down. Three plays later James rolled left on a keeper and kept on going down the left sideline, breaking four tackles on his way to a 40-yard touchdown. James performed an encore for the two-point conversion, and suddenly the Generals were back within range at 28–22, and the Lewisville fans began to get a bit concerned.

Their concerns grew to outright worry as the Farmers were forced to punt after three so-so plays following the latest MacArthur score. The Generals got the ball in decent field position at their own 33, after being penalized for holding, and all of a sudden they were within striking distance. Not only were they 67 yards away from the potential go-ahead touchdown, but the third quarter was dwindling with 1:35 left. The game had taken a different turn and the momentum had clearly shifted to the MacArthur side of the field.

James carried the ball on six of seven plays in the drive, including the last one, a 1-yard plunge for the dreaded score to tie the game at 28–28. Ramond Robinson kicked the extra point, and the Farmers fell behind for the first time in the contest, 29–28.

That score was familiar in the history of Lewisville Farmer football, one that brings back pleasant memories of the 1972 season 21 years earlier. Against McKinney, Lewisville had fallen behind 28–14, like MacArthur, and began a dramatic fourth quarter surge to win, as quarterback Joe Martin dove into the end zone with no time remaining, earning their first district championship since 1957. Now it appeared, at least for the moment, that the 29–28 score

A Dream Realized

The Rowdy Crowd celebrates after the Farmers regained the lead, 36–29, in the fourth quarter. Later, they would celebrate again, but not without a scare.

had come back to haunt the Farmers. The only hope they had was the 10:38 remaining in the contest.

The Farmers began a must-score drive at their own 30 and moved the ball as they had all day. The linemen blocked like they were on a mission, and Brazzell and Mitchell ran like they were possessed. A nice ball-controlling drive would accomplish two things: 1) it would gain the needed score to retake the lead and 2) it would use up some of the clock. Nelson and company accomplished what they set out to do with an eight-play drive climaxed by a 2-yard run by Brazzell. Instead of kicking, though, the Farmers elected to go for two, forcing the Generals to make a two-point conversion should they, God forbid, score again. Nelson kept the ball for the two points and the Farmers recaptured the lead at 36–29 with 6:58 remaining; plenty of time to play with the explosiveness of these two offensive units.

When the Farmers fell behind 29–28, Gage was not that concerned. He had confidence in the offense and the success they had demonstrated that day. That faith was realized with Lewisville bouncing right back to go ahead 36–29, and everything was fine again. Things were on target; the right team was winning. Had someone pulled the plug on the stadium clock at that moment Gage would have been pleased, as would the throngs that witnessed both in person and on television. They had seen a good ball game. How could it get any better?

Before it got better, though, things got worse for the Farmers; much worse.

MacArthur didn't know they weren't supposed to win. They didn't know, or at least they didn't care, that Lewisville had been deprived of a state championship they should have won 21 years earlier. This one was supposed to belong to the Farmers . . . but the Generals would have something to say about it.

Roach's kickoff sailed out of the end zone for the touchback, forcing MacArthur to have to drive 80 yards for the go-ahead score, and with 6:58 to go, off they went. Garner hit the middle of the line for 9 yards, then off left tackle for 7, and another first down. James kept up the middle for 1 yard, then rolled out right and left for 3 and 9 yards for yet another first down, and it didn't look like they could be stopped. The young sophomore was methodically dissecting the Farmer defense, managing to move swiftly down the field and simultaneously burn the clock. Gage was getting worried, as was the 10 or so thousand who had driven south on Interstate Highway 45 to witness first hand what they thought would be the first ever state championship for their Farmers. That dream seemed to be slowly slipping away, yard-by-yard, as the Generals neared the goal line. At their own 49 James hit Robinson for his fourth, and most important, catch of the day, a 19-yarder to the Farmer 32. James followed that with a 17-yard keeper to Lewisville's 15, and what everyone feared deep down in their hearts and minds would happen, was happening; the Farmers were losing their grip. At least it looked that way if they could not find a way to stop James.

From the Farmer 15 it took the Generals just two plays to get into the end zone for the potential winning score; it would take a two-point conversion to put them in front. On the drive James kept around the left side for a quick 7 and followed that with an 8-yard touchdown run through the heart of Farmer defense, to bring the Generals to within one, still behind at 36–35. Gage sank to his knees on the sideline to watch the conversion attempt. There was nothing else he or Defensive Coordinator Terry Goode could do but watch. The defense that had not allowed a single back to rush for 100 yards had allowed two to do so in this ballgame: Garner, with the 8-yard score, had rushed for 102 yards on 18 carries, while James almost doubled that with 189 yards on 25 tries—a tribute to just how good the young Aldine MacArthur Generals were. As the Generals lined up for the two-point attempt the crowd hushed to concentrate on the action. Gage, still kneeling, as if praying to the football gods for a miracle, was motionless. The moment of fear that had remained in Farmer history for 21 years had come.

As he had done so many times that afternoon, James kept on the two-point play and lumbered into the end zone to put the Generals ahead for the second time in the contest, 37–36, with 3:13 left to play. As Gage watched, his eyes shut with disbelief and his upper body bent forward with his forehead almost touching the turf. The hard work he, his coaches and team had gone through was seemingly coming to an unpleasant end. For the fans, the flashbacks of 1972 immediately came to mind, with images of the Farmer offense struggling to penetrate the end zone from a yard away, but being unsuccess-

A Dream Realized

Dan Merritt (bottom) and Jeff Branch (right) combine to stop Delbert Garner for a short gain, but could not keep the Generals out of the end zone on their final drive. MacArthur's touchdown and two-point conversion made it 37–36 with 3:13 to play.

ful in doing so. The frustration felt in '72 was multiplied when James crossed the goal line, and everyone wondered if it would be 21 more years before getting another chance at winning the big prize. As Gage was aware, opportunities at winning a state championship sometimes only came around once in a career, and for some, not even once.

But there was hope. With just over three minutes to play the Farmer offense would get another crack at it, and with the reliable leg of Topher Roach, about 50 to 60 yards would be all they would need to pull it out. After a moment of anguish, Gage quickly jumped to his feet to organize the final Farmer attack for the 1993 season. This game was far from being over, Gage knew, and his Farmers were going to have the last word.

MacArthur's Ramond Robinson kicked the ball through the end zone for a touchback, giving Lewisville the ball at their own 20-yard line with 3:13 to play. All eyes were fixed on Chad Nelson and Dwayne Brazzell, hoping the two could engineer the offense to a winning score. Nelson and Brazzell had combined to score 30 touchdowns between them entering the state playoff game. The two had combined for three scores thus far in the game, including Brazzell's touchdown on the Farmers' last possession, proving that this offense was capable of scoring at any time from anywhere.

The primary concern for the Lewisville fans was the time factor. The Steamroller offense's trademark was multi-play, long drives of 3- and 4-yard gains, capped by short touchdown runs. But with the triple option, Nelson was a threat to score from anywhere and turn what might normally be a seven or eight minute drive into one of one or two minutes. Regardless of the weapons in the Farmer arsenal, this situation would be a true test of character for the prolific offense, setting up the climax to what had been an already exciting contest.

Nelson kept on the first play of the final drive for a 10-yard gain, and the hope that had dissipated from the Lewisville fans during the MacArthur scoring drive, suddenly came back to life. Brazzell ran for 9 yards on the following play and it did not look like the Farmers would be denied. Nineteen yards in two plays was an encouragement to the Farmer contingent; the main concern would be in completing the drive within the remaining time frame.

On second-and-one MacArthur finally found a way to stop the Farmers. Nelson, avoiding a 5-yard loss while trying to turn the corner, was brought down by Aldine's Charlie Foster for no gain, with the clock still ticking. Facing third-and-one, Lewisville decided to try something different. The General defense was keying on both Nelson and Brazzell, so the Farmers opted to hand off to Reggie Crawford, anticipating that the attention Nelson and Brazzell attracted would free him to gain the first down. Instead of being fooled, Anthony Williams and Mister Johnson met Crawford at the line, stopping the Farmers for no gain on the second consecutive play, and Lewisville was forced to use its final-time out to set up a vital fourth-and-one situation at their own 39-yard line.

Gage, Pietrosky and Nelson conferred on the Farmer sideline to draw up a play which would hopefully gain the necessary yard. Forget about the field goal; this was the play of the game for Lewisville. Pietrosky had been a neutralizing factor for Gage on the sideline during the critical drive, keeping him apprised of the down, yards needed and the time remaining. All communications with the Farmer head coach were channeled through him, eliminating all distractions and allowing Gage to concentrate fully on the task at hand, which was to make a first down. The play decided upon was a naked bootleg, where Nelson would fake the handoff to Crawford on the right side and roll back to his left, unprotected. Nelson's speed would either make or lose the first down.

The play matched up well against MacArthur's defense. The Generals ran a 4-3 formation; four down linemen with three linebackers. Hopefully the fake would attract the defense to the middle, allowing Nelson enough room to get outside for the first down. As the offense lined up for the play, though, Gage noticed a fifth man on the defensive line, and right at the point of attack. When Gage saw that, he thought that it was over. "I thought the play was a mistake after seeing them shift to a 5-3 defense. I didn't think we had much of a chance at getting the first down. I was sick," Gage remembers.

As diagrammed, Nelson turned right and faked to Crawford and company barreling into the line. Chad continued to turn to his right, still holding

A Dream Realized

the ball, and came full circle with the bulk of the action going away from him. The defense, including the extra man, went for the fake, leaving Nelson and his sprinter's speed alone to pick up the yardage. Nelson had to dip about 5 yards behind the line to carry out the fake, giving him that much more yardage to gain. Once he cleared the mass of bodies piled up at the line, he spotted the place he needed to reach to make the first down. He darted to that spot, attracting attention from the secondary. From then on it was a foot race, with Nelson winning. He gained not only 1, but 6 yards, and the dream was still alive. Kermit Woods and Armin Love ganged up for the tackle, and Love grabbed Nelson's face mask on the way down, resulting in a 5-yard penalty. First down, Farmers!

Altogether the play gained 11 yards; 6 on the carry and 5 on the penalty. The play, a 24 blast keeper, worked for two reasons. It was the same one they had given to Crawford on the previous play for no gain, but Nelson had carried out the fake completely, making the actual play with him keeping more effective. Another reason it worked was that Nelson told only Crawford that he was keeping the ball. "I didn't tell the linemen I was keeping so that they would block as if it was a run to the right. I told Coach Gage I would get the yard on the keeper. We made it look like the blast, and I was able to use my speed to get outside," recalled the third-year Farmer quarterback.

The Farmer coaching staff can accept a portion of the credit for Nelson's first-down run. To ensure the success of the wishbone offense, each back must carry out the fake on every play as if they are going to get the ball. This forces the defense to divide its attention at several points of attack, increasing the offense's chances at picking up positive yardage. If, during practice, a back would not carry out the fake, the coaches would reprimand him for loafing and require him to run after practice, an incentive for carrying out the fake the next time. That had worked all year and contributed to the success of the Farmer wishbone attack. Nelson remembered that on the third-down play, and it paid off on the all-important fourth-down attempt.

Nelson carried for 3 yards on the next play, with MacArthur's Armin Love knocking him out of bounds and stopping the clock with 1:10 to play. The Farmers were still 20 yards away from Roach's field goal range. His longest successful field goal came against Abilene Cooper, a 43-yarder just before halftime, meaning Lewisville would have to reach the 27-yard line to equal that distance. Brazzell picked up 7 yards for another first down to reach the 40, with 1:04 remaining, and followed with a 2-yard run, setting up a second-and-eight situation. The clock was still running. Nelson spiked the ball on the next play to stop the clock, and Lewisville faced a third-and-eight situation with :33 remaining, still needing at least 18 yards to assure themselves of a reasonable field goal attempt.

Sophomore backup quarterback LaDarrin McLane brought the next play in from the bench, and immediately Nelson knew they would be abandoning the running game—at least for one play. Normally when McLane made an appearance in the game it was a pass play. McLane was being groomed to take Nelson's place at quarterback when he graduated, but his speed and hands were too valuable to wait until the 1994 season to be utilized, so McLane saw time at the wide receiver position, although he hadn't caught a pass all season. He had 11 rushes for 113 yards in the small amount of action he saw, but he did have a 34-yard scamper in the third game of the season against Newman Smith, showing that he, too, had the ability to make big plays. And at third-and-eight, with no time-outs and :33 seconds left in the state championship game, there would be no bigger play.

The play McLane brought in from Coach Gage was a "right pass, 36 throwback post." The Farmers were in their standard running formation, with Martin Simmons lined up at tight end on the right side and McLane split wide left, nearest the Farmer sideline. By design, Nelson would take the snap and start down the right side as if running the option—as they had done 52 times before that day—then drop back after faking to Brazzell. The fake would draw the defense to the line and hopefully create a passing lane for Nelson to hit either Simmons on an out-pattern to the right, or McLane on the post-pattern over the middle. If Nelson hit Simmons he would have been able to get out of bounds and stop the clock, giving the Farmers time to run at least two more plays to work themselves into field goal position. If Nelson could find McLane in single coverage over the middle, it would put the Farmers in much better shape; the ball would be much closer to the goal post, and it would be spotted in between the hash marks to give Roach a better angle. The key would be in executing the fake to "sell" the defense on the run.

MacArthur strong safety Armin Love had made three straight tackles during the drive before Nelson spiked the ball to stop the clock, an indication of how well the Farmer offensive line had controlled the line of scrimmage. Doing so had forced the MacArthur secondary to pay extra attention to the run, making tackles that the defensive line or linebackers normally would make. Nelson and Brazzell had penetrated the secondary often that day, with Nelson mostly breezing by the defenders and Brazzell delivering several punishing blows on his 25 carries throughout the ball game. The fake to the Farmer fullback would certainly get the attention of the MacArthur secondary.

The play could not have gone any better had Gage, Pietrosky and all the coaches suited up and entered the game to run it themselves. The offensive line fired off the ball and Nelson faked to Brazzell, and the defense converged on number 32 for a split second, until they realized the Farmer workhorse didn't have the ball. By that time Nelson had dropped back and began looking for a receiver. The wide receiver, McLane, was the primary receiver on the play, and the fake had produced the desired effect of single coverage on him. McLane got inside the coverage of free safety Kermit Woods, and he was more open than a co-dependency group session. Woods did not get any inside help from Love because he had fallen for the fake; hook, line and sinker. Nelson didn't even look at Simmons.

A Dream Realized

As LaDarrin broke inside, Nelson delivered the ball with precision to the MacArthur 12-yard line. McLane snared the critical pass and Woods brought him down at the General 10. The Farmers were now in excellent shape at the 10-yard line with :26 seconds remaining. Now all they had to do was run the clock down and kick the field goal. Roach had proven reliable from that range, and the last-second field goal would put Lewisville up by two at 39–37, allowing the Farmers to claim the elusive state trophy.

After the big play MacArthur's coach Bob Alpert ordered a time-out to allow his team to settle down. At that point they were down, but not out. Meanwhile the Farmer offensive unit was summoned to the sideline to confer with coaches Gage and Pietrosky to determine which play would be both the surest and best one to run in this situation. Gage had already sent in a play prior to the time-out, but the break allowed the coaches and players to reevaluate the situation and put a plan together. As several plays were discussed, offensive tackle Mike Anderson told Gage that he felt they should run the 30-trap, a play in which Dwayne Brazzell would carry the ball up the middle. What the Farmers needed to accomplish was to hold onto the ball, make a few yards, retain the position of the ball in the middle of the field and use up the clock. A 30-trap would accomplish just that, and the Farmers had used it successfully that day as recently as the two or three times during the final drive. Anderson convinced Gage and Pietrosky that he would get the job done, kind of a "Field of Dreams" of sorts. "If you run it, we will gain," guaranteed the massive offensive right tackle. Anderson's job on that play was to come off the line and block Nick Glenn, the MacArthur strong-side linebacker. Anderson had crushed the 190-pound senior already several times that day and felt he could do it again.

The 6-foot-3-inch, 242-pound senior had been a leader on the offensive line all season, with the bulk of the Farmer running attack going to his side. He, along with guard Buddy Phillips and tight end Martin Simmons, were the epitome of the Steamroller concept all season and proved effective against the Generals' best that day. Mika Clark was shifted from center to guard to replace Buddy Phillips, who was out with a second quarter injury, and Bret Johnson was inserted at center. As the offense approached the line of scrimmage, Anderson encouraged Clark to spend all of what remaining energy he had on the upcoming play. "Come on, man, let's do it," he whispered to Clark as he got in his stance. The rest was history.

The pass to McLane on the previous play had the MacArthur defense off balance to the extent that they didn't know what to expect next. At least it looked that way. As Nelson called the snap he pivoted 360 degrees to his left, handing the ball to Brazzell three-fourths of the way around. By turning to his left the defense reacted in that direction before realizing Brazzell had the ball on the right side behind Clark, Anderson, et. al. By the time they figured it out it was too late. Anderson fired off the line and MacArthur's Glenn didn't have a chance. Anderson blind-sided him, burying him under his 6-foot-3-

inch frame. Clark completed the trap block, providing a hole large enough to drive a team of oxen through at slow speed. All Brazzell had to do was keep his balance, after evading a grasping hand from underneath the pileup at the line of scrimmage. Once he broke through the line he didn't meet anyone until he reached the goal line, and then he plowed over Armin Love to reach the end zone. What had originally started out as a scheme to get the team in good field goal position had turned into a smash-mouth touchdown run. Topher Roach did get into the game later, but only for an extra point. His kick was good and the Farmers led once again, 43–37, with :21 seconds left on the clock. That would mean the Generals would get the ball one final time.

When the touchdown run was made and the extra point completed, strangers on the Farmer side were hugging and high-fiving each other with their mutual love for the Fighting Farmers as a unifying force. Somehow, some way their beloved team had found a winning combination . . . at least for the moment. Those who still had voices were yelling as loudly as they could, awaiting the ensuing kickoff that would put an end to this game so that their Farmers could finally grab that much desired state championship trophy. Things settled a bit as Roach got set to kick, then grew extremely anxious as MacArthur's David Patterson broke through much of the Farmer coverage and scooted down the sideline. He had one man to beat in order to deflate the Farmer balloon and regain the lead. But that was not to be. Lewisville's defensive end, Zeb Cornist, ran Patterson down in front of Coach Gage at the Farmer 40-yard line, a little too close for comfort. HSE color commentator Dave Elmendorf described Cornist's effort as "want to," and indeed it was. By knocking Patterson out of bounds the Generals had time enough to draw up one final play to top the miracle the Farmers had pulled off 14 game-seconds earlier. This game was not over yet.

Due to the running ability of Odell James the Farmers were forced to play a more controlled style of defense instead of free-lancing, as they had done against Abilene Cooper and Temple. That was part of the reason the MacArthur line had been able to get good blocks on them. Had they looped and stunted more often they may have been harder to block, but it would have also made it easier for James and Garner to break more big plays; they had broken enough as it was. Because of that, the Farmers' defensive play had become somewhat predictable to the General's offensive line, so Defensive Coordinator Terry Goode decided to turn his defensive front loose on the final play, hopefully to confuse the offensive line. After all, everybody knew it would be a pass into the end zone.

James never got the pass away. Somebody either forgot to block Dan Merritt, or couldn't get a block on him. As James dropped back to pass, Merritt charged through untouched and blind-sided the gifted sophomore from behind, causing him to fumble away their final chance. He didn't know what hit him. MacArthur's strong-side offensive tackle recovered the fumble and, bless his heart, tried his best to do what he could to keep his team's chances alive, but

A Dream Realized

Post game ceremony — Assistant UIL Athletic Director Charles Breithaupt (right) presents Ronnie Gage with the State Championship trophy as HSE's Craig Way looks on.

Pete Bonenberger was right there to wrap him up with :09 left... and ticking. There was no time left to do anything, and all the Aldine MacArthur fans could do was helplessly watch the clock run down to zero—too swiftly for MacArthur, but not soon enough for the Farmers.

Once the clock hit 00:00 the emotions pent up for over two decades exploded with the realization of claiming the state championship. A program that had drank from the trough of success for 21 years finally came away with its thirst quenched. Assistant UIL Athletic Director Charles Breithaupt was on hand to present Head Coach Ronnie Gage with the championship trophy, and Gage held it high overhead toward the Lewisville crowd. The crowd erupted again, almost as loudly as they did when Brazzell crossed the goal line. The ride back home would be joyous, with celebrations lasting the entire four-and-a-half hour trip. Some Farmer fans already had their shoe polish ready to spell out "State Champs," to let everyone know what team was the best team in Texas that day. It made for a short trip home.

As far as the residual effects from the championship, there were many. The Farmers dominated the post-season honors by having 18 players named to the District 6-5A All-District team; seven on the first team, eight on the second team and three on the honorable mention list. What stung the Farmer program a bit was that Lewisville was practically ignored when it came to the All-Area and All-State teams.

Aside from Topher Roach being named to the second team All-Area team, no Farmer landed a spot on the state-wide coaches' selection. Six Farmers did make the Texas Sports Writers Association Class 5A All-State Team, four on the first team and two on the second. Dan Merrit, Dwight Hunter and Dwayne and Shannon Brazzell made the first team, while Chad Nelson and Martin Simmons were named to the second team. What was encouraging to the immediate future of the Farmer program was that three of the six would be returning in 1994.

The accolades for Ronnie Gage poured in after the championship as well, beginning with the District 6-5A Co-Coach of the Year, an honor he shared with Grapevine Head Coach Mike Sneed. Sneed had led the Mustangs into the playoffs for the first time in several years on their way to a 7–4 record. A narrow loss to Keller in the bi-district game ended an otherwise brilliant sea-

Finally home — Coach Gage (above) holds the elusive trophy overhead to a roaring crowd as the Farmer faithful display their allegiance.

son for the Mustangs. Gage was named the University of North Texas Alumni Coach of the Year in February of 1994. He was also selected 5A Coach of the Year by the Alamo High School Extra Report, as well as the Fab-Knit 5A Division II Coach of the Year. But mostly Gage was thrilled with what the title did for the Farmer football program and the city of Lewisville. "It felt good for Lewisville with all the support they had given us. It felt good for all those

A Dream Realized

The Ninth Wonder of the World — The Lewisville Fighting Farmers were finally able to relax . . . after the game was over and the trophy was in hand.

people who came down to see it, and especially those who were disappointed in 1972; it really felt good to finally gain the notoriety and respect the program at Lewisville deserved," reflected the Farmer head coach.

Gage was the first to extend credit to the coaching staff for the success of the Farmer football program in 1993. "All the honors are a reflection of the coaching staff. I've been fortunate, since being a head coach, in having good people around me. The guys (the assistant coaches) are good for the kids. They love to motivate them. Not only are they teaching the game of football, but they're also teaching them the game of life," spoke Gage of the importance of a special coaching staff.

The Farmer football program at Lewisville High School dates back into the early 1920s and has featured some of the greatest moments in Texas high school football history. From Lee Preston's teams in the early '20s to their first state championship in 1993, the effort put forth by those fortunate enough to have been called Farmers have found a place in the heart of the citizens of Lewisville both past and present. Memorable moments from Hoss Williams directing the single wing offense in 1930–33, the powerful

The Tower says it all.

Friday Night Farmers

**The 1993 5A Division II State Champions
Lewisville Fighting Farmers**

running of Gordon Salsman, the leadership of Dan and Don Smith, the spectacular Paul Rice, the season-saving catch of Eugene Corbin, and the vivid scene of Dwayne Brazzell bursting in for the final touchdown in the 1993 State Championship game; all are images that have remained in the memory of Farmer fans for decades and have preserved a heritage that has been passed down from generation to generation. That heritage has given birth to pride and tradition that has withstood the test of time, having produced spirit and unity, which is what high school football is all about. With it, the 1993 Farmers were able to realize a dream that was unavailable to the early Lewisville football teams and elusive to the later ones. The 1993 season was truly a dream realized.

. . .

APPENDIX

YEAR-AT-A-GLANCE 1920–93

Year	District	Coach	Record	Homecoming Queen*
1920	N/A	Preston, Lee	0–1–0	
1921	N/A	Preston, Lee	N/A	
1922	N/A	Preston, Lee	0–1–0	
1923	N/A	Preston, Lee	0–1–0	
1924	N/A	Lowe, Ed	2–1–0	
1925	N/A	Lowe, Ed	1–3–1	
1926	N/A	Jones, Darrell	N/A	
1927	N/A	Jones, Darrell	7–2–0	
1928	N/A	Scarborough, Luther	1–2–0	
1929	N/A	Scarborough, Luther	6–2–2	
1930	5-B	Davis, R.O.	0–2–0	
1931	5-B	Davis, R.O.	0–2–1	
1932	5-B	Davis, R.O.	9–0–1	
1933	5-B	Elms, Roger	3–6–1	
1934	16-C	Dunsworth, Taft	0–1–0	
1935	16-C	Dunsworth, Taft	0–3–0	
1936	16-C	Mattingly, R.E.	6–1–1	
1937	16-C	Mattingly, R.E.	8–1–0	
1938	15-C	Mattingly, R.E.	8–0–1	
1939	13-B	Mattingly, R.E.	9–1–1	
1940	13-B	Mattingly, R.E.	9–1–0	
1941	13-B	Mattingly, R.E.	9–1–0	
1942	13-B	Delay, J.K.	1–2–0	
1943	9-B	Delay, J.K.	5–1–1	
1944	9-B	Delay, J.K.	1–4–1	
1945	9-B	Delay, J.K.	3–3–1	
1946	13-B	Delay, J.K.	10–2–0	
1947	13-B	Delay, J.K.	13–0–0	
1948	13-B	Hudson, A.J.	6–3–1	
1949	13-B	Bronaugh, J.H.	9–1–0	
1950	14-B	Bronaugh, J.H.	11–0–0	
1951	10-A	Bronaugh, J.H.	7–2–1	
1952	10-A	Kay, A.L.	6–4–0	
1953	10-A	Kay, A.L.	7–3–0	
1954	10-A	Kay, A.L.	9–1–0	Sue Mercer
1955	10-A	McReynolds, Lewis	10–1–0	Deloris Woolridge
1956	10-AA	McReynolds, Lewis	10–1–0	Helen Morgan
1957	10-AA	McReynolds, Lewis	8–3–0	Brenda Bryson
1958	12-AA	McReynolds, Lewis	6–4–0	Dixie Williams
1959	12-AA	Harmon, Ben	4–6–0	Anne Smith
1960	12-AA	Harmon, Ben	3–7–0	Sharon Kerbow
1961	12-AA	Harmon, Ben	5–5–0	Carolyn Frady
1962	11-AA	Harmon, Ben	5–5–0	Pam Polser
1963	11-AA	Harmon, Ben	4–6–0	Dianne Hulsey
1964	11-AA	Bottoms, Sherrill	6–4–0	Eileen Stewart
1965	11-AA	Bottoms, Sherrill	2–8–0	Pat Peabody
1966	6-AAA	Shipman, Bill	2–8–0	Yvonne "Suggie" Puls
1967	6-AAA	Shipman, Bill	1–9–0	Sandi Smith
1968	6-AAA	Shipman, Bill	6–4–0	Patty Alexander
1969	6-AAA	Poe, Don	6–4–0	Sallye Davis
1970	6-AAA	Poe, Don	5–5–0	Elaine Melrose

YEAR-AT-A-GLANCE 1920–93

Year	District	Coach	Record	Homecoming Queen*
1971	6-AAA	Shipman, Bill	2–7–1	Cathy Turner
1972	6-AAA	Shipman, Bill	12–2–0	Rita "Skeeter" Proctor
1973	6-AAA	Shipman, Bill	9–1–0	Connie Boyd
1974	13-AAAA	Visentine, David	5–5–0	Karen Gnuse
1975	13-AAAA	Visentine, David	4–4–2	Lisa Pike
1976	13-AAAA	Visentine, David	4–6–0	Yvonne Graham
1977	6-AAAA	Visentine, David	2–8–0	Kristi Matthews
1978	6-AAAA	Wilson, Neal	9–2–0	Marsha Saunders
1979	6-AAAA	Wilson, Neal	12–1–1	Tammie Keith
1980	6-AAAAA	Wilson, Neal	4–5–1	Anita Carpenter
1981	6-AAAAA	Wilson, Neal	10–1–1	Krista Legge
1982	12-AAAAA	Wilson, Neal	8–2–1	Sissy Messina
1983	12-AAAAA	Wilson, Neal	8–2–0	Desiree Babler
1984	12-AAAAA	Wilson, Neal	6–3–1	Holly Robinson
1985	12-AAAAA	Wilson, Neal	10–3–0	Crystal Bullock
1986	5-AAAAA	Mills, Chuck	6–4–0	Laci Williams
1987	5-AAAAA	Mills, Chuck	8–4–0	Melissa Gasperin
1988	5-AAAAA	Mills, Chuck	8–1–1	LaConda McLain
1989	5-AAAAA	Mills, Chuck	6–5–0	Tiffany Etheridge
1990	5-AAAAA	Mills, Chuck	7–3–0	Gema Salgado
1991	5-AAAAA	Gage, Ronnie	7–5–0	Brandy Wilson
1992	6-AAAAA	Gage, Ronnie	10–2–1	Kriste Hicks
1993	6-AAAAA	Gage, Ronnie	15–0–1	Amber Etter

Overall Record of Lewisville Fighting Farmers from 1920–1993:

421–214–25   Winning Percentage: .662

* Lewisville High School did not begin crowning Homecoming Queens until 1954, although the team elected Football Sweethearts prior to that year.

FARMER MASCOT FROM 1970–994

Year	BIG JOHN	Year	BIG JOHN
1970	Scott Jackson	1983	Doug Boyd
1971	Scott Jackson	1984	Doug Boyd
1972	Billy Merritt	1985	Pat Gaines
1973	Darrell Gaudin	1986	Pat Gaines
1974	T.J. Koehler	1987	Curtis Almond
1975	Kelly Philpot	1988	Curtis Almond
1976	Kelly Philpot	1989	Rick Emery
1977	Bobby Hoskins	1990	Mark Locke
1978	Brent Giesler	1991	Dax Gollaher
1979	Mark Miller	1992	Ryan Collinsworth
1980	Will Grider	1993	Derrick Redmon
1981	John Castro	1994	Derrick Redmon
1982	John Prochaska		

Friday Night Farmers
Schedules and Results from 1920–1993

1920*

Date	W/L	Opponent	Score
	L	Grapevine	40–6

Record: 0–1; Schedule incomplete.
Coach: Lee Preston

1922*

Date	W/L	Opponent	Score
11-4	L	Plano	66–7

Record: 0–1; Schedule incomplete.
Coach: Lee Preston

1923*

Date	W/L	Opponent	Score
	L	Highland Park	34–0

Record: 0–1; Schedule incomplete.
Coach: Lee Preston

1924*

Date	W/L	Opponent	Score
	L	Gainesville	64–0
	W	Sanger	20–13
	W	Sanger[a]	20–19

Record: 5–3; Schedule incomplete.
Coach: Ed Lowe

[a] County championship

1925

Date	W/L	Opponent	Score
	W	Sanger	6–0
	L	Masonic Lodge Orphans Home	21–0
	L @	Sanger	25–0
	Tie	Grapevine	0–0
	L @	Grapevine	48–0

Record: 1–3–1
Coach: Ed Lowe

1926*

Date	W/L	Opponent	Score

Record: Unavailable
Coach: Darrell Jones

1927

Date	W/L	Opponent	Score
9-30	W @	Justin	48–0
10-7	W	Celina	12–7
10-14	W @	Frisco	6–0
10-21	L @	Grapevine	14–0
10-28	W	Sanger	12–0
11-4	L	NTSTC[a]	12–7
11-11	W	Grapevine	14–6
11-18	W	Irving	20–0
11-24	W @	Grand Prairie	14–6

Record: 7–2
Coach: Darrell Jones

[a] Game three was played against the 3rd string of North Texas State Teachers College.

1928*

Date	W/L	Opponent	Score
	L	Irving	6–0
	W	Denton B	12–0
	L	Grapevine	9–0

Record: 1–2; Schedule incomplete.
Coach: Luther Scarborough

---

* Complete schedule was neither available from the UIL office in Austin nor from newspapers; the games listed are the only ones available. No Scores or Schedule reported for 1921 and 1926.
† Denotes District Games
‡ Represents Homecoming Games

1929 — District 5-B

Date	W/L	Opponent	Score
9-27	W	Sanger†	12–0
10-04	W	Denton	12–0
10-11	L	Irving†	6–0
10-18	W	Justin†	42–0
10-25	L	Grapevine†	9–0
11-01	Tie	Celina†	6–6
11-08	W	Grand Prairie	6–0
11-15	Tie	Irving†	6–6
11-22	W	Sanger†	32–7
11-28	W	Grapevine†	7–6

Record: 6–2–2
Coach: Luther Scarborough

1930* — District 5-B

Date	W/L	Opponent	Score
11-11	L	Handley	20–0
	L	Plano	19–0

Record: 0–2; Schedule incomplete.
Coach: Luther Scarborough

1931* — District 5-B

Date	W/L	Opponent	Score
	L	Arlington	34–0
10-2	Tie	@ Handley†	0–0
10-9	L	Plano†	13–0

Record: Schedule incomplete.
Coach: R.O. Davis

1932 — District 5-B

Date	W/L	Opponent	Score
	W	Sunset–Dallas	7–0
	W	Arlington	6–0
	W	Justin†	19–6
	W	Pilot Point†	45–0
	W	Tioga†	48–0
	W	Collinsville†	26–0
	Tie	Sanger†	0–0
	W	Celina†	19–0
	W	Grapevine†	6–0
Bi-District			
	W	Whitesboro	14–0

Record: 9–0–1; Bi-District Champions
Coach: R.O. Davis

Notes: Outscored opponents 190–6.
Bi-District playoff level was as far as Class B teams played; there was no state championship at this level.

1933 — District 5-B

Date	W/L	Opponent	Score
9-22	L	@ Justin	8–0
9-29	L	@ Grandview†	20–0
10-6	L	St. Joseph's Academy	12–7
10-13	L	@ Handley†	1–0[a]
10-27	L	@ Grand Prairie	25–13
11-2	L	@ Arlington†	31–7
11-10	W	@ Sanger	13–7
11-17	Tie	@ Tioga	6–6
11-24	W	Celina	72–12
11-30	W	Grapevine†	13–0

Record: 3–6–1
Coach: R.G. Elms

[a] Forfeit to Handley

1934* — District 16-C

Date	W/L	Opponent	Score
	L	Grand Prairie	19–0

Record: 0–1; Schedule incomplete
Coach: Taft Dunsworth

1935* — District 16-C

Date	W/L	Opponent	Score
9-28	L	@ Celina	46–0
11-1	L	@ Grapevine†	12–0
11-25	L	Grapevine†	25–0

Record: 0–3; Schedule incomplete.
Coach: Taft Dunsworth.

1936 — District 16-C

Date	W/L	Opponent	Score
9-25	W	Alvord†	12–6
10-2	Tie	Boyd†	7–7a
10-9	W	@ Valley View†	6–2
10-16	L	@ Forney	26–19
10-23	W	@ Birdville†	7–0
10-30	W	Justin†	51–0
11-6		Open	
11-13	W	Sanger†	33–0
11-20	W	Keller†	18–0
11-26	L	@ Grapevine†	7–0

Record: 6–1–1
Coach: R.E. Mattingly

aLHS awarded game on penetrations.

1937 — District 16-C

Date	W/L	Opponent	Score
9-24	W	@ Carrollton	18–2
10-1	W	@ Alvord†	12–0
10-8	W	Boyd†	45–0
10-15		Open	
10-22	L	@ Arlington	19–0
10-29	W	Birdville†	19–6
11-5	W	@ Keller†	28–6
11-12	W	@ Sanger†	13–6
11-19	W	Valley View†	73–0
11-25	W	Grapevine†	28–13

Record: 8–1; District Champions
Coach: R.E. Mattingly

1938 — District 15-C

Date	W/L	Opponent	Score
9-16	W	Boyd[1]	18–0
9-23	W	Carrollton	13–6
9-30	W	Era	21–6
10-7		Open	
10-14	W	Alvord†	32–0
10-21	W	Valley View†	46–0
10-28	W	@ Birdville	7–6
11-5		Open	
11-11	W ‡	Sanger†	28–0
11-18	W	Grapevine†	12–0
11-24	Tie	@ Grapevine†	0–0

Record: 8–0–1; District Co-Champions
Coach: R.E. Mattingly

1939 — District 13-B

Date	W/L	Opponent	Score
9-15	W	Celina	21–12
9-22	W	@ Carrollton	24–0
9-29		Open	
10-6	W	Wylie	31–0
10-13	W	Era	6–0
10-20	W	@ Alvord	40–0
10-27	W	Valley View	32–0
11-10	W	@ Sanger	32–0
11-17	L	Frisco	7–0
11-24	W	Frisco[2]	19–13
12-4	Tie	Grapevine	0–0
Bi–District		@ Mckinney	
12-8	W	Howe	32–6

Record: 9–1–1; Bi-District Champions
Coach: R.E. Mattingly

1940 — District 13-B

Date	W/L	Opponent	Score
9-13	W	Celina	61–0
9-20	W	@ Grapevine	12–0
9-27	W	Keller	18–0
10-4		Open	
10-11	W	Wylie†	13–0
10-18	L	@ Era†	13–6
10-25	W	Alvord†	67–0
11-1	W	@ Frisco†	29–0
11-8	W	Sanger†	45–0
11-15		Open	
11-22	W	Carrollton	14–7
Bi–District @ North Texas State Teachers College in Denton, Texas.			
11-29	W	Howe	46–6

Record: 9–1; Bi-Distrtct Champions
Coach: R.E. Mattingly

[1] First game under lights at Lewisville. Charlie Whitlock was responsible for the installation of lights at the Gin Lot, or Degan Field, where the Farmers played from 1921–1949.

[2] Game against Frisco on 11–24 was for sole possession of district championship instead of coin toss. Era beat Frisco which gave them one loss, causing a tie with Lewisville, who beat Era in game four.

1941 — District 13-B

Date	W/L	Opponent	Score
9-19	W	Grapevine	19–7
9-26	W	Forest B[a]	38–0
10-3	W	Valley View[†]	1–0
10-10	W	Wylie[†]	26–0
10-17	W	Era[†]	13–6
10-23	W	@ Alvord[†]	20–6
10-30	W	Frisco[†]	38–0
11-7	W	Birdville[†]	20–13
11-14	W	@ Sanger[†]	13–7
11-21	L	@ Carrollton[†]	38–0

Record: 9–1; Last in District due to use of ineligible player.[b]
Coach: R.E. Mattingly

[a] Second game against Forest B originally scheduled with Keller, but Keller had to call game off, therefore Forest B team was substituted.

[b] LHS finished with a 9–1 actual record but had to forfeit all but 1 game due to the use of an ineligible player. A council composed of representatives from each team they played voted that Lewisville had to forfeit all but game 1, giving them an official record of 1–9.

1942* — District 13-B

Date	W/L	Opponent	Score
10-30	W	@ Frisco[†]	14–7
11-13	L	Grapevine[†]	6–0
11-19	L	Wilmer-Hutchins[†]	45–13

Record: 1–2
Coach: J.K. Delay[1]

1943 — District 9-B

Date	W/L	Opponent	Score
10-15	W	@ Frisco[†]	14–6
10-22	W	Alvord[†]	62–0
10-28	W	@ Valley View[†]	23–12
11-5	Tie	@ Plano[†]	6–6
11-12	W	Sanger[†]	26–20
11-19	W	Boyd[†]	21–0
11-25	L	@ Carrollton[†]	7–6

Record: 5–1–1; District Champions
Coach: J.K. Delay

Notes: Lewisville outscored opponents 158–51.

1944 — District 9-B

Date	W/L	Opponent	Score
10-6	L	@ Era[†]	7–6
10-13	L	Frisco[†]	18–0
10-20	W	Alvord[†]	9–6
10-27	L	Valley View[†]	33–6
11-2	Open		
11-9	Tie	@ Boyd[†]	7–7
11-16	Open		
11-23	L	@ Sanger[†]	28–0

Record: 1–4–1
Coach: J.K. Delay

[1] This was Mr. Delay's first year as Superintendent. He came on October 1, 1942. Prior to the school year the coach, R.E. Mattingly, resigned one week before school began. The Superintendent prior to Mr. Delay resigned on the first day of school, leaving vacancies in both positions. Because of WWII there was a shortage of men to coach, so the school board voted to suspend all athletics until after the war and cancelled their 1942 schedule. Once hired, Mr. Delay was approached on his first day by some high school boys, including William T. Bolin, about the prospects of getting a team together. Mr. Delay pointed out the fact there was no coach or schedule, but the boys persisted, suggesting that he coach and call area teams to see if he could schedule some games. Finally, he gave in and, after the other teams in the district gave their approval, Mr. Delay agreed to coach, scheduling only the three games listed above. Interestingly, the first practice was on the Monday before the Frisco game.

1945 — District 9-B

Date	W/L	Opponent	Score
10-5		Era†	Rained Out
10-12	W	@ Bridgeport†	6–0
10-19	W	@ Alvord†	19–6
10-26	L	@ Valley View†	23–0
11-2	L	@ Grapevine†	19–6
11-9	W	Sanger†	8–2
11-16	Tie	Boyd†	6–6
11-22	L	Era (Make-up)†	25–0

Record: 3–3–1
Coach: J.K. Delay

1946 — District 13-B

Date	W/L	Opponent	Score
9-13	W	Grapevine†	7–0
9-20	W	Tioga	53–0
9-27	W	@ Alvord†	6–0
10-4	W	@ Frisco	7–0
10-11	W	Bridgeport†	40–13
10-18	W	@ Azle @ Lake Worth†	40–6
10-25	W	Valley View†	26–0
11-1	W	Era†	24–19
11-8		Open	
11-15	W	Sanger†	1–0[a]
11-22	W	Boyd†	1–0[a]
11-29	L	Plano†	40–6[b]
Bi-District		@ Denton	
12-6	L	Pilot Point	21–0

Record: 10–2; District Champions
Coach: J.K. Delay

[a] Forfeit due to flu
[b] Farmers had not played since 11-1-46, so they had a month without playing, therefore, they had trouble staying sharp. No alternate teams could be scheduled.

1947 — District 13-B

Date	W/L	Opponent	Score
9-12	W	@ Grapevine†	25–0
9-18	W	Mansfield	12–6
9-25	W	Bryson†	21–0
10-3	W	Frisco	27–9
10-10	W	@ Bridgeport†	25–0
10-17	W	Azle†	45–0
10-25	W	Valley View†	21–0
10-31	W	Era†	52–0
11-7	W	Tioga†[c]	41–0
11-14	W	@ Boyd†[d]	1–0
11-21	W	@ Sanger†	60–0
Bi-District		@ Denton	
11-28	W	Van Alstyne	27–0
Regional 5B Championship @ Garland[e]			
12-5	W	Richardson	13–12

Record: 13–0; Region 5 Champions
Coaches: J.K. Delay, Head; J.T. Watson

Notes: Lewisville outscored opponents 445–27.

[c] Lewisville B String
[d] Forfeit due to bad weather
[e] Class B ball played to Regional Championship Only

1948 — District 13-B

Date	W/L	Opponent	Score
9-17	W	North Dallas B	14–6
9-24	W	@ Bryson†	18–12
10-1	L	@ Frisco	24–0
10-8	L	Bridgeport†	12–6
10-15	Tie	@ Saint Jo†	6–6
10-22	W	Valley View†	20–13
10-29	W	@ Era†	19–0
11-5	W	Alvord†	20–7
11-12	L	@ Boyd†	12–0
11-19	W	Sanger†	20–6

Record: 6–3–1; Third in District
Coaches: A.J. Hudson, Head; M.R. Bogard

1949 — District 13-B

Date	W/L	Opponent	Score
9-16	L	Valley View of Iowa Park†	13–12
9-23	W	Bryson†	38–0
9-30	W	Frisco	12–0
10-7	W	@ Bridgeport†	7–0
10-14	W	Saint Jo†	7–6
10-21	W	@ Valley View†	25–0
10-28	W	Era†	42–0
11-4	W	@ Alvord†	21–0
11-11	W ‡	Boyd†	58–0
11-18	W	@ Sanger†	12–6

Record: 9–1; District Runner-up
Coaches: J.H. Bronaugh, Head; A.E. Cody

Notes: Outscored opponents 233–25.

1950 — District 14-B

Date	W/L	Opponent	Score
9-15	W	Grapevine	13–0
9-22	W	North Dallas B	13–6
9-29	W	@ Frisco	13–0
10-6		Open	
10-13	W	Bridgeport†	14–7
10-20	W	Valley View†	45–0
10-27	W	@ Era†	40–6
11-3	W	Northwest†	36–0
11-10	W	Boyd†	34–0
11-17	W ‡	Sanger†	12–0
Bi–District		@ Wichita Falls	
12-1	W	Valley View of Iowa Park	27–7
Regional		@ McKinney	
12-8	W	Farmersville	19–7

Record: 11–0; Regional 4-B Champions
Coaches: J.H. Bronaugh, Head; A.E. Cody

Notes: Moved into new high school, which is currently Delay Middle School.

1951 — District 10-A

Date	W/L	Opponent	Score
9-14	W	@ Era	42–0
9-21	W	Frisco	6–0
9-28	W	Azle†	45–0
10-5	L	Lake Worth†a	12–6
10-12	W	@ Northwest†	20–0
10-19	Tie	@ Sanger	12–12
10-26	W	Pilot Point†	38–0
11-2	W	@ Carrollton	21–6
11-9	W	@ Bridgeport†	40–7
11-16	L ‡	Grapevine†	7–6

Record: 7–2–1; Lost district in final game.
Coaches: J.H. Bronaugh, Head; Alvin Kinsey

a First loss for Farmers in 24 games.

1952 — District 10-A

Date	W/L	Opponent	Score
9-12	L	@ Frisco	7–0
9-19	W	Sanger	12–7
9-26	W	@ Azle†	19–6
10-3	L	Carrollton	20–6
10-10	L	@ Lake Worth†	7–6
10-17	W	Northwest†	19–0
10-24	W	Era	44–12
10-31	W	@ Pilot Point†	7–0
11-7		Open	
11-14	W ‡	Bridgeport†	33–12
11-21	L	Grapevine†	20–0

Record: 6–4; Tied for 2nd in district.
Coaches: A.L. Kay, Head; Lewis McReynolds

1953 — District 10-A

Date	W/L	Opponent	Score
9-11	W	Frisco	6–0
9-18	L	@ Sanger	14–0
9-25	W	@ Northwest	13–7
10-2	W	@ Plano	27–6
10-9	W	Lake Worth	19–0
10-15	L	@ Carrollton	13–0
10-23	W	Azle†	19–0
10-30	W ‡	Pilot Point†	19–7
11-6		Open	
11-13	W	@ Bridgeport†	40–0
11-20	L	Grapevine†	7–6

Record: 7–3
Coaches: A.L. Kay, Head; Lewis McReynolds

1954 — District 10-A

Date	W/L	Opponent	Score
9-10	W	@ Frisco	34–6
9-17	W	Sanger	26–0
9-24	W	Northwest	28–6
10-1	W	Plano	14–2
10-8	W	@ Mesquite	30–6
10-15	W	Carrollton	34–6
10-22	W	@ Azle†	7–0
10-29	L	@ Pilot Point†	21–20
11-5		Open	
11-12	W ‡	Bridgeport†	34–7
11-19	W	@ Grapevine†	13–0

Record: 9–1; 2nd in District
Coaches: A.L. Kay, Head; McReynolds, Thomas Coyle

1955 — District 10-A

Date	W/L	Opponent	Score
9-9	W	Frisco	47–6
9-16		Open	
9-24	W	Grapevine	26–7
9-30	W	@ Plano	34–6
10-7	W ‡	Mesquite	40–6
10-14	W	Carrollton	41–21
10-21	W	@ Springtown†	60–0
10-28	W	Northwest†	93–6
11-4	W	Azle†	65–0
11-11	W	Bridgeport†	51–6
11-18	W	Pilot Point†	58–0
Bi-District		@ Wichita Falls Coyote Field	
11-25	L	Chilicothe	20–7

Record: 10–1; District 10-AA Champions
Coaches: Lewis McReynolds, Head; Charles Measel, Donald Vernon, Robert Eargle
Notes: Lewisville Farmers were state's highest scoring team, outscoring opponents 522–78.

1956 — District 10-AA

Date	W/L	Opponent	Score
9-14	W	Itasca	30–13
9-21	W	@ Richardson	22–0
9-28	W	Plano	52–12
10-5	W ‡	Mansfield†	53–6
10-12	W	@ Azle†	19–0
10-18	W	@ Mesquite	19–0
10-26	W	Northwest†	53–7
11-2	W	@ Grapevine†	18–6
11-9	W	@ Lake Worth†	34–18
11-16	W	Whitesboro†	25–7
Bi-District		@ WichitaFalls	
11-22	L	Burkburnett	28–19

Record: 10–1; District 10-AA Champions
Coaches: Lewis McReynolds, Head; Eargle, Vernon, Kent Clark

1957 — District 10-AA

Date	W/L	Opponent	Score
9-6	L	@ Bowie	12–6
9-13		Open	
9-20	L	Richardson	12–7
9-27	W	@ Alvord[a]	46–0
10-4	W	@ Mansfield†	33–7
10-11	W ‡	Azle†	46–14
10-18	W	Mesquite	21–20
10-25	W	@ Northwest†[b]	1–0
11-1	W	Grapevine†	28–20
11-8	W	Lake Worth†	20–12
11-15	W	@ Whitesboro†	33–13
Bi-District		@ Bronco Field in Denton[c]	
11-22	L	Electra	32–7

Record: 8–3; District Champions
Coaches: Lewis McReynolds, Head; Eargle, Clark, Marshall Durham

1958 — District 12-AA

Date	W/L	Opponent	Score
9-5	L	Bowie	29–26
9-12	W	@ Northwest	36–6
9-19	L	Carrollton	13–12
9-26	W	@ Keller	7–6
10-3	L	@ Grapvine	13–6
10-10		Open	
10-17	W ‡	Whitesboro†	38–8
10-24	L	@ Bonham†	28–7
10-31	W	Commerce†	18–7
11-7	W	@ Plano†	23–6
11-14	W	Richardson†	18–13

Record: 6–4
Coaches: Lewis McReynolds, Head; Eargle, Durham, Clark

[a] Originally scheduled to play Plano, but flu epidemic forced LHS to schedule Alvord as substitute.
[b] Cancelled due to flu.
[c] Originally scheduled to be played at Fout's Field, but rain caused game to be switched to Bronco Field in Denton so as not to interfere with NTSC the following day.

1959 — District 12-AA

Date	W/L	Opponent	Score
9-4	L	@ Bowie	45–0
9-11	L	Northwest	15–13
9-18	L	@ Carrollton	39–8
9-25	W	Keller	12–0
10-2	L	Grapevine	22–8
10-9		Open	
10-16	W	@ Whitesboro†	42–14
10-23	L	‡ Bonham†	20–6
10-30	W	@ Commerce†	30–0
11-6	W	Plano†	21–14
11-13	L	@ Richardson†	34–8

Record: 4–6
Coaches: Ben Harmon, Head; Don Duke

1960 — District 12-AA

Date	W/L	Opponent	Score
9-2	L	@ Northwest	8–0
9-9	L	Bowie	14–0
9-16	L	Carrollton	22–8
9-23	L	@ Bonham	18–0
9-30	L	@ Grapevine	19–7
10-7		Open	
10-14	L	@ Commerce†	18–7
10-21	W	‡ Wilmer-Hutchins†	33–0
10-28	W	Rockwall†	35–6
11-4	W	@ Cooper†	45–14
11-11	L	Plano†	20–12

Record: 3–7
Coach: Ben Harmon, Head; Don Duke

1961 — District 12-AA

Date	W/L	Opponent	Score
9-1	W	Northwest	7–0
9-8		Open	
9-15	L	@ Carrollton	50–20
9-22	L	Bonham	13–12
9-29	L	Grapevine	34–19
10-6	W	@ Azle^a	1–0
10-13	L	‡ Commerce†	13–7
10-20	W	@ Wilmer-Hutchins	20–0
10-27	W	@ Rockwall†	20–6
11-3	W	Cooper†	22–0
11-10	L	@ Plano†	28–8

Record: 5–5; 2nd in District
Coaches: Ben Harmon, Head; Kent Clark, Bob Way
^a Forfeit

1962 — District 11-AA

Date	W/L	Opponent	Score
9-7	W	@ Northwest	20–6
9-14	L	Carrollton	32–13
9-21	L	@ Bonham	2–0
9-28	W	@ Grapevine	13–0
10-5	W	Azle	28–6
10-12		Open	
10-19	L	@ Commerce†	14–13
10-26	W	‡ Whitesboro†	21–0
11-2	L	Rockwall†	34–13
11-9	W	@ Cooper†	12–0
11-16	L	Plano†	13–6

Record: 5–5; Finished 4th in District 11–AA.
Coaches: Ben Harmon, Head; Sherrill Bottoms, William Davenport, Darwin Creagh, Jim Dieb, Kent Clark

1963 — District 11-AA

Date	W/L	Opponent	Score
9-6	W	Northwest	20–12
9-13	L	@ Carrollton	26–12
9-20	L	Bonham	32–0
9-27	L	Grapevine	14–7
10-4	L	@ Azle	12–6
10-11		Open	
10-18	W	‡ Commerce†	40–12
10-25	W	@ Whitesboro†	26–0
11-1	W	@ Rockwall†	36–0
11-8	W	Cooper†	24–8
11-15	L	@ Plano†	47–0

Record: 4–6
Coaches: Ben Harmon, Head; Bottoms, Davenport, Clark

1964 — District 11-AA

Date	W/L	Opponent	Score
9-4	W	@ Northwest	50–0
9-11	L	Bishop Dunne	7–0
9-18	L	@ Bonham	20–6
9-25	W	@ Grapevine	7–6
10-2	W	Azle^a	16–8
10-9	W	Bridgeport	40–8
10-16	L	‡ Rockwall†	21–13
10-23	W	@ Seagoville†	8–6
10-30	W	Wilmer-Hutchins†	41–40
11-6	L	@ Plano†	49–20

Record: 6–4
Coaches: Sherrill Bottoms, Head; Sam Harrison, Jerry Cantrell

^a Azle victory was first defeat of a 3A team for Lewisville.

1965 — District 11-AA

Date	W/L	Opponent	Score
9-3	W	Northwest	52–8
9-10	L	@ Bishop Dunne	33–0
9-17	L	Grapevine	21–8
9-24	L	Bonham	46–26
10-1	L	@ Azle	14–8
10-8	L	@ Bridgeport	28–20
10-15	L	@ Rockwall†	35–12
10-22	L	‡ Seagoville†	19–0
10-29	W	@ Wilmer-Hutchins†	8–0
11-5	L	Plano†	34–0
11-12		Open	

Record: 2–8
Coaches: Sherrill Bottoms, Head; Cantrell, Ronnie Daum, Pete Holby, Clark

1966 — District 6-AAA

Date	W/L	Opponent	Score
9-9	L	Duncanville	33–6
9-16	L	Waxahachie	19–0
9-23	W	Grapevine	9–0
9-30		Open	
10-7	L	@ Sulphur Springs†	28–6
10-14	L	‡ Lake Highlands†	27–6
10-21	W	@ Mt. Pleasant†	18–8
10-28	L	Bonham†	33–13
11-4	L	@ McKinney†	44–0
11-11	L	Gainesville†	21–0
11-18	L	@ Greenville†	34–7

Record: 2–8
Coaches: Bill Shipman, Head; Cantrell, Tommy Shields, Daum, James Hawes, James Freed, Ray Stickle, Terry Townzen, Elgin Conner

1967 — District 16-AAA

Date	W/L	Opponent	Score
9-8	L	@ Duncanville	28–0
9-15	L	Waxahachie	13–7
9-22		Open	
9-29	L	@ Grapevine	15–0
10-6	L	Sulpher Springs†	28–7
10-13	L	@ Lake Highlands†	40–0
10-20	W	‡ Mt. Pleasant†	37–14
10-27	L	@ Bonham†	6–0
11-3	L	McKinney†	24–0
11-10	L	@ Gainseville†	16–0
11-17	L	Greenville†	34–0

Record: 1–9
Coaches: Bill Shipman, Franklin Bons, Daum, Don Poe, Shields, Townzen, Billy Dyer, Billy Whitman, Max Goldsmith, Lars Berg

1968 — District 6-AAA

Date	W/L	Opponent	Score
9-13	W	@ Boswell	31–0
9-20	L	Waxahachie	21–7
9-27	W	Diamond Hill	24–12
10-4	W	@ Waco Midway	21–7
10-11	W	McKinney†	17–14
10-18	L	‡ Bonham†	21–14
10-25	W	@ Grapevine†	17–14
11-1	L	@ Plano†	31–0
11-8		Open	
11-15	W	J.J. Pearce†	21–0
11-22	L	@ Gainesville†	36–0

Record: 6–4
Coaches: Bill Shipman, Head; Poe, Townzen, Goldsmith, Whitman

1969 — District 6-AAA

Date	W/L	Opponent	Score
9-12	W	Boswell	12–0
9-19	L	@ Waxahachie	19–17
9-26	W	Diamond Hill	49–16
10-3		Open	
10-10	L	@ McKinney†	10–9
10-17	L	@ Bonham†	41–0
10-24	W	‡ Grapevine†	27–12
10-31	W	Plano†	7–6
11-7	W	North Dallas[a]	34–16
11-14	L	@ J. J. Pearce†	6–0
11-21	W	@ Gainesville†	27–14

Record: 6–4
Coaches: Don Poe, Head; Whitman, Townzen, Stan Williams, Foy Williams, Clayton Downing

[a] North Dallas was first 4-A team Farmers met.

1970 — District 6-AAA

Date	W/L	Opponent	Score
9-11	L	@ Boswell	6–0
9-18	W	Waxahachie	33–7
9-25	W	Wilmer-Hutchins	23–15
10-2		Open	
10-9	L	Plano†	48–0
10-16	L	@ McKinney†	49–0
10-23	W	‡ Grapevine†	13–8
10-30	W	@ Berkner†	46–14
11-6	L	Bonham†	21–12
11-13	W	@ Gainesville†	11–8
11-20	L	@ S. Grand Prairie†	24–14

Record: 5–5
Coaches: Don Poe, Head; S. Williams, Tony Mandina, Townzen

1971 — District 6-AAA

Date	W/L	Opponent	Score
9-10	L	Boswell	16–13
9-17	W	@ Waxahachie	22–14
9-24	Tie	@ Wilmer-Hutchins	6–6
9-30		Open	
10-8	L	@ Plano†	49–0
10-15	L	McKinney†	32–6
10-23	W	@ North Garland†	39–7
10-29	L	‡ Berkner†	14–0
11-5	L	@ Bonham†	35–6
11-12	L	Gainesville†	19–14
11-19	L	S. Grand Prairie†	13–12

Record: 2–7–1
Coaches: Bill Shipman, Head; Tommy Shields, Don Harvey, David Visentine

1972 — District 6-AAA

Date	W/L	Opponent	Score
9-8	W	@ Boswell	14–7
9-15	W	Waxahachie	29–0
9-22	W	@ Grapevine	32–6
9-29	W	‡ Burleson	48–15
10-7	W	@ S. Grand Prairie†	46–7
10-13	W	Berkner†	34–0
10-20	W	@ North Garland†	49–14
10-27	W	Bonham†	26–0
11-3	L	@ Gainesville†	9–6
11-10	W	McKinney†	29–28
11-17		Open	

Bi-District @ Birdville Stadium, Haltom City
| 11-24 | W | Boswell | 35–0 |

Quarter Finals @ Forrester Field, Mesquite
| 11-30 | W | Mt. Pleasant | 20–14 |

Semi-Finals @ Amon Carter Stadium, Ft. Worth
| 12-7 | W | Burkburnett | 34–0 |

State Finals @ Memorial Stadium, Austin
| 12-15 | L | Uvalde | 33–28 |

Record: 12–2; State Runner-up
Coaches: Bill Shipman, Head; Visentine, Harvey, Charles Bode, Shields, Bill Branum, Gary Petross

1973 — District 6-AAA

Date	W/L	Opponent	Score
9-7	W	Boswell	34–0
9-14	W	@ Waxahachie	27–6
9-21	W	Grapevine	43–13
9-28	W	Burleson	35–12
10-5	W	@ S. Grand Prairie†	38–19
10-12	W	Berkner†	20–7
10-19	W	@ North Garland†	40–18
10-26	W	‡ Bonham†	21–0
11-2	W	Gainesville†	48–6
11-9	L	@ McKinney†	28–21

Record: 9–1; District 6-AAA Runner-up
Coaches: Bill Shipman, Head; Visentine, Shields, Bode, Branum, Petross, Harvey

1974 — District 13-AAAA

Date	W/L	Opponent	Score
9-6	L	@ Trinity	21–7
9-13	L	Irving	28–14
9-20	W	Northside	14–13
9-27		Open	
10-4	L	@ Plano†	28–0
10-11	W	@ Denison†	21–14
10-18	L	‡ R.L. Turner†	7–2
10-25	W	@ Greenville†	19–14
11-1	L	@ Denton†	20–3
11-8	W	Sherman†	21–8
11-15	W	Paris†	21–13

Record: 5–5
Coaches: David Visentine, Head; Bode, Petross, Harvey, Geroge Boynton, Jewell Cope, Vick Rucker
Notes: First year for LHS in 4A competition.

1975 — District 13-AAAA

Date	W/L	Opponent	Score
9-6	W	Trinity	14–0
9-13	Tie	@ Jesuit	7–7
9-20	W ‡	Northside	30–0
9-27		Open	
10-3	L	Plano†	42–7
10-10	Tie	Denison†	13–13
10-17	L	@ R.L. Turner†	14–8
10-24	L	Greenville†	13–12
10-31	W	Denton†	28–6
11-7	L	@ Sherman†	28–14
11-14	W	@ Paris†	13–7

Record: 4–4–2
Coaches: David Visentine, Head; Bode, Cope, Harvey, Boynton, Petross, Willie Roten

1976 — District 13-AAAA

Date	W/L	Opponent	Score
9-3	L	Duncanville	21–12
9-10	L	@ Berkner	37–14
9-17	W	Western Hills	15–14
9-24	L	@ R.L. Turner	31–19
10-1	L	@ Trinity†	47–7
10-8	W ‡	W.F. High†	7–6
10-15	L	@ W.F.Rider†	23–6
10-22	L	L.D. Bell†	14–10
10-29	W	@ W. Falls Hirschi†	20–16
11-5		Open	
11-12	W	Denton†	17–0

Record: 4–6
Coaches: David Visentine, Head; Bode, Harvey, Petross, Boynton, Tom Kupper, Mike Tefatiller

1977 — District 6-AAAA

Date	W/L	Opponent	Score
9-2	L	@ Duncanville	31–16
9-9	L	Berkner	23–13
9-16	W	Western Hills	41–9
9-23	L	R.L. Turner	49–21
9-30	L	Trinity†	50–10
10-7	L	@ W.F. High†	14–7
10-14	L ‡	W.F. Rider†	20–17
10-21	L	@ L.D. Bell†	21–20
10-28	W	W.F. Hirschi†	20–13
11-4		Open	
11-11	L	@ Denton†	55–25

Record: 2–8
Coaches: David Visentine, Head; Harvey, Bode, Petross, Boynton, Teafitiller, Kupper

1978 — District 6-AAAA

Date	W/L	Opponent	Score
9-8	W	Duncanville	42–14
9-15	W	@ Berkner	37–6
9-22	W	Arlington Bowie	31–7
9-29	L	@ Arlington High	31–14
10-6	W ‡	Bishop Lynch	42–21
10-13	W	R.L. Turner†	68–15
10-20	W	W.F. High†	34–8
10-26		Open	
11-3	W	W.F. Rider†	13–9
11-10	W	Newman Smith†	35–7
11-17	W	@ Denton†	31–7

Bi-District @ Shotwell Stadium in Abilene
| 11-24 | L | Odessa Permian | 17–7 |

Record: 9–2; District Champions
Coaches: Neal Wilson, Head; Que Brittain, Billy Mitchell, Jim Smith, Tom Everest, Charles Hesse, Bobby Gentry

1979 — District 6-AAAA

Date	W/L	Opponent	Score
9-7	W	@ Duncanville	14–9
9-14	W	Berkner	16–7
9-21	W	@ Arlington Bowie	14–7
9-28	Tie	Arlington High	14–14
10-5	W ‡	Bishop Lynch	19–10
10-11	W	@ R.L. Turner†	34–0
10-19	W	W.F. High†	48–7
10-26		Open	
11-2	W	@ W.F. Rider†	48–9
11-9	W	Newman Smith†	40–0
11-16	W	Denton†	26–10

Bi-District @ Texas Stadium
| 11-23 | W | Abilene Cooper | 13–10 |

Regional Finals @ Texas Stadium
| 12-1 | W | Arlington Heights | 28–12 |

Quarter Finals @ Texas Stadium
| 12-8 | W | El Paso Coronado | 15–7 |

Semi-Finals @ Texas Stadium
| 12-15 | L | Temple | 3–0 |

Record: 12–1–1; Quarter Final Champions, State Semi-Finalists

Coaches: Neal Wilson, Head; Brittain, Smith, Mitchell, Everest, Hesse, Gentry

1980 — District 6-AAAAA

Date	W/L	Opponent	Score
9-5	Tie	Duncanville	21–21
9-12	L	@ Plano	28–7
9-19	W	Arlington Bowie	28–17
9-26	W	@ Arlington High	13–0
10-3	L ‡	Jesuit	7–3
10-10	L	@ W.F. High†	13–0
10-17	W	@ Denison†	45–0
10-24	L	Sherman†	10–6
10-31		Open	
11-7	W	W.F. Rider†	20–0
11-14	L	@ Denton†	13–12

Record: 4–5–1

Coaches: Neal Wilson, Head; Gentry, Brittain, Mitchell, Ronnie Gage, Gino Ristevski, Steve May, Eddie Brister

Notes: 1980 was the first year for the 5A division in Texas Schoolboy Division. LHS was picked number one in many pre-season polls, based on their strong finish in 1979, however, it proved to be a jinx as Duncanville tied the Farmers in game one, and the season unravelled from that point. This was Neal Wilson's only losing season in his eight years as head coach of the Farmers.

1981 — District 6-AAAAA

Date	W/L	Opponent	Score
9-4	W	@ Duncanville	32–18
9-11	W	Plano @ N.T.S.U.	38–21
9-18	W	@ Arlington Bowie	10–0
9-25	W ‡	Arlington High	20–15
10-2	W	@ Jesuit	35–6
10-9		Open	
10-16	W	W. F. High†	17–7
10-23	W	Denison†	49–13
10-30	W	@ Sherman†	14–0
11-6	W	@ W. F. Rider†	28–14
11-13	W	Denton†	13–6

Bi-District @ Odessa
| 11-21 | Tie | @ Odessa Permian | 14–14a |

Area Championship @ Texas Stadium
| 11-27 | L | Eastern Hills | 15–8 |

Record: 10–1–1; Area Finalists

Coaches: Neal Wilson, Head; Brittain, Gage, Tom Everest, Tommy Briggs, May, Mitchell, Gary Walton.

aFarmers advanced on first down totals (19–15) according to playoff format.

1982 — District 12-AAAAA

Date	W/L	Opponent	Score
9-3	W	Arlington High	21–14
9-10	L	Eastern Hills	19–6
9-17	W ‡	Jesuit	42–7
9-24	W	@ Lake Highlands†	21–14
10-1	W	@ Berkner†	27–7
10-8	Tie	Plano†	0–0b
10-15	W	@ Richardson†	20–10
10-22	W	Greenville†	35–21
10-29	W	@ Plano East†	24–14
11-5	W	J.J. Pearce†	19–0

Bi-District
| 11-12 | L | Dallas Carter | 9–7 |

Record: 8–2–1; District Champions

Coaches: Neal Wilson, Head; Briggs, Gage, Mitchell, May, Brittain, Walton, Everest

b Lewisville wins game five on penetrations according to playoff format.

1983 — District 12-AAAAA

Date	W/L		Opponent	Score
9-2	W	@	Arlington	27–6
(@ UTA's Maverick Stadium)				
9-9	W		Eastern Hills	6–0
9-16	W	‡	Jesuit	17–3
9-23	W		Lake Highlands†	14–3
9-30	W		Berkner†	41–0
10-7	L	@	Plano†	7–6
10-14	L		Richardson†	28–21
10-21	W	@	Greenville†	29–12
10-28	W		Plano East†	28–15
11-7	W	@	J.J. Pearce†	35–7

Record: 8–2; Third in District
Coaches: Neal Wilson, Head; Everest, Gage, Briggs, James Odoms, Gino Ristevski, Robert Mears, Brittain, Terry Goode

1985 — District 12-AAAAA

Date	W/L		Opponent	Score
9-6	W	@	Arlington	28–15
(@ UTA's Maverick Stadium)				
9-13	W		Eastern Hills	35–6
9-20	W	‡	Jesuit	35–3
9-27	W	@	Greenville†	34–9
10-4	W		Berkner†	33–13
10-11	W	@	Lake Highlands†	24–0
10-18	W		Richardson†	49–24
10-25	W	@	J.J. Pearce†	35–28
11-1	L		Plano†	22–7
11-8	L	@	Plano East†	24–23
Bi-District @ Loos Stadium, Farmers Branch				
11-16	W		Kimball	41–7
Area @ Texas Stadium				
11-23	W		North Mesquite	20–14
Regional @ Waco; Floyd Casey Stadium				
11-30	L		Cypress-Fairbanks	35–7

Record: 10–3; Regional Finalists
Coaches: Neal Wilson, Head; Gage, Brittain, Chuck Mills, Goode, Langston, Odoms, Briggs

1984 — District 12-AAAAA

Date	W/L		Opponent	Score
9-7	W		Arlington	21–0
9-14	W		Eastern Hills	45–6
9-21	W		Jesuit	31–7
9-28	W		Greenville†	46–14
10-5	W	@	Berkner†	14–0
10-12	Tie		Lake Highlands†	7–7
10-19	W	@	Richardson†	35–17
10-26	L	‡	J.J. Pearce†	8–7
11-2	L	@	Plano†	20–14
11-9	L		Plano East†	14–7

Record: 6–3–1
Coaches: Neal Wilson, Head; Brittain, Briggs, Odoms, Everest, Stan Langston, Goode, Gage, Ristevski

1986 — District 5-AAAAA

Date	W/L		Opponent	Score
9-5	W		Western Hills	19–0
9-12	W	@	Eastern Hills	39–0
(@ Ft. Worth's Clark Field)				
9-19	L		Jesuit	27–9
9-26	L	@	Denton†	17–6
(@ Fout's Field in Denton)				
10-3	W		Sherman†	56–6
10-10	W		Weatherford†	43–23
10-17	L	@	W.F. Rider†	25–14
10-24	L	@	W.F. High†	42–17
10-31	W	‡	Keller†	42–6
11-7	W		Marcus†(1)	42–0

Record: 6–4
Coaches: Chuck Mills, Head; Mike Campbell, Goode, Gage, Bill Peitrosky, Ristevski, Langston, Jim Bragg, Steve Herring

¹ First year for Battle For the Ax.

1987 — District 5-AAAAA

Date	W/L	Opponent	Score
9-4	L	@ Western Hills	1–0 [a]
9-11	W	Eastern Hills	28–14
9-18	L	Jesuit	17–14
9-25	L	Denton[†]	21–0
10-2	W	@ Sherman[†]	22–16
10-9	W	@ Weatherford[†]	56–13
10-17	W [‡]	W.F. Rider[†]	21–7
10-23	W	W.F. High[†]	24–18
10-30	W	@ Keller[†]	39–14
11-6	W	@ Marcus[†]	26–14

Bi-District @ Texas Stadium

11-13	W	Trimble Tech	41–20

Area @ Texas Stadium

11-20	L	Arlington High	21–3

Record: 8–4; Area Finalists

Coaches: Chuck Mills, Head; Goode, Langston, Pietrosky, Campbell, Fred Willis, Pat Smiley, Bucky Jones, Tim Oehrlein, Joe Paty, Jeff Harp

[a] Originally won game one 34–7, but had to forfeit due to ineligible player under House Bill 72.

1988 — District 5-AAAAA

Date	W/L	Opponent	Score
9-2	W	R.L. Turner	22–9
9-10	W	@ Newman Smith	28–17
9-16	W	Richland	22–7
9-23	L	@ Sherman[†]	16–7
9-30	W	@ W.F. Rider[†]	24–14
10-7	W	Denton[†]	35–0
10-14	W	Weatherford[†]	49–7
10-21	W	@ W.F. High[†]	38–6
10-29	W [‡]	Keller[†]	35–14
11-4	Tie	Marcus[†]	20–20 [b]

Record: 8–1–1

Coaches: Chuck Mills, Head; Goode, Langston, Pietrosky, Willis, Smiley, Jones, Oehrlein, Harp, Campbell, Mike Wren, David Warehime

[b] Marcus awarded game on first downs (17–15) under play-off format. Both teams had 3 penetrations each, which is first tie-breaker.

1989 — District 5-AAAAA

Date	W/L	Opponent	Score
9-8	L	@ R.L. Turner	21–7
9-15	L	Newman Smith	14–0
9-21	W	@ Richland	10–7
9-29	L	Sherman[†]	49–24
10-6	W	W.F. Rider[†]	21–6
10-13	W	@ Denton[†]	35–14
10-20	W	@ Weatherford[†]	27–23
10-28	W [‡]	W.F. High[†]	27–17
11-3	W	@ Keller[†]	28–7
11-10	L	@ Marcus[†]	23–15

Bi-District @ Pennington Field, Bedford

11-17	L	Trimble Tech	18–13

Record: 6–5; 2nd in District

Coaches: Chuck Mills, Head; Goode, Willis, Langston, Pietrosky, Smiley, Jones, Wren, Oehrlein, Campbell, Harp, Warehime

1990 — District 5-AAAAA

Date	W/L	Opponent	Score
9-7	W	R.L. Turner	24–0
9-14	W	@ Eastern Hills	45–0
9-21	W	Grand Prairie	17–0
9-28	W	@ Denton[†]	17–9

(@ Fout's Field in Denton)

10-5	W	Sherman[†]	34–10
10-12	W	@ W.F. Rider[†]	23–21
10-19	W	@ Keller[†]	35–9
10-26	L	Marcus[†]	35–31
11-2	L [‡]	Haltom City[†]	10–9
11-9	L	@ Richland[†]	22–14

Record: 7–3; Tied with Marcus for 3rd place in District; Marcus eliminates LHS from playoffs with win over LHS in week eight.

Coaches: Chuck Mills, Head; Campbell, Goode, Harp, Langston, Keith Mikeska, Warehime, Willis, Pietrosky, Smiley, Wren

1991 — District 5-AAAAA

Date	W/L	Opponent	Score
9-6	L	@ R.L. Turner	16–9
9-13	W	Eastern Hills	56–14
9-20	W	@ Grand Prairie	21–0
9-27	L	@ Denton†	28–25
(@ Fout's Field, Denton)			
10-4	L	@ Sherman†	26–7
10-11	W	W.F. Rider†	21–0
10-18	W ‡	Keller†	45–9
10-25	W	@ Marcus†	45–26
11-1	L	@ Haltom City†	27–20
11-8	W	Richland†	31–28
Bi-District @ Texas Stadium			
11-15	W	L.D. Bell	30–17
Area @ Texas Stadium			
11-22	L	Arl. Sam Houston	46–27

Record: 7–5; Area Finalists
Coaches: Ronnie Gage, Head; Goode, Willis, Pietrosky, Smiley, Warehime, Langston, Tim Wasson

1992 — District 6-AAAAA

Date	W/L	Opponent	Score
9-4	W	R.L. Turner	31–7
9-11	Tie	Plano East	14–14
9-18	W	@ Newman Smith	24–9
9-25	L	@ Grapevine†	28–14
10-2	W	Sherman†	41–21
10-9	W	@ W.F. Rider†	21–0
10-16	W	@ Denton†	17–7
(@ Fout's Field, Denton)			
10-23	W ‡	The Colony†	28–21
10-30	W	@ Allen†	35–28
11-6	W	Marcus†	35–10
Bi-District @ Texas Stadium			
11-13	W	Burleson	48–7
Area @ Texas Stadium			
11-20	W	South Grand Prairie	48–28
Regional @ Ratliff Stadium, Odessa			
11-28	L	@ Odessa Permian	28–0

Record: 10–2–1; Regional Finalists
Coaches: Ronnie Gage, Head; Willis, Smiley, Harp, Wasson, Pietrosky, Goode, Brian Brazil

1993 — District 6-AAAAA

Date	W/L	Opponent	Score
9-3	W	@ R.L. Turner	30–9
9-10	W	@ Plano East	14–7
9-17	W ‡	Newman Smith	51–7
9-24	W	Grapevine†	42–8
10-1	W	@ Sherman†	35–33
10-8	W	W.F. Rider†	17–6
10-15	W	Denton†	41–7
10-22	Tie	@ The Colony H S†	7–7
10-29	W	Allen†	52–0
11-05	W	@ Marcus‡	20–13
Bi-District @ Texas Stadium			
11-12	W	Burleson	43–7
Area @ Texas Stadium			
11-19	W	S. Grand Prairie	24–0
Regional @ Midland			
11-27	W	Midland Lee	44–30
Quarterfinals @ Texas Stadium			
12-4	W	Abilene Cooper	52–21
Semi-Finals @ Texas Stadium			
12-11	W	Temple	40–16
State Finals @ Houston Astrodome			
12-18	W	Aldine MacArthur	43–37

Record: 15–0–1; State Champions, 5A Division II
Coaches: Ronnie Gage, Head; Terry Goode, Bill Peitrosky, Pat Smiley, Billy Mitchell, Brian Brazil, Tim Wasson, Scott Osborn, Keith Mikeska, Mike Campbell, Ray White, Scott Ledbetter, Dugan Walker

COACHES CAREER — RECORDS AT LHS

Coach	Year(s)	Career Record Wins Losses Ties	Winning Percentage
Bottoms, Sherrill	1964–65	8–12–0	.400
Bronaugh, J.H.	1949–51	27–3–1	.900
Davis, R.O.	1930–32	9–4–2	.538*
Delay, J.K.	1942–47	33–12–3	.733
Dunsworth, Taft	1934–35	0–4–0	.000*
Elms, Roger	1933	3–6–1	.333
Gage, Ronnie	1991–93a	32–7–2	.821
Harmon, Ben	1959–63	21–29–0	.420
Hudson, A.J.	1948	6–3–1	.667
Jones, Darrell	1926–27	7–2–0	.778*
Kay, A.L.	1952–54	22–8–0	.733
Lowe, Ed	1924–25	3–4–1	.430*
Mattingly, R.E.	1936–41	49–5–3	.907
McReynolds, Lewis	1955–58	34–9–0	.791
Mills, Chuck	1986–90	35–17–1	.673
Preston, Lee	1920–23	0–3–0	.000*
Poe, Don	1969–70	11–9–0	.550
Scarborough, Luther	1928–29	7–4–2	.583*
Shipman, Bill	1966–68, 1971–73	32–31–1	.508
Visentine, David	1974–77	15–23–2	.395
Wilson, Neal	1978–85	67–19–5	.779

* Overall record incomplete due to unavailability of results. Percentage calculated on available results.
a Results through the 1993 season, including the state championship.

THE BAND THAT MARCHES WITH PRIDE

Year	Band Director	Drum Major(s)	Contest Rating
1958	Gordon Collins	Vivian Claytor	N/A
1959	Gordon Collins	Vivian Claytor	N/A
1960	Gordon Collins	Linda Banks	1
1961	Gordon Collins	Carolyn Stewart	2
1962	Gordon Collins	Kathy Rankin	2
1963	Vernon Denman	Kathy Rankin	1
1964	William Brady	Jill Morriss	1
1965	William Brady	Doug Coyle	1
1966	William Brady	Mary Stewart	1
1967	William Brady	Mary Stewart	1
1968	William Brady	Sandi Smith	1
1969	William Brady	Rodney Barton, Glenda Bassinger	1
1970	William Brady	Ronny Haygood, Cindy Mikel	1
1971	Rex White	Kathy Cochran, Cindy Mikel	1
1972	Rex White	Mike Kerbow, Debbie Stewart	1
1973	Rex White	Cindy Houston, Russell Kerbow	1
1974	Rex White	Dale Benson, Shirley Davis, Suzy Schlegel	1
1975	Rex White	Shirley Davis, Mike DeSimine, Jeff Herro	1
1976	Rex White	Mark Bogle, Sharna Mihleder, Elma Rios	1
1977	Rex White	Mary Harmon, Terry Whitmer	1
1978	Carol Allen	Mark Lee, John Nyquist, Mark Sessumes	1
1979	Bill McMath	Terri Keith, Bobby McKenzie, Elizabeth Rau	1
1980	Bill McMath	Elizabeth Rau, Jackie Walker	1
1981	Bill McMath	John Moates, Darla Moseley, Jackie Walker	1
1982	Bill McMath	Kristen Strobel, Alyson Wood	1
1983	Bob Brashears	Tim Germann, George Howard	1
1984	Bob Brashears	Kristi Keith, Tom Krauss	1
1985	Bill Morocco	DeAnne LaGrone, Craig Partin	1
1986	Bill Morocco	Becky Jameson, Tanya Richardson	1
1987	Bill Morocco	Sharron Aldermann, Michelle Roberts	1
1988	Bill Morocco	Rachel Elizabeth Dye, Mary Lou Moreno Larios	2
1989	Bill Morocco	Nikki Razey, Heather Sutton	1
1990	Bill Morocco	Brandi Davidson, Neil Grant, Nikki Razey	1
1991	Bill Morocco	Jennifer Billingsley, Rori Newcomb, Nicole Provost	2
1992	Bill Morocco	Heather Farha, Cari Lee Isom, Anh Thu Nguyen	2
1993	Brad Kent	Bandon Harvey, Josh Schnitzius	1

NICKNAMES OF FARMER OPPONENTS 1920–93

Team	Nickname
Allen	Eagles
Alvord	Bulldogs
Arlington High	Colts
Arlington Heights, Ft. Worth	Yellow Jackets
Azle	Hornets
Bell, L.D., Hurst	Blue Raiders
Berkner, Richardson	Rams
Birdville	Buffaloes
Bishop Dunne	Falcons
Bishop Lynch	Friars
Bonham	Purple Warriors
Boswell-Eagle Mt.-Saginaw	Pioneers
Bowie	Jack Rabbits
Bowie, Arlington	Volunteers
Boyd	Yellow Jackets
Bridgeport	Bulls
Bryson	Cowboys
Burkburnett	Bulldogs
Burleson	Elks
Carrollton	Lions
Carter, Dallas	Cowboys
Celina, 1927	Blue Blizzards
Celina	Bobcats
Chilicothe	Eagles
Collinsville	Pirates
Commerce	Tigers
Cooper	Bulldogs
Cooper, Abilene	Cougars
Coronado, El Paso	Thunderbirds
Cypress-Fairbanks	Bobcats
Denison	Yellow Jackets
Denton	Broncos
Diamond Hill, Ft. Worth	Eagles
Duncanville	Panthers
Eastern Hills, Ft. Worth	Highlanders
Electra	Tigers
Era	Hornets
Farmersville	Farmers
Forney	Jack Rabbits
Forest Avenue	Lions
Frisco	Coons
Gainesville	Leopards
Grand Prairie	Gophers
Grapevine	Mustangs
Greenville	Lions
Haltom	Buffaloes
Handley	N/A
Highland Park	Scots
Howe	Bulldogs
Irving	Tigers
Itasca	Wampuscats
J.J. Pearce, Richardson	Mustangs
Jesuit, Dallas	Rangers
Justin	Texans
Keller	Indians
Kimball, Dallas	Knights
Lake Highlands	Wildcats
Lake Worth	Bullfrogs
Lee, Robert E., Midland	Rebels
MacArthur, Aldine	Generals
Mansfield	Tigers
Marcus, Edward S., Flower Mound	Marauders
Masonic Lodge Orphans Home, Ft. Worth	Mighty Mites
McKinney	Lions
Mesquite	Skeeters
Midland Lee	Rebels
Midway, Waco	Panthers
Mt. Pleasant	Tigers
N.T.S.C., North Texas Freshma Team	Eagles
Newman Smith, Carrollton	Trojans
North Dallas	Bulldogs
North Garland	Raiders
North Mesquite	Stallions
Northside, Ft. Worth	Steers
Northwest, Justin	Texans
Odessa Permian	Panthers
Paris	Wildcats
Pilot Point	Bearcats
Plano	Wildcats
Plano East	Panthers
Richardson	Eagles
Richland	Rebels
Rockwall	Yellow Jackets
Saint Jo	Panthers
St. Joseph's Academy	Bloodhounds
Sam Houston, Arlington	Texans
Sanger	Indians
Seagoville	Dragons
Sherman	Bearcats
South Grand Prairie	Warriors
Springtown	Porcupines
Sulpher Springs	Bears
Sunset, Dallas	Bisons
Temple	Wildcats
The Colony High School	Cougars
Tioga	Bulldogs
Trimble, Green B. Technical, Ft. Worth	Bulldogs
Trinity, Euless	Trojans
Turner, R.L., Carrollton	Lions
Uvalde	Coyotes
Valley View	Eagles
Valley View, Iowa Park	Warriors
Van Alstyne	Panthers
Waxahachie	Indians
Weatherford	Kangeroos
Western Hills, Ft. Worth	Cougars
Whitesboro	Bearcats
Wichita Falls High	Coyotes
Wichita Falls Hirschi	Huskies
Wichita Falls Rider	Raiders
Wilmer-Hutchins	Eagles
Wylie	Pirates

NICKNAME OF FARMER OPPONENTS BY MASCOT

Nickname	School	Nickname	School
Bearcats	Pilot Point	Leopards	Gainesville
	Sherman	Lions	Carrollton
	Whitesboro		Forest Avenue
Bears	Sulpher Springs		Greenville
Bisons	Sunset, Dallas		McKinney
Bloodhounds	St. Joseph's Academy		R.L. Turner, Carrollton
Blue Blizzards	Celina, 1927	Marauders	Marcus, Edward S., Flower Mound
Blue Raiders	L.D. Bell, Hurst		
Bobcats	Celina	Mighty Mites	Masonic Lodge Orphans Home, Ft. Worth
	Cypress-Fairbanks		
Broncos	Denton	Mustangs	Grapevine
Buffaloes	Birdville		Pearce, J.J., Richardson
	Haltom City	Panthers	Duncanville
Bulldogs	Alvord		Odessa Permian
	Burkburnett		Plano East
	Cooper		Saint Jo
	Howe		Van Alstyne
	North Dallas		Waco Midway
	Tioga	Pioneers	Boswell-Eagle Mt.-Saginaw
	Trimble, Green B. Technical, Ft. Worth	Pirates	Collinsville
			Wylie
Bullfrogs	Lake Worth	Porcupines	Springtown
Bulls	Bridgeport	Purple Warriors	Bonham
Colts	Arlington High	Raiders	North Garland
Coons	Frisco		Wichita Falls Rider
Cougars	Cooper, Abilene	Rams	Berkner, Richardson
	The Colony High School	Rangers	Jesuit
	Western Hills, Ft. Worth	Rebels	Lee, Robert E., Midland
Cowboys	Bryson		Richland
	Carter, Dallas	Scots	Highland Park
Coyotes	Uvalde	Skeeters	Mesquite
	Wichita Falls High	Stallions	North Mesquite
Dragons	Seagoville	Steers	Northside, Ft. Worth
Eagles	Allen	Texans	Justin
	Chilicothe		Northwest
	Diamond Hill, Ft. Worth		Sam Houston, Arlington
	N.T.S.C., North Texas State College Freshman Team	Thunderbirds	Coronado, El Paso
		Tigers	Commerce
	Richardson		Electra
	Valley View		Irving
	Wilmer-Hutchins		Mansfield
Elks	Burleson		Mt. Pleasant
Falcons	Bishop Dunne	Trojans	Newman Smith, Carrollton
Farmers	Farmersville		Trinity, Euless
Friars	Bishop Lynch	Volunteers	Bowie, Arlington
Generals	MacArthur, Aldine	Wampuscats	Itasca
Gophers	Grand Prairie	Warriors	South Grand Prairie
Highlanders	Eastern Hills, Ft. Worth		Valley View, Iowa Park
Hornets	Azle	Wildcats	Lake Highlands
	Era		Paris
Huskies	Wichita Falls Hirschi		Plano
Indians	Keller		Temple
	Sanger	Yellow Jackets	Arlington Heights, Ft. Worth
	Waxahachie		Boyd
Jack Rabbits	Bowie		Denison
Kangeroos	Weatherford		Forney
Knights	Kimball, Dallas		Rockwall

Top Ten Biggest Wins in Farmer History

Farmers	Opponent	Score	Result	Year
93	Northwest	6	Win	1955
73	Valley View	0	Win	1937
72	Celina	12	Win	1932
68	R.L. Turner	15	Win	1978
67	Alvord	0	Win	1940
65	Azle	0	Win	1955
62	Alvord	0	Win	1943
61	Celina	0	Win	1940
60	Springtown	0	Win	1955
60	Sanger	0	Win	1947

Top Ten Point Total Given Up in Farmer History

Score	Opponent	Farmers	Result	Year
66	Plano	7	Loss	1922
64	Gainesville	0	Loss	1924
55	Denton	25	Loss	1977
50	Trinity	10	Loss	1977
50	Carrollton	20	Loss	1961
49	Sherman	24	Loss	1989
49	R.L. Turner	21	Loss	1977
49	Plano	0	Loss	1971
49	Plano	20	Loss	1964
49	McKinney	0	Loss	1970

LEWISVILLE FARMER ALL–TIME ROSTER 1920–94

A

Aaron, Alvin	1944–45
Aaron, Dan	1963–65
Aaron, DeVerne	1947
Aaron, Frank	1938–40
Aaron, Mike	1970
Aaron, Tommy	1958
Abrams, Robert	1993
Adams, Victor	1984
Adefope, Emmanuel	1994
Aguirre, Jason	1989–90
Akins, Chris	1988–89
Albert, Verlee	1984–85
Aldridge, Lance	1992–93
Alf, Robin	1975–76
Aljoe, Mike	1979–81
Allen Avery	1984–85
Allen, Danny	1973
Allen, Don	1958
Allen, George	1977
Allen, Jerry	1947–48
Allen, John	1967–69
Allen, LaDwanne	1990–91
Allen, Pat	1936–38
Allen, Paul	1941–43
Allen, Richard	1986
Allen, Ronald	1944
Allen, Stanford	1935, '37
Allen, Stewart	1954, 56
Allgood, Billy	1993–94
Allison, Bob	1965–66
Altom, Josh	1993
Aly, Mike	1949–52
Amason, Marvin	1950
Ambriz, Jesus	1991–92
Amdall, Steve	1979–80
Anderson, Eugene	1939–41
Anderson, Chuck	1951
Anderson, Gene	1952
Anderson, Joe	1953–56
Anderson, Randy	1968
Anderson, John	1972
Anderson, Johnny	1976
Anderson, Ronald	1980
Anderson, Mike	1992–93
Angeli, Mark	1972–73
Anthe, Ron	1981–83
Anwyll, Billy	1983–84
Archer, Cory	1989
Archer, Jim	1951–52
Arrambide, Tom	1978–79
Arthur, Brad	1977
Ashford, Robert	1976
Ashton, Gary	1958–60
Atkins, Bob	1945
Auringer, David	1978
Autwell, Gary	1971–72

B

Bacon, Brian	1983
Bacon, Bruce	1983
Bacon, Clyde	1949–50
Bacon, Eddie	1978–79
Bacon, Jimmy	1949
Bacon, Larry	1963–64
Bagley, Sean	1983
Bailey, Randy	1983–84
Bambridge, Chuck	1987–88
Baker, Aaron	1986
Baker, Greg	1991–92
Balderston, Robin	1956, 58
Banks, Brent	1979
Banks, Kenny	1986
Banks, Ted	1986–87
Barfnecht, Charles	1962–63
Barfnecht, Matt	1985
Barger, Mike	1992
Barnes, Rick	1963–65
Barnes, Tommy	1964
Barr, Ken	1975–76
Bartholomew, Michael	1986
Bassinger, Dennis	1967–68
Basurto, Albert	1984
Bateman, Joey	1994
Battenfield, Jake	1989–90
Battle, Marcel	1992–93
Baum, Daniel	1991
Baum, Geoff	1988–89
Baum, Johnny	1956–58
Bays, Herman	1927–30
Bays, Woodrow	1929–33
Beal, Bron	1980–81
Beck, Brian	1994
Beck, Pat	1951–54
Beck, Sidney	1940
Bedell, F.E.	1946–49
Bedell, Jerry	1948–51
Beggs, Steve	1974–75
Beisner, Jamie	1990–91
Bell, Bob	1982
Bedner, Frank	1982
Beremea, Anthony	1987
Bernard, Greg	1975–76
Berndt, Jack	1939

Berndt, Pete	1936	Brooks, Bart	1946–47
Berndt, Walter	1927	Brooks, Bobby	1977
Bernhard, Steve	1979–81	Brooks, Ervin	1935–37
Berryman, Steve	1973	Brooks, Jeff	1986
Berthelot, Greg	1983	Brown, Andre	1989–91
Bertrand, Milton	1950–51	Brown, Bobby	1952
Biggs, Tommy	1961	Brown, Bryan	1990–91
Birdsong, Charles	1961–63	Brown, Calvin	1982
Birdsong, Dennis	1956–58	Brown, Carlton	1987–88
Bishop, Curtis	1968–69	Brown, Dale	1977–78
Bishop, James	1972–73	Brown, Eric	1985–86
Bishop, Joe	1968–70	Brown, James	1967–68
Bisson, Mark	1990–91	Brown, Jonathan	1991
Blacketer, Allen	1993–94	Brown, Kenny	1993–94
Blackstone, Bret	1979	Brown, Lon	1941–43
Blalock, Tommy	1981	Brown, Vernon	1974–75
Boenker, Henry	1948	Brumley, Harrold	1924
Bohannon, Mike	1982	Bryant, Michael	1992
Bolin, Dana	1967–68	Bryce, Gary	1980
Bolin, Evert	1939–41, '43	Buchanan, Jack	1992
Bolin, William	1940–42	Buhler, Aaron	1994
Bond, Lee	1931–34	Burch, John	1991
Bonds, Jack	1921–25	Burel, Milton	1974–76
Bonenberger, Pete	1991–93	Bukrhardt, Andy	1993–94
Boren, James	1963–64	Burkhardt, Dean	1936–38
Bosley, Chris	1982	Burns, David	1987
Botello, Johnny	1986	Burns, John	1975–76
Bounds, Eldridge	1927	Burris, Bill	1969–70
Bounds, Ivan	1941–44	Burris, Bob	1965–66
Bowden, Ray	1972–73	Burris, Boyd	1963–64
Bowery, Raymond	1967–68	Burroughs, Tommy	1963–64
Bowman, Tarrance	1992	Burt, Mike	1978–80
Box, Jim	1982–83	Burton, David	1978
Boyd, Allman	1924	Buschow, Rusty	1991–92
Boyd, Johnny	1990	Bush, Charles	1956–57
Boyd, Pal	1930–32	Bush, Jimmy	1950–51
Boyd, Pat	1967–69	Bush, Ray	1965
Boyd, Sultan	1921–25	Butler, Will	1994
Boynton, Kenny	1968	Buysse, John	1984
Bradbury, Todd	1975–77		
Bradford, Herb	1929–31	**C**	
Bradford, Robert	1927–29	Cable, Ricky	1969
Bradshaw, Greg	1974	Cade, Randy	1971–73
Bragg, Billy Jack	1955–57	Cade, Rusty	1972–73
Bragg, Jim	1971–72	Cade, Terry	1973–74
Branch, Jeff	1992–93	Calvert, J.B.	1941
Brazzell, Dwayne	1991–93	Camp, Brian	1978–80
Brazzell, Shannon	1992–94	Camp, Gary	1985–86
Brent, Jackie	1965–67	Campbell, Glen	1979
Brinegar, Danny	1978	Cannon, R.T.	1930
Brodavsky, Jason	1981	Cantrell, Brett	1981
Brodsky, Aaron	1988	Cantrell, Jeff	1978
Brodsky, Jason	1986	Capehart, Tommy	1963–64
Brooks, Art	1974	Carlton, Danny	1947–49

Carpenter, Jimmy	1946–48	Collinsworth, Billy J.	1968
Carr, Bill	1968	Collinsworth, Ray	1987–88
Carr, Bobby	1960–62	Collinsworth, Robin	1974
Carreker, John	1980	Compton, H.L.	1965–66
Carrera, Greg	1978	Compton, Ted	1947–48, '50
Carroll, John	1993–94	Conklin, Jerry	1951
Carter, Charles	1938	Conway, Garland	1951
Carter, Doug	1949–50	Cook, Charles Ray	1945
Carter, Joe	1960	Cook, James	1929
Caruthers, S.N.	1929	Cook, Jimmy	1960–61
Cassidy, Sean	1979	Cordor, Douglas	1952
Cates, A.D.	1938–41	Cokran, Lynn	1984
Champion, Anthony	1978–79	Cornist, Zeb	1992–94
Champion, Manuel	1969–70	Cothrin, Gary	1972–73
Chappel, Bud	1950	Cotten, Jason	1992–93
Chavarria, Alex	1994	Cotter, Mike	1974–76
Cherigo, Carlos	1993	Cotter, Steve	1972
Chew, Bill	1964	Cottle, James	1956–57
Chew, Fred	1974–75	Cowell, Jason	1993–94
Childress, Casey	1982–84	Cox, Brett	1992–94
Christian, Paul	1994	Cox, Jared	1994
Christian, Reggie	1983–85	Cox, Jeff	1987
Christian, Roy	1981–82	Cox, Jim	1977–79
Christie, Edgar	1933	Cozby, Hubert	1936–38
Clair, Bill	1972–73	Cozby, James	1932–33
Clark, Doug	1981–82	Cravens, Bobby	1982
Clark, Eugene	1933	Crawford, Clyde	1939
Clark, Mika	1992–93	Crawford, Don	1953
Clark, Ronnie	1986	Crawford, James	1934–35
Clark, Steve	1981	Crawford, Mack	1940–42
Cleveland, Clark	1927–29	Crawford, Reggie	1992–94
Cleveland, Frank	1931	Crawford, R.L., Sr.	1934
Cleveland, Jason	1990	Crawford, R.L., Jr.	1954–57
Clifton, Walter	1939–41	Crawford, Walter	1924
Cluff, Ron	1980–81	Crawford, Wayne	1940–41
Coates, Billy	1973–74	Crow, J.W.	1944
Coats, Chris	1992	Crum, Noel	1986–87
Cobb, Howard	1921–25	Crum, Philip	1975–76
Cobb, Jerry	1958–60	Cruson, Billy	1957–59
Cobbs, Allan	1986	Cude, Billy	1976
Cody, Jimmy	1953–55	Cummings, Chad	1990–91
Cogbill, Dean	1954	Cummings, Gary	1986
Coil, Ruic	1982–83	Cummings, Ronnie	1967–70
Coker, Brian	1975	Cundieff, David	1948
Coker, David W.	1974	Cunningham, Bert	1951–52
Coker, J. David	1973–74	Cunningham, Charlie	1932
Coker, Geary	1956–57	Cunningham, Jack	1935
Coker, Steve	1971–72	Cunningham, Jerry	1972–73
Coker, Ted	1935	Cunignham, Taylor	1924
Cole, Michael	1984–85	Curry, David	1984
Cole, Rex	1979–80	Curtis, Barry	1984
Collette, John	1983	Curtis, Carl	1924
Collins, Matt	1992	Curtis, Cleve	1924
Collinsworth, Ben	1992–94	Curtis, Donald Ray	1957–59

D

D'Onofrio, Daron	1992
Dabboussi, Nadar	1985–86
Dabboussi, Nagi	1979
Dalton, John	1988
Daniels, Jeff	1984–85
Danielson, Mike	1988–89
Darnell, Danny	1985
Davidson, Roger	1953
Davis, Al	1962
Davis, Brent	1990
Davis, Butch	1968–69
Davis, Gary	1956–66
Davis, Jackie	1980–81
Davis, Jerry E.	1957
Davis, Jerry O.	1981–82
Davis, Jim	1944
Davis, Kevin	1967–68
Dawson, Chad	1992–93
Day, Richard	1975
Deaver, LeRoy	1974–75
DeBolt, Devon	1991
Degan, Dan	1974–75
Degan, James	1927
DeGrand, Darren	1974
Delena, Tony	1985
Delfts, Thomas	1940–41
Demers, Jeff	1983
Demers, Pete	1985
Denison, Ben	1982–83
Denison, Dave	1959–60
Denison, Everett	1933
Denison, Mike	1953–56
Denison, Nolan	1933–36
Denison, Tim	1963
Dewald, Jay	1988–89
DeWill, Jeff	1988
Dickens, Steve	1981
Dixon, David	1986
Dixon, Olin	1938–39
Dombroski, Frank	1990
Donald, R.L., Jr.	1924
Dorety, John	1970–71
Dorety, Terry	1966–67
Dowis, Larry	1969
Downing, Jason	1987
Draguicivich, Oscar	1986
Dubberly, Brent	1977
Duff, David	1967
Dunaway, Mike	1989
Duncan, Chris	1994
Dungan, B.L.	1944
Dungan, Carl	1950–51
Dunn, Mathis	1967–68
Durham, Marshall	1947–50
Durham, Rory	1978–79
Durham, Rudy	1972–73
Duvall, Duncan	1969
Duwe, Bill	1936
Duwe, Don	1946–49
Duwe, Gerald Wayne	1947
Duwe, Jack	1937–39
Duwe, Ronnie	1974
Dyer, Chuck	1977

E

Earle, Richard	1987
Early, Gene	1971
Eames, Marshall	1927–29
Earwood, Lanny	1975–76
Earwood, Marty	1971
Easton, Russell	1984
Eberhart, James	1963–65
Ebsen, Herby	1970
Ebsen, Steve	1963–64
Eckert, Lance	1994
Eden, Scott	1988–89
Edmonds, Clyde	1950–53
Edmonds, Jack	1939–40
Edmondson, Rick	1962
Edwards, Billy	1987–88
Eiffert, Michael	1986–87
Elbert, Jerry	1951–52
Ellis, David	1961–62
Ellis, Earnest	1956
Ellis, John Howard	1936–39
Ellis, Steve	1965–66
Emery, Raymond	1921–24
Emery, Ty	1927
English, Lee	1986–87
Ennis, Doug	1975–76
Ennis, Larry	1967
Ennis, Woody	1968
Eshleman, Jeff	1974–75
Eshleman, Robert	1970–71
Eshleman, Tim	1971–72
Estes, Lonnie	1929–30
Evans, Garry	1976
Evans, Larry	1976

F

Farha, Russell	1994
Favilla, Anthony	1989–90
Feagins, Gibson	1948–50
Feagins, Kenneth	1946
Fearnside, Rod	1978–80
Fellers, Ralph	1961
Ferguson, Logan	1982–83
Ferris, Eric	1979

Fields, Tracy	1983
Fiene, Tim	1986
Files, Ricky	1979
Fillingham, Mark	1979
Fincher, Mike	1990
Flanagan, Clay	1978–79
Flinn, Charlie	1989–90
Flowers, Mike	1972
Flynt, Jon	1983
Ford, Charlie	1986–87
Ford, Greg	1975
Ford, Rick	1987–88
Fox, Allen	1971–72
Frady, Wayne	1948
Franklin, Jim	1963–64
Frasier, Donald	1982–83
Fraze, David	1985–86
Frazier, Kyle	1978
Frazier, Mike	1991–93
Freed, James	1960–61
Freed, Mickey	1966
French, Doyle	1930–32
French, Jimmy	1960
Friday, Chris	1990
Fritcher, Brian	1988
Fulenwilder, Joel	1990

G

Galde, Danny	1959–60
Galde, Pete	1959–60
Galler, Jerry	1963–64
Garces, Johnny	1992
Garcia, Horatio	1990
Garcia, Jesse	1977–78
Garcia, Taddy	1980–82
Garrison, Alvin	1932, '34
Garrison, Bill	1957, '59
Garrison, John	1968–70
Garrison, W.L.	1936–38
Garrison, Walt	1959–61
Garth, Emory	1947
Garth, James	1937–38
Gaston, Frank	1947–50
Gaudin, Darrell	1972
Gaudin, Ronald	1974
Gentry, Billy Bob	1943–44
Gentry, Ronnie	1984–85
Genuit, Todd	1977–78
Gernigan, Mike	1978
Gibbons, Tim	1972–73
Gibson, Jerry	1968–69
Gibson, Richard	1970
Gilbert, Kevin	1988–89
Gilbreath, Danny	1956–66

Gilbreath, Johnny	1970–71
Giles, Reed	1982
Gipson, Tommy	1977
Gladen, Donald Ray	1953
Glass, Robbie	1970–71
Glover, Doug	1972
Glover, Mark	1973–74
Gober, George	1963–64
Godinez, Arthur	1989–90
Godinez, Gilbert	1988–89
Golden, Jason	1992
Goldsmith, Gary	1968
Goldsmith, Max	1938–39
Gomez, Joey	1975
Gooch, Mike	1973–75
Gooch, Wesley	1972–73
Gordon, James	1986
Gothard, Calvin	1991
Grace, John	1994
Grace, Tommy	1988–89
Graham, Billy	1972–74
Graham, Darren	1984
Graham, J.R.	1983–85
Graham, Johnny	1963–66
Graham, Mike	1981
Gravely, Bill	1969–70
Gray, Barry	1969
Green, Henry	1945–46
Green, Jerry	1946, 48
Green, Lance	1985–86
Greer, Johnny	1954–57
Greer, Virgil	1927
Gregory, George	1956–58
Grimes, Deacon	1990–91
Grimes, Dustin	1994
Grimes, James	1983
Grimes, Lloyd	1943
Grisham, Tommy	1962
Grissom, Monty	1965–66
Groening, Jerry	1953–54
Gorgan, Scott	1985–86
Gronfwold, Scott	1988
Groves, Jerry	1952
Grumbles, Bobby	1974
Guillen, Craig	1985–86
Gullick, Tim	1972
Gumbert, Bill	1980

H

Habern, Mike	1972–74
Haddad, Al	1984–85
Hagman, Scott	1974–75
Hahn, Max	1942–43
Hahn, Stewart	1943–44

Hale, Jerry	1967
Hales, Ken	1985
Hales, Kurt	1984
Hall, Chris	1979–80
Hall, Jeff	1975
Hamaker, Allen	1994
Hamby, Dave	1973
Hamby, Ronnie	1953–54, '56
Hamlin, Thomas	1940
Hammitt, Brad	1971
Hammond, George	1968
Hancock, Barry	1984
Hancox, Howard	1988–90
Hann, Wayne	1982
Hanson, Burt	1977
Hardy, Charlie	1987
Hare, Vince	1980–82
Harn, Billy Joe	1942–44
Harper, Mickey	1956–58
Harris, Calvin	1944
Harris, Jimmy	1981
Hart, Dennis	1964
Harvey, Brian	1984
Haskins, George	1981
Hastens, Eugene	1960
Hastens, Richard	1959–60
Havens, Eddie	1981
Hawkins, David	1990
Hay, Matt	1991
Hayes, Dick	1931–32
Hayes, Tony	1959–61
Haynes, Clyde	1994
Hearn, Norman	1974
Heath, James	1947–48
Heath, Roland	1931
Heath, Royce	1950–52
Helm, Aaron	1990
Henderson, Greg	1978
Henderson, Jerry	1959
Henley, Doug	1973
Henry, Paul "Doc"	1966–67
Henson, Edward	1948–49
Henson, Eddie	1978
Hernandez, Adam	1976–77
Herring, Blaine	1992–93
Hester, Carroll	1952
Hester, Charles	1948–50
Hicks, Felix	1994
Hicks, Frank	1954
Higgins, Roland	1930
Higgins, Warren	1974
Higgs, Don	1975
Hilliard, Billy	1963–65
Hilliard, Herman	1947–48
Hilliard, Ronnie	1961–63
Hinkle, Allen	1990
Hixon, Mark	1969
Hoadley, Allan	1983–84
Hofferber, Ron	1980–81
Hoffman, Jason	1985–86
Hogue, Doug	1962–63
Holcomb, Derek	1989–90
Holden, Joe Bob	1973
Holland, Pat	1977
Holland, Waylon	1992–94
Holley, Millard	1932–33
Holloway, Chris	1986
Holmes, Steve	1973–74
Honeycutt, Roger	1977
Hood, Don	1957–59
Hood, Keith	1965–66
Hood, Truman	1933–34
Hooten, Donald	1981–82
Horne, Jerry	1986
Horner, Greg	1985
Hoskins, John Henry	1921–25
Houdek, David	1979
Houston, H.L.	1936–38
Howard, Don	1953
Howard, Terry	1994
Howsley, Jeff	1977–78
Hubbard, Jeff	1982
Huckabee, James	1964
Hudson, John	1972
Huffines, J.L., Jr.	1939
Hughes, Kenny	1975–77
Hunnicut, Randy	1991–92
Hunsaker, Alan	1963
Hunter, Dwight	1992–94
Hunter, Greg	1982
Hunter, Richard	1972–73
Hunter, Steve	1978–79
Huston, Bud	1927
Huston, Maurice	1929
Hyder, Bullock	1924

I

Iiams, Charlie	1970
Imm, Andy	1985
Ingram, Jay	1983
Isom, Billy	1988
Ivy, Darrell	1979–80

J

Jackson, Darold	1991
Jackson, Harold	1991
Jackson, Mark	1971
Jackson, Patrick	1988–89

Jackson, Tommy	1968–69	King, Mark	1990–91
Jaillett, Mike	1994	King, Ricky	1976
Jasper, Robert	1931–33	Kinney, Art	1974
Jeffcoat, Chad	1983	Kirk, Kevin	1985–86
Jeffcoat, Shawn	1984–85	Kirkpatrick, Andy	1981
Jenkins, Gary	1963–64	Kjar, Chris	1987
Jenkins, Greg	1979	Knight, Willard	1924
Jenkins, Harry	1956	Koehler, Jerry	1984–85
Jenkins, Vince	1981–82	Koehler, Steve	1969–70
Jeter, Tommy	1973	Krastin, Bobby	1991
Johnson, Bret	1993–94	Krastin, Mike	1988
Johnson, Brett	1984	Kubas, Roan	1982–83
Johnson, Chip	1984	Kuykendall, Frank	1968
Johnson, Darrick	1992		
Johnson, Eddy	1950–51	**L**	
Johnson, Floyd	1938–39	Ladehoff, Niles	1971–72
Johnson, H.C.	1932	Landers, Bobby	1974
Johnson, Harvey	1953–54	Landers, Riscard	1990
Johnson, Jerry	1962	Landrum, James	1966–67
Johnson, Lawrence	1968–69	Landrum, Jason	1988–89
Johnson, M.H.	1939	Landrum, Robert	1963–64
Johnson, Steve	1974	Landrum, Todd	1992–94
Jones, Alvin	1944–47	Lankford, M.J.	1942–43
Jones, Bert	1983–85	Latham, Marc	1979–81
Jones, David	1979	Lavender, James	1966–67
Jones, Eric	1987–89	Lawson, E.F.	1974–75
Jones, Gary E.	1970	Ledbetter, David	1956–58
Jones, Gary D.	1981–82	Lee, Lyndal	1983
Jones, Gerald	1961	Lester, Pat	1950–51
Jones, Harry	1981	Ligon, Rayford	1929–30
Jones, Kevin	1985	Liles, Kenneth	1960
Jones, LaRue	1944–46	Loard, Carroll	1947–50
Jones, Perry	1981–82	Lockett, Eddie	1982
Jordan, John	1957	Lockett, Robert	1978–80
Jordan, Thomas	1984	Logston, J.T.	1947–49
Joyce, Marc	1985	Long, Mark	1981–82
		Long, Robbie	1984–85
K		Longshore, Art	1974–75
Kahue, Ryan	1991	Love, Earl	1984
Kammerer, Jeff	1978–80	Low, Charles	1963–64
Keith, Gene	1967–69	Lowe, Brett	1985
Keith, Sidney	1953–54	Lowe, Jim	1978
Kendrick, Clay	1978	Ludwig, John	1968–69
Kendrick, Rodney	1992	Lunow, Eddie	1960–62
Kennedy, Don	1954	Lunow, Jerry	1956–58
Kerbow, Gary	1975	Luster, Willie	1987
Key, Craig	1983	Lynn, Kyndal	1984
Killian, Mike	1989	Lyons, Robby	1987
Kilman, Tommy	1993–94		
Kim, Tommy	1986	**M**	
Kimberlin, Tim	1989	MacDougall, Nathan	1986
Kimmel, Bobby	1953–56	Maeker, Mark	1984
Kimmel, Garland	1961–62	Maeker, Matt	1986–87
Kindhart, Waylon	1989	Maeker, Mike	1989–90

Name	Year
Maimone, Wesley	1994
Marcom, Ben	1963–64
Marks, Kevin	1983–84
Marony, Tony	1982
Marshall, Scott	1977–78
Martin, Bill	1948–50
Martin, Chuck	1974–75
Martin, Eugene	1962
Martin, Joe	1972–73
Martin, Kennery	1988
Martin, Tim	1975
Martinez, Joe	1970–71
Martinez, John	1967
Martinez, Mike	1980–81
Martinez, Ray	1985
Martinez, Victor	1985
Martinez, George	1987–88
Mason, Jacky	1956–57
Massey, Bill (Cade)	1951–52
Massey, James	1937
Massey, Mike	1961
Massingill, Danny	1983–84
Massingill, Justin	1991
Matthews, Dean	1941
Matthews, Deron	1982–83
Matthews, Eugene	1945–46
Matthews, Garland	1957, '59
Maxson, Tanner	1994
Mayes, Randy	1971–72
Mayfield, Ray	1961–62
Mayo, Gerard	1988
Mayon, Kenneth	1994
Mays, Billy	1991
Mays, Jeff	1975
McAniley, John	1980
McBride, Joe	1983–84
McBride, Mike	1982
McCall, Bryan	1988–89
McClain, Harvey	1957–59
McCloyn, Mike	1978–80
McCool, Keith	1987–88
McCormick, Chris	1992
McCrary, Brian	1983
McCurley, Mark	1971–72
McCurrach, Scott	1987
McDaniel, Claude	1937
McDaniel, Curtis	1939
McDaniel, Choyce	1949–50, '52
McDaniel, Greg	1971
McDaniel, Jackie	1977
McDougal, Kevin	1982
McFarling, Bill	1972
McFarling, Bruce	1983
McGatlin, Donny	1965–66
McGatlin, Jimmy	1959–61
McGatlin, Ronald	1948–49
McGee, Allan	1952–53
McGee, Billy	1951–52
McGee, Jerry	1957–59
McGee, Tony	1962
McHenry, Metrick	1990–92
McInerney, Brian	1988
McKamy, Brian	1973
McKenzie, Bob	1952–54
McKenzie, Jimmy	1953–55
McKie, Scott	1975
McKinney, Greg	1980–81
McLane, LaDarrin	1993–94
McMahan, Mike	1994
McMinimy, Robert	1980
McWhorter, Mark	1972
Melendrez, Jose	1982–83
Melendrez, Mike	1984
Melledy, Jason	1988–89
Melton, Mike	1977
Melugin, David	1983
Merriman, Eddie	1970–71
Merriman, Freddie	1970–71
Merritt, Dan	1992–93
Merritt, Edward	1927
Merritt, James	1971–72
Merritt, Sam	1936
Messinger, Robbie	1969–70
Meyers, Al	1987
Miles, Jeff	1983–84
Miles, Vaden	1927
Miles, Verdie	1927
Miller, Albert	1944
Miller, Andre	1986
Miller, Dewey	1977
Miller, Dub	1929
Miller, Terrance	1984–85
Mills, Tommy	1963
Minor, Charles	1942–43
Mitchell, Byron	1992–94
Mitchell, Deron	1982–83
Moody, Danny	1975
Moody, Glenn	1993–94
Moody, Tim	1988–89
Moore, Alvin	1936–37
Moore, Jason	1989–90
Moore, Speck	1932
Morgan, Hamlin	1953
Morgan, Michael	1987–88
Morris, J.W.	1927
Morris, Lynn	1936–38
Morriss, Ralph	1949–51
Morriss, Richard	1952–55

Morriss, Walter	1954–57	Orr, Garland	1921–25
Morrow, Glen	1983–84	Osborn, Scott	1983
Morrow, Teddy	1952	Otsuji, Eric	1993
Morse, Van	1962	Owens, Randy	1976–77
Moseley, Darrell	1976	Owens, Scott	1989–90
Mosley, Dwayne	1980–81		
Moushon, Mike	1982	**P**	
Mueller, Craig	1986	Painter, Fred	1941–43
Mullins, Bill	1943	Painter, Sam	1936–37
Mullins, Eddie	1971–72	Pair, Ernest	1924
Murphy, Brandon	1987–88	Pannell, Eddie	1962–63
Murphy, Duwane	1980–81	Parker, Alvin	1929–31
Murphy, Edward	1978–79	Parker, Bobby	1956, 58
Murphy, Marvin	1981–82	Parker, Darrell	1948–50
Murphy, Rodney	1981–83	Parker, James	1953–55
Murrau, Matt	1982–83	Parker, Josh	1990–91
Music, Chuck	1992	Parker, Scott	1977
Myers, Clarence	1952–55	Parks, Billy Lee	1944–45
Myers, Jeff	1989–90	Parks, Terry Don	1953–55
N		Parrish, John	1987
Nailing, John	1968	Parrott, Bruce	1968
Naphi, Ted	1972	Parrott, Forrest	1970–71
Nations, Tommie	1964	Patterson, Donald	1976
Neander, Todd	1988–90	Patton, Charles	1959
Neely, Edwin	1921–25	Payne, Jimmy	1960–61
Neely, Sidney	1927–29	Peabody, Billy	1960–61
Neilson, Brad	1984–85	Pearson, Bobby	1958
Nelson, Chad	1991–93	Pearson, Charles	1953–56
Nelson, Spence	1970	Pendergast, Ross	1986
Newman, Lee	1966	Pennington, Brent	1984–85
Newman, Paul	1968–69	Perez, Anthony	1991
Newsome, Michael	1992–93	Perry, Arvin	1924
Nichols, Clayton	1959	Perry, Billy Joe	1943
Nichols, Mike	1971–73	Perry, Clyde	1939–41
Nickelson, Bryan	1987	Perry, Doyal	1956–58
Nix, Curtis	1935	Perry, Hubert	1924
Nix, Jimmy	1953–55	Perry, Johnny	1963–65
Nix, Neal	1980–81	Perry, Roy	1960
Nixon, James	1978	Peters, Randy	1984–85
Noguera, Robert	1985–86	Peterson, Kirk	1980
Nowak, Jeff	1982	Phillips, Buddy	1991–93
Nowak, Matt	1985	Phillips, Robbie	1985
Nowlin, Gene	1948–49	Phillips, Scott	1982–83
Nowlin, Urby	1937–39	Piburn, John	1967
		Pierce, Pat	1987
O		Plair, Orrin	1994
O'Bannon, David	1986	Poirier, John, Sr.	1951–52
Odle, Michael	1994	Poirier, John, Jr.	1977
O'Donnell, Mark	1983	Pollock, Clark	1975–77
O'Steen, Derek	1989–90	Polser, Aubrey, Sr.	1927
Odneal, Curt	1978	Polser, Aubrey, Jr.	1957–60
Odneal, Dean	1982	Polser, David	1983–84
Ogburn, Chris	1987	Polser, Eugene	1927–29
Olson, Randy	1975	Polser, James	1956–58

Pomykal, Parker	1983	Rodgers, Matt	1985–86
Pomykal, Preston	1987–88	Romine, Joe	1980
Ponath, Danny	1974	Rosse, Tony	1982
Porter, S.W.	1948	Routh, Kyle	1975–76
Poteet, Jason	1993	Rowe, Kent	1978
Potter, Curtis	1987	Runnels, Rocky	1962–64
Potter, Mark	1990–91	Runnels, Steve	1963
Powell, Lynn	1982	Ruple, Robert	1993
Prewitt, Rusty	1969	Rush, Terry	1971
Price, Jeff	1987	Rutherford, Jon	1981
Price, Mickey	1983–85	Rutledge, Mike	1968–69
Pruitt, Tim	1969–70	Ryan, Mark	1972
Puls, George	1967–69		

Q

Querner, Jim	1969–70

R

Ragsdale, Dean	1966	Salsman, Ronnie	1960–62
Rains, Gaylon	1977	Salter, Jeff	1986
Ramsey, Doug	1977	Sampley, Robert	1979–80
Ramsey, Jeff	1978–79	Sampson, Eric	1979–80
Ramsey, Jimmy	1952–53	Sampson, Lester	1973–75
Ramsey, Kelley	1975–76	Sampson, Nick	1985
Ramsey, Mike	1955–56	Sampson, Rodney	1984
Rankin, Gary	1965–66	Sampson, Steve	1975–76
Ratliff, Carl	1921–25	Sandlin, Mark	1968–69
Ratliff, Frank	1937	Sargent, Darwin	1950
Ratliff, Joe	1931	Sargent, Eddie	1927–29
Ratliff, Olin	1933–34	Sargent, Stephen	1936–37
Redmon, Edgar	1964	Sarine, David	1979–80
Reed Hoyt	1945–47	Savage, Glen	1946–47
Reed, Mike	1989	Scheibelhut, John	1987–88
Reed, Pat	1968–69	Scheibelhut, Tim	1989–90
Reed, Tim	1976	Schnell, Lee	1974
Remy, Chris	1961	Schreiber, Harold	1941
Reynolds, Cade	1983	Sciotti, Chalee	1984
Reynolds, Everett	1951–54	Seagraves, Clark	1933
Reynolds, Mark	1969–70	Seagraves, James	1933
Rheudasil, Booker	1976–77	Seagraves, Joe	1944–46
Rice, Paul	1972–74	Seagraves, Mack	1939
Richardson, Mickey	1969	Seagraves, Raymond	1933
Richardson, Steve	1965	Seaman, Mark	1973–74
Ridinger, Eugene	1959–61	Searcy, Russell	1955
Ridinger, Ray	1989	Sergent, Jeff	1979 80
Riley, Mike	1970–71	Sergent, John	1980
Roach, Mickey	1987	Sewell, Larry	1963
Roach, Topher	1992–93	Shafer, Joe Bailey	1938–40
Robbins, Claudie	1938, '40	Shafer, Raymond	1941–42
Robbins, J.W.	1938–40	Shafer, Wylie	1940–43
Roberts, Eddie	1971	Sharr, Paul	1987
Roberts, Jeff	1983	Shaw, Obert	1924
Robertson, Lester	1930	Shaw, Otis	1921–25
Rogers, Donnie	1989	Shelley, David	1983

S

Salgado, Eloy	1987
Salmon, Nolen	1938–39
Salmon, Sam	1921–25
Salsman, Gordon	1952–55

Name	Year
Shelley, Doug	1979
Shelton, Fred	1944
Shelton, Poss	1945
Sheppard, Greg	1981
Shields, James	1987–88
Shields, P.J.	1990–92
Shipman, Walt	1972–73
Shoemake, Jeff	1976–78
Shost, Sam	1979
Shovlin, Nick	1984
Shovlin, Pat	1980
Sigler, Billy	1940–41
Sigler, Dale	1961
Sigler, Foster	1934
Sigler, Jimmy	1968–69
Sigler, Larry	1956–58
Sigler, Sammy	1958–61
Sigler, Woodrow	1931–33
Siler, Richard	1980–81
Silk, Otho	1921
Simmons, James	1937–38
Simmons, Martin	1992–94
Simpson, Lee	1973
Simpson, W.C. Buddy	1946–47
Sims, Dabney	1933
Sirianni, Mike	1981
Sisk, Billy	1952–55
Sisk, Stephen	1954–57
Skaggs, Allen	1994
Skalski, John	1981–82
Skipworth, Phil	1965–66
Slater, Gerald	1951–54
Slater, Jimmy	1953–55
Smart, Dale	1978
Smart, Dwain	1982
Smith, Andrew	1976
Smith, Calvin	1973
Smith, Chris	1989–90
Smith, Dan	1953–56
Smith, Don R.	1949–52
Smith, L. Don	1962
Smith, Elbert	1935–37
Smith, Greg	1976
Smith, James	1948–49
Smith, Jeff	1986
Smith, Leroy	1935
Smith, Loren	1988
Smith, Mike	1967
Smith, Tino	1987–88
Snowden, Mark	1971
Sonntag, Cornelius	1930–35
Sonntag, E.O.	1936–37
Sonntag, J.C.	1940–42
Sornsen, Rob	1978
Soto, Chris	1991–92
Sparks, Robert	1935
Sparks, Tommy Ray	1945–48
Speed, Troy	1988–89
Stalcup, Jim	1976
Steele, Ricky	1979–81
Stephens, James	1963
Stevenson, Randy	1959–61
Steward, Jack	1937–39
Stewart, Bo	1973–75
Stewart, Hal	1978–79
Stewart, Howard	1933
Stewart–Perry, Lee	1993–94
Stewart, Reveau	1935–37
Stewart, Travis	1991
Stimmel, Walter	1985
Stockard, Alfred	1951
Stockard, Bill	1941–43
Stockard, Roy	1941
Stockard, Tommy	1952–54
Stockard, Uel Ray	1946–47
Stone, Gene	1951
Stouffe, John	1980–81
Stout, Scout	1986–87
Strawser, Charlie	1988–89
Stubblefield, Benny	1950–52
Stubblefield, Scotty	1953–56
Sullivan, Fred	1967–69
Swindell, Donald	1953
Sycks, Steve	1983–84

T

Name	Year
Tackett, Dean	1986
Talley, Dan	1952–55
Talley, Jim	1936–40
Talley, Martin	1938–39
Tanner, Carlton	1977
Tate, Gordon	1927–29
Taylor, Bobby	1946–47
Taylor, Greg	1983–85
Taylor, Herbert	1951–54
Taylor, Luke	1994
Tefatiller, Melvin	1982
Temple, Dean	1936
Testa, Rick	1962–64
Testerman, Weldon	1947–50
Tharp, Richard	1972–73
Theide, Bennett	1942–44
Theide, Sammy	1965–67
Thomas, Billy	1949–51
Thomas, Brad	1979–80
Thomas, J.H., Jr.	1945–48
Thomas, James	1988–89
Thomas, Jason	1991

Thomas, Phillip	1977
Thompson, Kenny	1986
Thompson, Mike	1985–86
Threadgill, Gene	1959–60
Thurmond, Arno, Jr.	1942
Tillery, Bart	1989
Tillery, David	1962–64
Tillman, Eddie	1977–78
Timmons, Carey	1969
Tiner, Jerry	1961
Tittle, Ted	1981–82
Todd, Hoyt	1980
Tolleson, Monte	1962–64
Torres, Johnny	1984
Tourk, Thomas	1984
Townsend, Tom	1980
Travelstead, Wallace	1946–48
Traynor, David	1974
Treadway, Gary	1969
Tucker, Billy	1957–59
Tucker, Johnny	1936–37
Turner, Alvin	1975
Turner, Kelvan	1979
Turner, Lamont	1990–91
Turner, Zachary	1974–75
Twitty, Arvil	1945
Tyler, Darin	1992

U

Ulichnie, Jason	1992
Underwood, David	1936–37
Underwood, Edwin	1930
Underwood, Pete	1954–57
Uppole, Matt	1988–89

V

Van Zandt, Gaylon	1987–88
Vance, Henry	1931–33
Vandergriff, Paul	1979
Vandenburg, Allan	1984
Vaughn, Bobby	1988–89
Verba, Chris	1985
Vestal, Jon	1981
Vickery, Kent	1968
Vielma, Dino	1989–90
Vielma, Dion	1994
Vierra, Fred	1986
Vigue, Shane	1989–90
Vincent, Chester	1941
Vinson, Eddie	1963–64
Vittrup, James	1973–74
Vorin, Dennis	1970–71
Voss, Chad	1990–91
Voss, Floyd	1971–72
Voss, Jason	1993
Voss, Sammie	1972–73

W

Wade, Chris	1994
Waggoner, Bruce	1963
Waite, Cliff	1971–72
Waldrip, Bud	1930–32
Waldrip, Jay	1962–63
Waldroup, Jeff	1984
Walker, Bryan	1971
Walker, Joe	1968
Wallace, Ricky	1978, '80
Wallen, Shannon	1986
Warder, Tommy	1986
Ware, Nathan	1982–83
Warford, Gary	1992
Warmouth, Jonathan	1991–92
Warnick, Bobby	1950
Warren, Albert	1979
Washington, Manuel	1971
Washington, Wayne	1950
Watson, J.T.	1921–25
Webb, Horace	1990
Webb, Tim	1976–78
Webb, Todd	1982–83
Webster, Brad	1984–85
Weger, Johnny	1959–60
Weiss, Cory	1986
Welch, Carl	1979–80
Weldon, Jay	1984–85
Wells, Freddie	1978–79
Wells, Weldon	1934
Welton, Zack	1992–93
Westbrook, David	1977
Westbrook, Don	1977
Westbrook, Joe	1951
Whatley, Don	1957–59
Whatley, Johnny	1949–51
Wheadon, Richard	1979–80
White, Billy	1944–45
White, Charlie	1980
White, Donald	1952
White, Eris	1993–94
White, George	1959–60
White, Randy	1975–76
White, Tommy	1971
Whitlock, Charlie	1921–25
Whitlock, Joe	1954
Wilcox, Kent	1986
Wilcox, Mike	1967–69
Wilcox, Terry	1972–73
Wiley, Eddie	1957–58
Willard, Buford	1934–35

Willard, Wesley	1987–89	Wolters, Bill	1958–59
Williams, Bobby	1951–54	Wolters, David	1960–62
Williams, Dale	1953–55	Wolters, Mike	1927
Williams, Doyle	1970	Wood, J.K.	1972, '74
Williams, Fred "Hoss"	1930–33	Wood, Johnny	1988–89
Williams, Jerry	1985–86	Wood, Rob	1994
Williams, Joe	1977	Wood, Shawn	1973–75
Williams, Kenneth	1948–49	Wood, Steven	1977
Williams, Kevin	1986	Woodall, Frank	1963–64
Williams, Wesley	1947–48	Woods, Bob	1950
Williams, Willie	1984	Wooldridge, Gaylon	1955–57
Willmond, Roy	1957	Wooten, Brent	1978
Wilson, Clifton	1935	Wooten, David	1982
Wilson, Colby	1989–90	Worthington, Daymond	1977
Wilson, Darrell	1983–84	Wotlin, Dallas	1978–79
Wilson, Dwayne	1977–78	Wright, Charles	1993
Wilson, Freddie	1993	Wulfjen, Ralph	1939–41
Wilson, Joey	1984		
Wilson, Lance	1985–86	**Y**	
Wilson, Robert	1975	Yost, Matt	1991–92
Wilson, Sammie	1944–47	Young, Bill	1951
Windham, Mike	1981	Young, Bud	1951–52
Winget, Wesley	1972–74	Young, Kenny	1994
Winiger, Steve	1979	Young, Kevin	1984
Winkler, Bill	1972		
Winters, Jimmy	1961–62	**Z**	
Witmer, Todd	1979–80	Zagagoza, Jamie	1989
Wolfe, Kirk	1977–79	Zeliff, Victor	1992–93
Wolfe, Randy	1982–84	Zepka, Johnny	1989–90
Wolters, Albert	1929	Zuspan, Norman	1951, '53–54

FARMER POST SEASON HONORS 1939–93

1939
First Team: A.D. Cates, Olin Dixon, John Ellis, Max Goldsmith, Jack Steward.
Second Team: Frank Aaron, J.W. Robbins.

1940
None

1941
First Team: Evert Bolin, Thomas Delfs, Raymond Shafer, J.C. Sonntag.

1942
None

1943
First Team: Bill Mullins, Fred Painter, Wylie Shafer.

1944
None

1945
None

1946
None

1947
First Team: Jimmy Carpenter, Henry Green, Joe Seagraves, Tommy Sparks, Uel Ray Stockard, Bobby Taylor, Sammy Wilson.

1948
First Team: Jerry Green, Tommy Sparks.

1949
First Team: F.E. Bedell, Danny Carlton, Marshall Durham, Don Duwe.

1950
First Team: Marshall Durham, Don Smith, Weldon Testerman.
Second Team: Clyde Bacon.
Honorable Mention: Marvin Amason, Gibson Feagins, Frank Gaston, Carroll Loard, Ralph Morriss, Darrell Parker, Johnny Whatley.

1951
First Team: Mike Aly, Don Smith, Johnny Whatley.
Second Team: Bert Cunningham.
Honorable Mention: Jerry Bedell, Jimmy Bush, Ralph Morriss, Benny Stubblefield.

1952
First Team: Mike Aly, Don Smith.
Second Team: Jim Archer, Bert Cunningham, Benny Stubblefield.

1953
First Team: Jerry Groening, Clarence Myers, Jimmy Ramsey, Billy Sisk, Norman Zuspan.
Second Team: Pat Beck, Gordon Salsman.
Honorable Mention: Everett Reynolds.

1954
First Team: Pat Beck, Jerry Groening, Bob McKenzie, Clarence Myers, Everett Reynolds, Gordon Salsman, Billy Sisk, Gerald Slater, Dan Smith, Norman Zuspan.

1955
First Team: Mike Denison, Gordon Salsman, Billy Sisk.
Second Team: Dan Smith, Scotty Stubblefield.
All-State: Gordon Salsman, Billy Sisk.
All-American: Gordon Salsman.

1956
First Team: Joe Anderson, Dan Smith, Scotty Stubblefield.
Second Team: Mike Denison, Walter Morriss, Charles Peterson, Pete Underwood.
Honorable Mention: R.L. Crawford Jr., Johnny Greer, Bobby Kimmel.
All-State: Joe Anderson.
All-State Honorable Mention: Dan Smith, Scotty Stubblefield.

1957
First Team: R.L. Crawford Jr., David Ledbetter, Pete Underwood.
Second Team: Steve Sisk, Johnny Greer, Walter Morriss.

1958
None

1959
First Team: Gary Ashton, Billy Cruson, Don Hood, Harvey McClain, Jerry McGee, Billy Tucker, Don Whatley.

1960
First Team: Gary Ashton, Sammy Sigler, Gene Threadgill.
Honorable Mention: Walt Garrison, Richard Hasten, Johnny Weger.

1961
First Team: Billy Peabody, Sammy Sigler.
Honorable Mention: Bobby Carr, Walt Garrison, Eugene Ridinger, Ronnie Salsman, Randy Stevenson, David Wolters.

1962
First Team: Bobby Carr, Eddie Lunow, Ronnie Salsman, David Wolters.

1963
First Team: Ronnie Hilliard, Jay Waldrip.
Honorable Mention: Doug Houge, Eddie Pannell.

1964
First Team: Jerry Galler, Rocky Runnels, Monte Tolleson.
Honorable Mention: Tommy Capehart, James Eberhart, Jim Franklin, Edgar Redmon, Rick Testa, Eddie Vinson.
All-State: Monte Tolleson.

1965
First Team: Billy Hilliard.
Honorable Mention: Steve Allen, James Eberhart, Steve Ellis, John Graham.

1966
First Team: John Graham.
Honorable Mention: Steve Ellis, Monty Grissom.

1967
First Team: Jerry Hale, Paul (Doc) Henry.

1968
First Team: Ronnie Cummings, Gary Goldsmith, Fred Sullivan.
Honorable Mention: James Brown, Mathis Dunn, George Puls.

1969
First Team: Ronnie Cummings.
Honorable Mention: John Allen, Joe Bishop, John Garrison, Barry Gray, Gene Keith, George Puls, Fred Sullivan.

1970
First Team: Ronnie Cummings, Robbie Messenger.
Second Team: Joe Bishop, Spence Nelson, Mike Riley.
Honorable Mention: John Garrison, Robbie Glass.

1971
First Team: None
Second Team: Mike Riley.
Honorable Mention: Jim Bragg, John Dorety, Robbie Glass, Brad Hammit, Forrest Parrott.
6-3A Sophomore of the Year: Randy Cade.

1972
First Team: Mark Angeli, Jim Bragg, Steve Coker, Randy Mayes, Mark McCurley, Eddie Mullins, Paul Rice, Floyd Voss, Sammie Voss.
Second Team: Gary Autwell, Rudy Durham, Allen Fox, Joe Martin, Mike Nichols, Richard Tharp.
6-3A Offensive Player of the Year: Paul Rice.
6-3A Defensive Player of the Year: Sammie Voss.
6-3A Sophomore of the Year: Paul Rice.
6-3A Coach of the Year: Bill Shipman.
All-State: Jim Bragg, Allen Fox, Paul Rice.
All-State Second team: Steve Coker.
Texas 3-A Coach of the Year: Bill Shipman.
All-American: Paul Rice.

1973
First Team: Rudy Durham, Joe Martin, Paul Rice, Walt Shipman, Richard Tharp, Sammie Voss.
Second Team: Mark Angeli, Randy Cade, Mike Nichols, Wesley Winget.
All-State: Randy Cade, Paul Rice, Richard Tharp, Sammie Voss.
All-American: Paul Rice.

1974
First Team: LeRoy Deaver, Paul Rice, Wesley Winget.
All-American: Paul Rice.

1975
First Team: Steve Beggs, LeRoy Deaver, Greg Ford, Steve Sampson.
Second Team: Mike Gooch, Lester Sampson, Bo Stewart.

1976
First Team: John Burns, Steve Sampson, Randy White.
Honorable Mention: Ken Barr, Kenny Hughes.

1977
First Team: Dale Brown, Jesse Garcia.
Honorable Mention: Adam Hernandez, Kenny Hughes, Booker Rheudasil, Tim Webb, Joe Williams.

1978
First Team: Dale Brown, Jesse Garcia, Scott Marshall, Edward Murphy, Jeff Shoemake, Tim Webb, Freddie Wells.
Second Team: Eddie Bacon, Danny Brinegar, Greg Carrera, Anthony Champion, Rory Durham, Clay Flanagan, Todd Geniut, Robert Gunnoe, Clay Kendrick, James Nixon, Curt Odneal, Dwayne Wilson.
6-4A Offensive Player of the Year: Dale Brown.
6-4A Sophomore of the Year: Mike Burt.
6-4A Coach of the Year: Neal Wilson.

1979
First Team: Mike Burt, Brian Camp, Rory Durham, Rod Fearnside, Clay Flanagan, Steve Hunter, Greg Jenkins, Jeff Kammerer, Robert Lockett, Edward Murphy, Hal Stewart, Freddie Wells, Kirk Wolfe; Dallas Wotlin, Punter.
Honorable Mention: Mike Aljoe, Eddie Bacon, Brent Banks, Anthony Champion, Rex Cole, Jim Cox, Eugene Corbin, Eric Ferris, Mike McCloyn, Jeff Ramsey, Eric Sampson, Ricky Steele, Kelvin Turner, Dallas Wotlin.
6-4A Offensive Player of the Year: Freddie Wells.
6-4A Defensive Player of the Year: Edward Murphy.
6-4A Coach of the Year: Neal Wilson.
All-State: Rory Durham, Freddie Wells.
All-State Second Team: Rod Fearnside, Edward Murphy, Dallas Wotlin.

1980
First Team: Steve Amdall, Mike Burt, Brian Camp, Rod Fearnside, Jeff Kammerer, Robert Lockett, Mike McCloyn, Robert Sampley, Eric Sampson, Ricky Steele.
Honorable Mention: Ronald Anderson, Rex Cole, Chris Hall, Vince Hare, Darrell Ivy, Marc Latham, Dwayne Mosley, Duwane Murphy, John Stouffe.
All-American: Brian Camp.

1981
First Team: Mike Aljoe (Off), Bron Beal, Ron Cluff, Vince Hare, Marc Latham, Mike Martinez, Greg McKinney, Dwayne Mosley, Duwane Murphy, John Skalski; Bron Beal, Punter.
Honorable Mention: Mike Aljoe (Def), Steve Bernhard, Tommy Blalock, Roy Christian, Doug Clark, Ron Cluff, Jerry Davis, Steve Dickens, Jimmy Harris, Donald Hooten, Vince Jenkins, Gary Jones, Harry Jones, Marvin Murphy, Rodney Murphy, Neal Nix, Richard Siler, John Stouffe.
6-5A Offensive Player of the Year: Duwane Murphy.
6-5A Sophomore of the Year: Rodney Murphy.
6-5A Coach of the Year: Neal Wilson.
All-State Second Team: Mike Aljoe.

1982
First Team: Donald Hooten, Vince Jenkins, Mike McBride, Rodney Murphy, John Skalski.
Second Team: Jerry Davis, Gary Jones, Todd Webb.
Honorable Mention: Ron Anthe, Bob Bell, Doug Clark, Vince Hare, Mark Long.
All-Metro: Teddy Garcia, Kicker; John Skalski.

1983
First Team: Jim Box, Rodney Murphy, Matt Murray, Todd Webb.
Second Team: Ben Denison, Logan Ferguson, Scott Phillips.
Honorable Mention: Bruce Bacon, Terrance Brown, Ruic Coil, Jeff Demers, Don Frazier, Danny Massingill, Deron Matthews, Jose Melendrez, Mickey Price, David Shelley.

1984
First Team: Allan Hoadley, Danny Massingill, Joe McBride, Terrance Miller.
Second Team: David Polser, Darrell Wilson, Randy Wolfe.
12-5A Defensive Player of the Year: Joe McBride.

1985
First Team: Avery Allen, J.R. Graham, Ken Hales, Bert Jones, Terrance Miller, Brent Pennington, Mickey Price, Greg Taylor.
Second Team: Verlee Albert, Eric Brown, Reggie Christian, Al Haddad.
Honorable Mention: Gary Camp, Ronnie Gentry, Lance Green, Craig Guillen, Robbie Long, Brad Neilson, Robert Noguera, Randy Peters, Robbie Phillips, Matt Rodgers, Rodney Sampson, Jerry Williams, Lance Wilson.
12-5A Coach of the Year: Neal Wilson.

1986
First Team: Eric Brown, Gary Camp, Craig Guillen.

1987
First Team: David Burns, Noel Crum.
Second Team: Chuck Bambridge, Ted Banks, Jeff Cox, Charley Ford, Brian Nickelson, Chris Ogburn, Scott Stout.
Honorable Mention: Jason Downing, Mike Eiffert, Lee English, George Martinez, Jeff Price, Gaylon Van Zandt.
5-5A Co-Defensive Player of the Year: David Burns.
5-5A Co-Coach of the Year: Chuck Mills.
All-State: David Burns, Noel Crum.

1988
First Team: Chuck Bambridge, Carlton Brown, George Martinez, Mike Morgan, Preston Pomykal, Tino Smith, Johnny Wood.
Second Team: Aaron Brodsky, Mike Danielson, Jay Dewald, Rick Ford, Keith McCool, Brandon Murphy.
Honorable Mention: Ray Collinsworth, Gaylon Van Zandt.
All-Area: Chuck Bambridge, Carlton Brown, George Martinez, Preston Pomykal.
All-State: Johnny Wood.

1989
First Team: Michael Danielson, Arthur Godinez, Eric Jones, Mike Reed.
Second Team: Chris Akin, Andre Brown, Mike Dunaway, Pat Jackson, Charlie Strawser.
Honorable Mention: Michael Danielson, Tommy Grace, Howard Hancox, Tim Moody, Bobby Vaughn, Wes Willard.
5-5A Sophomore of the Year: Andre Brown.
All-Area: Michael Danielson, Eric Jones.
All-Area Second Team: Andre Brown, Arthur Godinez, Mike Reed.
All-Area Honorable Mention: Mike Dunaway, Charlie Strawser.

1990
First Team: Andre Brown, Todd Neander, Derek O'Steen, Dino Vielma.
Second Team: Mark Bisson, Anthony Favilla, Jeff Myers, Shane Vigue, Colby Wilson.
Honorable Menton: Jake Battenfield, Charlie Flinn, Arthur Godinez, Howard Hancox, Scott Owens, Tim Scheibelhut.
All-Area: Andre Brown, Dino Vielma.
All-Area Second Team: Todd Neander, Derek O'Steen.
All-State: Todd Neander, Dino Vielma.

1991
First Team: Andre Brown, Josh Parker, Lamont Turner.
Second Team: LaDwane Allen, Metrick McHenry, P.J. Shields, Matt Yost.
Honorable Mention: Mark Bisson, Bryan Brown, Rusty Buschow, Chad Cummings, Mark King, Mark Potter, Bobby Krastin.
5A Co-Offensive Player of the Year: Metrick McHenry.

1992
First Team: Dwayne Brazzell, Mike Frazier, Jason Golden, Metrick McHenry (Off), P.J. Shields, Matt Yost.
Second Team: Greg Baker, Metrick McHenry (Def), Buddy Phillips, Jason Ulichnie.
6-5A Sophomore of the Year: Martin Simmons.
6-5A Offensive Player of the Year: Metrick McHenry.
6-5A Coach of the Year: Ronnie Gage.

1993

First Team: Mike Anderson, Dwayne Brazzell, Zeb Cornist, Dwight Hunter, Dan Merritt, Chad Nelson, Martin Simmons.

Second Team: Pete Bonenberger, Shannon Brazzell, Mike Frazier, Waylon Holland, Byron Mitchell, Buddy Phillips, Topher Roach, Zack Welton.

Honorable Mention: Jeff Branch, Jason Cotten, Blaine Herring.

6-5A Co-Coach of the Year: Ronnie Gage.

All-Area Second Team: Topher Roach.

Texas Sports Writers Association Class 5A All-State First Team: Dwayne Brazzell, Shannon Brazzell, Dwight Hunter, Dan Merritt.

Texas Sports Writers Association Class 5A All-State Second Team: Chad Nelson, Martin Simmons.

Texas Sports Writers Association Class 5A Coach of the Year: Ronnie Gage.

Fab-Knit 5A Division II Coach of the Year: Ronnie Gage.